Table of Contents

INTRODUCTION

Welcome to the World of Psychology!

PSYCHOLOGY: The systematic study of behavior and mental processes; *psychology is a science*. As such, it can be defined as a set of procedures for systematically observing facts about behavior and for organizing these facts into generalizations, or laws, that seek to explain why human beings and other animals act as they do. In addition, *psychology is a means of promoting human welfare*, a body of information that can be applied to help solve a variety of individual and group problems. Regardless of a student's academic and career goals, psychology is one of the most relevant disciplines to an individual's daily life. While you may be most familiar with the term psychology as it relates to mental illness, psychology also plays an important role in education, business, parenting, relationships, medicine, law, technology, and life itself.

Remember the old adage, "an ounce of prevention is worth a pound of cure." A major focus of modern psychology is the promotion of health-enhancement behaviors, both mental and physical. Psychology includes coverage of topics like overeating, drug and alcohol abuse, the effects of inheritance, the family structure, and peer pressure. In a way, the term psychology is more a cover title for a variety of related fields of inquiry and application. As an individual discipline, psychology has a relatively short life and yet, a very long history. The first psychologists probably predate history, as the great philosophers posed difficult questions about human nature that were pondered and debated. Many of these same questions still result in energetic discussion today as psychology continues to search the mysteries of our mental experience, the wondrous complexities of the brain, and the many ways we express ourselves through our physical and verbal behaviors. And there is controversy! As you read the text you will discover many different ways of examining and offering solutions to the problems of psychology. Sometimes theories will appear to be completely opposite of each other. At times it may appear that what one theory proclaims is simply a different way of stating the same thing as another theory. The problem for many students of psychology is that they see the inherent value in every theory and wonder why there needs to be so many theories to explain one phenomenon. The truth is that theories do not mean proof. In other words, because of the difficulty of studying the unique creature that is the human animal, psychologist often begin their work toward a practical theory by taking educated guesses. That does not mean that we don't have any answers—but we certainly don't have all the answers.

Psychology is often said to have been born of philosophy and physiology in the 19th century when early psychologists attempted to measure mental experience through the methods used in the physical sciences of the day. While much of the stuff of early psychology has been abandoned as new approaches have dawned, there remains a strong emphasis on our mental experience and its relationship to behavior. Others would strongly assert that the only true science of psychology is one that ignores completely anything that is mind oriented and that only overt behaviors should be considered in understanding how and why we do what we do. Some theorists see our behavior and futures as predestined while others view humans as the executors of free will and choice. The controversy continues into the realm of mental health and illness also. Are the problems of life we call psychological disorders the result of complex and dynamic psychological systems or is mental illness just another kind of physical disease? This argument will influence the way we treat the problems of life and often will define that field of medicine we call psychiatry. There are also concerns over the methods we use to collect information for knowledge in psychology. These concerns include the extent to which such endeavors are really scientific, and issues such as using animals in research.

Finally, how should we use the knowledge gained from psychological research? Can the wrong people misuse it? The information is used numerous ways by a diverse group of people. Madison Avenue knows the power of the right stimulus in the right place when it comes to influencing millions of people to buy the items advertisers spend millions of dollars selling each day. Modern psychologists can be found in a myriad of different clinical and professional settings. In addition to the traditional role in health care and mental illness, today's psychologist may be involved in activities ranging from designing better car dash boards to teaching industry how to maintain employee moral while keeping productivity high. Psychology is a fascinating subject and you will be surprised at the ways it soon will, and already does touch your life. As you read The World of Psychology and attend your classes, you will be amazed as you discover the many ways you and those around you use psychology every day.

Study Guide

for

Wood and Wood

The World of Psychology

Third Edition

Dan Kelts · Guy Aylward

Illinois Central College

Allyn and Bacon
Boston · London · Toronto · Sydney · Tokyo · Singapore

About this Study Guide

This study guide is designed to make your voyage of discovery one that will lead to many dividends in your personal, academic, and professional life. As an accompaniment to your text, The World of Psychology, this study guide will help you be successful in your introductory psychology class. We hope our enthusiasm for the subject matter, along with the insights we have gained through our years of work in the field, will help you towards the achievement of a good grade in your class. More importantly though, we also hope that this study guide will assist you in developing an appreciation for the important and beneficial role psychology plays in your life. We have set forth several strategies and goals in this study guide that we believe will help in this goal. First, we believe the study guide will compliment the didactic information in the text through a variety of activities designed to expose you to the many different and practical ways that psychology is used in our lives. As you gain an appreciation for the real life applications of psychology we believe you will develop a deeper understanding of the material. A more functional understanding of the material will help you have a more comfortable command of tests or other class activities. Second, we believe that the more different ways you handle a piece of information, the more ways it will be available for you on the test. To this end, we have designed a variety of activities designed to personalize your familiarization of the information. We also believe that learning can be more fun than just cramming away in a study cubicle or dorm room hoping to memorize enough detail to be able to get by. We hope you will enjoy using this valuable resource, that you will be encouraged by its content and structure to engage yourself fully, and that such use will promote a sense of comfort with the information. There are, we believe, a number of added advantages to this process. They are: 1) as you develop confidence with the material, you will suffer less from test anxiety, 2) you will avoid the tendency to procrastinate studying until it is too late to really benefit from that study, and 3) as you discover how effective this kind of elaborate class preparation can be for your grade, you may generalize the techniques to other classes you are taking. In the long run, you will discover advantages to taking this class you may have never imagined! Psychology is a subject you will want to not only know for tests, but that you will find yourself using in many ways throughout the rest of your life.

The Objectives-Mastery Self-Evaluation (OMSE) System of Study

This book is designed around a self-paced, objective study program. Each chapter is divided into OMSE sections corresponding to major topics headings in the text. For each OMSE section there are presented a number of learning objectives and activities. Also, each OMSE section has a Learning Mastery Scorecard. It is recommended that you complete each OMSE section as an individual entity, starting with the first section and following in order each subsequent section. As you complete the activities and attain a sense of mastery over the objectives, record your progress on the scorecard. There are several advantages to this approach. These include approaching the often-complex chapter materials from a more manageable perspective rather than viewing the chapter as one overwhelming task. In addition, you will be able to set an objectives-mastery time plan and keep a record of your progress as you complete the learning activities and meet your goals. You will also gain a sense of accomplishment and confidence as you complete the score cards and move from one OMSE section to the next.

Each OMSE section includes the following activities:

QUICK QUIZ

After you have read the text corresponding to the OMSE and have worked with the key terms and concepts (see above), you can check your understanding of the material with the QUICK QUIZ. Take the quiz and then check your answers against the information in the text. Record the date of the quiz and your score. If you missed questions, review the material and key terms/concepts. After you have restudied the information, take the quiz again. Continue this process until you answer all the questions correctly. While answer keys are provided at the end of each chapter, it is recommended you do not use this key until you have searched the text for the correct answers and then re-quiz yourself two or three times.

PREPARE A LECTURE

The old adage, "the best way to learn something is to teach it," may serve you well as you prepare for your text and other class activities. As has been suggested, the more different ways you handle the information, the more different ways you know the information. Another bit of wisdom, "practice makes perfect," may or may not be true for all things but it is a great way to solidify information and enhance recall. Good teachers know that a well-organized lecture is one important mode of teaching that will provide information to students in a way that will help them learn. Teachers will often report that writing a lecture is also a good way to refresh their own knowledge of the topics. In writing an effective lecture one will handle the information in a variety of ways. Lecture preparation usually includes deciding on topic priorities, organizing the material, and integrating the relationship of concepts and applications to other subjects or life in general. Writing the notes for a lecture and assembling supplementary materials will assist in information mastery and recall. Writing a quiz or test over the lecture content is another form of "handling" the information. Finally, talking about the information (teaching it to someone else and then answering questions) can both solidify the fund of knowledge and serve as a kind of test of knowledge in and of itself.

This activity is designed to offer you an opportunity to take advantage of this valuable mode of learning. Each OMSE section will include a lecture exercise. Once you have finished each OMSE section you may want to write a lecture over the entire chapter. Once you have written the lecture for your current OMSE section, you can enhance your learning by also writing a quiz covering the material. Now it is time to find some willing and inquisitive audience members. Your roommates or family may be a great place to start. Present them the lecture as if you are teaching a class in Introduction to Psychology. Remember to ask for questions and give your students the quiz following the lecture. As you present the lecture and go over the quiz you will not only solidify your information and ability to use that information, but you may discover you know a lot more about the topics covered than you realized. This can do wonders for overcoming test anxiety. Each OMSE section includes a lecture preparation template you can use for this exercise.

This exercise can also serve to turn a *study-buddy* group into a very productive way to prepare for the test. Each member of the group can take different OMSE sections for their lecture/teacher role while the rest of the group serves as the class. The discussion of questions and answers along with the quiz will transform what is often simply another exercise in rote memory (or the study session that deteriorates in to a chat session) into a profitable and fun way to master the information.

THE OMSE SCORE CARDS

Update your score card as you work through the various sections of the chapter. First, find and define key terms and concepts included in each section and note the page number(s) from the text that contain important references to the material. Next, gain a practical understanding of the concepts by considering the Laboratory to Life scenarios and thinking of at least one original example of how the concept might apply in real life. Complete the *Objective-Mastery Self-Evaluation* (OMSE) exercises for this section and record your scores. Revisit the exercises, recording your score and the date completed until you have attained mastery (100%). Finally, decide how you would prepare a lecture on each objective using the template provided, outline the lecture, and practice presenting it. Keep an honest tally of your achievements and, when finished, you will have developed learning mastery through elaborate rehearsal.

Each chapter includes:

Information Integration and Application Exercises

KEY TERMS AND CONCEPTS

The key terms and concepts are presented in the order of their appearance in the text. Space is provided for you to include a personalized definition or example of each term or concept in your own words. As you encounter each term in the text, make a note of its meaning and context. You should also note the page of the text where the term or concept is found and record it on the scorecard. Next, conceptualize the meaning of the term in a way that makes the most sense to you. You can also think about examples of the term from your own life. Write your definition and/or example in the space provided next to the word in this book. The KEY TERMS pages in this book are designed in a way to help you self-quiz your mastery of the definitions. First lay a sheet of paper over the terms and concepts side of the page so that you only see the definitions. Read the definition and try to recall the term or concept. Mark all those you are unable to answer so you can restudy them. When you have learned all of the terms and concepts in this way, move the paper to the definition side so that you can see only the term or concept, try to recall both the textbook definition and your personal version. Repeat this until you know all of the terms and concepts by definition and personal understanding.

FROM THE LABORATORY TO REAL LIFE

This exercise will enhance your understanding of the subject matter as you read brief real-life examples and respond to the questions following each. You will also generalize your knowledge to different situations. It is likely that your unit examination will present a variety of ways to think about and use the concepts and terms in the text chapters. Answer keys are provided at the end of the chapter.

FROM THEORY TO PRACTICE

Psychology deals with information and theory that often results in controversy. Whether you agree or disagree with a particular issue, it is important that you understand the issue and be able to communicate your opinions in an articulate manner. This exercise will provide you an opportunity to use your knowledge of the chapter material in an applied manner – the assertion and support of opinions regarding controversial issues. This activity will add a new dimension to your command of the subject matter and should make you more prepared to be successful on tests and other classroom activities. Read each item and then respond to the issues posed by that item. This is another great way to take advantage of study-buddy groups as you discuss different ways to think about and support your opinions regarding the various issues.

COMPREHENSIVE PRACTICE TEST

Once you have mastered the objectives in each chapter OMSE, test your knowledge of the chapter as a whole. Take the test and then check your answers. Once again, it is advised you check your answers by finding them in your reading prior to using the chapter KEY.

1

INTRODUCTION TO PSYCHOLOGY

Psychology is defined as the scientific study of behavior and mental processes.

CHAPTER OVERVIEW

I can still remember my freshman year of college. Since I lived off campus, I participated in a car pool. On the way to campus one day, a fellow passenger asked about my major. When I told her I was studying psychology she replied, "Oh, we had better be careful, you can probably read our minds." At the time, I wasn't quite sure how to respond to this statement. In fact, at that time I wasn't certain what psychology was and what it was not. I knew that, so far, we had not talked about mind reading in class. As a matter of fact, after two weeks into the semester, it didn't seem like we had talked much about psychology at all! We were going to have an exam soon and I was still trying to figure out the difference between the mean, the mode, and the median. What was this thing called psychology?

I soon learned that psychology had absolutely nothing to do with reading minds. I also learned that psychology was much more than I had anticipated. Psychology seemed to be a part of just about everything that happened in the world, from personal relationships to world politics, and from education to economics. I became fascinated with the ways in which psychology could influence and shape our world. Well, I never did learn to read minds, but I did learn many innovative and provocative ways in which to look at and understand behavior—and so will you.

This chapter will help you gain a more functional understanding of psychology as an individual science, its history, and current trends in psychology. The materials are divided into two Objective-Mastery Self-Evaluation (OMSE) sections, 1) psychology as a science, and 2) the history of psychology (including current status). You will be introduced to some of the major theoretical approaches in psychology today as you proceed through your introduction to psychology. These include the psychoanalytical approach, behaviorism, the cognitive perspective, and humanism. Become familiar with the names and concepts associated with these major approaches as you will encounter them often as you proceed through the various issues and concerns addressed in class and in the textbook. Now is the time to build a basic knowledge of each perspective, as this understanding will serve as a foundation upon which to begin to build your understanding of human development, personality, psychological disorders, and therapy.

TIMELINE

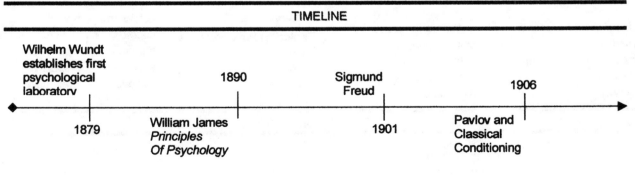

Wilhelm Wundt establishes first psychological laboratory — 1879

1890 — William James *Principles Of Psychology*

Sigmund Freud — 1901

1906 — Pavlov and Classical Conditioning

CHAPTER OUTLINE

Psychology: An Introduction
Psychology: Science or Common Sense?
The Goals of Psychology
Critical Thinking: Thinking Like A Scientist
Descriptive Research Methods
Naturalistic Observation: Caught in the Act of Being Themselves
The Case Study Method: Studying a Few Subjects in Depth
Survey Research: The Art of Sampling and Questioning
The Experimental Method: Searching for Causes
Independent and Dependent Variables
Experimental and Control Groups: The Same Except for the Treatment
Generalizing the Experimental Findings: Do the Findings Apply to Other Groups?

Potential Problems in Experimental Research
Advantages and Limitations of the Experimental Method
Other Research Methods
The Correlational Method: Discovering Relationships, Not Causes
Psychological Tests: Assessing the Subject
Meta-analysis: Combining the Results of Many Studies
Participants in Psychological Research
Ethics in Research: Protecting the Participants
Human Participants in Psychological Research
Bias in Psychological Research
The Use of Animals in Research

Exploring Psychology's Roots
Wilhelm Wundt: The Founding of Psychology
Titchener and Structuralism
Functionalism: The First American School of Psychology
Gestalt Psychology: The Whole Is More Than Just the Sum of Its Parts
Behaviorism: Never Mind the Mind
Psychoanalysis: It's What's Down Deep That Counts
Humanistic Psychology: Looking at Human Potential
Cognitive Psychology: Focusing on Mental Processes
Psychology Today
Modern Perspectives in Psychology: Current Views on Behavior and Thinking
Psychologists at Work
Apply It! Study Skills and Critical Thinking
Thinking Critically
Chapter Summary and Review

TERMS AND CONCEPTS

Introduction to Psychology
psychology
scientific method
theory
basic research
applied research
critical thinking
Descriptive Research Methods
descriptive research methods
naturalistic observation
case study
survey

population
sample
representative sample
The Experimental Method: Searching for Causes
experimental method
hypothesis
independent variable
dependent variable
experimental group
control group
selection bias
random assignment
placebo effect

placebo
experimenter bias
double-blind technique
Other Research Methods
correlational method
correlation coefficient
reliability
validity
replication
meta-analysis
Exploring Psychology's Roots
structuralism
functionalism

behaviorism
psychoanalysis
Gestalt psychology
humanistic psychology
cognitive psychology
Psychology Today
biological perspective
neuroscience
psychoanalytic perspective
behavioral perspective
cognitive perspective
humanistic perspective
evolutionary perspective
sociocultural perspective

TIMELINE

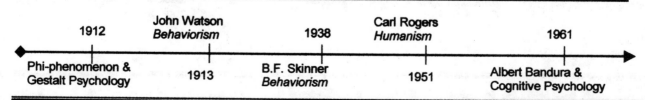

| 1912 | John Watson *Behaviorism* | 1938 | Carl Rogers *Humanism* | 1961 |

Phi-phenomenon & Gestalt Psychology   1913   B.F. Skinner *Behaviorism*   1951   Albert Bandura & Cognitive Psychology

OMSE # 1: PSYCHOLOGY AS A SCIENCE

LEARNING OBJECTIVES:

1. What is the scientific method?
2. What are the four goals of psychology?
3. What is naturalistic observation, and what are some of its advantages and limitations?
4. What is the case study method, and for what purposes is it particularly well suited?
5. What are the methods and purposes of survey research?
6. What is a representative sample, and why is it essential in a survey?
7. What is the main advantage of the experimental method?
8. What is the difference between the independent variable and the dependent variable?
9. How do experimental groups and control groups differ?
10. What is selection bias, and what technique do researchers use to control for it?
11. What is the placebo effect, and how do researchers control for it?
12. What is experimenter bias, and how is it controlled?
13. What is the correlational method, and when is it used?
14. What is a correlation coefficient?
15. What is meta-analysis?
16. What are some ethical guidelines governing the use of human subjects in research?
17. Why are animals used in research?

LEARNING MASTERY SCORECARD: Update your score card as you work through the various sections of the chapter. First, find and define key terms and concepts included in each section and note the page number(s) from the text that contain important references to the material. Next, gain a practical understanding of the concepts by considering the Laboratory to Life scenarios and thinking of at least one original example of how the concept might apply in real life. Complete the *Objective-Mastery Self-Evaluation* (OMSE) exercises for this section and record your scores. Revisit the exercises, recording your score and the date completed until you have attained mastery (100%). Finally, decide how you would prepare a lecture on each objective using the template provided, outline the lecture, and practice presenting it. Keep an honest tally of your achievements and, when finished, you will have developed learning mastery through elaborate rehearsal.

Key terms & concepts	Page #	Key terms & concepts	Page #
psychology	_____	dependent variable	_____
scientific method	_____	experimental group	_____
theory	_____	control group	_____
basic research	_____	selection bias	_____
applied research	_____	random assignment	_____
critical thinking	_____	placebo effect	_____
descriptive research methods	_____	placebo	_____
naturalistic observation	_____	experimenter bias	_____
case study	_____	double-blind technique	_____
survey	_____	correlational method	_____
population	_____	correlation coefficient	_____
sample	_____	reliability	_____
representative sample	_____	validity	_____
experimental method	_____	replication	_____
hypothesis	_____	meta-analysis	_____
independent variable	_____		

Quick Quiz

Date	Score	Date	Score	Date	Score
_/_/_	_____	_/_/_	_____	_/_/_	_____
_/_/_	_____	_/_/_	_____	_/_/_	100%

Elaborate Rehearsal

Lecture Preparation	Completion Date
Key Terms, Persons, & Concepts	__/__/__
Learning Objectives	__/__/__
Lecture Notes	__/__/__

Quick Quiz

1. Which of the following was NOT listed as a goal of psychology?
    a) description
    b) manipulation
    c) prediction
    d) control

2. A theory serves to organize facts and _____ _____.

3. Basic research is to _____ as applied research is to _____:
    a) correlation; statistics
    b) naturalistic observation; case study
    c) new knowledge; problem solving
    d) control group; experimental group

4. The most valuable aspect of naturalistic observation is that we can infer cause-effect conclusions from our observations.
    a) True
    b) False

5. One way to gather information in psychology is to study a single individual or small number of persons in great depth, over an extended period of time. This technique is called the _____ _____ method.

6. In a typical psychological experiment, we study members of the _____ and hope to be able to generalize our findings to the _____.
    a) population; sample
    b) control group; experimental group
    c) sample; population
    d) experimental group; control group

7. Imagine that a survey was being undertaken of students at your school. The findings of this survey would result in information and decisions that could effect the entire student body. You would hope that the survey would tap a _____ sample of students in order to accurately reflect the opinions of the student body.

8. Professor Smith is interested in the difference between student attention span just before lunch and just after lunch. She randomly assigns students to one of two groups. One group will listen to a lecture on global warming at 11 AM, followed by a lecture comprehension test. The second group will hear the same lecture and take the same test at 1 PM. She would use the test scores to help answer the question about attention span. In this experiment, the independent variable is _____ and the dependent variable is _____.
    a) students; group assignment
    b) time of day; test scores
    c) group assignment; students
    d) test scores; time of day

9. A pharmaceutical company is interested in improving their current allergy medication. They hope the improved version will help sufferers find more relief from symptoms. Two groups of allergy sufferers are randomly assigned to either the current medicine condition or the new medicine condition. After a period of time, all subjects are asked to rate levels of symptom relief. In this experiment, the control group will receive the _____ medicine and the experimental group will receive the _____ medicine.

10. A random sample is used to control for:
    a) the independent variable
    b) random subjects
    c) the experimental group
    d) selection bias

11. A researcher found a strong positive correlation between scores on a driving simulator game and scores on an eye-hand coordination test. This means that practicing the driving simulator game causes better eye-hand coordination.
    a) True
    b) False

12. A psychologist wants to determine if talk therapy alone is as effective as talk therapy combined with anti-anxiety medicine for treating agoraphobia. He decides to run an experiment where some participants receive talk therapy alone and some receive both talk therapy and the medicine. However, in order to treat both groups the same, the talk therapy group receives a sugar pill at the same time the other subjects are receiving their anti-anxiety medicine. The sugar pill was identified in the book as a(n) _____.

13. In the above experiment, the psychologist does not know which group is receiving the therapy and real medicine, and which group is receiving the therapy and a sugar pill. This strategy was referred to in your text as the _____ technique and is used to control for _____.
    a) placebo; participant selection
    b) double-blind; participant expectations
    c) placebo; experimenter bias
    d) double-blind; experimenter bias

14. When a test yields consistent results we would say it is _____. When a test measures what it is intended to measure, we say it is _____.

15. When it comes to ethics in research, it is clear that there is little controversy regarding issues such as subject deception and the use of animals.
    a) True
    b) False

Throughout history, psychology has been the subject of discussion for philosophers and a topic of curiosity for others. It was not until 1879, however, that psychology emerged as a science when Wilhelm Wundt put human consciousness under the laboratory microscope.

B. Matching

_____	1.	Entire group of interest	a)	Independent Variable
_____	2.	Relationship between two variables	b)	Dependent Variable
_____	3.	A prediction	c)	Theory
_____	4.	The variable that is manipulated	d)	Hypothesis
_____	5.	Sub-group of the population that is studied	e)	Control Group
_____	6.	Method to determine cause-effect relationship	f)	Experimental Group
_____	7.	A general principle	g)	Population
_____	8.	Exposed to the independent variable	h)	Sample
_____	9.	The variable that is measured	i)	Experiment
_____	10.	Not exposed to the independent variable	j)	Correlation

C. Review Methods for Gathering Information in Psychology

Select from the *response menu* those items that most accurately describe each of the following methods for gathering information in psychology. Some items may take more than one response and some responses may be used more than once.

1. Naturalistic Observation		2. Laboratory Observation		3. Case Study		4. Survey	
Description:	_____	Description:	_____	Description:	_____	Description:	_____
Advantages:	_____	Advantages:	_____	Advantages:	_____	Advantages:	_____
Disadvantages:	_____	Disadvantages:	_____	Disadvantages:	_____	Disadvantages:	_____

5. Experimental Method		6. Correlational Method		7. Psychological Tests		8. Meta-analysis	
Description:	_____	Description:	_____	Description:	_____	Description:	_____
Advantages:	_____	Advantages:	_____	Advantages:	_____	Advantages:	_____
Disadvantages:	_____	Disadvantages:	_____	Disadvantages:	_____	Disadvantages:	_____

Response Menu

Description	Advantages	Disadvantages
a) statistical method to combine results of research studies	a) assess strength of a relationship	a) tests may not be reliable or valid
b) randomly assign subjects to groups for comparison	b) accurate information about large numbers of people	b) findings may be no more reliable than the original research
c) interview or questionnaire from a group of people	c) identify cause – effect relationships	c) possible observer bias
d) observe under more controlled conditions	d) estimate of combined effect of many studies	d) little control over conditions
e) observe behavior in its natural setting	e) provide data for a variety of decision making settings	e) does not demonstrate cause and effect
f) used to determine the relationship between two variables	f) more control than naturalistic observation	f) interviewer may influence subject responses
g) tests used to measure a variety of psychological traits or characteristics	g) source of information for rare or unusual conditions or events	g) information may not be representative of condition or event
h) in-depth study of one or a few subjects	h) provides descriptive information	h) possible inaccurate responses and may not be a representative sample

PREPARE A LECTURE: This activity is designed to offer you an opportunity to take advantage of a valuable mode of learning, elaborate rehearsal. Once you have finished the OMSE section, write a lecture using the instructional guide provided below. After your lecture is prepared, you can enhance your learning by writing a quiz covering the material. Now it is time to find some willing and inquisitive audience members. Your roommates or family may be a great place to start. Present them the lecture as if you are teaching a class. Remember to ask for questions and give your students the quiz following the lecture. This exercise can also serve to turn a *study-buddy* group into a very productive way to prepare for the test. Each member of the group can take different OMSE sections for their lecture/teacher role while the rest of the group serves as the class.

I. Key Terms, Names, Dates, and Concepts you will include in this lecture:

1. _____   5. _____   9. _____
2. _____   6. _____   10. _____
3. _____   7. _____   11. _____
4. _____   8. _____   12. _____

II. Learning Objectives (what do you want the student to know and be able to do as a result of your lecture):

1. _____
2. _____
3. _____
4. _____
5. _____

III. Lecture Notes (notes should be brief cues and serve as a guide).

Major topic #1: _____

   Sub-topics and notes: _____

   _____

   _____

   _____

Major topic #2: _____

    Sub-topics and notes: _____

_____

_____

_____

Major topic #3: _____

    Sub-topics and notes: _____

_____

_____

_____

OMSE # 2: THE HISTORY OF PSYCHOLOGY

LEARNING OBJECTIVES

1. What was Wundt's contribution to psychology?
2. What were the goals and method of structuralism, the first school of psychology?
3. What was the goal of the early school of psychology known as functionalism?
4. What is the emphasis of Gestalt psychology?
5. How did behaviorism differ from previous schools of psychology?
5. What was the role of the unconscious in psychoanalysis, Freud's approach to psychology?
6. What is the focus of humanistic psychology?
7. What is the focus of cognitive psychology?
8. What are the seven major perspectives in psychology today?
9. What are some specialists in psychology, and in what settings are they employed?

LEARNING MASTERY SCORECARD: Update your score card as you work through the various sections of the chapter. First, find and define key terms and concepts included in each section and note the page number(s) from the text that contain important references to the material. Next, gain a practical understanding of the concepts by considering the Laboratory to Life scenarios and thinking of at least one original example of how the concept might apply in real life. Complete the *Objective-Mastery Self-Evaluation* (OMSE) exercises for this section and record your scores. Revisit the exercises, recording your score and the date completed until you have attained mastery (100%). Finally, decide how you would prepare a lecture on each objective using the template provided, outline the lecture, and practice presenting it. Keep an honest tally of your achievements and, when finished, you will have developed learning mastery through elaborate rehearsal.

Key terms & concepts	Page #	Key terms & concepts	Page #
structuralism	_____	biological perspective	_____
functionalism	_____	psychoanalytic perspective	_____
behaviorism	_____	behavioral perspective	_____
psychoanalysis	_____	cognitive perspective	_____
Gestalt psychology	_____	humanistic perspective	_____
humanistic psychology	_____	evolutionary perspective	_____
cognitive psychology	_____	sociocultural perspective	_____

Quick Quiz

Date	Score	Date	Score	Date	Score
_/_/_	_____	_/_/_	_____	_/_/_	_____
_/_/_	_____	_/_/_	_____	_/_/_	100%

Elaborate Rehearsal

Lecture Preparation	Completion Date
Key Terms & Concepts	_/_/_
Learning Objectives	_/_/_
Lecture Notes	_/_/_

A. Quick Quiz

1. Which psychologist is generally considered the "father of psychology?"
   a) Freud
   b) Titchener
   c) Watson
   d) Wundt

2. The most famous student of the first school of psychology was which of the following:
   a) Freud
   b) Titchener
   c) Watson
   d) Wundt

3. The first psychological laboratory set up in the United States was established under which school of thought in psychology:
   a) psychoanalysis
   b) structuralism
   c) behaviorism
   d) functionalism

4. When the new psychology of structuralism came to America, a more pragmatic approach, influenced by the work of Charles Darwin, gained acceptance and was known as:
   a) psychoanalysis
   b) functionalism
   c) evolutionary
   d) behaviorism

5. Watson's basic ideas (mental processes are not observable and therefore not appropriate for the science of psychology) became known as:
   a) psychoanalysis
   b) humanism
   c) behaviorism
   d) functionalism

6. Watson espoused the view that behavior is determined primarily by factors in the environment
   a) True
   b) False

7. B. F. Skinner continued the behaviorist tradition through his studies in _____ conditioning.

8. Freud's theory of personality and his therapy for the treatment of psychological disorders share a common name. It is:
   a) psychoanalysis
   b) humanism
   c) behaviorism
   d) functionalism

9. According to Freud's theory, the _____ is the most important determinant of behavior.
   a) conscious
   b) subconscious
   c) preconscious
   d) unconscious

10. The leader of the Gestalt movement in psychology was:
    a) Freud
    b) Wertheimer
    c) Watson
    d) Skinner

11. Gestalt psychology emphasized the importance of:
    a) analysis of the mind
    b) introspection
    c) the principles of perceptual organization
    d) measurable behaviors

12. The humanistic school of psychology has tended to emphasize:
    a) the uniqueness of human beings
    b) the human capacity for growth
    c) the human capacity for free choice
    d) all of the above

13. The focus of this school of psychology is on mental processes, decision making, language, and perception:
    a) cognitive
    b) humanism
    c) behaviorism
    d) psychoanalysis

14. This psychological perspective focuses on biochemistry, genetics, and the brain:
    a) cognitive perspective
    b) biological perspective
    c) behaviorist perspective
    d) psychoanalytic perspective

15. This view of psychology stresses the roles of social and cultural influences on behavior:
    a) behavioral perspective
    b) psychoanalytic perspective
    c) cognitive perspective
    d) sociological perspective

B. MATCHING

_____	1. Freud	a) behaviorism
_____	2. Titchener	b) cognitive
_____	3. James	c) humanistic
_____	4. Wertheimer	d) psychoanalysis
_____	5. Wundt	e) introspection
_____	6. Watson	f) structuralism
_____	7. Information-processing approach	g) Gestalt
_____	8. Maslow and Rogers	h) functionalism

C. COMPLETE THE DIAGRAM: Fill in the theorist or the psychological perspective as indicated.

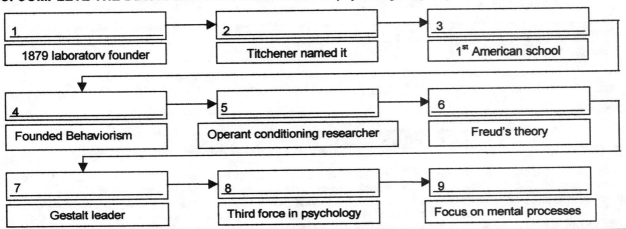

1. _____	2. _____	3. _____
1879 laboratory founder	Titchener named it	1st American school

4. _____	5. _____	6. _____
Founded Behaviorism	Operant conditioning researcher	Freud's theory

7. _____	8. _____	9. _____
Gestalt leader	Third force in psychology	Focus on mental processes

> So many theories—so little time! How will I ever know which is right? Relax—each theory overlaps with the next in some way. There are major differences, but you do not have to decide that one is absolute. Try to apply the concepts to your own life and decide what fits you the best. There, now isn't that better?

PREPARE A LECTURE: This activity is designed to offer you an opportunity to take advantage of a valuable mode of learning, elaborate rehearsal. Once you have finished the OMSE section, write a lecture using the instructional guide provided below. After your lecture is prepared, you can enhance your learning by writing a quiz covering the material. Now it is time to find some willing and inquisitive audience members. Your roommates or family may be a great place to start. Present them the lecture as if you are teaching a class. Remember to ask for questions and give your students the quiz following the lecture. This exercise can also serve to turn a *study-buddy* group into a very productive way to prepare for the test. Each member of the group can take different OMSE sections for their lecture/teacher role while the rest of the group serves as the class.

I. Key Terms, Names, Dates, and Concepts you will include in this lecture:

1. _____   5. _____   9. _____
2. _____   6. _____   10. _____
3. _____   7. _____   11. _____
4. _____   8. _____   12. _____

II. Learning Objectives (what do you want the student to know and be able to do as a result of your lecture):

1. _____
2. _____
3. _____
4. _____
5. _____

III. Lecture Notes (notes should be brief cues and serve as a guide).

Major topic #1: _____

   Sub-topics and notes: _____

_____

_____

_____

Major topic #2: _____

   Sub-topics and notes: _____

_____

_____

_____

Major topic #3: _____

   Sub-topics and notes: _____

_____

_____

_____

_____

KEY TERMS AND CONCEPTS EXCERCISE

The key terms and concepts are presented in the order of their appearance in the text. Space is provided for you to include a personalized definition or example of each term or concept. As you encounter each term in the text, make a note of its meaning and context. Next, conceptualize the meaning of the term in a way that makes the most sense to you. You can also think about examples of the term from your own life. Write your definition and/or example in the space provided next to the word in this book. The KEY TERMS exercise utilizes a modified *T-note* design so that you can self-evaluate your mastery of the definitions. First lay a sheet of paper over the terms and concepts side of the page so that you only see the definitions. Read the definition and try to recall the term or concept. Mark all those you are unable to answer so you can restudy them. When you have learned all of the terms and concepts in this way, move the paper to the definition side so that you can see only the term or concept, try to recall both the textbook definition and your personal version. Repeat this until you know all of the terms and concepts by definition and personal understanding.

Psychology	The scientific study of behavior and mental processes. Since psychologists can neither read a person's thoughts, nor capture and weigh a person's mental processes, behaviors are the best available source of understanding and inferring psychological processes. _____ _____ _____
Scientific Method	The orderly, systematic procedures researchers follow as they identify a research problem, design a study to investigate the problem, collect and analyze their data, draw conclusions, and communicate their findings. _____ _____ _____
Theory	A general principle or set of principles proposed in order to explain how a number of separate facts are related to one another. For example, you will study Piaget's theory of cognitive development later in this class. Piaget watched his children grow and change according to what appeared to be stages. He put together the facts and offered a theory to help explain the process. _____ _____ _____

Basic Research	Research conducted for the purpose of advancing knowledge rather than for its practical application. Recent advances in technology (e.g., PET scan and fMRI) have aided scientists in researching potential genetic precursors to such disorders as Alzheimer's disease and schizophrenia. _____
Applied Research	Research conducted for the purpose of solving practical problems. Once basic research has pinpointed certain potential causes of an illness, applied researchers can begin the task of researching the most effective treatment methods. _____
Critical Thinking	The ability and determination to reach conclusions and make judgements based on objective evidence. _____
Descriptive Research Methods	Research methods that yield descriptions of behavior rather than causal explanations. Because psychology is a relatively young science, there are many unanswered questions regarding behavior and mental processes. Observation and description is generally the best place to begin searching for answers. _____
Naturalistic Observation	A research method in which the researcher observes and records behavior in its natural setting, without attempting to influence or control it. TV shows like 60 minutes have made their reputation and maintained their ratings by filming people without their knowledge. Often we see the behavior of greed played out on our TV screens. _____
Case Study	An in-depth study of one or a few subjects consisting of information gathered through observation, interview, and perhaps psychological testing. Freud developed his theory of personality based almost entirely on his studies of individual cases. _____
Survey	A method in which researchers use interviews and/or questionnaires to gather information about the attitudes, beliefs, experiences, or behaviors of a group of people. If you watch the news, especially at election time, you have no doubt seen the political opinion polls.
Population	The entire group of interest to researchers and to which they wish to generalize their findings; the group from which a sample is selected. If you wanted to learn about the study habits of all students at your school, you would probably only study a segment, or sample, of the student population. If the sample were selected properly, you would then be able to generalize those findings to the entire population—all students at the school. _____

Sample	The portion of any population that is selected for study and from which generalizations are made about the larger population. Samples must be representative of the population before generalizations can be made. If you were studying all students at your school, you wouldn't select a sample of all White males and expect to generalize to the entire population.
Representative Sample	A sample of subjects selected from the larger population in such a way that important subgroups within the population are included in the sample in the same proportion as they are found in the larger population. Samples are usually chosen to include correct proportions in regard to race, gender, age and other important determinants of attitudes and beliefs.
Experimental Method	The research method in which researchers randomly assign subjects to groups and control all conditions other than one or more independent variables, which are then manipulated to determine their effect on some behavioral measure—the dependent variable in the experiment. *Experimental is the only method that can be used to identify cause-effect relationships.*
Hypothesis	A prediction about the relationship between two or more variables. One hypothesis you may be familiar with is—the more effort you put into studying, the better your grades will be.
Independent Variable	In an experiment, the factor or condition that the researcher manipulates in order to determine its effects on another behavior or condition known as the dependent variable. Let's say you currently study 3 hours per week, carry a 2.5 GPA, and are interested in learning what effect studying 12 hours per week will have on your GPA. The independent variable in your experiment would be the amount of study time. GPA would be the dependent variable.
Dependent Variable	The variable that is measured at the end of an experiment and is presumed to vary as a result of manipulations of the independent variable. See the scenario above.
Experimental Group	In an experiment, the group of subjects that is exposed to the independent variable, or the treatment. If you wanted to learn more about the effects of increased study on college students as a population, you would select a representative sample and divide that sample into two groups, the experimental group and the control group. The experimental group would increase the hours spent studying while the control group would continue to study at the same rate as always. All conditions would remain equal except study hours.

Control Group	In an experiment, a group that is similar to the experimental group and is exposed to the same experimental environment but is not exposed to the independent variable; used for purposes of comparison. See the above scenario. _____ _____ _____ _____
Selection Bias	The assignment of subjects to experimental or control groups in such a way that systematic differences among the groups are present at the beginning of the experiment. For example, in the study proposed above, if most or all of the subjects in the experimental group already have GPA's of 3.5 or higher and most or all of the subjects in the control group have current GPA's of 2.5 or lower, the results of the experiment could be skewed. _____ _____ _____ _____
Random Assignment	In an experiment, the assignment of subjects to experimental and control groups by using a chance procedure, which guarantees that all subjects have an equal probability of being placed in any of the groups; a control for selection bias. If the total population under investigation consists of 5000 students, and you want two randomly assigned groups of 50 students each, you must ensure that each of the 5000 students has an equal opportunity of being selected for both groups. _____ _____ _____
Placebo Effect	The phenomenon that occurs when a person's response to a treatment or response on the dependent variable in an experiment is due to expectations regarding the treatment rather than the treatment itself. Many studies on the effectiveness of drugs for treating specific disorders or symptoms include a placebo group. This differentiates between the placebo effect and the true effects of the experimental manipulation or independent variable. _____ _____ _____ _____
Experimenter Bias	A phenomenon that occurs when the researcher's preconceived notions in some way influence the subjects' behavior and/or the interpretation of experimental results. If a particular professor wanted to experimentally demonstrate the effectiveness of a new teaching method, she may unintentionally communicate her expectations to subjects or interpret the data in such a way as to skew the results in favor of her hypothesis. _____ _____ _____
Double-Blind Technique	An experimental procedure in which neither the subject nor the experimenter knows who is in the experimental or control groups until after the results have been gathered; a control for experimenter bias. Often the lead researcher on a project will assign research assistants to administer the experimental manipulation, collect and record data, and analyze the data. Since they are blind (in the dark) as to the nature of the expectations, bias is controlled for. _____ _____ _____
Correlational Method	A research method used to establish the relationship (correlation) between two characteristics, events, or behaviors. As healthy children mature, they grow taller and heavier. Does the height increase cause the weight increase or vice versa? No, but there is certainly a strong positive correlation between the two. _____ _____ _____ _____

Correlation Coefficient	A numerical value that indicates the strength and direction of the relationship between two variables; ranges from +1.00 (a perfect positive correlation) to −1.00 (a perfect negative correlation). There is a strong negative correlation between amount of alcohol ingested and reaction time. As alcohol intake goes up, reaction time goes down. _____ _____ _____ _____ _____
Reliability	The ability of a test to yield nearly the same scores when the same people are tested and then retested using the same test or an alternate form of the test. For a test to be reliable it must be consistent. A scale that fluctuates by 2 or 3 pounds with each use is still measuring weight, but it is not measuring the weight reliably. _____ _____ _____ _____
Validity	The ability of a test to measure what it is intended to measure. If your psychology professor decided to give you a pop quiz on chapter 1, but inadvertently included ten questions on chapter 7, the quiz would not be measuring what it is intended to measure—your knowledge of chapter 1—and would, therefore, not be valid. _____ _____ _____ _____
Replication	The process of repeating a study with different subjects and preferably a different investigator to verify research findings. Perhaps you've noticed that there have been several promising advances in HIV research announced over the past decade. Some of these advances have been reported as the cure for AIDS, only to disappoint when tested by another or several other researchers. _____ _____ _____ _____
Meta-analysis	A complex statistical procedure used by researchers to combine the results of many studies on the same topic in order to determine the degree to which a hypothesis can be supported. In a study heralded as a landmark because of the early use of meta-analysis, two researchers supported the hypothesis that psychotherapy was an effective method of treatment. _____ _____ _____
Structuralism	The first formal school of psychology, aimed at analyzing the basic elements, or structures, of conscious mental experience through the use of introspection. _____ _____ _____ _____
Functionalism	An early school of psychology that was concerned with how mental processes help humans and animals adapt to their environments. _____ _____ _____ _____
Behaviorism	The school of psychology founded by John B. Watson that views observable, measurable behavior as the appropriate subject matter for psychology and emphasizes the key role of environment as a determinant of behavior. _____ _____ _____ _____

Psychoanalysis	The term Freud used for both his theory of personality and his therapy for the treatment of psychological disorders; the unconscious is the primary focus of the psychoanalytic theory.
Gestalt Psychology	The school of psychology that emphasizes that individuals perceive objects and patterns as whole units and that the perceived whole is greater than the sum of its parts.
Humanistic Psychology	The school of psychology that focuses on the uniqueness of human beings and their capacity for choice, growth, and psychological health.
Cognitive Psychology	A specialty that studies mental processes such as memory, problem solving, decision making, perception, language, and other forms of cognition; often uses the information-processing approach.
Biological Perspective	A perspective that emphasizes the role of biological processes and heredity as the key to understanding behavior.
Neuroscience	A field that combined the work of psychologists, biologists, biochemists, medical researchers, and others in the study of the structure and function of the nervous system.
Psychoanalytic Perspective	A perspective initially proposed by Freud that emphasizes the importance of the unconscious and of early childhood experiences as the keys to understanding behavior and thought.
Behavioral Perspective	A perspective that emphasizes the role of environment in shaping behavior.
Cognitive Perspective	A perspective that emphasizes the role of mental processes that underlie behavior.
Humanistic Perspective	A perspective that emphasizes the importance of an individual's subjective experience as a key to understanding behavior.
Evolutionary Perspective	A perspective that focuses on how humans have evolved and adapted behaviors required for survival against various environmental pressures over the long course of evolution.

Sociocultural Perspective	A perspective that focuses on social and cultural influences on human behavior and stresses the importance of understanding those influences when we interpret the behavior of others.

FROM THE LABORATORY TO LIFE

DESIGN AN EXPERIMENT

Imagine you are a psychology major in an experimental psychology class. As an assignment for this class you are to design an experiment. You are interested in the effects of stress on witness recall. Your experiment will divide subjects into two groups. Each group will watch five different videos involving incidents such as a car accident and a fight between two spectators at a sporting event. After each video, subjects will respond to questions regarding what they just observed. One group (group A) will watch the videos while sitting in a comfortable chair in a quiet room. The other group (Group B) will watch the videos while sitting in an uncomfortable chair in a room that has a variety of visual and audio distractions. In addition, the temperature in the quiet room is 70 degrees Fahrenheit while the other room has a temperature of 95 degrees Fahrenheit. Following this exercise, you will compare the average number of correct responses to the questions for each group.

1. What is the independent variable in this experiment?_____

2. What is the dependent variable in this experiment? _____

3. Which group (A or B) is the control group? _____ Which group (A or B) is the experimental group? _____

4. In order to control for selection bias, you should use _____ assignment when you decide who will be members of which group.

5. You are doing this experiment to test the _____ (prediction) that the subjects in group-A will score higher on correct responses than the subjects in group-B.

6. From your text, the above procedures sound most like the _____ method of research in psychology.

CHOOSING A CAREER IN PSYCHOLOGY

Imagine that, as a psychology major, you are in the process of selecting a specialty area in which you will work once you have completed your psychology training. As a precursor to deciding on your specialty, you visit a variety of work settings to gather information about each potential specialty area. What you observe is contained in the brief descriptions below.

Read each description and select the specialty from the list that is most accurately depicted by each description. Place the appropriate letter on the line provided.

Specialty Codes

A) Educational Psychology	C) Physiological Psychology	E) Developmental Psychology
B) Counseling Psychology	D) Experimental Psychology	F) Industrial/Organizational

Specialty Descriptions

1. Workers here study the structure and function of the brain and nervous system to determine the relationship between these structures and behavior.	_____
2. Workers here study the relationship between people and their work environment. Goals include increased productivity for the employer and increased job satisfaction for the employee.	_____
3. Workers here study the processes involved in how people grow, develop, and change throughout the life span. Some of these workers are known as child psychologists and some are known as gerontologists.	_____
4. Workers here help people with adjustment problems. They also sometimes provide academic or vocational counseling. This is a non-medical setting.	_____

5. You now visit a laboratory where workers are seeking new information in a variety of specialization areas. The laboratory setting allows precise control in a manner to isolate the effects of independent variables on dependent variables.	_____
6. Workers here are studying the processes of teaching and learning. A lot of their work is in a school where they do things like test students, and counsel students or teachers on a variety of school-related problems.	_____

PSYCHOLOGICAL TIME TRAVELER

Imagine that you can travel back in time and meet the people responsible for psychology's evolution. Read each statement below and then, in the blank that follows identify the person with whom you are talking.

1. I became the first African American president of the APA.   _____

2. I did research on operant conditioning and the effects of reinforcement on behavior._____

3. I disagreed with Freud on his male-based theory of personality.   _____

4. I established the first psychological laboratory in Leipzig, Germany.   _____

5. I wrote the book *Principles of Psychology* and advocated *functionalism*.   _____

6. I was the first African American to earn a Ph.D. in psychology in the U.S.   _____

7. I opposed the mind-oriented psychology of my time and promoted *behaviorism*. _____

8. I wrote about *social learning* and helped begin the *cognitive revolution*. _____

9. I founded the American Psychological Association in 1882.   _____

FROM THEORY TO PRACTICE

IS PSYCHOLOGY REALLY A SCIENCE?

Throughout its brief history, psychology has undergone many changes. It seems as though each decade of psychology's evolution has brought with it new criticisms and radical proposals for change. For example, Wundt was convinced that the human mind could best be understood by grasping the complexities of the elements of consciousness. He went about demonstrating the validity of his belief by having individuals practice introspection. When Wundt's theory became better known, there was widespread reaction to it. The Gestalt school opposed the concept of limiting the understanding of humanity to a group of independent structures. The functionalists, inspired by the work of Charles Darwin, declared function, not structures, to be the key to understanding the human mind. Watson and the behaviorists scoffed at the idea of studying hypothetical constructs and calling it science. Over the past three decades, technological advances have provided support for the biological perspective, and clinical trials have shown cognitive-behavioral therapy to be a successful treatment for many psychological disorders. Freud's psychoanalysis still has a loyal following and humanistic psychology has received acclaim from many practitioners.

So who had or has the right idea? Is psychology even a science? Have you ever seen a mind or a personality? Of course not and neither has anybody else. These are intangibles—hypothetical constructs that are never seen and always inferred. Below, three theorists are listed. Record the key concepts of their work that point to ways of understanding the human mind. Answer the questions that follow based on your reading.

Sigmund Freud   _____

John B. Watson   _____

Abraham Maslow   _____

How do you think the mind differs from the brain? _____

_____

Do you believe the study of the human mind is really a science? Why or why not? _____

_____

_____

Which of the psychological perspectives discussed in this chapter makes the most sense to you, and why? _____

_____

_____

HAPPINESS: WHAT'S UP WITH THAT?

Students take psychology for many different reasons. Some students take psychology because it is required. Others take it because they have a drive to understand things unknown. Still others have a more personal reason for studying psychology. Many people are troubled by the notion that they are different from most other people. Some have a family history of alcoholism or other mental illness and want to know more about the various disorders and their etiology. Having polled many students over the years, I have found more than a handful who wish to understand themselves better so that they may find their personal path to happiness. Is there such a path? That's a tough question to answer. Certainly some people seem to be happy most of the time, while others seem to be happy almost never. Where do you fit into this picture? Can you define happiness, or for that matter unhappiness? For many, it is easier to define and describe the people, places, and things that make them unhappy than it is to put a finger on the things that make them happy. Would a lot of money make you happy? There seem to be a lot of depressed rich people out there. If money is the answer, why are they not happy?

List below the things that make you unhappy. Keep in mind that stress, guilt, shame, resentment, false pride, and low self-worth are feelings that become unhappiness. Taking personal responsibility, describe what appropriate action you might take to eliminate or mitigate each source of unhappiness in your life. Perfect happiness may be a myth, but working toward our vision of it can take us a long way from unhappiness.

SOURCE	ACTION	GOAL
Person, place, or event	What I'll do, when, and how	Short, mid, or long-term

COMPREHENSIVE PRACTICE TEST

1. Which of the following psychological perspectives likened human mental life to an iceberg?
    a) behaviorism
    b) Gestalt
    c) humanistic
    d) structuralism

2. Which of the following psychological perspectives spoke of concepts including the uniqueness of human beings and their capacity for choice and growth?
    a) behaviorism
    b) Gestalt
    c) humanistic
    d) cognitive

3. _____ psychology focuses on mental processes such as memory, concept formation, and decision making.
   a) Gestalt
   b) cognitive
   c) functionalism
   d) behavioral

4. _____ is the approach to psychology that believed the study of the mind and consciousness was not scientific.
   a) structuralism
   b) behaviorism
   c) functionalism
   d) humanistic

5. Functionalism is known as the first American school of psychology and was interested in how the mind functioned to help humans and animals adapt to their environment.
   a) True
   b) False

6. Structuralism was the name of the school of psychology developed by:
   a) Freud
   b) Wundt
   c) Watson
   d) Titchener

7. Which perspective in psychology is interested in the role of social and cultural influences on behavior?
   a) humanistic
   b) cognitive
   c) evolutionary
   d) sociocultural

8. The _____ perspective in psychology would explain behavior through an understanding of the brain and the central nervous system.
   a) evolutionary
   b) functionalism
   c) biological
   d) behavioral

9. Which of the following probably had the most influence on the evolutionary perspective in psychology?
   a) Darwin
   b) Watson
   c) Wundt
   d) Freud

10. A social psychologist would be most interested in how individuals behave in isolated settings such as alone in their home.
    a) True
    b) False

11. A _____ psychologist specializes in the diagnosis and treatment of mental and behavior disorders.
    a) social
    b) organizational
    c) educational
    d) clinical

12. "The whole thus perceived is greater than the sum of its parts," is a quote you would most expect to hear from a _____ psychologist.
    a) behavioral
    b) cognitive
    c) Gestalt
    d) humanistic

13. Which of the following would be best matched with behaviorism?
    a) Wundt
    b) Rogers
    c) Freud
    d) Watson

14. Which of the following would be best matched with psychoanalysis?
    a) Skinner
    b) Freud
    c) Maslow
    d) Binet

15. Which of the following would be best matched with intelligence testing?
    a) Binet
    b) Rogers
    c) Titchener
    d) Pavlov

16. Which of the following is credited with establishing the first psychological laboratory?
    a) Freud
    b) Skinner
    c) Rogers
    d) James

17. Which of the following would be best matched with the humanistic perspective in psychology?
   a) Freud
   b) Watson
   c) Titchener
   d) Maslow

18. Description, explanation, prediction, and control of behavior and mental processes were identified as the _____ of psychology.
   a) reasons
   b) goals
   c) perspectives
   d) methods

19. A _____ was defined in the book as a general principle or set of principles proposed to explain how a number of separate facts are related to one another.
   a) perspective
   b) goal
   c) theory
   d) reason

20. Basic research is conducted for the purpose of solving practical problems and improving the quality of life.
   a) True
   b) False

21. Unobtrusively observing people who are eating in a fast-food restaurant in order to determine how frequently they take bites is an example of:
   a) naturalistic observation
   b) the case study method
   c) the experimental method
   d) the survey method

22. If I want to produce evidence for cause-effect relationships, I would use:
   a) naturalistic observation
   b) correlation
   c) the survey method
   d) the experimental method

23. Subjects are assigned to take math tests in either a crowded classroom or an almost empty classroom. Test scores are then examined to determine whether these conditions affected performance. In this experiment, the independent variable is:
   a) math skills
   b) how crowded the classroom was
   c) test scores
   d) subjects

24. In an experiment, I would use the *double blind* approach to control for:
   a) selection bias
   b) placebo bias
   c) random bias
   d) experimenter bias

25. We are interested in comparing the effects of a therapy technique alone on treating anxiety and a therapy technique combined with anti-anxiety medicine. In this experiment, the control group is the group that receives both therapy and medicine.
   a) True
   b) False

26. In an experiment I will study a _____ of subjects in order to generalize my findings to the _____.
   a) sample; control group
   b) control group; sample
   c) population; sample
   d) sample; population

27. The ability to provide an overall estimate of the combined effects of many studies on the same topic was listed as an advantage of the _____ method of research.
   a) meta-analysis
   b) case study
   c) correlational
   d) laboratory observation

28. The issues of reliability and validity were discussed in reference to the _____ method of research.
   a) correlational
   b) survey
   c) meta-analysis
   d) psychological testing

29. For current research in psychology, the majority of subjects come from mental hospitals.
   a) True
   b) False

30. Often, animals are used in psychological research instead of human participants because there is no controversy related to studying animals like there is when studying humans.
    a) True   b) False

31. Deception in psychological research may be acceptable if certain conditions are met. One of these conditions is that subjects must be debriefed immediately following the experiment.
    a) True   b) False

32. Which of the following best defines a science?
    a) the subject matter   c) the methods used to gather information
    b) the goals set forth   d) the kinds of questions asked

OMSE # 1 Answer Key: Psychology as a Science

A. Quick Quiz	B. Matching	C. Methods: Table Completion
1. b	1. g	1. c, h, d, or c
2. guide research	2. j	2. d, f, c
3. c	3. d	3. h, f, g
4. false	4. a	4. c, b, h
5. case study	5. h	5. b, c, g
6. c	6. i	6. f, a, e
7. representative	7. c	7. g, e, a
8. b	8. f	8. a, d, b
9. current; new	9. b	
10. d	10. e	
11. false		
12. placebo		
13. d		
14. reliable; valid		
15. false		

OMSE # 2 Answer Key: The History of Psychology

A. Quick Quiz		B. Matching	C. Complete the Diagram	
1. d	9. d	1. d	1. Wundt	6. Psychoanalysis
2. b	10. b	2. f	2. Structuralism	7. Wertheimer
3. b	11. c	3. h	3. Functionalism	8. Humanistic
4. b	12. d	4. g	4. Watson	9. Cognitive
5. c	13. a	5. e	5. Skinner	
6. true	14. b	6. a		
7. operant	15. d	7. b		
8. a		8. c		

ANSWER KEY: LABORATORY TO REAL LIFE

Design an Experiment	Choosing a Career	Psychological Time Traveler
1. environmental conditions—level of stress	1. c	1. Kenneth B. Clark
2. number of correct responses	2. f	2. B.F. Skinner
3. Group A; Group B	3. e	3. Karen Horney
4. random	4. b	4. Wilhelm Wundt
5. hypothesis	5. d	5. William James
6. experimental	6. a	6. Francis Sumner
		7. John B. Watson
		8. Albert Bandura

ANSWER KEY: LABORATORY TO REAL LIFE

Design an Experiment	Choosing a Career	Psychological Time Traveler
1. environmental conditions—level of stress	1. c	1. Kenneth B. Clark
2. number of correct responses	2. f	2. B.F. Skinner
3. Group A; Group B	3. e	3. Karen Horney
4. random	4. b	4. Wilhelm Wundt
5. hypothesis	5. d	5. William James
6. experimental	6. a	6. Francis Sumner
		7. John B. Watson
		8. Albert Bandura

ANSWER KEY: COMPREHENSIVE PRACTICE EXAM

1. d	9. a	17. d	25. false
2. c	10. false	18. b	26. d
3. b	11. d	19. c	27. a
4. b	12. c	20. false	28. d
5. true	13. d	21. a	29. false
6. d	14. b	22. d	30. false
7. d	15. a	23. b	31. true
8. c	16. b	24. d	32. c

2

BIOLOGY AND BEHAVIOR

Biology is the source of all that we do and are. All of our actions, thoughts, feelings, memories, and dreams occur only with the aid of a complex network of biological processes. Biological psychology seeks to explain behavior in terms of the physiology, development, evolution, and function of the nervous system.

CHAPTER OVERVIEW

When I was 16 years old, following a serious car accident, I awoke from a 14-day coma to discover that, among other things, I had received 180 stitches in my forehead. It was not until I took my first college psychology courses that I realized the importance of the injury and the possible consequences it could have had on my behavior. I was fortunate. While I had suffered a serious blow to the head resulting in concussion, coma, and three broken vertebrae, I seemed to have little more than some irritating memory problems for long-term effects. In graduate school I would shudder when I watched films of closed head injury patients and the kinds of problems they suffered as a result of their injuries. It was then that I gained an interest in and appreciation for the important relationship between the brain and behavior. Everything we do, think, feel, want, wish, experience, or wonder is irrevocably tied to the activity of our brain. If we are going to have anything close to a true and comprehensive understanding of behavior, we must first understand the brain and nervous system and how these are related to that behavior.

This chapter will help you gain a more practiced and functional understanding of the relationship between the brain and nervous system and behavior. The materials are divided into four OMSE sections, 1) neurons and the central nervous system, 2) cerebral hemispheres and specialization of the cerebral hemispheres, 3) brain mysteries and brain damage, and 4) the peripheral nervous system and the endocrine system. You will gain an understanding of the anatomy and physiology of this important influence on behavior. You will also gain an understanding of how these different biological systems not only influence behavior but how behavior and the environment can have an impact on these systems. Future chapters or units of study in your text and class will build upon this basic information as you examine topics such as sensation and perception, human development, states of consciousness, and psychological disorders.

By completing the exercises provided, you should gain a thorough understanding of the information provided in your text. In other words, you should be better prepared for tests, quizzes, class participation, and life itself.

TIMELINE

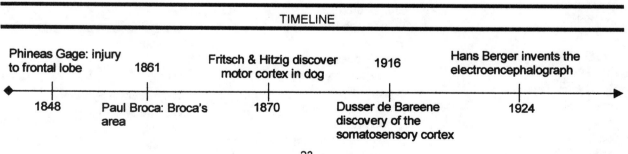

Phineas Gage: injury to frontal lobe

1861

Fritsch & Hitzig discover motor cortex in dog

1916

Hans Berger invents the electroencephalograph

1848

Paul Broca: Broca's area

1870

Dusser de Bareene discovery of the somatosensory cortex

1924

CHAPTER OUTLINE

The Neurons and the Neurotransmitters

The Neurons: Billions of Brain Cells

Neurotransmitters: The Chemical Messengers of the Brain

The Effects of Drugs on Neural Transmission

The Variety of Neurotransmitters

The Rate of Neural Firing and the Speed of the Impulse

Glial Cells: The Neurons' Helper Cells

The Central Nervous System

The Spinal Cord: An Extension of the Brain

The Brainstem: The Most Primitive Part of the Brain

The Cerebellum: A Must for Graceful Movement

The Thalamus: The Relay Station Between Lower and Higher Brain Centers

The Hypothalamus: A Master Regulator

The Limbic System: Primitive Emotion and Memory

The Cerebral Hemispheres

The Lobes of the Brain

Specialized Functions of the Left Hemisphere: Language, First and Foremost

Specialized Functions of the Right Hemisphere: The Leader in Visual-Spatial Tasks

The Split Brain: Separate Halves or Two Separate Brains?

Discovering the Brain's Mysteries

The EEG and the Microelectrode

The CT scan and Magnetic Resonance Imaging

The PET scan, fMRI, and Other Imaging Techniques

Brain Damage: Causes and Consequences

Stroke

Head Injury

Recovering From Brain Damage

The Peripheral Nervous System

The Endocrine System

Apply it! Handedness—Does It Make a Difference?

Thinking Critically

Chapter Summary and Review

KEY TERMS

The Neurons and the Neurotransmitters
neuron
cell body
dendrites
axon
synapse
resting potential
action potential
neurotransmitter
receptor site
reuptake
acetylcholine
dopamine
norepinephrine
serotonin
endorphins
myelin sheath
glial cells

The Central Nervous System
central nervous system
spinal cord
brainstem
medulla
reticular formation

cerebellum
thalamus
hypothalamus
limbic system
amygdala
hippocampus

The Cerebral Hemispheres
cerebrum
cerebral hemispheres
corpus callosum
cerebral cortex
association areas
frontal lobes
motor cortex
Broca's area
Broca's aphasia
aphasia
parietal lobes
somatosensory cortex
occipital lobes
primary visual cortex
temporal lobes
primary auditory cortex
Wernicke's area

Wernicke's aphasia
lateralization
left hemisphere
right hemisphere
split-brain operation

Discovering The Brain's Mysteries
electroencephalogram
beta wave
alpha wave
delta wave
microelectrode
CT scan
MRI
PET scan
fMRI

Brain Damage: Causes and Consequences
stroke
plasticity

The Endocrine System
endocrine system
hormone
adrenal gland

OMSE # 1: NEURONS & THE CENTRAL NERVOUS SYSTEM

LEARNING OBJECTIVES

1. What is a neuron, and what are its three parts?
2. What is a synapse?
3. What is the action potential?
4. What are neurotransmitters, and what role do they play in the transmission of signals from one neuron to another?
5. What are some of the ways in which neurotransmitters affect behavior, and what are some of the major neurotransmitters?
6. How can the body tell the difference between a very strong and a very weak stimulus?
7. Why is an intact spinal cord important to normal functioning?
8. What are the crucial functions handled by the brainstem?
9. What are the primary functions of the cerebellum?
10. What is the primary role of the thalamus?
11. What are some of the processes regulated by the hypothalamus?
12. What is the role of the limbic system?

LEARNING MASTERY SCORECARD: Update your score card as you work through the various sections of the chapter. First, find and define key terms and concepts included in each section and note the page number(s) from the text that contain important references to the material. Next, gain a practical understanding of the concepts by considering the Laboratory to Life scenarios and thinking of at least one original example of how the concept might apply in real life. Complete the *Objective-Mastery Self-Evaluation* (OMSE) exercises for this section and record your scores. Revisit the exercises, recording your score and the date completed until you have attained mastery (100%). Finally, decide how you would prepare a lecture on each objective using the template provided, outline the lecture, and practice presenting it. Keep an honest tally of your achievements and, when finished, you will have developed learning mastery through elaborate rehearsal.

Key terms & concepts	Page #	Key terms & concepts	Page #	Key terms & concepts	Page #
neuron		reuptake		cell body	
acetylcholine		dendrites		dopamine	
axon		norepinephrine		synapse	
serotonin		resting potential		endorphins	
action potential		myelin sheath		neurotransmitter	
glial cells		receptor site		spinal cord	
brainstem		hypothalamus		medulla	
limbic system		reticular formation		amygdala	
cerebellum		hippocampus		thalamus	
central nervous system		reticular formation		limbic system	
spinal cord		cerebellum		amygdala	
brainstem		thalamus		hippocampus	
medulla		hypothalamus			

Quick Quiz

Date	Score	Date	Score	Date	Score
__/__/__	_____	__/__/__	_____	__/__/__	_____
__/__/__	_____	__/__/__	_____	__/__/__	100%

Elaborate Rehearsal

Lecture Preparation	Completion Date
Key Terms, Persons, & Concepts	__/__/__
Learning Objectives	__/__/__
Lecture Notes	__/__/__

TIMELINE

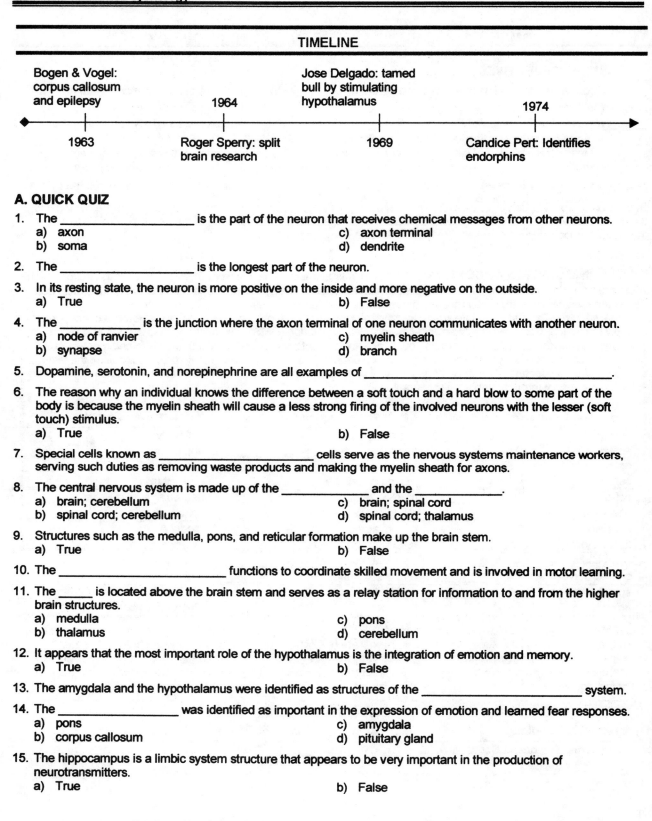

Bogen & Vogel:
corpus callosum
and epilepsy

1964

Jose Delgado: tamed
bull by stimulating
hypothalamus

1974

1963

Roger Sperry: split
brain research

1969

Candice Pert: Identifies
endorphins

A. QUICK QUIZ

1. The _____ is the part of the neuron that receives chemical messages from other neurons.
    a) axon
    b) soma
    c) axon terminal
    d) dendrite

2. The _____ is the longest part of the neuron.

3. In its resting state, the neuron is more positive on the inside and more negative on the outside.
    a) True
    b) False

4. The _____ is the junction where the axon terminal of one neuron communicates with another neuron.
    a) node of ranvier
    b) synapse
    c) myelin sheath
    d) branch

5. Dopamine, serotonin, and norepinephrine are all examples of _____.

6. The reason why an individual knows the difference between a soft touch and a hard blow to some part of the body is because the myelin sheath will cause a less strong firing of the involved neurons with the lesser (soft touch) stimulus.
    a) True
    b) False

7. Special cells known as _____ cells serve as the nervous systems maintenance workers, serving such duties as removing waste products and making the myelin sheath for axons.

8. The central nervous system is made up of the _____ and the _____.
    a) brain; cerebellum
    b) spinal cord; cerebellum
    c) brain; spinal cord
    d) spinal cord; thalamus

9. Structures such as the medulla, pons, and reticular formation make up the brain stem.
    a) True
    b) False

10. The _____ functions to coordinate skilled movement and is involved in motor learning.

11. The _____ is located above the brain stem and serves as a relay station for information to and from the higher brain structures.
    a) medulla
    b) thalamus
    c) pons
    d) cerebellum

12. It appears that the most important role of the hypothalamus is the integration of emotion and memory.
    a) True
    b) False

13. The amygdala and the hypothalamus were identified as structures of the _____ system.

14. The _____ was identified as important in the expression of emotion and learned fear responses.
    a) pons
    b) corpus callosum
    c) amygdala
    d) pituitary gland

15. The hippocampus is a limbic system structure that appears to be very important in the production of neurotransmitters.
    a) True
    b) False

B. MATCHING: Place the appropriate letter in the space provided.

_____	1. Metabolize glucose, energy during exercise	a) acetylcholine
_____	2. Relief from pain, feelings of pleasure	b) dopamine
_____	3. Movement, learning, memory, REM sleep	c) norepinephrine
_____	4. Learning, attention, movement	d) epinephrine
_____	5. Eating and sleep	e) serotonin
_____	6. Neural inhibition	f) GABA
_____	7. Mood, sleep, appetite, aggression	g) endorphins

C. DIAGRAM EXERCISE:

In the space provided below, draw a neuron from memory. As you draw the neuron, imagine you are explaining this biological component to someone else. Describe in detail the purpose and function of the neuron as well as each individual component of the neuron. Remember the following parts of the neuron:

a) Dendrite   b) Cell Body   c) Axon
d) Myelin Sheath   e) Nodes of Ranvier   f) Axon Terminal

After you have drawn the neuron, write in the appropriate corresponding letter to indicate each of the above parts. Finally, draw an arrow indicating the direction of the neural impulse.

Draw and Label a Neuron

PREPARE A LECTURE: NEURONS & THE CENTRAL NERVOUS SYSTEM

This activity is designed to offer you an opportunity to take advantage of a valuable mode of learning, elaborate rehearsal. Once you have finished the OMSE section, write a lecture using the instructional guide provided below. After your lecture is prepared, you can enhance your learning by writing a quiz covering the material. Now it is time to find some willing and inquisitive audience members. Your roommates or family may be a great place to start. Present them the lecture as if you are teaching a class. Remember to ask for questions and give your students the quiz following the lecture. This exercise can also serve to turn a *study-buddy* group into a very productive way to prepare for the test. Each member of the group can take different OMSE sections for their lecture/teacher role while the rest of the group serves as the class.

I. Key Terms, Names, Dates, and Concepts you will include in this lecture:

1. _____	5. _____	9. _____
2. _____	6. _____	10. _____
3. _____	7. _____	11. _____
4. _____	8. _____	12. _____

II. Learning Objectives (what do you want the student to know and be able to do as a result of your lecture):

1. _____
2. _____
3. _____
4. _____
5. _____

III. Lecture Notes (notes should be brief cues and serve as a guide).

Major topic #1: _____

   Sub-topics and notes: _____

_____

_____

_____

Major topic #2: _____

   Sub-topics and notes: _____

_____

_____

_____

Major topic #3: _____

   Sub-topics and notes: _____

_____

_____

_____

OMSE # 2: CEREBRAL HEMISPHERES & SPECIALIZATION

LEARNING OBJECTIVES

1. What are the cerebral hemispheres, the corpus callosum, and the cerebral cortex?

2. What are some of the main areas within the frontal lobes and what are their functions?

3. What are the primary functions of the parietal lobes in general and the somatosensory cortex in particular?

4. What are the primary functions of the occipital lobes in general and the primary visual cortex in particular?

5. What are the major areas within the temporal lobes and what are their functions?

6. What are the main functions of the left hemisphere?

7. What are the primary functions of the right hemisphere?

8. What is the significance of the split-brain operation?

LEARNING MASTERY SCORECARD: Update your score card as you work through the various sections of the chapter. First, find and define key terms and concepts included in each section and note the page number(s) from the text that contain important references to the material. Next, gain a practical understanding of the concepts by considering the Laboratory to Life scenarios and thinking of at least one original example of how the concept might apply in real life. Complete the *Objective-Mastery Self-Evaluation* (OMSE) exercises for this section and record your scores. Revisit the exercises, recording your score and the date completed until you have attained mastery (100%). Finally, decide how you would prepare a lecture on each objective using the template provided, outline the lecture, and practice presenting it. Keep an honest tally of your achievements and, when finished, you will have developed learning mastery through elaborate rehearsal.

Key terms	Page #	Key terms	Page #	Key terms	Page #
cerebrum	_____	Broca's aphasia	_____	primary auditory cortex	_____
cerebral hemispheres	_____	aphasia	_____	Wernicke's area	_____
corpus callosum	_____	parietal lobes	_____	Wernicke's aphasia	_____

cerebral cortex	_____	somatosensory cortex	_____	lateralization	_____
association areas	_____	occipital lobes	_____	left hemisphere	_____
frontal lobes	_____	primary visual cortex	_____	right hemisphere	_____
motor cortex	_____	temporal lobes	_____	split-brain operation	_____
Broca's area	_____				

Quick Quiz

Date	Score	Date	Score	Date	Score
_/_/_	_____	_/_/_	_____	_/_/_	_____
_/_/_	_____	_/_/_	_____	_/_/_	100%

Elaborate Rehearsal

Lecture Preparation	Completion Date
Key Terms, Persons, & Concepts	_/_/_
Learning Objectives	_/_/_
Lecture Notes	_/_/_

A. QUICK QUIZ

1. The largest structure of the human brain, consisting of two cerebral hemispheres connected by the corpus callosum and covered by the cerebral cortex is the:
    a) cerebellum
    b) motor cortex
    c) parietal lobe
    d) cerebrum

2. This structure makes possible the transfer of information and the synchronization of activity between the two cerebral hemispheres:
    a) cerebellum
    b) corpus callosum
    c) parietal lobe
    d) motor cortex

3. The left hemisphere controls language functions in over 95% of people.
    a) True
    b) False

4. This structure, which accounts for approximately 40% of the human brain's total weight, is primarily responsible for the higher mental processes of language, memory, and thinking:
    a) the cerebral cortex
    b) the corpus callosum
    c) the cerebellum
    d) the hypothalamus

5. Areas of the cerebral cortex that house memories and are involved in thought, perception, learning, and language are known as:
    a) sensory input areas
    b) motor areas
    c) association areas
    d) corpus areas

6. In each cerebral hemisphere there are four lobes. Which of the following is NOT one of the four lobes?
    a) frontal lobe
    b) temporal lobe
    c) caudal lobe
    d) parietal lobe

7. The _____ _____ is the strip of tissue at the rear of the frontal lobes that controls voluntary body movements.

8. A person who has lost the ability to speak, or who can verbalize only a few poorly articulated words with great effort, might be diagnosed with which of the following:
    a) a hypothalamic lesion
    b) Wernicke's aphasia
    c) aphasia
    d) Broca's aphasia

9. Damage to this brain structure might result in a person still being able to speak words fluently while making no sense to the listener. The words are clear and distinguishable but the content is either vague or incomprehensible to the listener.
    a) thalamus
    b) Wernicke's area
    c) aphasic cortex
    d) Broca's area

10. The _____ hemisphere is, in most people, specialized for visual-spatial perception and for interpreting nonverbal behavior.

11. When you hear a favorite "oldie" on the radio, you recognize it instantly even though you have not heard it for years. In which lobe is found the special association area where old melodies are stored?
    a) temporal lobe   c) parietal lobe
    b) occipital lobe   d) frontal lobe

12. The part of the temporal lobes where hearing registers is known as the _____.

13. The strip of tissue at the front of the parietal lobes where touch, pressure, temperature, and pain register in the cerebral cortex is which of the following:
    a) the somatosensory cortex   c) the motor cortex
    b) the sensorial lobe   d) the kinesthetic cortex

14. In extreme cases of epilepsy, surgeons have severed the corpus callosum in a drastic procedure known as the
    _____.

15. The downside of the procedure referred to in question # 14 is that it results in major changes in intelligence, personality, and behavior.
    a) True   b) False

B. MATCHING (Place the appropriate letter in the blank).

_____	1. Covered by the cerebral cortex and connected by the corpus callosum	a) Wernicke's area
_____	2. Convoluted covering of the cerebral hemispheres	b) parietal lobes
_____	3. Lobes that control voluntary body movement, speech, & thinking	c) occipital lobes
_____	4. These lobes are where touch, temperature, pressure, and pain register	d) Broca's area
_____	5. Language area in the temporal lobe involved in comprehension	e) lateralization
_____	6. Area in the frontal lobe that controls the production of speech sounds	f) temporal lobes
_____	7. Lobes that contain the primary visual cortex	g) cerebral cortex
_____	8. Lobes that contain the primary auditory cortex	h) cerebral hemispheres
_____	9. Specialization of one hemispheres to handle a particular function	i) frontal lobes

C. COMPLETE THE DIAGRAM: Place the letter representing the correct lobe or cortex in the space provided.

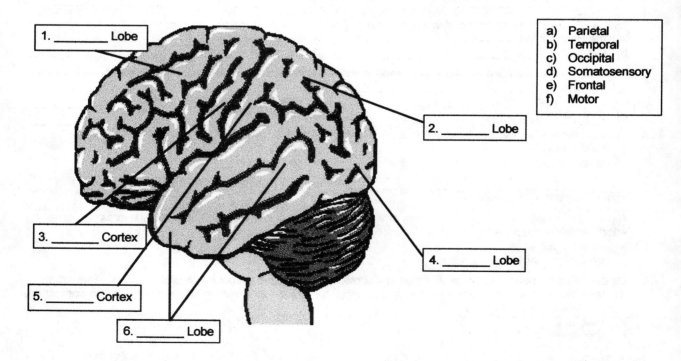

1. _____ Lobe

2. _____ Lobe

3. _____ Cortex

4. _____ Lobe

5. _____ Cortex

6. _____ Lobe

a) Parietal
b) Temporal
c) Occipital
d) Somatosensory
e) Frontal
f) Motor

PREPARE A LECTURE: This activity is designed to offer you an opportunity to take advantage of a valuable mode of learning, elaborate rehearsal. Once you have finished the OMSE section, write a lecture using the instructional guide provided below. After your lecture is prepared, you can enhance your learning by writing a quiz covering the material. Now it is time to find some willing and inquisitive audience members. Your roommates or family may be a great place to start. Present them the lecture as if you are teaching a class. Remember to ask for questions and give your students the quiz following the lecture. This exercise can also serve to turn a *study-buddy* group into a very productive way to prepare for the test. Each member of the group can take different OMSE sections for their lecture/teacher role while the rest of the group serves as the class.

I. Key Terms, Names, Dates, and Concepts you will include in this lecture:

1. _____   5. _____   9. _____

2. _____   6. _____   10. _____

3. _____   7. _____   11. _____

4. _____   8. _____   12. _____

II. Learning Objectives (what do you want the student to know and be able to do as a result of your lecture):

1. _____

2. _____

3. _____

4. _____

5. _____

III. Lecture Notes (notes should be brief cues and serve as a guide).

Major topic #1: _____

Sub-topics and notes: _____

_____

_____

_____

Major topic #2: _____

Sub-topics and notes: _____

_____

_____

_____

Major topic #3: _____

Sub-topics and notes: _____

_____

_____

_____

OMSE # 3: BRAIN MYSTERIES & BRAIN DAMAGE

LEARNING OBJECTIVES

1. What are some methods that researchers have used to learn about brain function?

2. What is the electroencephalogram (EEG), and what are three of the brain-wave patterns it reveals?

3. Why is a stroke so serious?

4. What must occur in the brain for there to be some recovery from brain damage?

How many billions of neurons will have to release how many neurotransmitters across how many synaptic clefts before you receive your diploma? How many others will lose this opportunity by using brain chemistry-altering drugs?

LEARNING MASTERY SCORECARD: BRAIN MYSTERIES AND BRAIN DAMAGE

Update your score card as you work through the various sections of the chapter. First, find and define key terms and concepts included in each section and note the page number(s) from the text that contain important references to the material. Next, gain a practical understanding of the concepts by considering the Laboratory to Life scenarios and thinking of at least one original example of how the concept might apply in real life. Complete the *Objective-Mastery Self-Evaluation* (OMSE) exercises for this section and record your scores. Revisit the exercises, recording your score and the date completed until you have attained mastery (100%). Finally, decide how you would prepare a lecture on each objective using the template provided, outline the lecture, and practice presenting it. Keep an honest tally of your achievements and, when finished, you will have developed learning mastery through elaborate rehearsal.

Key terms	Page #	Key terms	Page #	Key terms	Page #
electroencephalogram	___	microelectrode	___	fMRI	___
beta wave	___	CT scan	___	stroke	___
alpha wave	___	MRI	___	plasticity	___
delta wave	___	PET scan	___		

Quick Quiz

Date	Score	Date	Score	Date	Score
_/_/_	___	_/_/_	___	_/_/_	___
_/_/_	___	_/_/_	___	_/_/_	100%

Elaborate Rehearsal

Lecture Preparation	Completion Date
Key Terms, Persons, & Concepts	_/_/_
Learning Objectives	_/_/_
Lecture Notes	_/_/_

A. QUICK QUIZ

1. Beta waves are associated with mental or physical activities while alpha waves are associated with:
   a) deep sleep
   b) deep relaxation
   c) concentration
   d) extreme wakefulness

2. Slow wave sleep is associated with the _____ wave.

3. The first attempts to study the brain were through autopsies.
   a) True
   b) False

4. The CT scan uses X-rays to provide clear pictures of the brain while the _____ produces higher resolution without exposing patients to X-rays.
   a) PET
   b) EEG
   c) MRI
   d) ECG

5. The PET scan has the advantage of providing information about activity in various parts of the brain.
   a) True
   b) False

6. According to the book, _____ is the most common cause of damage to the adult brain.

7. It appears that, at birth, we have about two thirds of the total number of neurons we will have as adults.
   a) True
   b) False

8. Impaired motor coordination and _____ ability are the most obvious results of head injury.
   a) music
   b) visual
   c) language
   d) hearing

9. Many people who suffer head injury will develop _____ that includes either Grand mal or Petit mal seizures.

10. Plasticity refers to the brain's ability to:
    a) understand two languages at the same time
    b) process more that one piece of information
    c) compensate for damage
    d) remain active in old age

B. MATCHING: Place the appropriate letter in the space provided.

_____	1.	High resolution images of the structure of the brain	a) EEG
_____	2.	Record of brain wave images	b) CT scan
_____	3.	A new technique that measures magnetic changes in the brain	c) MRI
_____	4.	Cross section images of the brain	d) PET scan
_____	5.	Reveals activity in various parts of the brain	e) SQUID

C. COMPLETE THE DIAGRAM

Complete the following diagram by drawing the brain wave pattern seen in each of the following levels of brain activity. After you have drawn in the patterns, briefly describe each level of activity in the space corresponding to the activity level as indicated below.

Beta	
Alpha	
Theta	
Delta	

Brief Description

Beta: _____

Alpha: _____

Theta: _____

Delta: _____

PREPARE A LECTURE: This activity is designed to offer you an opportunity to take advantage of a valuable mode of learning, elaborate rehearsal. Once you have finished the OMSE section, write a lecture using the instructional guide provided below. After your lecture is prepared, you can enhance your learning by writing a quiz covering the material. Now it is time to find some willing and inquisitive audience members. Your roommates or family may be a great place to start. Present them the lecture as if you are teaching a class. Remember to ask for questions and give your students the quiz following the lecture. This exercise can also serve to turn a *study-buddy* group into a very productive way to prepare for the test. Each member of the group can take different OMSE sections for their lecture/teacher role while the rest of the group serves as the class.

I. Key Terms, Names, Dates, and Concepts you will include in this lecture:

1. _____	5. _____	9. _____
2. _____	6. _____	10. _____
3. _____	7. _____	11. _____
4. _____	8. _____	12. _____

II. Learning Objectives (what do you want the student to know and be able to do as a result of your lecture):

1. _____

2. _____

3. _____

4. _____

5. _____

III. Lecture Notes (notes should be brief cues and serve as a guide).

Major topic #1: _____

   Sub-topics and notes: _____

_____

_____
_____

Major topic #2: _____
    Sub-topics and notes: _____
_____
_____
_____

Major topic #3: _____
    Sub-topics and notes: _____
_____
_____
_____

OMSE # 4: PERIPHERAL NERVOUS AND ENDOCRINE SYSTEMS

LEARNING OBJECTIVES

1. What is the peripheral nervous system?

2. What are the roles of the sympathetic and parasympathetic nervous systems?

3. What is the endocrine system and what are some of the glands within it?

LEARNING MASTERY SCORECARD: Update your score card as you work through the various sections of the chapter. First, find and define key terms and concepts included in each section and note the page number(s) from the text that contain important references to the material. Next, gain a practical understanding of the concepts by considering the Laboratory to Life scenarios and thinking of at least one original example of how the concept might apply in real life. Complete the *Objective-Mastery Self-Evaluation* (OMSE) exercises for this section and record your scores. Revisit the exercises, recording your score and the date completed until you have attained mastery (100%). Finally, decide how you would prepare a lecture on each objective using the template provided, outline the lecture, and practice presenting it. Keep an honest tally of your achievements and, when finished, you will have developed learning mastery through elaborate rehearsal.

Key terms & concepts	Page #	Key terms & concepts	Page #
peripheral nervous system	_____	hormone	_____
sympathetic nervous system	_____	pituitary gland	_____
parasympathetic nervous system	_____	adrenal glands	_____
endocrine gland	_____		

Quick Quiz

Date	Score	Date	Score	Date	Score
_/_/_	_____	_/_/_	_____	_/_/_	_____
_/_/_	_____	_/_/_	_____	_/_/_	100%

Elaborate Rehearsal

Lecture Preparation	Completion Date
Key Terms, Persons, & Concepts	_/_/_
Learning Objectives	_/_/_
Lecture Notes	_/_/_

A. QUICK QUIZ

1. The human nervous system consists of two major subdivisions. They are the:
    a) central & peripheral nervous systems
    b) sympathetic & parasympathetic nervous systems
    c) somatic & autonomic nervous systems
    d) reticular & hypothalamic nervous systems

2. The peripheral nervous system has two subdivisions. They are the _____ nervous systems:
   a) somatic & sympathetic
   b) autonomic & parasympathetic
   c) somatic & autonomic
   d) sympathetic & parasympathetic

3. The somatic nervous system consists of:
   a) all sensory and motor nerves
   b) the brain and spinal cord only
   c) all organs and glands
   d) all neuronal and endocrine systems

4. The autonomic nervous system transmits messages between the central nervous system and the glands, the cardiac muscle, and the smooth muscles that are not ordinarily under voluntary control.
   a) True
   b) False

5. The autonomic nervous system is divided into two parts—they are the _____ nervous systems:
   a) somatic & sympathetic
   b) central & peripheral
   c) somatic & autonomic
   d) sympathetic & parasympathetic

6. If you are walking through the woods and are suddenly confronted by a large grizzly bear, your _____ _____ _____ will probably ready your body for action by mobilizing your body's resources.

7. The term coined by Walter Cannon to describe the state of physiological arousal produced by a threatening or stressful experience like meeting an unfriendly grizzly bear is _____-___-_____ response.

8. The internal feedback system, composed of ductless glands, that maintains hormonal balance is called:
   a) the pituitary network
   b) the receptive aphasia
   c) the positron emission
   d) the endocrine system

9. This endocrine gland, located in the brain and often called the "master gland," releases hormones that control or "turn on" other endocrine glands and also releases a growth hormone. It is the:
   a) adrenal gland
   b) pituitary gland
   c) thyroid gland
   d) parathyroid gland

10. Some of the same chemical substances that are _____ also act as hormones.

11. The _____ gland(s), located just below the larynx , produce(s) the hormone _____, which is responsible for maintaining the body's metabolic balance.
    a) pineal; corticoid
    b) pancreas; insulin
    c) thyroid; thyroxin
    d) gonads; androgens

12. The adrenal glands release the hormones, _____ and _____, that prepare the body for the "fight-or-flight" response.

13. When the threat is resolved, the _____ nervous system acts to restore the heightened bodily responses back to normal, thus switching off the fight-or-flight response.

14. The _____ release hormones that are responsible for reproduction as well as secondary sex characteristics.

15. Males have more of the sex hormones called _____, and females have more _____.

The "fight-or-flight" response was probably much more necessary when we served saber-toothed tiger for dinner than it is now. Can you gain control over the activation of the response? Consider trying to gain control the next time you're stuck in traffic.

B. MATCHING: Place the appropriate letter in the space provided.

_____	1. This system makes it possible for us to sense our environment and move	a) parasympathetic
_____	2. The heart muscle operates under the control of this system	b) pituitary
_____	3. The state of physiological arousal identified by Walter Cannon	c) hormone
_____	4. This system mobilizes the body's resources for action	d) autonomic
_____	5. This system restores the body's balance once the threat is removed	e) sympathetic
_____	6. The master gland, about the size of a pea	f) adrenal glands
_____	7. Travels through the bloodstream to target receptor cells	g) somatic
_____	8. Produce epinephrine and norepinephrine	h) fight-or-flight

C. COMPLETE THE DIAGRAM

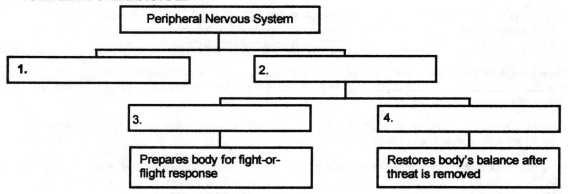

PREPARE A LECTURE: This activity is designed to offer you an opportunity to take advantage of a valuable mode of learning, elaborate rehearsal. Once you have finished the OMSE section, write a lecture using the instructional guide provided below. After your lecture is prepared, you can enhance your learning by writing a quiz covering the material. Now it is time to find some willing and inquisitive audience members. Your roommates or family may be a great place to start. Present them the lecture as if you are teaching a class. Remember to ask for questions and give your students the quiz following the lecture. This exercise can also serve to turn a *study-buddy* group into a very productive way to prepare for the test. Each member of the group can take different OMSE sections for their lecture/teacher role while the rest of the group serves as the class.

I. Key Terms, Names, Dates, and Concepts you will include in this lecture:

1. _____   4. _____   9. _____

2. _____   5. _____   10. _____

3. _____   6. _____   11. _____

4. _____   7. _____   12. _____

II. Learning Objectives (what do you want the student to know and be able to do as a result of your lecture):

1. _____

2. _____

3. _____

4. _____

5. _____

III. Lecture Notes (notes should be brief cues and serve as a guide).

Major topic #1: _____

    Sub-topics and notes: _____

_____

_____

_____

_____

Major topic #2: _____
    Sub-topics and notes: _____
_____
_____
_____

Major topic #3: _____
    Sub-topics and notes: _____
_____
_____
_____

KEY TERMS AND CONCEPTS EXERCISE

The key terms and concepts are presented in the order of their appearance in the text. Space is provided for you to include a personalized definition or example of each term or concept. As you encounter each term in the text, make a note of its meaning and context. Next, conceptualize the meaning of the term in a way that makes the most sense to you. You can also think about examples of the term from your own life. Write your definition and/or example in the space provided next to the word in this book. The KEY TERMS exercise utilizes a modified *T-note* design so that you can self-evaluate your mastery of the definitions. First lay a sheet of paper over the terms and concepts side of the page so that you only see the definitions. Read the definition and try to recall the term or concept. Mark all those you are unable to answer so you can restudy them. When you have learned all of the terms and concepts in this way, move the paper to the definition side so that you can see only the term or concept, try to recall both the textbook definition and your personal version. Repeat this until you know all of the terms and concepts by definition and personal understanding.

Neuron	A specialized cell that conducts impulses through the nervous system and contains three major parts—a cell body, dendrites, and an axon. Everything we do, think, and feel can be traced to neuronal activity. _____
Cell Body	The part of the neuron, containing the nucleus, that carries out the metabolic functions of the neuron. _____
Dendrites	The branchlike extensions of a neuron that receive signals from other neurons. Dendrites act like antenna of your car radio. They receive messages across space without actually being physically connected to the transmitter. _____
Axon	The slender, tail-like extension of the neuron that transmits signals to the dendrites or cell body of other neurons or to the muscles or glands. Like the radio station transmits messages across space to be picked up by radios tuned to the correct frequency, the axon delivers a signal into a space where it is picked up by receivers designed to recognize and accept that electrochemical message. _____
Synapse	The junction where the axon of a sending neuron communicates with a receiving neuron across the synaptic cleft. _____

Resting Potential	The membrane potential of a neuron at rest, about −70 millivolts. The neuron at rest contains more negative ions inside and more positive ions outside. _____
Action Potential	The firing of a neuron that results when the charge within the neuron becomes more positive than the charge outside the cell's membrane. When a neuron is stimulated, it fires all the way. Like a gun, how hard or fast you squeeze the trigger does not matter. If you squeeze the trigger, it will fire. _____
Neurotransmitter	A chemical that is released into the synaptic cleft from the axon terminal of the sending neuron, crosses the synapse, and binds to appropriate receptor sites on the dendrites or cell body of the receiving neuron, influencing the dell either to fire or not to fire. The action of neurotransmitters is either excitatory or inhibitory. Certain neurotransmitters produce both excitatory and inhibitory effects. _____
Receptor Site	A site on the dendrite or cell body of a neuron that will receive only certain neurotransmitters. Receptor sites work like locks while neurotransmitters work like keys. Only a certain key will fit a certain lock and the same is true with receptor sites. There may be hundreds of neurotransmitters in a given synapse, but only those that are recognized will bind to the site. _____
Reuptake	The process by which neurotransmitter molecules are taken from the synaptic cleft back into the axon terminal for later use, thus terminating their excitatory or inhibitory effect on the receiving neuron. _____
Acetylcholine	A neurotransmitter that plays a role in learning, memory, & rapid eye movement (REM) sleep, and causes the skeletal muscles to contract. A deficiency of acetylcholine in the brain has been implicated in the kind of memory loss found in Alzheimer's patients. _____
Dopamine	A neurotransmitter that plays a role in learning, attention, and movement; a deficiency of dopamine is associated with Parkinson's disease, and an oversensitivity to it is associated with some cases of schizophrenia. The high associated with cocaine use is a result of the cocaine blocking the reuptake of dopamine. _____
Norepinephrine	A neurotransmitter affecting eating and sleep; a deficiency of norepinephrine is associated with depression. Studies show that people who suffer from depression appear to have lowered levels of activation at the norepinephrine synapses. _____
Serotonin	A neurotransmitter that plays an important role in regulating mood, sleep, aggression, and appetite; a serotonin deficiency is associated with anxiety, depression, and suicide. One category of antidepressant medications is the Serotonin-Selective Reuptake Inhibitors. _____

Endorphins	Chemicals produced naturally by the brain that reduce pain and positively affect mood. Endorphins are the body's natural opiates; they block pain and stimulate the brain reward system or pleasure center. _____
Myelin Sheath	The white fatty coating wrapped around some axons that acts as insulation and enables impulses to travel much faster. Consider the electrical wires or speaker cables in your home. Imagine the difference in the signal if these wires were not insulated. _____
Glial Cells	Cells that make the brain more efficient by holding the brain together, removing waste products such as dead neurons, making the myelin coating for the axons, and performing other manufacturing, nourishing, and clean-up tasks. Glial cells are also known as neuroglial cells and neuroglial literally means "nerve glue." _____
Central Nervous System	That part of the nervous system that is made up of the brain and the spinal cord, contains billions of neurons, and is the center for all activity. _____
Spinal Cord	An extension of the brain, reaching from the base of the brain through the neck and spinal column, that transmits messages between the brain and the peripheral nervous system.
Brainstem	The structure that begins at the point where the spinal cord enlarges as it enters the brain and that includes the medulla, the pons, and the reticular formation. The brainstem is considered the most primitive part of the brain and controls functions that are critical to our survival. _____
Medulla	The part of the brainstem that controls the heartbeat, blood pressure, breathing, coughing, and swallowing. The medulla performs its duties without conscious awareness of us. Fortunately, these processes occur automatically. If we had to think about breathing in order to breathe, we would have great difficulty sleeping. _____
Reticular Formation	A structure in the brainstem that plays a crucial role in arousal and attention and that screens sensory messages into the brain. Also known as the reticular activating system, this structure acts as a filter for sensory messages, discarding extraneous, unnecessary sensations and forwarding important messages to the appropriate brain structure. _____
Cerebellum	The brain structure that executes smooth, skilled body movements and regulates muscle tone and posture. Even the simplest everyday functioning, like taking notes in class or raising a glass to your mouth, would be impossible without a functioning cerebellum. _____

Thalamus	The structure, located above the brainstem, that acts as a relay station for information flowing into or out of the higher brain centers. A diverse brain structure, the thalamus also appears to play a role in the learning of new information, the regulation of sleep, and the production of language. _____
Hypothalamus	A small but influential brain structure that controls the pituitary gland and regulates hunger, thirst, sexual behavior, body temperature, and a wide variety of emotional behaviors. Studies have demonstrated an ability to turn off aggression and produce sensations of pleasure by stimulating parts of the hypothalamus. _____
Limbic System	A group of structures in the brain, including the amygdala and hippocampus, that are collectively involved in emotion, memory, and motivation. _____
Amygdala	A structure in the limbic system that plays an important role in emotion, particularly in response to aversive stimuli. The amygdala is involved in learning fear responses which assists us in avoiding dangerous situations and aversive consequences. _____
Hippocampus	A structure in the limbic system that plays a central role in the formation of long-term memories. Damage to the hippocampus can make it impossible to store or recall new information. For example, you could learn to play tennis today, but tomorrow, you would have no knowledge of tennis. _____
Cerebrum	The largest structure of the human brain, consisting of the two cerebral hemispheres connected by the corpus callosum and covered by the cerebral cortex. _____
Cerebral Hemispheres	The right and left halves of the cerebrum, covered by the cerebral cortex and connected by the corpus callosum. _____
Corpus Callosum	The thick band of nerve fibers that connects the two cerebral hemispheres and makes possible the transfer of information and the synchronization of activity between them. _____
Cerebral Cortex	The gray, convoluted covering of the cerebral hemispheres that is responsible for higher mental processes such as language, memory, and thinking. _____
Association Areas	Areas of the cerebral cortex that house memories and are involved in thought, perception, learning, and language. _____

Frontal Lobes	The lobes that control voluntary body movements, speech production, and such functions as thinking, motivation, planning for the future, impulse control, and emotional responses. They contain the motor cortex, Broca's area, and the frontal association areas. _____ _____ _____
Motor Cortex	The strip of tissue at the rear of the frontal lobes that controls voluntary body movement. Damage to the motor cortex can cause paralysis, impaired coordination, and the grand mal seizures of epilepsy. _____ _____ _____
Broca's Area	The area in the frontal lobe, usually in the left hemisphere that controls the production of speech sounds. Broca's area is involved in directing the pattern of muscle movement required to produce the speech sounds. _____ _____ _____
Broca's Aphasia	An impairment in the ability physically to produce the speech sounds, or in extreme cases, the inability to speak at all; caused by damage to Broca's area. Broca's aphasia is primarily a deficit in producing language, not in understanding it. _____ _____ _____
Aphasia	A loss or impairment of the ability to understand or communicate through the written or spoken word, which results from damage to the brain. _____ _____ _____
Parietal Lobes	The lobes that contain the somatosensory cortex (where touch, pressure, temperature, and pain register) and other areas that are responsible for body awareness and spatial orientation. _____ _____ _____
Somatosensory Cortex	The strip of tissue at the front of the parietal lobes where touch, pressure, temperature, and pain register in the cerebral cortex. This cortex also makes us aware of movement in our body and the positions of our body parts at any given moment. _____ _____ _____
Occipital Lobes	The lobes that contain the primary visual cortex, where vision registers, and association areas involved in the interpretation of visual information. _____ _____ _____
Primary Visual Cortex	The area at the rear of the occipital lobes where vision registers in the cerebral cortex. Each eye is connected to the primary visual cortex in both the right and left occipital lobes. _____ _____ _____
Temporal Lobes	The lobes that contain the primary auditory cortex, Wernicke's area, and association areas for interpreting auditory information. _____ _____ _____
Primary Auditory Cortex	The part of the temporal lobes where hearing registers in the cerebral cortex. Damage to one of these areas results in reduces hearing in both ears, and the destruction of both areas results in total deafness. _____ _____ _____

Wernicke's Area	The language area in the temporal lobe involved in comprehension of the spoken word and in formulation of coherent speech and written language. In about 95 percent of people, Wernicke's area is in the left hemisphere. _____ _____ _____
Wernicke's Aphasia	Aphasia resulting from damage to Wernicke's area, in which the patient's spoken language is fluent, but the content is either vague or incomprehensible to the listener. While the spoken words of a Wernicke's aphasia sufferer may clearly articulated, the actual message makes no sense to the listener (e.g., My dad the green hair of albatross noon by evening). _____ _____ _____
Lateralization	The specialization of one of the cerebral hemispheres to handle a particular function. Functions are not handled exclusively by one hemisphere or the other. There is always cooperation between hemispheres. _____ _____ _____
Left Hemisphere	The hemisphere that controls the right side of the body, coordinates complex movements, and in 95 % of people, controls the production of speech and written language. _____ _____ _____
Right Hemisphere	The hemisphere that controls the left side of the body, and that, for most people, is specialized for visual-spatial perception and for interpreting nonverbal behavior. _____ _____ _____
Split-brain Operation	An operation performed in severe cases of epilepsy, in which the corpus callosum is cut, separating the cerebral hemispheres and usually lessening the severity and frequency of grand mal seizures. This surgery causes no major changes in personality, intelligence, or behavior. _____ _____ _____
Electroencephalogram EEG)	A record of brain-wave activity made by the electroencephalograph, a machine invented by Hans Berger in 1924 that amplifies a million times the electrical activity occurring in the brain. _____ _____ _____
Beta Wave	The brain wave associated with mental or physical activity. _____ _____ _____
Alpha Wave	The brain wave associated with deep relaxation. _____ _____
Delta Wave	The brain wave associated with slow-wave (deep) sleep. _____ _____ _____
Microelectrode	An electrical wire so small that it can be used to monitor the electrical activity of a single neuron or to stimulate activity within it. _____ _____ _____

CT scan (computerized axial tomography)	A brain scanning technique involving a rotating X-ray scanner and a high-speed computer analysis that produces slice-by-slice, cross-sectional images of the structure of the brain. The CT scan illustrates the structures of the brain and reveals abnormalities, injuries, and damage from strokes. _____
Magnetic Resonance Imaging (MRI)	A diagnostic scanning technique that produces high-resolution images of the structures of the brain. _____
PET scan (positron-emission tomography)	A brain imaging technique that reveals brain activity in various parts of the brain, based on the amount of oxygen and glucose consumed. The PET scan allows researchers to actually see the brain working, thinking, and remembering, and has revealed much about the effects of drugs on the brain. _____
Functional MRI (fMRI)	A neuroimaging technique that reveals both brain structure and brain activity. _____
Stroke	The major cause of damage to the adult brain that occurs when an artery in the brain is blocked, cutting off the blood supply to the affected area, or when a blood vessel bursts. _____
Plasticity	The ability of the brain to reorganize and compensate for brain damage. Once neurons are destroyed, they are not replaced. However, it is sometimes possible for adjacent neurons to sprout new dendrites and assume some of the functions of the cells that were lost. _____
Peripheral Nervous System (PNS)	The nerves connecting the central nervous system to the rest of the body. Basically, the PNS is everything other than the Central Nervous System. The PNS contains two major subdivisions, the somatic and autonomic nervous systems. _____
Sympathetic Nervous System	The division of the autonomic nervous system that mobilizes the body's resources during stress, emergencies, or heavy exercise, preparing the body for action (fight-or-flight response). _____
Parasympathetic Nervous System	The division of the autonomic nervous system that is associated with relaxation and the conservation of energy and that brings the heightened bodily responses back to normal following an emergency. _____
Endocrine System	A system of ductless glands in various parts of the body that manufacture and secrete hormones into the bloodstream or lymph fluids, thus affecting cells in other parts of the body. _____

Hormone	A substance manufactured and released in one part of the body that affects other parts of the body. Some of the same substances that act as neurotransmitters act as hormones as well.
Pituitary Gland	The endocrine gland located in the brain and often referred to as the "master gland," which releases hormones that control other endocrine glands and also releases a growth hormone.
Adrenal Glands	A pair of endocrine glands that release hormones that prepare the body for emergencies and stressful situations and also release small amounts of the sex hormones. _____

FROM THE LABORATORY TO LIFE

TALKING TO THE BRAIN

For me, one of the best things about college was the opportunity to be introduced to all the new ideas and interesting ways of doing things—especially in graduate school as I investigated different ways of practicing psychotherapy. One approach that gained a lot of attention in the 1980's was based on the different ways in which the hemispheres of the brain process information. The theory suggested that one hemisphere of the brain would be more willing than the other hemisphere to accept certain therapeutic ideas and suggestions. This was based on the fact that the other side of the brain was too analytical and calculating to be able to appreciate the big picture of the message. New techniques of therapeutic communication were developed that utilized the telling of stories or metaphors geared to affect the side of the brain that would most benefit from these messages. The counselor was to deliver therapy in a manner designed to avoid the client's hemispherical tendency toward overanalyzing or resisting the information. Many books were published giving therapists ideas for stories or therapeutic fables that would be useful in various counseling situations. The moral of this story, as it turned out, is that there exists no panacea or magic bullet for the ills of human emotion. While good communication skills are necessary to the therapeutic relationship, don't be fooled by a promise of easy solutions for the complex issues of life!

1. In the above passage and according to the counseling theory discussed, which hemisphere of the brain are counselors attempting to communicate with when they use stories and metaphors? _____

2. Which hemisphere of the brain is recognized as the center of language for most people? _____

3. If the above theory were correct, which hemisphere of the brain would I want to talk to if I were going to use mathematical examples? _____

4. If the patient can not understand the deep meaning of a proverb such as "still water runs deep"; the patient probably has damage to the _____ hemisphere.

THE BRAIN – BEHAVIOR AND EXPERIENCE

1. I awoke this morning and felt very hungry—actually craving scrambled eggs and hash browns. Which part of my brain is most responsible for my motivation to eat? _____

2. I was hit in the head and actually saw stars for a few seconds. Which part of my brain probably sustained the brunt of the hit? _____

3. There is a story of an accident where a fencing enthusiast (a kind of sword fighting sport) was injured when the tip of the fencing sword entered his brain through his nose. From this point on he could no longer transfer information from short-term to long-term memory. What part of the brain was probably injured in this accident?

_____

4. Alice lives near an airport and it took a long time for her to get used to the noise. At first she would be awake half the night but she has finally gotten to the point that she can get a good night's sleep. Recently she had a baby. The interesting thing is that while she can still sleep through the noise of the air traffic, the slightest noise from the nursery seems to wake her immediately. This ability to discriminate between the airport noise and her newborn is under the control of the _____ system.

5. Joe was so excited on his first official day as the neighborhood's new paperboy that he awoke early and started his route before first light. As he approached one house he suddenly heard the sound of what appeared to be a large and unfriendly dog. He suddenly felt a rush of energy and other changes in his body, including an increased heart rate and quickened breathing. Joe was experiencing the effects of his _____ nervous system.

6. Frank seems to be unusually thin and doesn't understand why. He eats as much as other people his age and is not all that active. Recently, a friend suggested that Frank may have a glandular condition. Which gland was the friend probably referring to? _____

THEORY TO PRACTICE

Playing Doctor

Your text includes descriptions of the various brain structures in terms of what functions they control and, in some cases, the probable outcome of damage to each area. It also provides descriptions of many of the neurotransmitters and their various roles in everyday functioning. Below is a list of brief case studies involving people who are suffering from various problems. Follow the theoretical direction supplied in your text to diagnose these cases. Identify the most probable cause for the disorders listed below. Indicate the most likely **diagnosis** (unless already given), the **probable disturbance in neurotransmitter activity,** and/or the **location of possible brain damage**.

Select your responses from the answer key included below the exercise. Some items may have more than one correct response.

♦ Miriam is exhibiting language deficits. In particular, her words, though fluent, are incomprehensible to you.

♦ Juan displays spastic motor coordination and is diagnosed as having Parkinson's disorder.

♦ Neal, a 72-year-old retired carpenter, has gradually seen his everyday memory deteriorate badly. Sometimes he can't even find his way home from the grocery store a few blocks away. He is diagnosed as having Alzheimer's disease.

♦ Camille is highly irrational, has poor contact with reality, and reports hallucinations. She is given a diagnosis of Schizophrenic disorder.

♦ Cedric has expressed feelings of hopelessness and worthlessness and reports feeling that he'd be better off dead.

Case	Diagnosis	Neurotransmitter	Brain Structure
Miriam	1)	———————————	2)
Juan	Parkinson's	3)	Substantia nigra
Neal	Alzheimer's	Acetylcholine	4)
Camille	Schizophrenia	5)	Enlarged ventricles
Cedric	6)	7)	———————————

Answer Key

Diagnoses	Neurotransmitters	Brain Structures
a) Bipolar Disorder	e) Acetylcholine	i) Hippocampus
b) Broca's aphasia	f) Dopamine deficiency	j) Wernicke's area
c) Depression	g) Norepinephrine & Serotonin	k) Broca's area
d) Wernicke's Aphasia	h) Dopamine oversensitivity	l) Medulla

Stop Needling Me

Endorphins are a neurotransmitter with a chemical makeup like that of opiates. The endorphins function to relieve pain and produce feelings of pleasure. From the ancient Chinese art of healing comes a practice that has grown in popularity with Western cultures over the last several years—acupuncture. In the acupuncture procedure, very fine needles are inserted into the skin at various locations. How can being stuck with a needle help relieve pain?

_____

Describe the process. _____

_____

_____

_____

COMPREHENSIVE PRACTICE TEST

1. Phineas Gage changed from a polite, dependable, well-liked railroad foreman to a rude and impulsive person who could no longer plan realistically for the future. In a railroad construction accident, Gage had seriously damaged his:
   a) occipital lobe
   b) frontal lobe
   c) medulla
   d) cerebellum

2. Afferent is to efferent as:
   a) sensory is to sensation
   b) sensation is to perception
   c) motor is to sensory
   d) sensory is to motor

3. _____ neurons carry information between neurons in the brain, and between neurons in the spinal cord.
   a) afferent
   b) efferent
   c) myelinated
   d) inter

4. The junction where the axon terminal of a sending neuron communicates with a receiving neuron is known as the:
   a) dendritic bud
   b) synaptic cleft
   c) action potential perimeter
   d) efferent cleft

5. Communication between neurons is accomplished by:
   a) depolarization
   b) ion exchange
   c) neurotransmitters
   d) deionization potentials

6. Endorphins, norepinephrine, dopamine, and serotonin are all examples of:
   a) hormones
   b) neurotransmitters
   c) neuropeptides
   d) neuromodulators

7. A deficiency in _____ has been associated with Parkinson's disease, a disease characterized by tremors and rigidity in the limbs.
   a) dopamine
   b) norepinephrine
   c) acetylcholine
   d) GABA

8. Both _____ and _____ have been associated with positive moods while deficiencies in both have been associated with depression.
   a) serotonin; acetylcholine
   b) glutamate; acetylcholine
   c) endorphin; GABA
   d) norepinephrine; serotonin

9. Neurons can conduct messages faster if they have:
   a) an axon with a myelin sheath
   b) a positive resting potential
   c) more than one cell body
   d) fewer dendrites

10. When a neuron changes from the resting potential to the _____ potential, its electrical characteristics change from about –70 millivolts to about + 50 millivolts.
   a) charged
   b) impulse
   c) action
   d) reversal

11. The nervous system is first divided into the _____ and the _____ systems.
   a) central; autonomic
   b) central; peripheral
   c) somatic; autonomic
   d) somatic; sympathetic

12. The central nervous system is divided into the _____ and the _____.
   a) brain; cerebellum
   b) brain; spinal cord
   c) spinal cord; endocrine system
   d) somatic system; autonomic system

13. The functions of _____ cells include forming myelin sheaths, removing waste products, and other maintenance tasks.
   a) endorphin
   b) dendrite
   c) neuro-recombinant
   d) glial

14. This structure is located above the brain stem and it serves as a relay station for information to and from the higher brain centers.
   a) pituitary gland
   b) cerebellum
   c) thalamus
   d) amygdala

15. This structure is located in the brain stem and is important for basic life functions such as heartbeat and breathing.
   a) pons
   b) medulla
   c) hypothalamus
   d) hippocampus

16. Sometimes people refer to this brain structure as the body's thermostat because it controls things like temperature, hunger, thirst, and emotional behaviors.
   a) corpus callosum
   b) pituitary gland
   c) pons
   d) hypothalamus

17. This brain structure is important for the control of smooth movements, muscle tone, and posture.
   a) cerebellum
   b) limbic system
   c) parietal lobe
   d) occipital lobe

18. The lobe that contains the primary visual cortex and association areas involved in the interpretation of visual information is which of the following?
   a) frontal lobe
   b) parietal lobe
   c) occipital lobe
   d) temporal lobe

19. This lobe houses the motor cortex.
   a) frontal lobe
   b) parietal lobe
   c) occipital lobe
   d) temporal lobe

20. This lobe contains the primary auditory cortex.
   a) frontal lobe
   b) parietal lobe
   c) occipital lobe
   d) temporal lobe

21. The thick band of nerve fibers that connects the two cerebral hemispheres and makes possible the transfer of information between them is the _____.
   a) pituitary structure
   b) corpus callosum
   c) reticular activating system
   d) limbic system

22. This part of the brain is involved in the comprehension of spoken words and the formulation of written and spoken language.
   a) Broca's Area
   b) right hemisphere
   c) Wernicke's Area
   d) left hemisphere

23. The cerebral cortex is located just below the brain stem and is important for functions such as sleep and wakefulness and response to novel stimuli.
   a) True
   b) False

24. Damage to Broca's Area will result in a type of aphasia where patients know what they want to say but can not speak.
    a) True   b) False

25. The left hemisphere was identified as controlling visual-spatial perception and interpreting non-verbal behaviors.
    a) True   b) False

26. While the left hemisphere seems to be most important in general language abilities, the right hemisphere seems to allow us to detect emotion or anger in someone's verbal behavior.
    a) True   b) False

27. If I am interested in getting information regarding the brain's activity based on the amount of oxygen and glucose consumed as a function of that activity, I should use a(n):
    a) MRI   c) PET
    b) EEG   d) CT

28. The _____ system controls skeletal muscles and communicates with the external environment.
    a) autonomic   c) sympathetic
    b) spinal   d) somatic

29. The _____ system mobilizes the body for action through what has come to be known as fight-or-flight.
    a) reticular activating   c) parasympathetic
    b) sympathetic   d) limbic

30. The pituitary gland is known as the master gland of the _____ system.
    a) hypothalamic   c) endocrine
    b) sympathetic   d) reticular activating

31. The adrenal glands are important in the body's fight-or-flight response through the release of _____.
    a) insulin   c) androgens
    b) corticoids   d) endorphins

32. According to the *APPLY IT* feature in this chapter, handedness has now been shown to be most influenced by the neonatal environment.
    a) True   b) False

OMSE # 1 ANSWER KEY: NEURONS AND THE CENTRAL NERVOUS SYSTEM

A. Quick Quiz	B. Matching	C. Complete The Diagram
1. d	1. d	
2. axon	2. g	
3. false	3. a	
4. b	4. b	
5. neurotransmitters	5. c	
6. false	6. f	
7. glial	7. e	
8. c		
9. true		
10. cerebellum		
11. c		
12. false		
13. limbic		
14. c		
15. false		

Dendrites
Cell Body
Myelin Sheath
Nodes of Ranvier
Axon
Axon Terminal

OMSE # 2 Answer Key: Cerebral Hemispheres and Specialization

A. Quick Quiz	B. Matching	C. Complete the Diagram
1. d	1. h	1. e
2. b	2. g	2. a
3. true	3. i	3. f
4. a	4. b	4. c
5. c	5. a	5. d
6. c	6. d	6. b
7. motor cortex	7. c	
8. d	8. f	
9. b	9. e	
10. right		
11. a		
12. primary auditory cortex		
13. a		
14. split-brain operation		
15. false		

OMSE # 3 Answer Key: Brain Mysteries and Brain Damage

A. Quick Quiz	B. Matching
1. b	1. c
2. delta	2. a
3. true	3. e
4. c	4. b
5. true	5. d
6. stroke	
7. false	
8. c	
9. epilepsy	
10. c	

The brain still holds many mysteries. As technology is advanced, so is the opportunity to better understand the human brain. Recent advances have unlocked many of the secrets of the brain in a relatively short span. What will be the next major breakthrough?

C. Complete the Diagram

Beta	
Alpha	
Theta	
Delta	

Beta: The brain wave associated with mental or physical activity.

Alpha: The brain wave associated with deep relaxation.

Theta: The brain wave associated with light sleep.

Delta: The brain wave associated with slow-wave (deep) sleep.

OMSE # 4 Answer Key: Peripheral Nervous System and Endocrine System

A. Quick Quiz		B. Matching	C. Complete the Diagram
1. a	9. b	1. g	1. somatic nervous system
2. c	10. neurotransmitters	2. d	2. autonomic nervous system
3. a	11. c	3. h	3. sympathetic nervous system
4. true	12. epinephrine;	4. e	4. parasympathetic nervous system
5. d	norepinephrine	5. a	
6. sympathetic nervous	13. parasympathetic	6. b	
system	14. gonads	7. c	
7. fight-or-flight	15. androgens; estrogens	8. f	
8. d			

Answer Key: Laboratory to Real Life

Talking to the Brain	Behavior and Experience
1. right	1. hypothalamus
2. left	2. occipital lobe
3. left	3. hippocampus
4. right	4. reticular activating system
	5. sympathetic
	6. thyroid

Answer Key: Theory to Practice

Playing Doctor	Stop Needling Me
1. d	Endorphins are being released.
2. j	Since endorphins are released in response to pain, the acupuncturist's needles are bringing
3. f	about a natural remedy. The endorphins are released into the system as the needles affect
4. i	nerve endings in the dermis. The natural pain killing effect of the endorphins, combined with
5. h	stimulation of pleasurable sensations, is enough to make many people come back for more
6. c	needling.
7. g	

COMPREHENSIVE PRACTICE EXAM

1. b	17. a
2. d	18. c
3. d	19. a
4. b	20. d
5. c	21. b
6. b	22. c
7. a	23. false
8. d	24. true
9. a	25. false
10. c	26. true
11. b	27. c
12. b	28. d
13. d	29. b
14. c	30. c
15. b	31. b
16. d	32. false

3

SENSATION AND PERCEPTION

Sensation describes all that we see, hear, feel, smell, and taste in our environment. Every stimulus that we come into contact with becomes a part of our sensory experience. Perception allows us to interpret and understand that multitude of stimuli.

CHAPTER OVERVIEW

Ahhhhh, the memories! Waking up on Thanksgiving morning with the smell of roasting turkey already wafting through the house! To this day, every time I smell turkey roasting I am reminded of those wonderful childhood holidays. At times, the smells of Thanksgiving take me all the way back to my youth. Similarly, a favorite old tune can carry me back to another time in my life—puberty and adolescence. It seems that this time of life is often defined and remembered by the music we listened to as we discovered our world and ourselves. Even today, when I hear one of those old songs, I am returned to some vivid, happy or sometimes sad memory. Madison Avenue certainly knows the importance of a well placed sensory memory when it comes to convincing us that we need this or that product on our friendly grocery or electronics store shelf. The never-ending barrage of oldies-but-goodies that accompanies retailer's product pitches has geometrically increased in the last decade or two. It has been within that same period of time that we have really begun to understand the relationship between our sensory/perceptual experience and things like mood and performance. For example, can the type of smells or lighting in a factory or busy office help workers feel better, fight fatigue, and be more productive? Can we use smells and different kinds of lighting to help people deal with depression? Can smell be used to help people lose weight? These questions and many others have increased interest and aided in advancing psychology's research in the area of sensation and perception.

Of course, sensation and perception add up to much more than a way to tap the fond memories of childhood. Imagine what life would be like without the ability to interact with the environment through our senses. Fortunately, our ability to communicate with the environment turns out to be a robust process. People who have lost one sense seem to experience an improvement in one or more of the other senses, thereby accommodating that loss and enabling most people to get on with their lives. When I think of the human spirit I am often reminded of Helen Keller–what a wonderful example of our brain's ability to do what it takes to help us live life to its fullest!

This chapter will help you gain a more practiced and functional understanding of the relationship between our sensory abilities, our perceptual processes, and our behavior. The information has been divided into three OMSE sections, 1) sensation and basic sensory processes, 2) the major sensory systems, and 3) the processes of perception. You will gain an understanding of the physiological and cognitive processes involved in sensation and perception and you will come to appreciate the complex mechanism that is the human body. This chapter will combine with the previous chapter to give you a complete understanding of how our bodies work with the outside environment to create for us the experience of living life to its fullest.

By completing the exercises provided, you should gain a thorough understanding of the information provided in your text. In other words, you should be better prepared for tests, quizzes, class participation, and life itself.

CHAPTER OUTLINE

KEY TERMS

OMSE # 1: SENSATION: THE SENSORY WORLD

LEARNING OBJECTIVES

1. What is the difference between sensation and perception?
2. What is the difference between absolute threshold and difference threshold?
3. How are the sensory stimuli in the environment experienced as sensations?

LEARNING MASTERY SCORECARD: Update your score card as you work through the various sections of the chapter. First, find and define key terms and concepts included in each section and note the page number(s) from the text that contain important references to the material. Next, gain a practical understanding of the concepts by considering the Laboratory to Life scenarios and thinking of at least one original example of how the concept might apply in real life. Complete the *Objective-Mastery Self-Evaluation* (OMSE) exercises for this section and record your scores. Revisit the exercises, recording your score and the date completed until you have attained mastery (100%). Finally, decide how you would prepare a lecture on each objective using the template provided, outline the lecture, and practice presenting it. Keep an honest tally of your achievements and, when finished, you will have developed learning mastery through elaborate rehearsal.

Key Terms & Concepts	Page #		Key Terms & Concepts	Page #
sensation	____		Weber's law	____
perception	____		signal detection theory	____
absolute threshold	____		sensory receptors	____
difference threshold	____		transduction	____
just noticeable difference	____		sensory adaptation	____

Quick Quiz

Date	Score	Date	Score	Date	Score
_/_/_	____	_/_/_	____	_/_/_	____
_/_/_	____	_/_/_	____	_/_/_	100%

Elaborate Rehearsal

Lecture Preparation	Completion Date
Key Terms, Persons, & Concepts	_/_/_
Learning Objectives	_/_/_
Lecture Notes	_/_/_

TIMELINE

1660	Thomas Young: trichromatic theory of color vision	1834	August Seeback: frequency theory of hearing	1878
Robert Boyle: no sound in a vacuum	1802	Ernst Weber: Weber's Law and JND	1840s	Ewald Hering: opponent-process theory of color vision

A. QUICK QUIZ

1. Sensation is to _____ as perception is to _____:
   a) stimuli detection; sensory interpretation
   b) difference threshold; absolute threshold
   c) absolute threshold; difference threshold
   d) sensory interpretation; detect stimuli

2. Weber's Law is used to determine the value of the absolute threshold.
   a) True
   b) False

3. The _____ threshold is a measure of the smallest change in a physical stimulus required to produce a noticeable difference in sensation 50 percent of the time.

4. The smallest change in sensation that we are able to detect 50 percent of the time is known as:
   a) absolute threshold
   b) just noticeable difference
   c) perceptual difference
   d) sensate threshold

5. The absolute threshold for vision has been determined to be a candle flame 30 miles away on a clear night.
   a) True
   b) False

6. Researchers in sensory psychology and _____ study phenomena related to sensation such as the least amount of stimuli required for detection.

7. One important issue when studying sensation is the fact that what and how we detect a stimulus will be influenced by more than the actual physical event. Other things involved in the process include motivation, previous experience, and all of the other sensory stimuli occurring at the time of the detection. The book referred to *all of the other stimuli* as:
   a) sensory interference
   b) figure-ground phenomena
   c) perceptual disturbance
   d) background noise

8. While signal detection theory has proven to be an interesting topic for academic research, few practical applications for the information gained from that research have been identified.
   a) True
   b) False

9. _____ refers to the process by which a physical sensory stimulus is changed by the sensory receptors into neural impulses.

10. As a part of his training in personnel relations, Ted had to spend a whole day in a very noisy factory. While the sound seemed almost painful at first, he noticed by the end of the day that it didn't seem so loud anymore. This is an example of _____ _____.

B. MATCHING

_____	1. Change from physical to neural	a) sensation
_____	2. Least amount needed to detect a change	b) perception
_____	3. What does it mean	c) absolute threshold
_____	4. It doesn't seem so warm in here anymore	d) difference threshold
_____	5. What is it	e) transduction
_____	6. Least amount to detect it is there	f) sensory adaptation

C. COMPLETE THE DIAGRAM:
This exercise will combine what you learned in Chapter Two with what you are learning now in Chapter Three, *Sensation and Perception*. Locate each of the primary areas for the senses–vision, hearing, touch, taste, and smell—on the picture of the brain below. Place the letter representing the correct answer in the appropriate box.

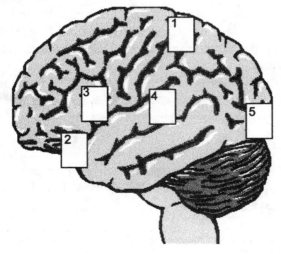

a) vision

b) hearing

c) touch

d) taste

e) smell

PREPARE A LECTURE: THE SENSORY WORLD: This activity is designed to offer you an opportunity to take advantage of a valuable mode of learning, elaborate rehearsal. Once you have finished the OMSE section, write a lecture using the instructional guide provided below. After your lecture is prepared, you can enhance your learning by writing a quiz covering the material. Now it is time to find some willing and inquisitive audience members. Your roommates or family may be a great place to start. Present them the lecture as if you are teaching a class. Remember to ask for questions and give your students the quiz following the lecture. This exercise can also serve to turn a *study-buddy* group into a very productive way to prepare for the test. Each member of the group can take different OMSE sections for their lecture/teacher role while the rest of the group serves as the class.

I. Key Terms, Names, Dates, and Concepts you will include in this lecture:

1. _____
2. _____
3. _____
4. _____

5. _____
6. _____
7. _____
8. _____

9. _____
10. _____
11. _____
12. _____

II. Learning Objectives (what do you want the student to know and be able to do as a result of your lecture):

1. _____
2. _____
3. _____
4. _____
5. _____

III. Lecture Notes (notes should be brief cues and serve as a guide).

Major topic #1: _____
    Sub-topics and notes: _____
_____
_____
_____

Major topic #2: _____
    Sub-topics and notes: _____
_____
_____
_____

Major topic #3: _____
    Sub-topics and notes: _____
_____
_____
_____

Does the light of a single candle change the brightness in a well-lit room? Can you really spot the flame of a single candle from 30 miles away on a clear night? What is the difference between *absolute threshold* and *difference threshold*? _____

_____
_____
_____
_____
_____

OMSE # 2: THE SENSES

LEARNING OBJECTIVES

1. How do the cornea, the iris, and the pupil function in vision?
2. What are the lens and the retina?
3. What roles do the rods and cones play in vision?
4. What path does the neural impulse take from the retina to the primary visual cortex?
5. What are the three dimensions that combine to provide the colors we experience?
6. What two main theories attempt to explain color vision?
7. What determines the pitch and loudness of a sound, and how is each quality measured?
8. How do the outer, middle, and inner ears function in hearing?
9. What two major theories attempt to explain hearing?
10. What are some major causes of hearing loss?
11. What are some major causes of hearing loss?
12. What path does a smell message take on its journey from the nose to the brain?
13. What are the four primary taste sensations, and how are they detected?
14. How does the skin provide sensory information?
15. What beneficial purpose does pain serve?
16. What is the gate-control theory of pain?
17. What are endorphins?
18. What kind of information does the kinesthetic sense provide, and how is this sensory information detected?
19. What is the vestibular sense, and where are its sensory receptors located?

LEARNING MASTERY SCORECARD: Update your score card as you work through the various sections of the chapter. First, find and define key terms and concepts included in each section and note the page number(s) from the text that contain important references to the material. Next, gain a practical understanding of the concepts by considering the Laboratory to Life scenarios and thinking of at least one original example of how the concept might apply in real life. Complete the *Objective-Mastery Self-Evaluation* (OMSE) exercises for this section and record your scores. Revisit the exercises, recording your score and the date completed until you have attained mastery (100%). Finally, decide how you would prepare a lecture on each objective using the template provided, outline the lecture, and practice presenting it. Keep an honest tally of your achievements and, when finished, you will have developed learning mastery through elaborate rehearsal.

Key Terms & Concepts	Page #	Key Terms & Concepts	Page #	Key Terms & Concepts	Page #
visible spectrum		opponent-process theory		frequency theory	
cornea		afterimage		bone conduction	
lens		color blindness		olfaction	
accommodation		frequency		olfactory epithelium	
retina		amplitude		olfactory bulbs	
rods		decibel		gustation	
cones		timbre		taste buds	
fovea		audition		tactile	
dark adaptation		outer ear		gate-control theory	
optic nerve		middle ear		endorphins	
feature detectors		inner ear		naloxone	
hue		cochlea		kinesthetic sense	
saturation		hair cells		vestibular sense	
brightness		place theory		semicircular canals	
trichromatic theory					

Quick Quiz

Date	Score	Date	Score	Date	Score
__/__/__	___	__/__/__	___	__/__/__	___
__/__/__	___	__/__/__	___	__/__/__	100%

Elaborate Rehearsal

Lecture Preparation	Completion Date
Key Terms, Persons, & Concepts	__/__/__
Learning Objectives	__/__/__
Lecture Notes	__/__/__

A. QUICK QUIZ

1. The most important human sensory system to everyday perceptual functioning is:
   a) smell
   b) vision
   c) taste
   d) hearing

2. One of the major parts of the eye, the _____, performs the first step in vision by bending the light rays inward through the pupil.
   a) cornea
   b) lens
   c) iris
   d) retina

3. In Chapter 2 you learned that stimuli are picked up at the senses by groups of specialized cells called receptors. There are two types of receptors in the eye. They are:
   a) fovea & trichromatic
   b) cones & hues
   b) hues & rods
   d) cones & rods

4. The lens of the eye changes shape as it focuses objects on the retina. This process is called:
   a) adaptation
   b) accommodation
   c) saturation
   d) feature detection

5. Which of the following is NOT one of the three dimensions that combine to provide the colors we experience?
   a) hue
   b) saturation
   c) adaptation
   d) brightness

6. According to the _____ theory of color vision, certain cells in the visual system increase their rate of firing to signal the opposing color.

7. An important characteristic of sound, _____ is determined by the number of cycles completed by a sound wave in one second.
   a) frequency
   b) pitch
   c) amplitude
   d) timbre

8. One of two major theories of hearing, this theory proposes that each pitch we hear is determined by the particular spot along the basilar membrane of the cochlea that vibrates the most:
   a) frequency theory
   b) conduction theory
   c) place theory
   d) transduction theory

9. This sensory system sends information to the limbic system, an area in the brain that plays an important role in memory and emotion.
   a) vision
   b) olfactory system
   c) auditory system
   d) gustatory system

10. The two types of hearing loss and deafness are identified as:
    a) amplitude and ossicular
    b) conductive and neural
    c) conductive and timbre
    d) perceptive and sequential

11. Gustation gives us four distinct kinds of sensations. They are:
    a) sweet, acrid, hot, & cold
    b) hot, cold, salty, & sweet
    c) sweet, sour, salty, & bitter
    d) sweet, sour, salty, & acrid

12. A sense influenced by temperature, smell, color, & texture is _____.

13. When you inadvertently lay your hand on a hot stove, at which brain structure is the neural message of heat and pain received?
    a) motor cortex
    b) occipital lobe
    c) somatosensory cortex
    d) hypothalamus

14. This sense provides information about relative position and movement of body parts.
    a) gustation
    b) vestibular sense
    c) olfaction
    d) kinesthetic sense

15. The sense that provides information about movement and our orientation in space is called:
    a) gustation
    b) vestibular sense
    c) olfaction
    d) kinesthetic sense

B. MATCHING

_____	1. The thin brand of electromagnetic waves that we can see	a) gate-control theory
_____	2. Transparent covering of the colored part of the eye	b) gustation
_____	3. Theory of color vision that suggests there are three types of cones	c) ossicles
_____	4. Measurement of loudness of sound based on amplitude	d) naloxone
_____	5. Distinctive quality of a sound	e) bone conduction
_____	6. In the ear, the three smallest bones in your body	f) visible spectrum
_____	7. The sensation of hearing	g) tactile
_____	8. Theory that hair cell receptors vibrate at the same rate as the sound	h) cornea
_____	9. Chewing ice is heard in the head via this process	i) frequency theory
_____	10. Can usually be helped by a hearing aid	j) taste buds
_____	11. Home for 10 million receptor cells for smell	k) trichromatic theory
_____	12. The sensation of taste	l) olfactory epithelium
_____	13. Receptor cells for taste reside here	m) timbre
_____	14. Pertaining to the sense of touch	n) decibel
_____	15. Theory that pain signals travel slowly	o) audition
_____	16. Drug that blocks the action of endorphins	p) conductive hearing loss

C. COMPLETE THE DIAGRAM: Place the letter corresponding to the appropriate answer in the box.

a) lens
b) retina
c) blind spot
d) fovea
e) pupillary opening
f) cornea
g) iris
h) optic nerve

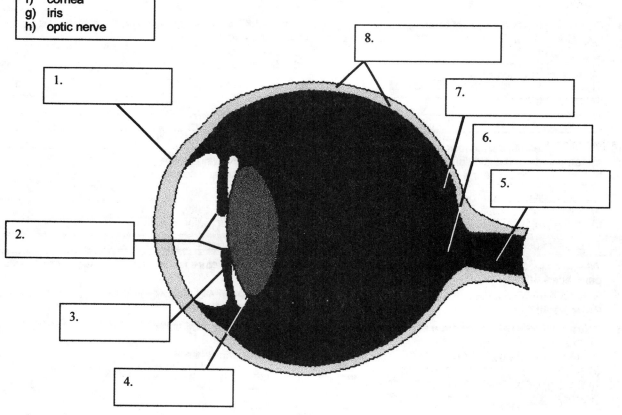

8.

1.

7.

6.

5.

2.

3.

4.

PREPARE A LECTURE: THE SENSES: This activity is designed to offer you an opportunity to take advantage of a valuable mode of learning, elaborate rehearsal. Once you have finished the OMSE section, write a lecture using the instructional guide provided below. After your lecture is prepared, you can enhance your learning by writing a quiz covering the material. Now it is time to find some willing and inquisitive audience members. Your roommates or family may be a great place to start. Present them the lecture as if you are teaching a class. Remember to ask for questions and give your students the quiz following the lecture. This exercise can also serve to turn a *study-buddy* group into a very productive way to prepare for the test. Each member of the group can take different OMSE sections for their lecture/teacher role while the rest of the group serves as the class.

I. Key Terms, Names, Dates, and Concepts you will include in this lecture:

1. _____
2. _____
3. _____
4. _____

5. _____
6. _____
7. _____
8. _____

9. _____
10. _____
11. _____
12. _____

II. Learning Objectives (what do you want the student to know and be able to do as a result of your lecture):

1. _____
2. _____
3. _____
4. _____
5. _____

III. Lecture Notes (notes should be brief cues and serve as a guide).

Major topic #1: _____
   Sub-topics and notes: _____
   _____
   _____
   _____

Major topic #2: _____
   Sub-topics and notes: _____
   _____
   _____
   _____

Major topic #3: _____
   Sub-topics and notes: _____
   _____
   _____
   _____

OMSE # 3: PERCEPTION AND SUBLIMINAL PERCEPTION

LEARNING OBJECTIVES

1. What are the Gestalt principles of perceptual organization?
2. What is perceptual constancy and what are its four types?
3. What are the binocular depth cues?
4. What are seven monocular depth cues?
5. In what types of situations do we rely on bottom-up processing or top-down processing?
6. What are some psychological factors that affect our perception?
7. Is subliminal perception effective in influencing our behavior?
8. What is extrasensory perception, and have the claims of psychics been verified scientifically?

LEARNING MASTERY SCORECARD: Update your score card as you work through the various sections of the chapter. First, find and define key terms and concepts included in each section and note the page number(s) from the text that contain important references to the material. Next, gain a practical understanding of the concepts by considering the Laboratory to Life scenarios and thinking of at least one original example of how the concept might apply in real life. Complete the *Objective-Mastery Self-Evaluation* (OMSE) exercises for this section and record your scores. Revisit the exercises, recording your score and the date completed until you have attained mastery (100%). Finally, decide how you would prepare a lecture on each objective using the template provided, outline the lecture, and practice presenting it. Keep an honest tally of your achievements and, when finished, you will have developed learning mastery through elaborate rehearsal.

Key Terms & Concepts	Page #	Key Terms & Concepts	Page #	Key Terms & Concepts	Page #
perception	____	color constancy	____	illusion	____
Gestalt	____	depth perception	____	bottom-up processing	____
figure-ground	____	binocular depth cues	____	top-down processing	____
innate	____	convergence	____	perceptual set	____
perceptual constancy	____	binocular disparity	____	subliminal persuasion	____
size constancy	____	monocular depth cues	____	subliminal perception	____
retinal image	____	apparent motion	____	extrasensory perception	____
shape constancy	____	phi phenomenon	____	parapsychology	____
brightness constancy	____				

Quick Quiz

Date	Score	Date	Score	Date	Score
_/_/_	____	_/_/_	____	_/_/_	____
_/_/_	____	_/_/_	____	_/_/_	100%

Elaborate Rehearsal

Lecture Preparation	Completion Date
Key Terms, Persons, & Concepts	_/_/_
Learning Objectives	_/_/_
Lecture Notes	_/_/_

A. QUICK QUIZ

1. _____ psychologists studied perception guided by the principle that "the whole is more than just the sum of its parts."
   a) Sensory
   b) Gestalt
   c) Perceptual
   d) Extrasensory perception

2. That we seem to perceive our environment in terms of an object standing out in the midst of a background is known as the _____ _____ principle.

3. The principle of *similarity* refers to the idea that we organize our perceptual experience based, in one way, on how objects contrast with each other.
   a) True
   b) False

4. When we group objects in accordance to their relative closeness in time or space, we are organizing our perceptual experience according to the principle of:
   a) continuity
   b) similarity
   c) spatial relativity
   d) proximity

5. Ted, an artist, always enjoyed creating pictures that led viewers to fill in gaps in the lines thereby forming a perceptual experience that created a whole pattern. When Ted did this, he was taking advantage of the principle of _____.

6. The fact that we tend to perceive people and objects as the same size, shape, brightness, and color even at different angles, distances, and lighting conditions is known as the *phi-phenomenon*.
   a) True
   b) False

7. If our _____ were given a literal interpretation, we would believe that Joe, who was five feet and seven inches tall, and who stood three feet away from us, were taller than John, who was six feet tall but was a block away.
   a) proximinal image
   b) distal image
   c) retinal image
   d) binocular image

8. Sometimes the brilliant moonlight can change considerably the shades of red on my horse barn. However, even under these conditions, I still perceive the barn as its "much-in-need-of-paint" shade of red. This tendency to perceive the correct color of familiar objects even under different conditions of illumination is known as _____ _____.

9. One interesting fact about depth perception is that, while we see the object in three dimensions, our eyes provide only two-dimensional information.
   a) True
   b) False

10. As an object comes closer, our eyes turn inward in order to maintain accurate perception. This in known as:
   a) binocular divergence
   b) dispergence
   c) monocular disparity
   d) convergence

11. One important contribution to our three dimensional perception is _____ _____, the phenomena where each eye receives a slightly different view of the objects we are watching.

12. *Interposition* is a dimensional cue that works by placing smaller objects behind larger objects in our perceptual field.
   a) True
   b) False

13. One day at an antique store, I found myself looking at a curious object without a clue as to its identity. However, after careful examination of its individual parts I was able to conclude that what I was looking at was an early version of a turning lathe (a machine for shaping decorative wood products like table legs). To make this determination I used which of the following:
   a) top-down processing
   b) perceptual construction
   c) bottom-up processing
   d) sensory construction

14. If you have been to Las Vegas, or at least seen videos of downtown Las Vegas at night, then you have seen what appears at first glance to be buildings that are alive with motion. The synchronous flashing of hundreds of neon lights offers arrows and figures moving all about the sides of buildings and tall signs. This illusion of apparent motion by stationary lights is known as the _____ _____.

15. Have you ever found yourself riding in a car at night and wondering if the moon was following you? If so, then you have experienced a phenomenon known as *motion parallax*.
   a) True
   b) False

B. MATCHING

_____	1. False perception of actual stimuli	a)	ambiguous figures
_____	2. Information from other than sensory channels	b)	impossible figures
_____	3. Old woman/young woman	c)	illusions
_____	4. Expectations affect perception	d)	Muller-Lyer & Ponzo
_____	5. Three-pronged trident	e)	subliminal perception
_____	6. Below absolute threshold	f)	extrasensory perception
_____	7. The farther the longer	g)	perceptual set

C. COMPLETE THE DIAGRAM: Binocular and monocular depth cues

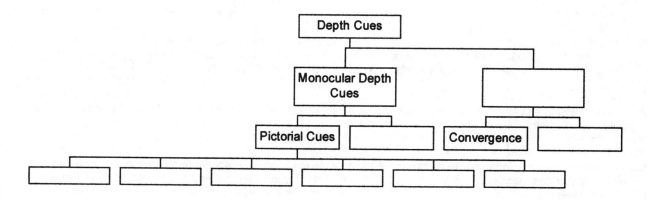

PREPARE A LECTURE: THE SENSES: This activity is designed to offer you an opportunity to take advantage of a valuable mode of learning, elaborate rehearsal. Once you have finished the OMSE section, write a lecture using the instructional guide provided below. After your lecture is prepared, you can enhance your learning by writing a quiz covering the material. Now it is time to find some willing and inquisitive audience members. Your roommates or family may be a great place to start. Present them the lecture as if you are teaching a class. Remember to ask for questions and give your students the quiz following the lecture. This exercise can also serve to turn a *study-buddy* group into a very productive way to prepare for the test. Each member of the group can take different OMSE sections for their lecture/teacher role while the rest of the group serves as the class.

I. Key Terms, Names, Dates, and Concepts you will include in this lecture:

1. _____   5. _____   9. _____
2. _____   6. _____   10. _____
3. _____   7. _____   11. _____
4. _____   8. _____   12. _____

II. Learning Objectives (what do you want the student to know and be able to do as a result of your lecture):

1. _____
2. _____
3. _____
4. _____
5. _____

III. Lecture Notes (notes should be brief cues and serve as a guide).

Major topic #1: _____

   Sub-topics and notes: _____

   _____

   _____

   _____

Major topic #2: _____

   Sub-topics and notes: _____

   _____

   _____

   _____

Major topic #3: _____

    Sub-topics and notes: _____

_____

_____

_____

KEY TERMS AND CONCEPTS EXERCISE

The key terms and concepts are presented in the order of their appearance in the text. Space is provided for you to include a personalized definition or example of each term or concept. As you encounter each term in the text, make a note of its meaning and context. Next, conceptualize the meaning of the term in a way that makes the most sense to you. You can also think about examples of the term from your own life. Write your definition and/or example in the space provided next to the word in this book. The KEY TERMS exercise utilizes a modified *T-note* design so that you can self-evaluate your mastery of the definitions. First lay a sheet of paper over the terms and concepts side of the page so that you only see the definitions. Read the definition and try to recall the term or concept. Mark all those you are unable to answer so you can restudy them. When you have learned all of the terms and concepts in this way, move the paper to the definition side so that you can see only the term or concept, try to recall both the textbook definition and your personal version. Repeat this until you know all of the terms and concepts by definition and personal understanding.

Sensation	The process through which the senses pick up visual, auditory, and other sensory stimuli and transmit them to the brain; sensory information that has registered in the brain but has not been interpreted. _____
Perception	The process by which sensory information is actively organized and interpreted by the brain. _____
Absolute Threshold	The minimum amount of sensory stimulation that can be detected 50 percent of the time. In other words, if you look at a candle flame from 30 miles away and see the flame every time, then it's not a threshold. If you cannot see the flame at all, it is also not a threshold. _____
Difference Threshold	The smallest increase or decrease in a physical stimulus required to produce a difference in sensation that is noticeable 50 percent of the time. _____
Just Noticeable Difference	The smallest change of sensation that we are able to detect 50 percent of the time. If you light a match in a well-lit room, is there a noticeable increase in the brightness of the room? _____
Weber's Law	The law stating that the just noticeable difference for all our senses depends on a proportion or percentage of change in a stimulus rather than on a fixed amount of change. If you were holding a 50-pound weight and a fly landed on it, you would not notice the difference—unless of course the fly weighed approximately one pound. _____

Signal Detection Theory	The view that detection of a sensory stimulus involves both discriminating a stimulus from background "noise" and deciding whether the stimulus is actually present. _____ _____ _____
Sensory Receptors	Specialized cells in each sense organ that detect and respond to sensory stimuli—light, sound, odors, etc.—and transduce (convert) the stimuli into neural impulses. _____ _____ _____
Transduction	The process by which sensory receptors convert sensory stimulation—light, sound, odors, etc.—into neural impulses. _____ _____ _____
Sensory Adaptation	The process of becoming less sensitive to an unchanging sensory stimulus over time. For example, you may sleep just fine next to a noisy fan after you have adapted to that sound, but an equally loud unfamiliar noise may startle you awake instantly. _____ _____ _____
Visible Spectrum	The narrow band of electromagnetic rays, 380–760 nm in length, that are visible to the human eye. _____ _____ _____
Cornea	The transparent covering of the colored part of the eye that bends light rays inward through the pupil. _____ _____ _____
Lens	The transparent structure behind the iris that changes in shape as it focuses images on the retina. _____ _____ _____
Accommodation	The changing in shape of the lens as it focuses objects on the retina, becoming more spherical for near objects and flatter for far objects. _____ _____ _____
Retina	The tissue at the back of the eye that contains the rods and the cones and onto which the retinal image is projected. _____ _____ _____
Rods	The light-sensitive receptors in the retina that provide vision in dim light in black, white, and shades of gray. _____ _____ _____
Cones	The receptor cells in the retina that enable us to see color and fine detail in adequate light, but do not function in dim light. _____ _____ _____
Fovea	A small area of the retina, 1/50th of an inch in diameter, that provides the clearest and sharpest vision because it has the largest concentration of cones. _____ _____ _____

Dark Adaptation	The eye's increasing ability to see in dim light; results from the recombining of molecules of rhodopsin in the rods and the dilation of the pupils. _____
Optic Nerve	The nerve that carries visual information from the retina to the brain. _____
Feature Detectors	Neurons in the brain that respond to specific features of a sensory stimulus (for example, to lines or angles). _____
Hue	The property of light commonly referred to as color (red, blue, green, etc.), determined primarily by the wavelength of light reflected from a surface. _____
Saturation	The degree to which light waves producing a color are of the same wavelength; the purity of a color. _____
Brightness	The dimension of visual sensation that is dependent on the intensity of light reflected from a surface and that corresponds to the amplitude of the light wave. _____
Trichromatic Theory	The theory of color vision suggesting that there are three types of cones, which are maximally sensitive to red, green, or blue, and that varying levels of activity in these receptors can produce all of the colors. _____
Opponent-Process Theory	The theory that certain cells in the vision system increase their firing rate to signal one color and decrease their firing rate to signal the opposing color (red/green, yellow/blue, white/black).
Afterimage	The visual sensation that remains after a stimulus is withdrawn. _____
Color Blindness	The inability to distinguish some or all colors in vision, resulting from a defect in the cones.
Frequency	Measured in the unit hertz, the number of sound waves or cycles per second, determining the pitch of the sound. _____
Amplitude	Measured in decibels, the magnitude or intensity of a sound wave, determining the loudness of a sound; in vision the amplitude of a light wave affects the brightness of a stimulus.

Decibel	A unit of measurement of the loudness or intensity of sound based on the amplitude of the sound wave. _____ _____ _____
Timbre	The distinctive quality of a sound that distinguishes it from other sounds of the same pitch and loudness. _____ _____ _____
Audition	The sensation of hearing; the process of hearing. _____ _____ _____
Outer Ear	The visible part of the ear, consisting of the pinna and the auditory canal. _____ _____ _____ _____
Middle Ear	The portion of the ear containing the ossicles, which connect the eardrum to the oval window and amplify the vibrations as they travel to the inner ear. _____ _____ _____
Inner Ear	The innermost portion of the ear, containing the cochlea, the vestibular sacs, and the semicircular canals. _____ _____ _____
Cochlea	The snail-shaped, fluid-filled organ in the inner ear that contains the hair cells (the sound receptors). _____ _____ _____
Hair Cells	Sensory receptors for hearing, found in the cochlea. _____ _____ _____
Place Theory	The theory that sounds of different frequency or pitch cause maximum activation of hair cells at certain locations along the basilar membrane. _____ _____ _____
Frequency Theory	The theory that hair cell receptors vibrate the same number of times as the sounds that reach them, thereby accounting for how variations in pitch are transmitted to the brain. _____ _____ _____ _____
Bone Conduction	The transmission of vibrations along the bones of the skull or face directly to the cochlea. _____ _____ _____
Olfaction	The sensation of smell; the process of smell. _____ _____ _____
Olfactory Epithelium	Two 1-inch square patches of tissue, one at the top of each nasal cavity, which together contain about ten million olfactory neurons, the receptors for smell. _____ _____ _____

Olfactory Bulbs	Two matchstick-sized structures above the nasal cavities, where smell sensations first register in the brain. _____
Pheromones	Body chemicals excreted by humans and other animals that act as signals and elicit certain patterns of behavior from members of the same species. _____
Gustation	The sensation of taste. _____
Taste Buds	The structures that are composed of about 60 to 100 sensory receptors for taste. _____
Tactile	Pertaining to the sense of touch. _____
Gate-Control Theory	The theory that the pain signals transmitted by slow-firing nerve fibers can be blocked at the spinal gate if fast-firing fibers get their messages to the gate first, or if the brain itself inhibits transmission of the pain messages. This theory attempts to explain why pressure, ice, and heat are capable of relieving pain. _____
Endorphins	Chemicals, produced naturally by the pituitary gland, that reduce pain and positively affect mood. The chemical makeup of endorphins is highly similar to that of heroin and morphine.
Naloxone	A drug that blocks the action of endorphins. Naloxone has been used to positively establish the pain-reducing effect of endorphins. _____
Kinesthetic Sense	The sense providing information about relative position and movement of body parts.
Vestibular Sense	Sense that provides information about movement and our orientation in space through sensory receptors in the semicircular canals and the vestibular sacs, which detect changes in the movement and orientation of the head. _____
Semicircular Canals	Three fluid-filled tubular canals in the inner ear that provide information about rotating head movements. _____
Perception	The process by which sensory information is actively organized and interpreted by the brain.

Gestalt	A German word roughly meaning "form" or "pattern." The Gestalt Psychologists maintained that we can not understand our perceptual world by studying the components of sensation and perception. The Gestalt psychologists insisted that "the sum is greater than the whole of its parts." _____
Figure-Ground	A principle of perceptual organization whereby the visual field is perceived in terms of an object (figure) standing out against a background (ground). _____
Innate	Inborn, unlearned. Generally, in psychology, the term innate is used to qualify the origin of a particular characteristic, trait, or ability. For example, many psychologists believe that the figure-ground perceptual ability is innate. _____
Perceptual Constancy	The tendency to perceive objects as maintaining stable properties, such as size, shape, brightness, and color despite differences in distance, viewing angle, and lighting. _____
Size Constancy	The tendency to perceive objects as the same size regardless of changes in the retinal image. As objects or people move farther away from us we continue to perceive them as being about the same size. _____
Retinal Image	The image of objects in the visual field projected onto the retina. _____
Shape Constancy	The tendency to perceive objects as having a stable or unchanging shape regardless of differences in viewing angle. _____
Brightness Constancy	The tendency to see objects as maintaining the same brightness regardless of differences in lighting conditions. _____
Color Constancy	The tendency to see objects as maintaining about the same color regardless of differences in lighting conditions. _____
Depth Perception	The ability to see in three dimensions and to estimate distance. _____
Binocular Depth Cues	Depth cues that depend on two eyes working together; convergence and binocular disparity. _____
Convergence	A binocular depth cue in which the eyes turn inward as they focus on nearby objects—the closer an object, the greater the convergence. _____

Binocular Disparity	A binocular depth cue resulting from differences between the two retinal images cast by objects at distances up to about twenty feet. _____ _____ _____
Monocular Depth Cues	Depth cues that can be perceived by only one eye. _____ _____ _____ _____
Apparent Motion	The perception of motion when none is occurring (as in the phi phenomenon or in stroboscopic movement). _____ _____ _____
Phi Phenomenon	An illusion of movement occurring when two or more stationary lights are flashed on and off in sequence, giving the impression that the light is actually moving from one spot to the next. _____ _____ _____
Illusion	A false perception of actual stimuli involving a misperception of size, shape, or the relationship of one element to another. _____ _____ _____
Bottom-Up Processing	Information processing in which individual components or bits of data are combined until a complete perception is formed. _____ _____ _____ _____
Top-Down Processing	Application of previous experience and conceptual knowledge to first recognize the whole of a perception and thus easily identify the simpler elements of that whole. _____ _____ _____ _____
Perceptual Set	An expectation of what will be perceived, which can affect what actually is perceived. _____ _____ _____
Subliminal Persuasion	Sending persuasive messages below the recipient's level of awareness. _____ _____ _____
Subliminal Perception	Perceiving sensory stimuli that is below the absolute threshold. _____ _____ _____
Extrasensory Perception	Gaining awareness of or information about objects, events, or another's thoughts through some means other than the known sensory channels. _____ _____ _____ _____
Parapsychology	The study of psychic phenomena including extrasensory perception. _____ _____ _____ _____

FROM THE LABORATORY TO REAL LIFE

THE SWEET SMELL OF SUCCESS

In the town where I live and work, there is a factory that produces ethanol, a fuel additive that is made by refining corn. I understand that this company is very successful on the world market, and I imagine their success smells sweet to them. However, the smell that results from the refining process is so pungent that, on a humid day, there is often no escape. My office is across the river and about 5 miles from the plant, so you would think the aroma would dissipate before it reached campus. That is not the case. When the plant first opened, the smell was enough to drive me indoors and keep me there. After a few months though, I noticed that the odor was only strong enough to bother me once or twice a month, and even then, it was tolerable. Oddly, every time out of town guests would arrive at my office, they were sure to comment on the horrendous odor that had assailed their nostrils on the way in. Funny—I had not noticed the odor on those days.

1.   What is the name of the sensation described in the above scenario? _____

2.   What part of the anatomy must odor molecules reach before they are sensed?   _____
_____

3.   Where do the smell sensations *first* register in the brain?   _____

4.   Why did I find the odor to be barely detectable while my guests found it to be so strong? _____
_____

5.   When there are competing smells in the air, what is the theory that best explains my recognition of the ethanol

fumes against the background of the other smells? _____

STOP THE PRESSES

My father-in-law, Joe, a healthy 80-year-old, wears hearing aids in both ears. He feels they help a little, but he asserts that they have not restored his hearing, and that he tends to wear them more often to please his wife than for their intended use. In fact, he often wears them turned off. Joe worked for a commercial printer for 40 years after fighting in the infantry in World War II. His job was to operate a printing press. He described his press as follows, "It was as big as a bedroom and as loud as the war." For 40 years that press pounded away at Joe's ears for 40 hours each week. Is it any wonder he has hearing problems?

1.   Is Joe's hearing loss a function of growing older? _____ Could the noisy printing press be the
culprit? _____

2.   What type of hearing loss do you think Joe suffers from? _____

3.   Why do you suppose Joe's hearing aids are ineffective? _____

4.   What probably happened inside Joe's ears that he is now having hearing problems? _____
_____

5.   Is there any hope for people with hearing problems like Joe's? _____ Why? _____

FROM THEORY TO PRACTICE

SUBLIMINAL PERCEPTION AND PERSUASION

I often visit the bookstores at the local mall. As psychology is my chosen field, I usually find myself looking in the psychology and self-help sections. Over the past few years I have noticed an increase in the number of offerings that assert that listening to an enclosed cassette tape will help the listener accomplish everything from stopping smoking, to having better self esteem, and even living a more fulfilling life. What a wonderful thing! All we need to do is listen to a tape and our lives can become nearly perfect! Subliminal perception/persuasion is not new. There was a scandal in the 1950s regarding the use of subliminal messages to persuade moviegoers to buy candy and popcorn. People became so alarmed at this new method of "mind control" that laws were passed to prohibit such "advertising." Department stores today often play subliminal messages over their sound systems asking patrons to consider the errors of shoplifting. What do you think? Can we really influence everything from criminality to health-enhancing behaviors by communicating with the unconscious? Is it possible to change our lives just by listening to a tape? If subliminal perception/persuasion is real why do we not take greater advantage of this powerful panacea in front line medicine? If it is not really all that effective, why are promoters selling so many tapes?

_____

_____

_____

_____

_____

PARAPSYCHOLOGY: FACT, FICTION, OR FRAUD?

I work late sometimes and I am amused at the number of psychic infomercials run in the wee hours of the morning. For just a few dollars per minute you can call a special number and meet someone who can tell you all you need to know about yourself! ESP (as well as a variety of other "special power" methods of guiding people) has been around for a very long time. Some people base their lives on the guidance of psychics and would become distressed or even angry at the suggestion that such a phenomenon did not really exist. However, science seems to have found little real evidence for this special perceptual power. What do you think? Do such abilities exist—at least in some? If so, how might we scientifically provide the kind of documentation that will stand up to our need for empirical evidence? Finally, should there be laws restricting the advertising of such powers until we can show that this is a genuine phenomenon, and not a fraud?

_____

_____

_____

_____

_____

PAIN – DO WE NEED IT?

What if we devised a way to make pain go away—something we could do to the brain that would result in the complete removal of the sensation of pain. Would that be a good idea? Is the sensation of pain important for our survival? Would the removal of all pain change the way we "feel" about pleasurable stimuli? Would there be at least some special circumstances when this would be a good idea? What do you think?

_____

_____

_____

_____

COMPREHENSIVE PRACTICE TEST

1. The process by which we detect visual, auditory, and other stimuli is known as _____.
   a) perception
   b) transduction
   c) sensation
   d) threshold

2. The process of organizing and interpreting the information we gather through vision, hearing, and the other senses is known as _____.
   a) perception
   b) absolute threshold
   c) transduction
   d) sensory induction

3. The _____ _____ is that level of stimulus intensity that defines the minimum amount of stimulus that can be detected 50% of the time.
   a) difference reaction
   b) absolute reaction
   c) difference threshold
   d) absolute threshold

4. The _____ _____ is a measure of the smallest change in a physical stimulus required to detect a change in the stimulus 50% of the time.
   a) difference reaction
   b) absolute difference
   c) difference threshold
   d) sensory threshold

5. You are waiting to meet your blind date at the restaurant and hope you will recognize the right person when she or he comes through the door. You are searching a sea of faces as you search for the one that best matches the description given to you by your friend. You watch carefully as you consider the consequences of either approaching the wrong person or not greeting the right person. This sounds like the process known as _____ discussed in the book.
   a) recognition threshold
   b) signal detection theory
   c) absolute recognition
   d) sensory adaptation

6. If I see, hear, taste, smell, or feel, my specific sense organ has specialized cells called _____ that detect and respond to the particular stimulus.
   a) sensory detectors
   b) sensory receptors
   c) perceptual responders
   d) perceptual receptors

7. When I see, hear, taste, smell, or feel a stimulus, the physical energy that caused this stimulus is changed to neural impulses that are processed in my brain. This process is known as _____.
   a) sensory adaptation
   b) absolute threshold
   c) perceptual organization
   d) transduction

8. Joe bought a new pool last spring and set it up right away. His wife thought he was crazy to mess with a pool when it was still early spring and pretty cool outside. The first day it seemed even a little warm Joe jumped in the water to enjoy his new pool. Once in he realized just how cold the water really was but he was going to use his new pool no matter what! As he continued to "enjoy" the water it seemed to become less cold and even comfortable. The was probably due to a process the book called _____.
   a) sensory adaptation
   b) difference threshold
   c) sensory threshold
   d) perceptual adaptation

9. If someone tells you they love the color of your eyes, they are actually talking about the _____.
   a) pupil
   b) cornea
   c) iris
   d) retina

10. Rods are to cones as _____ is to _____.
    a) dim light; color
    b) color; dim light
    c) bright light; color
    d) color; bright light

11. The blind spot in the back of the eye is where:
    a) the rods and cones come together
    b) the retina converges on the fovea
    c) the optic nerve leaves the eye
    d) the blood supply enters the eye

12. When I read a book, my lens is probably a little more spherical, and when I gaze out upon the stars at night the lens becomes flatter. This is due to a process known as _____.
    a) retinal disparity
    b) lens reactivity
    c) accommodation
    d) adaptation

13. Sally told me the other day that the reason we see color is that our cones can see one of three colors—blue, green, or red, and that each makes a maximum chemical response to their respective color. It is obvious Sally has been reading about the _____ theory of color vision.
    a) opponent-process
    b) trichromatic
    c) relative disparity
    d) complimentary color

14. When we talk about the number of cycles completed by a sound wave in one second, we are talking about _____.
    a) decibel
    b) timbre
    c) amplitude
    d) frequency

15. The job of the _____, also known as the hammer, the anvil, and the stirrup, is to amplify the sound as it moves from the eardrum to the oval window.
    a) ossicles
    b) cochlear bones
    c) hair cells
    d) timbre bones

16. Sally has also been talking about hearing lately. She says that we hear different pitch based on the spot along the basilar membrane that vibrates the most. She is talking about the _____ theory of hearing.
    a) frequency
    b) position
    c) cochlea
    d) place

17. I usually believe the things Sally tells me, but today she told me that I can sometimes hear as a result of vibration of the bones in my face and skull! I told her she had to be wrong here—there is no way we would hear something without the sound moving through our eardrum. Did I finally catch Sally making a wrong statement?
    a) Yes
    b) No

18. Olfaction refers to:
    a) the sense of taste
    b) the sense of smell
    c) the ability to detect skin temperature
    d) the ability to differentiate sounds

19. Sally threw me another curve today. Ever since grade school I have been told that our tongue has specific places to detect sweet, sour, salty, and bitter. We even had to learn the tongue map in biology. Now Sally says this is wrong—that all parts of the tongue seem to detect these tastes. Should I believe her?
    a) Yes
    b) No

20. *Tactile* is a term used in reference to the sense of _____.
    a) smell
    b) balance
    c) taste
    d) touch

21. The gate-control theory of pain would suggest that slow-conducting nerve fibers carry pain messages and that these messages can be stopped by fast-conducting nerve fibers that carry other sensory messages.
    a) True
    b) False

22. We were watching gymnastics on the sports channel the other day and were amazed at the grace with which the athletes could move on the parallel bars. Then Sally piped in again with all her knowledge. She said this ability is due to our _____ sense. She was right.
    a) tactile
    b) olfactory
    c) kinesthetic
    d) Eustachian

23. Finally I decided to show Sally that I knew something about the world also. I told her that our vestibular sense provides information that allows us to know that a red door is still red even in a dark room. She looked this one up in her textbook. Did I impress her with my knowledge?
    a) Yes
    b) No

24. I remember watching the half-time show at a football game one day. There seemed to be a hundred people marching on the field—all in different colored uniforms. Then I noticed that they took on a formation and suddenly all the red colored uniforms spelled out the initials of the home team school. Gestalt psychology would suggest I detected this clever trick due to the principle of _____.
    a) similarity
    b) continuity
    c) closure
    d) constancy

25. Which of the following is not discussed in the book as a principle of grouping?
    a) closure
    b) similarity
    c) constancy
    d) proximity

26. As an artist, I sometimes find it difficult to convince the viewer of my paintings that a familiar shape really is that shape even from a different perspective. I know that I perceive things like size, shape, and brightness the same even under different conditions in real life, and I try to cast that on my canvas. In perception this is known as perceptual _____.
    a) equilibrium
    b) constancy
    c) continuity
    d) reliability

27. If I move my finger closer and closer to my nose and focus on perceiving only one image of the finger even when it is almost touching my nose, my eyes begin to feel uncomfortable as they seem to turn more inward. This eye movement is known as _____.
    a) disparity
    b) monocular adjustment
    c) congruity
    d) convergence

28. Depth cues, such as interposition, linear perspective, and relative size are known as _____ depth cues.
    a) binocular
    b) divergent
    c) monocular
    d) bimodal

29. The phi-phenomenon refers to the perception of movement depicted by stationary lights flashing on and off in a specific sequence.
    a) True
    b) False

30. Sally wanted to bet me that I could not detect the difference between the lengths of different lines. One had diagonals extending outward on both ends and one had diagonals pointing inward. I said the first one was longer and Sally showed me that they were really of equal length! This clever illusion is called the _____ illusion.
    a) Ponzo
    b) Muller-Lyer

31. Bottom-up processing is to top-down processing as _____ is to _____:
    a) unfamiliar; familiar
    b) familiar; unfamiliar

32. When I was a kid I loved hotdogs. One day, when visiting family friends, I was thrilled to find out we were going to have hotdogs for lunch. When lunch was served I was horrified to discover a hotdog colored very different from the familiar reddish tint of my favorite brand. It tasted terrible to me! Given that the new hotdog was in reality as good as my old favorite, what would explain my distaste for this unpleasant luncheon surprise?
    a) perceptual constancy
    b) parapsychology
    c) perceptual persuasion
    d) perceptual set

ANSWER KEYS

OMSE # 1 ANSWER KEY: THE SENSORY WORLD

A. Quick Quiz	B. Matching	C. Complete the Diagram
1. a	1. e	1. c
2. false	2. d	2. e
3. difference	3. b	3. d
4. b	4. f	4. b
5. true	5. a	5. a
6. psychophysics	6. c	
7. d		
8. false		
9. transduction		
10. sensory adaptation		

OMSE # 2 ANSWER KEY: THE SENSES

A. Quick Quiz	B. Matching	C. Complete the Diagram
1. b	1. f	1. f
2. a	2. h	2. e
3. d	3. k	3. g
4. b	4. n	4. a
5. c	5. m	5. h
6. opponent-process	6. c	6. c
7. a	7. o	7. d
8. c	8. i	8. b
9. b	9. e	
10. b	10. p	
11. c	11. l	
12. taste	12. b	
13. c	13. j	
14. d	14. g	
15. b	15. a	
	16. d	

OMSE # 3 ANSWER KEY: PERCEPTION AND SUBLIMINAL PERCEPTION

A. Quick Quiz		B. Matching
1. b	9. true	1. c
2. figure-ground	10. d	2. f
3. false	11. binocular disparity	3. a
4. d	12. false	4. g
5. closure	13. c	5. b
6. false	14. phi-phenomenon	6. e
7. c	15. true	7. d
8. color constancy		

C. COMPLETE THE DIAGRAM

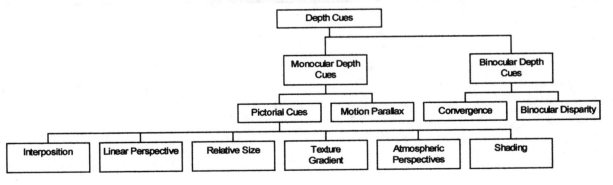

FROM THE LABORATORY TO LIFE

The Smell of Success

1. Olfactory

2. Olfactory epithelium

3. Olfactory bulbs

4. Sensory adaptation

5. Signal detection theory is the view that detection of a sensory stimulus—odor—involves both discriminating that particular aroma from background "noise" (other smells in the air) and deciding whether the stimulus is actually present. Deciding whether the odor is actually in the air depends partly on the probability that the stimulus will occur. It is a pretty safe bet that the multi-billion dollar business down the road will be operating at full stink on a daily basis.

Stop the Presses

1. Probably not; Yes

2. Neural hearing loss

3. Hearing aids do not usually help neural hearing loss or nerve deafness.

4. Continual, long-term exposure to high decibel sound brought about the gradual deterioration of the auditory nerve.

5. Yes, recent studies have shown that the inner ear hair cells of mammals can be restored.

Comprehensive Practice Test

1. c	9. c	17. no	25. c
2. a	10. a	18. b	26. b
3. d	11. c	19. yes	27. d
4. c	12. c	20. d	28. c
5. b	13. b	21. true	29. true
6. b	14. d	22. c	30. b
7. d	15. a	23. no	31. a
8. a	16. d	24. a	32. d

STATES OF CONSCIOUSNESS

Consciousness is defined as an awareness of our perceptions, thoughts, feelings, sensations, and our external environment.

CHAPTER OVERVIEW

Throughout history, consciousness has remained a major source of interest and controversy to both the philosophical and the scientific communities. More recently, consciousness has driven research and theoretical orientation in psychology and human behavior. Beginning with our philosophical roots, the subject of consciousness has inspired the asking of particularly difficult questions. What is consciousness? How does the electrical-chemical activity of our brain translate into that special sense of self-awareness? Freud maintained that we have three levels of consciousness, while Watson asserted his view that the topic of consciousness had no place in the scientific realm of psychology. Regardless of the tenuous nature with which we treat the definition of consciousness, we (humans) do seem to be relentlessly attracted to the idea of changing our levels of consciousness. We attempt to alter our states of consciousness through a variety of means, some more reckless than others. Mind-altering methods of choice over the last few decades have included the use of meditation, hypnosis, and drugs or alcohol. A better understanding of consciousness may not lessen our affinity toward attempting to alter it, but it may well provide clues, if not answers, to some of the enduring mysteries of the human experience.

This chapter will help you gain a more practiced and functional understanding of the issues related to consciousness, sleep, and some of the major ways we alter our level of awareness. The materials are divided into two OMSE sections, 1) Circadian Rhythms and Sleep, and 2) Altered States of Consciousness. You will also learn the important links between behavior, consciousness, and health. Drug abuse and dependence is one of the most important health issues facing our country today. Gaining a better understanding of the effects of drugs and the effects drugs have on our bodies and levels of consciousness can be an important step toward prevention and solution.

By completing the exercises provided, you should gain a thorough understanding of the information provided in your text. In other words, you should be better prepared for tests, quizzes, class participation, and life itself.

TIMELINE

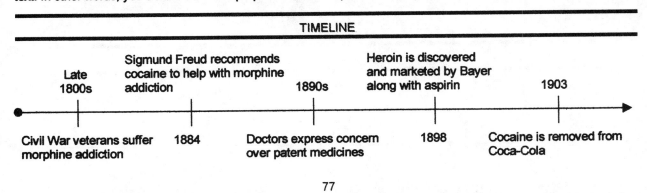

CHAPTER OUTLINE

What is Consciousness

Circadian Rhythms: Our 24-Hour Highs and Lows

The Suprachiasmatic Nucleus: The Body's Timekeeper

Jet Lag: Where Am I and What Time Is It?

Shift Work: Working Day and Night

Taking Melatonin as a Sleep Aid

Sleep: That Mysterious One-Third of Our Lives

NREM and REM Sleep: Watching the Eyes

Sleep Cycles: The Nightly Pattern of Sleep

Variations in Sleep: How We Differ

Sleep Deprivation: How Does It Affect Us?

The Functions of Sleep: The Restorative and Circadian Theories

Dreaming: Mysterious Mental Activity While We Sleep

Sleep Disorders

Parasomnias: Unusual Behaviors during Sleep

Major Sleep Disorders

Altering Consciousness through Concentration and Suggestion

Meditation: Expanded Consciousness or Relaxation?

Hypnosis: Look into My Eyes

Culture and Altered States of Consciousness

Altered States of Consciousness and Psychoactive Drugs

Variables Influencing Individual Responses to Drugs

Drug Addiction: Slave to a Substance

Stimulants: Speeding Up the Nervous System

Depressants: Slowing Down the Nervous System

Hallucinogens: Seeing, Hearing, and Feeling What Is Not There

How Drugs Affect the Brain

Apply It! Battling Insomnia

Thinking Critically

Chapter Summary and Review

TERMS AND CONCEPTS

What is Consciousness

consciousness
altered state of consciousness

Circadian Rhythms: Our 24-Hour Highs and Lows

circadian rhythm
suprachiasmatic nucleus
melatonin
subjective night

Sleep: That Mysterious One-Third of Our Lives

NREM sleep
REM sleep
Sleep cycle
delta wave
slow-wave sleep

Stage-4 sleep
restorative theory
circadian theory
microsleep
REM dreams
NREM dreams
lucid dreams
REM rebound

Sleep Disorders

somnambulism
sleep terror
nightmare
narcolepsy
sleep apnea
insomnia

Altering Consciousness through Concentration and Suggestion

meditation
hypnosis
sociocognitive theory
neodissociation theory

Altered States of Consciousness and Psychoactive Drugs

psychoactive drug
illicit drug
physical drug dependence
drug tolerance
withdrawal symptoms
psychological drug dependence

stimulants
amphetamines
cocaine
crash
crack
depressants
alcohol
barbiturates
minor tranquilizers
narcotics
heroin
hallucinogens
LSD
flashback
MDMA (Ecstasy)
marijuana
THC

TIMELINE

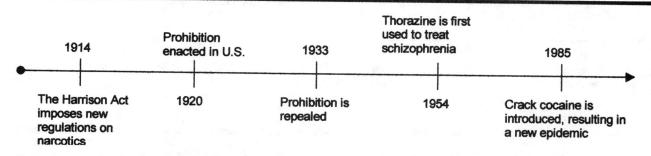

1914 — The Harrison Act imposes new regulations on narcotics

1920

Prohibition enacted in U.S.

1933 — Prohibition is repealed

1954

Thorazine is first used to treat schizophrenia

1985 — Crack cocaine is introduced, resulting in a new epidemic

OMSE # 1: CIRCADIAN RHYTHM AND SLEEP

LEARNING OBJECTIVES

1. What are some different states of consciousness?
2. What is circadian rhythm, and which rhythms are most relevant to the study of sleep?
3. What is the suprachiasmatic nucleus?
4. What are some problems experienced by people who work rotating shifts?
5. How does a sleeper react physically during NREM sleep?
6. How does the body respond physically during REM sleep?
7. What is the progression of NREM stages and REM sleep that a person follows in a typical night of sleep?
8. How do sleep patterns change over the life span?
9. What factors influence our sleep needs?
10. What are the two main theories that attempt to explain the function of sleep?
11. How do REM and NREM dreams differ?
12. In general, what have researchers found regarding the content of dreams?
13. What happens when people are deprived of REM sleep? What function does REM sleep appear to serve?
14. What are the characteristics common to sleepwalking and sleep terrors?
15. What is a sleep terror?
16. How do nightmares differ from sleep terrors?
17. What are the major symptoms of narcolepsy?
18. What is sleep apnea?
19. What is insomnia?

LEARNING MASTERY SCORECARD: Update your score card as you work through the various sections of the chapter. First, find and define key terms and concepts included in each section and note the page number(s) from the text that contain important references to the material. Next, gain a practical understanding of the concepts by considering the Laboratory to Life scenarios and thinking of at least one original example of how the concept might apply in real life. Complete the *Objective-Mastery Self-Evaluation* (OMSE) exercises for this section and record your scores. Revisit the exercises, recording your score and the date completed until you have attained mastery (100%). Finally, decide how you would prepare a lecture on each objective using the template provided, outline the lecture, and practice presenting it. Keep an honest tally of your achievements and, when finished, you will have developed learning mastery through elaborate rehearsal.

Key Terms	Page #	Key Terms	Page #	Key Terms	Page #
consciousness	____	delta wave	____	lucid dreams	____
altered state of consciousness	____	slow-wave sleep	____	REM rebound	____
circadian rhythm	____	Stage-4 sleep	____	somnambulism	____
suprachiasmatic nucleus (SCN)	____	restorative theory	____	sleep terror	____
melatonin	____	circadian theory	____	nightmare	____
subjective night	____	microsleep	____	narcolepsy	____
NREM sleep	____	REM dreams	____	sleep apnea	____
REM sleep	____	NREM dreams	____	insomnia	____
Sleep cycle	____				

Quick Quiz

Date	Score	Date	Score	Date	Score
__/__/__	____	__/__/__	____	__/__/__	____
__/__/__	____	__/__/__	____	__/__/__	100%

Elaborate Rehearsal

Lecture Preparation	Completion Date
Key Terms, Persons, & Concepts	__/__/__
Learning Objectives	__/__/__
Lecture Notes	__/__/__

QUICK QUIZ

1. In a normal 24-hour period, many of our bodily functions, such as energy level and mood, fluctuate from high to low. These fluctuations are known as:
   - a) cognitive levels
   - b) circadian rhythms
   - c) circadian levels
   - d) cognitive rhythms

2. While the subject may feel tired, the phenomenon of subjective night does not seem to affect performance and safety.
    a) True   b) False

3. The book defined _____ as an awareness of our perceptions, thoughts, feelings, sensations, and of our external environment.

4. When you are in the midst of a four-hour sleep stage where there is slow, regular respiration and heart beat, accompanied by a 24-hour low in blood pressure and brain activity, you are in _____ sleep.
    a) REM   c) NREM
    b) circadian   d) EMG

5. One interesting fact regarding REM sleep is that, in a way, you are paralyzed, at least in terms of large muscles.
    a) True   b) False

6. The _____ wave is the deepest brain wave and is found in Stage 3 and 4 sleep.

7. I often work late into the night, and I seem to get by pretty well on only a few hours sleep. However, I notice that I seem to occasionally nod off for a few seconds, sometimes in the middle of a thought. I am experiencing:
    a) REM rebound   c) latent sleep
    b) microsleeps   d) apnea

8. As we get older we sleep more than when we were younger. We also sleep deeper with more REM sleep.
    a) True   b) False

9. When we lose REM sleep due to factors like illness or drug use, we might experience _____ when we recover from our sleep deprivation.

10. I have a friend who says he is aware of his dreams as they occur and can even change the content of his dreams. This was discussed in the book as a _____ dream.
    a) REM   c) latent
    b) narcoleptic   d) lucid

11. The nice thing about REM dreams is the fact that they are usually very pleasant.
    a) True   b) False

12. An individual who experiences phenomena like sleepwalking or sleeptalking is suffering from a classification of sleep disturbances collectively known as _____.

13. Sleepwalking is more formally known as:
    a) somnambulism   c) ambulism
    b) somniloquy   d) latent sililoquy ambulatory syndrome

14. While insomnia is a problem for many people, it usually self-corrects within 24 to 48 hours.
    a) True   b) False

15. With regards to the difference between *larks* and *owls*, it appears that the performance of _____ declines as the day progresses while the performance of _____ seems to improve.

B. MATCHING

_____	1. Partially awaken in a panic state	a) sleep walking
_____	2. Daytime sleepiness and sudden REM sleep	b) sleep terror
_____	3. Difficulty falling or staying asleep	c) nightmare
_____	4. Somnambulism	d) narcolepsy
_____	5. A very frightening dream	e) sleep apnea
_____	6. Breathing stops during sleep	f) insomnia

Suffering from insomnia? Don't worry; in most cases the body resolves insomnia all by itself. Of course, where and when this happens might sometimes prove embarrassing or a bit uncomfortable. Narcoleptics can fall into uncontrollable attacks of REM sleep anywhere and anytime. Insomnia doesn't seem so bad in light of that—does it?

C. COMPLETE THE DIAGRAM: Fill in the blanks. Write in the sleep stage and/or draw the brain wave pattern.

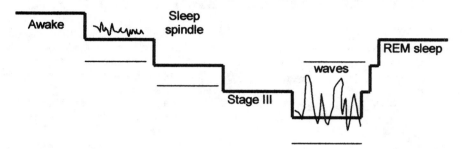

PREPARE A LECTURE: This activity is designed to offer you an opportunity to take advantage of a valuable mode of learning, elaborate rehearsal. Once you have finished the OMSE section, write a lecture using the instructional guide provided below. After your lecture is prepared, you can enhance your learning by writing a quiz covering the material. Now it is time to find some willing and inquisitive audience members. Your roommates or family may be a great place to start. Present them the lecture as if you are teaching a class. Remember to ask for questions and give your students the quiz following the lecture. This exercise can also serve to turn a *study-buddy* group into a very productive way to prepare for the test. Each member of the group can take different OMSE sections for their lecture/teacher role while the rest of the group serves as the class.

I. Key Terms, Names, Dates, and Concepts you will include in this lecture:

1. _____
2. _____
3. _____
4. _____

5. _____
6. _____
7. _____
8. _____

9. _____
10. _____
11. _____
12. _____

II. Learning Objectives (what do you want the student to know and be able to do as a result of your lecture):

1. _____
2. _____
3. _____
4. _____
5. _____

III. Lecture Notes (notes should be brief cues and serve as a guide).

Major topic #1: _____
    Sub-topics and notes: _____
    _____
    _____
    _____

Major topic #2: _____
    Sub-topics and notes: _____
    _____
    _____
    _____

Major topic #3: _____
    Sub-topics and notes: _____
    _____
    _____
    _____

OMSE # 2: ALTERED STATES OF CONSCIOUSNESS

LEARNING OBJECTIVES

1. For what purpose is meditation used?
2. What is hypnosis, and when is it most useful?
3. What are the two main theories that have been proposed to explain hypnosis?
4. What is the difference between physical and psychological drug dependence?
5. How do stimulants affect the user?
6. What effects do amphetamines have on the user?
7. How does cocaine affect the user?
8. What are some of the effects of depressants, and what drugs comprise this category?
9. What are the general effects of narcotics, and what are several drugs in this category?
10. What are the main effects of hallucinogens, and what are three psychoactive drugs classified as hallucinogens?
11. What are some harmful effects associated with heavy marijuana use?

LEARNING MASTERY SCORECARD: Update your score card as you work through the various sections of the chapter. First, find and define key terms and concepts included in each section and note the page number(s) from the text that contain important references to the material. Next, gain a practical understanding of the concepts by considering the Laboratory to Life scenarios and thinking of at least one original example of how the concept might apply in real life. Complete the *Objective-Mastery Self-Evaluation* (OMSE) exercises for this section and record your scores. Revisit the exercises, recording your score and the date completed until you have attained mastery (100%). Finally, decide how you would prepare a lecture on each objective using the template provided, outline the lecture, and practice presenting it. Keep an honest tally of your achievements and, when finished, you will have developed learning mastery through elaborate rehearsal.

Key Terms	Page #	Key Terms	Page #	Key Terms	Page #
meditation (concentrative)		psychological drug dependence		minor tranquilizers	
hypnosis		stimulants		narcotics	
sociocognitive theory		amphetamines		heroin	
neodissociation theory		cocaine		hallucinogens	
psychoactive drugs		crash		LSD	
illicit drug		crack		flashback	
physical drug dependence		depressants		MDMA (Ecstasy)	
drug tolerance		alcohol		marijuana	
withdrawal symptoms		barbiturates		THC	

Quick Quiz

Date	Score	Date	Score	Date	Score
_/_/_		_/_/_		_/_/_	
_/_/_		_/_/_		_/_/_	100%

Elaborate Rehearsal

Lecture Preparation	Completion Date
Key Terms, Persons, & Concepts	_/_/_
Learning Objectives	_/_/_
Lecture Notes	_/_/_

A. QUICK QUIZ

1. Psychoactive drugs are considered to be any of a group of substances that:
   a) will get a person high
   b) are sold and consumed illegally
   c) are in the illicit drug group
   d) alter normal mental functioning

2. _____ consists of a group of techniques designed to block out all distractions and achieve an altered state of consciousness.

3. Generally, while under hypnosis, subjects will do whatever they are told to, even if they are told to do something that violates their moral values.
   a) True
   b) False

4. A compulsive pattern of drug use in which the user develops a tolerance coupled with unpleasant withdrawal symptoms is referred to as:
   a) physical drug dependence
   b) psychological drug dependence
   c) drug tolerance
   d) drug craving

5. According to your text, what is the most highly correlated factor in the use of illicit drugs by adolescents?
   a) poverty
   b) peer influence
   c) family addiction pattern
   d) low self-esteem

6. The number one drug problem in the United States of America is:
   a) cocaine
   b) marijuana
   c) heroin
   d) alcohol

7. The most popular central nervous system depressant in the nation is:
   a) cocaine
   b) Valium
   c) heroin
   d) alcohol

8. Irene has recently discovered that she is pregnant and has decided to stop snorting heroin because of the danger to her unborn child. Soon after discontinuation of heroin use, Irene begins to experience nausea, diarrhea, depression, and stomach cramps. Irene (and no doubt the fetus) is experiencing _____ .
   a) tolerance
   b) cravings
   c) withdrawal
   d) flashbacks

9. Which physical problem has NOT been attributed to heavy marijuana use?
   a) respiratory damage
   b) reproductive problems
   c) loss of motivation
   d) increased risk of heart attack & stroke

10. To which drugs do non-human animals become most easily addicted?
    a) cocaine
    b) marijuana
    c) heroin
    d) alcohol

11. The euphoric high from cocaine lasts only a short time and is followed by an equally intense phenomenon called a _____, which is marked by depression, anxiety, agitation, and a powerful craving for more cocaine.

12. Cocaine's action in the human brain includes blocking the reuptake of the neurotransmitter, _____, thereby bringing about the continual (albeit short-lived) excitatory stimulation of the reward pathways in the brain.
    a) serotonin
    b) dopamine
    c) epinephrin
    d) endorphin

13. Long-term, regular marijuana use has been shown to be relatively harmless, and heavy marijuana use has been proven to be much safer for the respiratory system than cigarettes.
    a) True
    b) False

14. Heroin is addictive only when taken intravenously, and the newer practice of snorting heroin is relatively safe and non-addictive.
    a) True
    b) False

15. LSD, a hallucinogen, has regained popularity among adolescents in the U.S. in the past decade. One of the reasons for the steady increase in the use of LSD is that it causes no dangerous side effects.
    a) True
    b) False

Trying drugs as an experiment, or because—"Gee dude, everybody's doin' it"—may *seem* harmless at first. However, the lure of the high can quickly take control. Many of the illicit substances on the market today are capable of taking from you all that you have and all that you are in a very short time. Addiction to any substance is a ball and chain that you don't want to have a hold on you. If you refuse to slip yourself into the shackle by trying drugs, then you have nothing to fear from drugs.

B. MATCHING

_____ 1. Two methods are yoga and Zen
_____ 2. Uses the power of suggestion
_____ 3. Alters mood, perception, or thought
_____ 4. An illegal drug
_____ 5. Tolerance and withdrawal characterize it
_____ 6. Larger doses are required for the same effect
_____ 7. Irresistible urge for a drug's effects
_____ 8. Speed up the CNS
_____ 9. World's most widely used drug
_____ 10. Sniffed, injected, or smoked as crack
_____ 11. Marijuana's _high_ ingredient
_____ 12. Highly addictive poppy product
_____ 13. Number one U.S. drug problem
_____ 14. Cocaine slows its reuptake
_____ 15. Heroin mimics this brain chemical

a) stimulants
b) alcohol
c) endorphin
d) caffeine
e) meditation
f) heroin
g) dopamine
h) hypnosis
i) THC
j) illicit drug
k) psychoactive drug
l) physical dependence
m) cocaine
n) psychological dependence
o) tolerance

C. COMPLETE THE DIAGRAM

DRUGS	METHODS OF INGESTION	PRINCIPLE MEDICAL USES	EFFECTS	HEALTH RISKS
Narcotics				
Sedatives				
Stimulants				
Hallucinogens				
Marijuana				
Alcohol				

PREPARE A LECTURE: This activity is designed to offer you an opportunity to take advantage of a valuable mode of learning, elaborate rehearsal. Once you have finished the OMSE section, write a lecture using the instructional guide provided below. After your lecture is prepared, you can enhance your learning by writing a quiz covering the material. Now it is time to find some willing and inquisitive audience members. Your roommates or family may be a great place to start. Present them the lecture as if you are teaching a class. Remember to ask for questions and give your students the quiz following the lecture. This exercise can also serve to turn a *study-buddy* group into a very productive way to prepare for the test. Each member of the group can take different OMSE sections for their lecture/teacher role while the rest of the group serves as the class.

I. Key Terms, Names, Dates, and Concepts you will include in this lecture:

1. _____   5. _____   9. _____
2. _____   6. _____   10. _____
3. _____   7. _____   11. _____
4. _____   8. _____   12. _____

II. Learning Objectives (what do you want the student to know and be able to do as a result of your lecture):

1. _____
2. _____
3. _____
4. _____
5. _____

III. Lecture Notes (notes should be brief cues and serve as a guide).

Major topic #1: _____
   Sub-topics and notes: _____
   _____
   _____
   _____

Major topic #2: _____
   Sub-topics and notes: _____
   _____
   _____
   _____
   _____

Major topic #3: _____
   Sub-topics and notes: _____
   _____
   _____
   _____

KEY TERMS AND CONCEPTS EXCERCISE

The key terms and concepts are presented in the order of their appearance in the text. Space is provided for you to include a personalized definition or example of each term or concept. As you encounter each term in the text, make a note of its meaning and context. Next, conceptualize the meaning of the term in a way that makes the most sense to you. You can also think about examples of the term from your own life. Write your definition and/or example in the space provided next to the word in this book. The KEY TERMS exercise utilizes a modified *T-note* design so that you can self-evaluate your mastery of the definitions. First lay a sheet of paper over the terms and concepts side of the page so that you only see the definitions. Read the definition and try to recall the term or concept. Mark all those you are unable to answer so you can restudy them. When you have learned all of the terms and concepts in this way, move the paper to the definition side so that you can see only the term or concept, try to recall both the textbook definition and your personal version. Repeat this until you know all of the terms and concepts by definition and personal understanding.

Consciousness	An awareness of our perceptions, thoughts, feelings, sensations, and of our external environment. _____
Altered State Of Consciousness	A mental state other than ordinary waking consciousness, such as sleep, meditation, hypnosis, or a drug-induced state. _____
Circadian Rhythm	Within each 24-hour period, the regular fluctuations from high to low points of certain bodily functions. There are certain times of the day when you will be more likely to retain information from studying, and times when you will find study retention to be low. This is a function of circadian rhythms. _____
Suprachiasmatic Nucleus (SCN)	A tiny structure in the brain's hypothalamus that controls the timing of our circadian rhythms; our biological clock. _____
Melatonin	A hormone secreted by the pineal gland which acts to reduce activity and induce sleep. _____
Subjective Night	The time during a 24-hour period when your body temperature is lowest and when your biological clock is telling you to go to sleep. More errors in judgement and most accidents occur during the night shift. _____
NREM Sleep	Non-rapid eye movement sleep, consisting of the four sleep stages and characterized by slow, regular respiration and heart rate, an absence of rapid eye movements, and blood pressure and brain activity that are at a 24-hour low point. _____
REM Sleep	Sleep characterized by rapid eye movements, paralysis of large muscles, fast and irregular heart rate and respiration rate, increased brain-wave activity, and vivid dreams. _____
Sleep Cycle	A cycle of sleep lasting about 90 minutes and including one or more stages of NREM sleep followed by a period of REM sleep. _____
Delta Wave	The slowest brain-wave pattern; associated with stage 3 sleep and stage 4 sleep. _____
Slow-Wave Sleep	Stage 3 and stage 4 sleep; deep sleep. _____
Stage-4 Sleep	The deepest NREM stage of sleep, characterized by an EEG pattern of more than 50 percent delta waves. _____
Restorative Theory	The theory that sleep functions to restore body and mind. _____

Circadian Theory	The theory that sleep evolved to keep us out of harm's way during the night, with our sleepiness ebbing and flowing according to a circadian rhythm. _____ _____ _____
Microsleep	A momentary lapse from wakefulness into sleep, usually occurring when one has been sleep deprived. Maybe you have experienced microsleeps in the form of a few lost moments while trying to pull an all-nighter while studying for finals. _____ _____
REM Dreams	A type of dream having a dreamlike and storylike quality and occurring almost continually during each REM period; often associated with unpleasant dreams or nightmares. _____ _____ _____
NREM Dreams	Mental activity occurring during NREM sleep that is more thoughtlike in quality than REM dreams are. _____ _____
Lucid Dreams	A dream during which the dreamer is aware of dreaming and is often able to influence the content of the dream while it is in progress. _____ _____
REM Rebound	The increased amount of REM sleep that occurs after REM deprivation; often associated with unpleasant dreams or nightmares. _____ _____
Somnambulism	Sleepwalking that occurs during a partial arousal from Stage 4 sleep. _____ _____ _____
Sleep Terror	A sleep disturbance in which a person partially awakens from Stage 4 sleep with a scream, dazed and groggy, in a panic state, and with a racing heart. _____ _____
Nightmare	A very frightening dream occurring during REM sleep. _____ _____
Narcolepsy	A serious sleep disorder characterized by excessive daytime sleepiness and sudden, uncontrollable attacks of REM sleep. _____ _____
Sleep Apnea	A sleep disorder characterized by periods when breathing stops during sleep and the person must awaken briefly in order to breathe; major symptoms are excessive daytime sleepiness and loud snoring. _____ _____
Insomnia	A sleep disorder characterized by difficulty falling or staying asleep or by light, restless, or poor sleep, and causing distress and impaired daytime functioning. _____ _____ _____

Meditation	A group of techniques that involve focusing attention on an object, a word, one's breathing, or body movement in order to block out all distractions and achieve an altered state of consciousness. _____
Hypnosis	A procedure through which one person, the hypnotist, uses the power of suggestion to induce changes in thoughts, feelings, sensations, perceptions, or behavior in another person, the subject. _____
Sociocognitive Theory of Hypnosis	A theory suggesting that the behavior of hypnotized subjects is a function of their expectations about how a person behaves under hypnosis and their motivation to be good subjects. _____
Neodissociation Theory of Hypnosis	A theory proposing that hypnosis works by causing a split or dissociation between two aspects of consciousness that are ordinarily linked—the planning and the monitoring functions. _____
Psychoactive Drug	A drug that alters normal mental functioning—mood, perception, or thought; if used medically, called a controlled substance. _____
Illicit Drug	An illegal drug. _____
Physical Drug Dependence	A compulsive pattern of drug use in which the user develops a drug tolerance coupled with unpleasant withdrawal symptoms when the drug is discontinued. _____
Drug Tolerance	A condition in which the user becomes progressively less affected by the drug so that larger and larger doses are necessary to maintain the same effect. _____
Withdrawal Symptoms	The physical and psychological symptoms (usually the opposite of those produced by the drug) that occur when a regularly used drug is discontinued and that terminate when the drug is taken again. _____
Psychological Drug Dependence	A craving or irresistible urge for a drug's pleasurable effects. _____
Stimulants	A category of drugs that speed up activity in the central nervous system, suppress appetite, and cause a person to feel more awake, alert, and energetic; also called "uppers." _____
Amphetamines	A class of CNS stimulants that increase arousal, relieve fatigue, and suppress the appetite. _____

Cocaine	A type of stimulant that produces a feeling of euphoria; cocaine blocks or significantly slows the reuptake of the neurotransmitter dopamine thereby increasing the excitatory stimulation at the brain's reward center synapses. _____
Crash	The feelings of depression, exhaustion, irritability, and anxiety that occur following an amphetamine, cocaine, or crack high. _____
Crack	The most potent, inexpensive, and addictive form of cocaine, and the form that is smoked. _____
Depressants	A category of drugs that decrease activity in the central nervous system, slow down bodily functions, and reduce sensitivity to outside stimulation; also known as "downers." _____
Alcohol	A central nervous system depressant, alcohol is the number one drug problem in the U.S. _____
Barbiturates	A class of addictive depressants used as sedatives, sleeping pills, and anesthetics; overdoses can cause coma or death. _____
Minor Tranquilizers	A central nervous system depressant that calms the user. _____
Narcotics	A class of depressant drugs that are derived from the opium poppy, and have pain-relieving and calming effects; highly addictive. _____
Heroin	A highly addictive, partly synthetic narcotic derived from morphine. _____
Hallucinogens	A category of drugs, sometimes called psychedelics, that alter perception and mood and can cause hallucinations. _____
LSD	(lysergic acid diethylamide): A powerful hallucinogen with unpredictable effects ranging from perceptual changes and vivid hallucinations to states of panic and terror. _____
Flashback	The brief recurrence, occurring suddenly and without warning at a later time, of effects a person has experienced while taking LSD. _____
MDMA (Ecstasy)	A hallucinogenic designer drug that produces permanent damage of the serotonin neurons. _____

Marijuana	A hallucinogen with effects ranging from relaxation and giddiness to perceptual distortions and hallucinations. _____ _____ _____
THC	(Tetrahydrocannabinol): The principle psychoactive ingredient in marijuana and hashish. _____ _____ _____

FROM THE LABORATORY TO REAL LIFE

DRUGS AND SELF-DESTRUCTIVE BEHAVIORS

Drug and alcohol addiction is one of the most serious medical and mental health problems facing society today. Addiction is a relapse-prone disease, and success rates for those who reach certain levels of addiction severity are tenuous at best. Those unfortunates have a very difficult time stopping use and maintaining a life of recovery. One of the most dangerous aspects of addiction is that it is neither predictable nor discerning. I have worked with many people from all walks of life who have at least one thing in common by the time I meet them—they have lost just about everything in life, except life itself. While we continue to search for genetic and other biological causes, and develop theories about the family, social, and emotional factors related to addiction, many basically "normal" people begin and continue a very dangerous and self-destructive life-style under the control of addiction. I have often suggested that "normal" people do not self-destruct just because it feels good. By this I mean that part of the process aimed at stopping the progression of addiction is the discovery of the underlying payoffs that drive the addict's continued use in the face of so many negative consequences. When it comes to addiction the old adage, "An ounce of prevention is worth a pound of cure," may offer the greatest hope for our society.

Test your knowledge about drugs and addiction as you respond to the following questions.

1. One important warning sign that *drug use* is becoming *drug dependence* is the development of _____, marked by a need to increase the quantity consumed in order to obtain the desired effects.

2. The withdrawal syndrome associated with drugs such as cocaine and heroin can be very uncomfortable. However, with proper medical and social support, the patient can get through this difficult period. Often, the problem is that the patient continues to experience strong drug cravings, leading to intense anxiety and feelings of being overwhelmed. This is known as _____ dependence and is usually the greatest hurdle in interrupting or overcoming the addiction process.

3. People often run into trouble when they convince themselves that legal drugs must be safe or they wouldn't be available over the counter or from the doctor. List three drugs discussed in the book that are legal but can also lead to addiction if misused.

   _____   _____   _____

4. A patient enters the emergency room with the following drug use symptoms:
   - hyperexcitability
   - a state of suspiciousness and nervousness that resembles paranoia
   - very talkative, with disorganized speech and behavior
   - a racing heart and increased blood pressure.

   The patient is probably on either _____ or _____.

5. A patient is complaining of severe withdrawal symptoms including:
   - nausea
   - diarrhea
   - depression
   - intense physical pain in the stomach and legs.

   The patient is probably suffering withdrawal from _____.

A NIGHT IN THE LIFE.......

For me it had been a very long day. I finally decided to go to bed after hitting the wrong button on my computer. Instead of clicking the "save" icon, I closed the program and lost two hours of work. I seem to follow very strange work hours and am continually challenging my sleep/wake cycles. On weekends I sleep in late and stay up late while on weekdays I rise early and start getting tired around nine or ten in the evening. While I teach on a regular day shift basis, on weekends I am often working well into the early hours of the next morning. When I do this, I sometimes find myself nodding off for a few seconds—sometimes even in the middle of typing a sentence! I wonder if this is what happened last night when I hit the wrong button. I should know better than to juggle my sleep patterns, and I should be especially aware of the problems created by going several nights in a row with only three or so hours of sleep. I have a truck-driving friend who reportedly has a very difficult time driving at night. He believes he just isn't a safe driver as he rolls down the highway into the wee hours of the morning (I'm sure he's right).

I have worked with numerous clients whose life-styles have had negative effects on their sleep patterns. Cocaine and other stimulant addicts, who deprive themselves of regular sleep, will often sleep for long periods once they have stopped using drugs. One problem that stimulant abusers often report is the occurrence of bad dreams or drug-use nightmares during this *catch-up* sleep.

1. The sleep/wake cycles I refer to as I express concern for my strange work habits are an important aspect of what sleep researchers call _____ rhythms.

2. It appears that on weekdays I am most like a(n) _____ and on weekends I am most like a(n) _____.
    a) lark; owl   b) owl; lark

3. When I am working late at night and have been missing a lot of sleep I find myself nodding off. Sleep experts call this _____.

4. When my truck-driving friend and I work all night, our bodies may not be all that happy with us. We are working while our biological clock is telling us to sleep. The text called this _____ _____.

5. When the cocaine user was deprived of sleep for long periods of time he noticed that he had many unpleasant dreams when finally able to sleep. These dreams are probably what we call REM _____ dreams.

6. While my truck driver friend is concerned, and he probably would feel better if he had more normal sleep patterns, the fact seems to be that he is really no more likely to have an accident under these conditions than if he were driving on a normal first shift pattern.
    a) True   b) False

FROM THEORY TO PRACTICE

I'M LIKE—TRIPPIN' DUDE

Throughout history, there has been a general trend toward seeking an altered state of consciousness. Some ancient Chinese used opium; South Americans chewed coca leaves; Central and North American natives utilized organic hallucinogens in their religious rituals. In the United States, in the 1960's, consciousness expansion began to emerge as a nationwide trend in a broader way than ever before. Marijuana smoking reached epidemic proportions. Timothy Leary, the LSD guru of the sixties, expressed the belief that LSD expanded the consciousness of its users, thereby allowing them to be more intelligent, knowledgeable, and creative. Many of those who sought expanded consciousness without the use of drugs turned to methods out of the eastern philosophies, such as transcendental meditation, Zen, and yoga. The methods that have been espoused by the self-proclaimed gurus of mind expansion are too numerous and diverse to include herein. A few methods that have survived into the nineties are meditation, hypnosis, and drug use. Unfortunately there are many myths regarding hypnosis, meditation requires more initial effort and time than many are prepared to invest, and drugs produce dangerous, sometimes lethal side-effects.

Is there really a benefit to trying any of the above mentioned methods of mind expansion? From your reading, explain the potential benefits and/or risks of each of the following techniques for altering consciousness.

Meditation: _____
_____
_____
_____
_____

Hypnosis: _____
_____
_____
_____
_____

Drugs & alcohol: _____
_____
_____
_____
_____

DREAMING MYSELF SICK!

No doubt, if you have not seen any of the nightmare-based movies, you've at least heard of them. They feature a cantankerous character that shows up in another dimension (or something like that) when certain people in a small town fall asleep and dream. I have not actually seen any of these movies, but I understand the character is frightening primarily because he so badly needs a manicure. It seems that this poorly-dressed thug with long, dirty fingernails pops into peoples' dreams and torments, tortures, or kills them until somebody figures out that, if this is happening in dreamland, the dreamers should be able to break from their physical constraints and meet this menace on his terms. In other words, they should be able to fly, change shape, grow automatic weapons where arms used to be, and so on. Fortunately, the movies are fantasy and not reality. However, the films (if my son's description is accurate) do include some basis in psychological theory. For example, recurrent bad dreams can feel like torture to us, and taking control of our dreams to promote a happy ending does appear to be possible if we realize we are dreaming.

Consider the previous scenario in a real-life version—recurring nightmares that rob us of sleep and from which we awaken confused, shaken, and unable to return to our night's rest. Now, building from the terms and concepts below, demonstrate your understanding by piecing the scenario in where it best fits.

Nightmare: _____
_____
_____
_____
_____

REM sleep: _____
_____
_____
_____
_____
_____

REM rebound: _____

_____

_____

_____

_____

_____

Insomnia: _____

_____

_____

_____

_____

Microsleeps: _____

_____

_____

_____

_____

Lucid dream: _____

_____

_____

_____

_____

COMPREHENSIVE PRACTICE TEST

1. People seem to sleep best when their temperature is _____ and are more alert when their temperature is _____.
   a) higher; lower   b) lower; higher

2. While we usually think of jet lag as an affliction that affects world travelers, the same basic problem can be experienced by shift workers.
   a) True   b) False

3. People who work when their biological clock is telling them it is time to sleep can suffer lowered efficiency and productivity. The reason for this is known as:
   a) REM rebound   c) circadian rebound
   b) subjective night   d) narcolepsy

4. Research has suggested that a shift worker who gets _____ hours of bright light on one night can improve performance and lessen sleepiness the following night.
   a) 2   c) 4
   b) 1   c) 6

5. REM sleep appears as the _____ stage of sleep in a typical sleep cycle.
   a) first
   b) second
   c) last
   d) middle

6. Delta waves appear primarily in stage _____ sleep.
   a) 1
   b) 2
   c) 3
   d) 4

7. Another name for slow-wave sleep is _____:
   a) light sleep
   b) deep sleep
   c) REM sleep
   d) dream sleep

8. Larks are to owls as _____ are to _____.
   a) morning people; night people
   b) night people; morning people

9. Which of the following was NOT suggested as a possible function of REM sleep?
   a) maturation of the brain in infants
   b) facilitate learning
   c) muscle relaxation
   d) mental housecleaning

10. REM dreams seem to be more _____ while NREM dreams are more _____.
    a) scary in nature; related to pleasant memories
    b) visual, vivid, and emotional; thoughtlike
    c) thoughtlike; visual, vivid, and emotional
    d) related to pleasant memories; scary in nature

11. Some people complain about recurring dreams. The two most common themes in these dreams are:
    a) killing someone or being killed
    b) being persecuted or being arrested
    c) being embarrassed in public or marital infidelity
    d) falling or being chased

12. Freud believes dreams function to satisfy unconscious _____ and _____ urges.
    a) parental; childhood
    b) sexual; superego
    c) aggressive; violent
    d) sexual; aggressive

13. J. Allan Hobson believes dreams are merely the brain's attempt to make sense of the random firing of brain cells. This is known as the _____.
    a) Hobson Dream Hypothesis
    b) somniloquy hypothesis
    c) activation-synthesis hypothesis
    d) physiological activation hypothesis

14. The technical term for sleepwalking is _____.
    a) somniloquy
    b) mobile insomnia
    c) narcolepsy
    d) somnambulism

15. Sleepwalking usually occurs during REM sleep.
    a) True
    b) False

16. People who talk in their sleep often get in to trouble for revealing secrets or strong negative opinions.
    a) True
    b) False

17. Which of the following is NOT listed as a possible cause for a sleep attack in a person with narcolepsy?
    a) listening to music
    b) eating a big meal
    c) lovemaking
    d) sunbathing

18. Some people suffer a sleep disorder where they stop breathing and then need to wake for a brief time in order to start breathing again. This is known as:
    a) narcolepsy
    b) apnea
    c) somniloquy
    d) somnambulism

19. The sleep disorder characterized by either difficulty falling asleep or frequent waking is known as _____.
    a) amnea
    b) insomnia
    c) somnambulism
    d) REM rebound

20. Jack pleaded not guilty to his public indecency charges. He claimed he would never do such a thing in his right mind and that he was the victim of the effects of hypnosis. Would a psychologist probably support this claim?
    a) no
    b) yes

21. Elizabeth reports that she had been bothered by a troubling childhood memory. She says she went to a local hypnotist and was cured through age regression hypnosis. Her friend suggested that her sense of relief probably came from the belief that the hypnosis would help, but that age regression has not been shown to be all it has been made out to be. Who is probably more correct?
    a) Elizabeth
    b) her friend

22. Which of the following was NOT identified as a factor that influences the addictive potential of a drug?
    a) how fast the drugs effects are felt
    b) degree of discomfort to stopping use
    c) the cost of the drug
    d) how long the pleasurable feeling lasts

23. In general, the withdrawal syndrome of a drug is the opposite of the effect of the drug.
    a) True
    b) False

24. While caffeine is considered a relatively harmless stimulant in most cases, evidence suggests that some people can experience anxiety, depression, or hostility following use.
    a) True
    b) False

25. Drugs like LSD, MDMA, and marijuana are classified as:
    a) narcotics
    b) stimulants
    c) hallucinogens
    d) depressants

26. One reason for the popularity of "crack" cocaine is its _____.
    a) price
    b) legal status
    c) reduced risk
    d) depressant effects

27. Of all the drugs of abuse, one category that is still commonly used in medicine is amphetamines.
    a) True
    b) False

28. Which of the following drugs seems to produce its effect by mimicking endorphins?
    a) marijuana
    b) cocaine
    c) alcohol
    d) heroin

29. Which of the following is used in medicine as a tranquilizer or muscle relaxer?
    a) morphine
    b) valium
    c) barbiturates
    d) alcohol

30. Drugs like cocaine and amphetamine seem to produce their effect in part by _____ the reuptake of the neurotransmitter dopamine.
    a) facilitating
    b) speeding up
    c) enhancing
    d) slowing down

ANSWER KEYS

Answer Key OMSE # 1: Circadian Rhythms and Sleep

A. Quick Quiz	B. Matching
1. b	1. b
2. false	2. d
3. consciousness	3. f
4. c	4. a
5. true	5. c
6. delta	6. e
7. b	
8. false	
9. REM rebound	
10. d	
11. false	
12. parasomnia	
13. a	
14. false	
15. larks; owls	

C. Complete the Diagram

Answer Key OMSE # 2: Altered States of Consciousness

A. Quick Quiz		B. Matching	
1. d	9. d	1. e	9. d
2. meditation	10. a	2. h	10. m
3. false	11. crash	3. k	11. i
4. a	12. b	4. j	12. f
5. b	13. false	5. l	13. b
6. d	14. false	6. o	14. g
7. d	15. false	7. n	15. c
8. c		8. a	

C. Complete the Diagram

DRUGS	METHODS OF INGESTION	PRINCIPLE MEDICAL USES	EFFECTS	HEALTH RISKS
Narcotics	transdermal (patch), oral (pills, liquid), inject, sniff, and smoke (opium)	relieve pain and diarrhea	produce euphoria, relax muscles, suppress pain, cause constipation	addiction and overdose; may be fatal
Sedatives	oral, injection	sedative or sleeping aid	drowsiness, confusion, impairment of thinking, judgement, coordination, and reflexes	accidents, possible fatal overdose
Stimulants	oral, inject or sniff (crank), and smoke (ice)	treatment of narcolepsy and ADD/ADHD	increase arousal, relieve fatigue, suppress appetite, boost energy and performance	confused and disorganized behavior, paranoia, delusions and hallucinations, aggressiveness, antisocial behavior, and manic behavior
Hallucinogens	usually oral; can be taken transdermally (absorbed through the skin)	none	distort perceptions, alter mood, cause hallucinations, anxiety, and/or depression	injury to self or others, panic, terror, suicide, flashbacks
Marijuana	smoked or ingested orally	treatment of glaucoma, nausea, and loss of appetite	promotes sense of well-being and relaxation, relieves anxiety	adversely affects concentration, thinking, memory, motivation, reaction time, sex hormone production; causes respiratory damage
Alcohol	oral	none	relaxes, slows reaction time, poor coordination, aggressiveness	alcohol poisoning (can be fatal), accidents, black outs

Answer Key: Laboratory to Real Life

Drugs and Self-destructive Behaviors
1. tolerance
2. psychological
3. caffeine, nicotine, some amphetamines, alcohol, minor tranquilizers, some narcotics,
4. cocaine; amphetamines
5. heroin

A Night in the Life
1. circadian
2. lark; owl
3. microsleeps
4. subjective night
5. rebound
6. false

COMPREHENSIVE PRACTICE EXAM

1. b	11. d	21. b
2. true	12. d	22. c
3. b	13. c	23. true
4. c	14. d	24. true
5. c	15. false	25. c
6. d	16. false	26. a
7. b	17. a	27. false
8. a	18. b	28. d
9. c	19. b	29. b
10. b	20. a	30. d

5

LEARNING

Learning is defined as a relatively permanent change in behavior, capability, or attitude that is acquired through experience and cannot be attributed to illness, injury, or maturation.

CHAPTER OVERVIEW

Behavioral psychology (behaviorism) has been called the second force in psychology and is founded on the basic principles of *learning theory*. While early proponents highlighted behaviorism's opposition to the "mind" orientation of the psychoanalytic approach (known as the first force in psychology), theorists such as Kohler and Bandura illustrated the important role of cognitive processes in learning and behavior. Behaviorism has also claimed a dominant role in bringing psychology into respectability as a legitimate science. The practical applications of learning theory and behavioral psychology are many and varied, and have become increasingly more apparent through a major theoretical approach to applied psychology known as *behavior modification*.

This chapter will help you gain a more practiced and functional understanding of learning theory as it is presented in the text. The materials are divided into three OMSE areas: 1) classical conditioning, 2) operant conditioning, and 3) cognitive learning. Each OMSE area is further subdivided into easy to manage work sections designed to facilitate user understanding through elaborate rehearsal techniques. Each section contains easy to understand instructions and objective mastery self-evaluations and score cards so you may track your learning progress toward mastery.

By completing the exercises provided, you should gain a thorough understanding of the information presented in your text. In other words, you should be better prepared for tests, quizzes, class participation, and life itself.

CHAPTER OUTLINE

KEY TERMS

TIMELINE

Charles Darwin relates humans to other animals

1898

Pavlov identifies the unconditioned stimulus

1913

1859

Pavlov's work in classical conditioning

1906

John B. Watson—*Psychology as the Behaviorist Views It*

OMSE # 1: CLASSICAL CONDITIONING

1. What was Pavlov's major contribution to psychology?
2. How was classical conditioning accomplished in Pavlov's experiments?
3. How does extinction occur in classical conditioning?
4. What is generalization?
5. What is discrimination in classical conditioning?
6. How did Watson demonstrate that fear could be classically conditioned?
7. According to Rescorla, what is the critical element in classical conditioning?
8. What exceptions did Garcia and Koelling find to two traditional ideas about classical conditioning?
9. What are four factors that influence classical conditioning?
10. What type of responses can be acquired through classical conditioning?

LEARNING MASTERY SCORECARD: Update your score card as you work through the various sections of the chapter. First, find and define key terms and concepts included in each section and note the page number(s) from the text that contain important references to the material. Next, gain a practical understanding of the concepts by considering the Laboratory to Life scenarios and thinking of at least one original example of how the concept might apply in real life. Complete the *Objective-Mastery Self-Evaluation* (OMSE) exercises for this section and record your scores. Revisit the exercises, recording your score and the date completed until you have attained mastery (100%). Finally, decide how you would prepare a lecture on each objective using the template provided, outline the lecture, and practice presenting it. Keep an honest tally of your achievements and, when finished, you will have developed learning mastery through elaborate rehearsal.

Key terms & concepts	Page #	Key terms & concepts	Page #
Stimulus	_____	Conditioned Response (CR)	_____
Learning	_____	Extinction	_____
Classical Conditioning	_____	Spontaneous Recovery	_____
Reflex	_____	Generalization	_____
Conditioned Reflex	_____	Discrimination	_____
Unconditioned Response (UR)	_____	Higher-Order Conditioning	_____
Unconditioned Stimulus (US)	_____	Taste Aversion	_____
Conditioned Stimulus (CS)	_____		

Quick Quiz

Date	Score	Date	Score	Date	Score
__/__/__	_____	__/__/__	_____	__/__/__	_____
__/__/__	_____	__/__/__	_____	__/__/__	100%

Elaborate Rehearsal

Lecture Preparation	Completion Date
Key Terms, Persons, & Concepts	__/__/__
Learning Objectives	__/__/__
Lecture Notes	__/__/__

TIMELINE

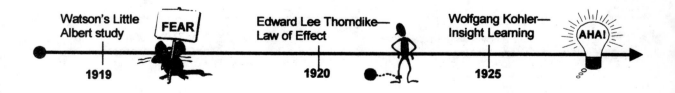

Watson's Little Albert study — FEAR — 1919

Edward Lee Thorndike— Law of Effect — 1920

Wolfgang Kohler— Insight Learning — 1925 — AHA!

A. QUICK QUIZ

1. A relatively permanent change in behavior or knowledge that occurs as a result of experience is known as:
   a) a conditioned response (CR)
   b) an unconditioned response (UR)
   c) acquisition
   d) learning

2. Henry, a long-time heroin addict, made it a habit to always use his drugs in the basement of his apartment. After three years of this practice, Henry was evicted from his apartment and found temporary refuge with another drug user. The first night there, Henry prepared and used his regular amount of the narcotic. Sadly, Henry suffered an overdose that evening. Classical conditioning proponents would probably attribute Henry's overdose to
   _____.

Read the following account of Watson's research and use the information to answer questions 3 – 9.

Watson introduced an 11-month-old boy, referred to as Little Albert, to a harmless white rat. Initially, Albert expressed no fear or other strong emotion while in the presence of the white rat, and even seemed to enjoy its company. At Albert's next meeting with the white rat, and at several subsequent meetings, Watson used a makeshift gong to create a loud, unpleasant sound from behind Albert each time the child reached for the rat, or when the rat approached. Later, after several pairings of the noise with the rat, Watson found that Albert was terrified of the rat even when the harsh noise was not present. Watson viewed Albert's fear of the rat as a relatively permanent change.

3. In the beginning, the white rat was viewed by Albert as a _____ stimulus.

4. The banging sound made by Watson was the _____ stimulus.

5. After several pairings with the noise, the rat became a _____ stimulus.

6. Albert's learned fear of the rat was the :
   a) conditioned response
   b) unconditioned response
   c) unconditioned stimulus
   d) conditioned stimulus

7. If after being conditioned to respond with fear to the rat, Albert were presented with the white rat repeatedly without the presence of the loud noise, this process would probably result in which of the following:
   a) acquisition
   b) delayed conditioning
   c) extinction
   d) trace conditioning

8. An interesting phenomenon resulted from Watson's work with Little Albert. Watson learned that Albert was not only frightened of the rat, but of anything white and furry. The process whereby Albert associated all things white and furry with his fear of the rat is called:
   a) discrimination
   b) acquisition
   c) generalization
   d) extinction

9. Had Watson taken the care to successfully complete the process of extinction with Little Albert, it is just possible that Albert's fear of white rats may have resurfaced at a later date. Had this happened, it would be an example of:
   a) second-order conditioning
   b) delayed conditioning
   c) spontaneous recovery
   d) extinction

10. If you have a dog, perhaps you've noticed that he or she runs around excitedly whenever you pull into your driveway. Does the dog act this way when other cars stop nearby? Probably not—the dog has learned to distinguish the difference between your car and most others because the arrival of your car is followed closely by your appearance at the front door. This process is known as _____.

11. In the above scenario (#10) identify the following:
    a) UCS _____
    b) CS _____
    c) UCR _____

12. Assume that after Albert was conditioned to fear the rat, Watson had repeatedly presented the rat to Albert without the original unconditioned stimulus (US). However, this hypothetical presentation occurred in a room that was lit just prior to and during the presentation of the rat by a single red light. Albert probably would have associated the red light with his conditioned response of fear. This process is known as:
    a) delayed conditioning
    b) spontaneous recovery
    c) higher-order conditioning
    d) second-order conditioning

13. Watson worked with a three-year-old boy named Peter to extinguish the child's fear of rabbits. The effort was a complete success and Peter's fear was extinguished. If, after a month or so, Peter were playing in his yard when a rabbit happened along, and Peter responded with fear only slightly weaker than he had prior to the treatment, we would call this phenomenon _____.

14. Scott is a young man whose passion is literature. He took his first high school literature class only to discover that the teacher was extremely rigid and demanding. Scott, an honor student, received his first failing grade ever. Now, Scott becomes angry when he walks past the literature classroom, and even when he hears other students discussing the class. Even more disconcerting is the fact that classic works of literature, formerly his favorites, have become a source of ill feelings such as anger and resentment. Scott's story is an example of:
a) delayed conditioning
b) spontaneous recovery
c) higher-order conditioning
d) second-order conditioning

15. Sometimes, alcoholics are administered a drug that produces severe nausea and vomiting when the user drinks any alcohol. This practice may serve as an example of:
a) taste aversion
b) spontaneous recovery
c) drug tolerance
d) second-order conditioning

B. Matching: Place the appropriate letter in the blank provided.

_____	1. An involuntary response to a particular stimulus.	a)	Higher-order conditioning
_____	2. The weakening or eventual disappearance of a conditioned response.	b)	Watson
_____	3. An event that produces a reflexive response.	c)	Discrimination
_____	4. Responding to stimuli similar to the original conditioned stimulus.	d)	Unconditioned response
_____	5. The learned ability to distinguish between similar stimuli.	e)	Extinction
_____	6. Association of a neutral stimulus to an already conditioned stimulus.	f)	Unconditioned stimulus
_____	7. Believed fears were classically conditioned.	g)	Generalization

TIMELINE

1932
Edward Tolman—Latent
Learning

1938
B. F. Skinner—*The
Behavior of Organisms*

1969
Albert Bandura—Observational
Learning

C. COMPLETE THE DIAGRAM

Stacey, a 47-year-old woman recounted this example of emotional response being acquired through classical conditioning. She wrote:

> I first met Bob when I was a junior in high school. We began dating and after a time, we got around to parking and necking. Bob was my first kiss and my first love. I can remember the feeling I had the first night we went out—when I got home I was floating on air. At the time I had never even kissed a boy. When we met, I wasn't really into music but I liked the popular (Top 40) stuff okay. Bob was really into a band named "The Doors" and he played their tapes all the time, especially when we were parking and making out. We went together all through high school and finally drifted apart when I went to college and he went to the military. I hadn't thought about Bob in years until recently. I was watching television when one of the characters turned on the stereo and out came an old Doors tune. At first I didn't recognize the music. I just suddenly felt weak in the knees and had that floating on air sensation. Then I realized that it was the music that sent me there.

Using information from Stacey's story, complete the following diagram by filling in the blanks: Include the neutral stimulus (NS), unconditioned stimulus (US), conditioned stimulus (CS), unconditioned response (UR), and conditioned response (CR).

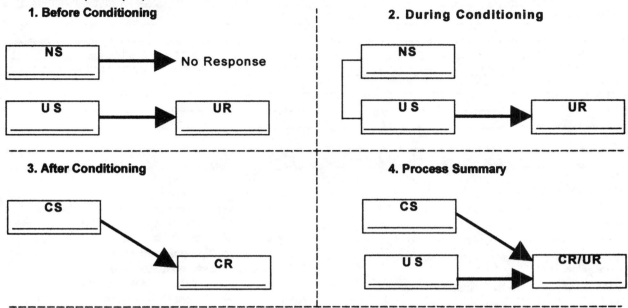

1. Before Conditioning

NS → No Response

US → UR

2. During Conditioning

NS

US → UR

3. After Conditioning

CS → CR

4. Process Summary

CS

US → CR/UR

PREPARE A LECTURE: This activity is designed to offer you an opportunity to take advantage of a valuable mode of learning, elaborate rehearsal. Once you have finished the OMSE section, write a lecture using the instructional guide provided below. After your lecture is prepared, you can enhance your learning by writing a quiz covering the material. Now it is time to find some willing and inquisitive audience members. Your roommates or family may be a great place to start. Present them the lecture as if you are teaching a class. Remember to ask for questions and give your students the quiz following the lecture. This exercise can also serve to turn a *study-buddy* group into a very productive way to prepare for the test. Each member of the group can take different OMSE sections for their lecture/teacher role while the rest of the group serves as the class.

I. Key Terms, Names, Dates, and Concepts you will include in this lecture:

1. _____
2. _____
3. _____
4. _____

5. _____
6. _____
7. _____
8. _____

9. _____
10. _____
11. _____
12. _____

II. Learning Objectives (what do you want the student to know and be able to do as a result of your lecture):

1. _____
2. _____
3. _____
4. _____
5. _____

III. Lecture Notes (notes should be brief cues and serve as a guide).

Major topic #1: _____

Sub-topics and notes: _____

_____

_____

_____

Major topic #2: _____
    Sub-topics and notes: _____
_____
_____
_____

Major topic #3: _____
    Sub-topics and notes: _____
_____
_____
_____

OMSE # 2: OPERANT CONDITIONING

LEARNING OBJECTIVES

1. What is Thorndike's major contribution to psychology?
2. What is Skinner's major contribution to psychology?
3. How are responses acquired through operant conditioning?
4. How is shaping used to condition a response?
5. How does extinction occur in operant conditioning?
6. What is the goal of both positive reinforcement and negative reinforcement, and how is the goal accomplished with each?
8. What are the four major schedules of reinforcement, and which schedule yields the highest response rate and the greatest resistance to extinction?
9. What is the partial reinforcement effect?
10. What three factors, in addition to the schedule of reinforcement, influence operant conditioning?
11. How does punishment differ from negative reinforcement?
12. What are some disadvantages of punishment?
13. What three factors increase the effectiveness of punishment?
14. What are some applications of operant conditioning?

LEARNING MASTERY SCORECARD: Update your score card as you work through the various sections of the chapter. First, find and define key terms and concepts included in each section and note the page number(s) from the text that contain important references to the material. Next, gain a practical understanding of the concepts by considering the Laboratory to Life scenarios and thinking of at least one original example of how the concept might apply in real life. Complete the *Objective-Mastery Self-Evaluation* (OMSE) exercises for this section and record your scores. Revisit the exercises, recording your score and the date completed until you have attained mastery (100%). Finally, decide how you would prepare a lecture on each objective using the template provided, outline the lecture, and practice presenting it. Keep an honest tally of your achievements and, when finished, you will have developed learning mastery through elaborate rehearsal.

Key terms	Page	Key terms	Page	Key terms	Page
Trial-and-Error Learning	_____	Law of Effect	_____	Reinforcement	_____
Extinction	_____	Operant Conditioning	_____	Partial-Reinforcement Effect	_____
Reinforcer	_____	Punishment	_____	Positive Reinforcement	_____
Negative Reinforcement	_____	Shaping	_____	Biofeedback	_____
Continuous Reinforcement	_____	Skinner Box	_____	Partial Reinforcement	_____
Schedule of Reinforcement	_____	Primary Reinforcer	_____	Fixed-Ratio Schedule	_____
Secondary Reinforcer	_____	Successive Approximations	_____	Variable-Ratio Schedule	_____
Fixed-Interval Schedule	_____	Avoidance Learning	_____	Learned Helplessness	_____
Behavior Modification	_____	Variable-Interval Schedule	_____	Discriminative Stimulus	_____
Token Economy	_____				

Quick Quiz

Date	Score	Date	Score	Date	Score
__/__/__	____	__/__/__	____	__/__/__	____
__/__/__	____	__/__/__	____	__/__/__	100%

Elaborate Rehearsal

Lecture Preparation	Completion Date
Key Terms, Persons, & Concepts	__/__/__
Learning Objectives	__/__/__
Lecture Notes	__/__/__

QUICK QUIZ

1. A continuous reinforcement schedule leaves the behavior more resistant to extinction than does a partial reinforcement schedule.
   a) True
   b) False

2. Primary reinforcement is to _____ as secondary reinforcement is to _____.
   a) acquired value; biological drives
   b) increase behavior; decrease behavior
   c) biological drives; acquired value
   d) decrease behavior; increase behavior

3. A behavior modification technique where the patient is taught to control the activity of the autonomic nervous system through relaxation training and immediate information regarding the effect on autonomic functions is called _____.

4. A good example of partial reinforcement schedule would be hitting the ball 3 times for every ten swings of the bat.
   a) True
   b) False

5. A consequence is a _____ if it increases the likelihood of repeating the behavior that preceded it.
   a) discriminative stimulus
   b) punisher
   c) reinforcer
   d) Skinnerian consequence

6. Providing reinforcement every time a subject performs the target behavior is using the _____ schedule of reinforcement.

7. Another, more technical, term for punishment is negative reinforcement.
   a) True
   b) False

8. Seligman found that dogs exposed to shock with no means for escape eventually just give up. He called this:
   a) avoidance learning
   b) learned helplessness
   c) negative reinforcement
   d) trial and error learning

9. Every time little Johnny and his mother get to the checkout lane at the grocery store, Johnny asks for a candy bar. Some times his mother says "yes" and sometimes she says "no." This is an example of the _____ schedule of reinforcement.

10. In operant conditioning, extinction refers to always presenting the conditioned stimulus while never presenting the unconditioned stimulus.
    a) True
    b) False

11. According to learning theory, a consequence that involves the presentation of an unpleasant stimulus or the removal of a pleasant stimulus is called _____.

12. Using the theories and concepts of learning theory to help a client change a problem behavior is known as:
    a) trial and error learning
    b) problem modification
    c) countercontigency learning
    d) behavior modification

13. Mom says "no" to little Johnny when he asks for a candy bar, and Johnny throws a tantrum. Finally, mom gives in and buys him the candy bar. Mom just reinforced a negative behavior using positive reinforcement.
    a) True
    b) False

14. Of the following, which is the best example of the fixed-interval schedule of reinforcement?
    a) slot machine
    b) shaping a rat to lever press
    c) turning on a light switch when the bulb is burned out
    d) weekly paycheck

15. The client reports that he has had many bad consequences after a night of drinking alcohol. He is confused as to why, given the bad consequences, he continues to go on drinking binges. The clinician asks the client what he experiences at the time of the drinking behavior and the client reports that he feels good and forgets his problems. The clinician believes he has the answer and explains that the apparently good consequences of the drinking behavior are outweighing the bad consequences that happen the next day. Your text refers to this factor that seems to be influencing the client's behavior as the _____ of reinforcement.

B. MATCHING

_____	1. Law of Effect	a)	money
_____	2. Primary Reinforcer	b)	reduce behavior
_____	3. Secondary Reinforcer	c)	like a reward
_____	4. Punishment	d)	Skinner
_____	5. Positive Reinforcement	e)	Seligman
_____	6. Negative Reinforcement	f)	Thorndike
_____	7. Reinforcement Theory	g)	successive approximations
_____	8. Learned Helplessness	h)	token economy
_____	9. Shaping	i)	remove aversive stimulus
_____	10. Acceptable behaviors earn privileges	j)	food

C. COMPLETE THE DAGRAM

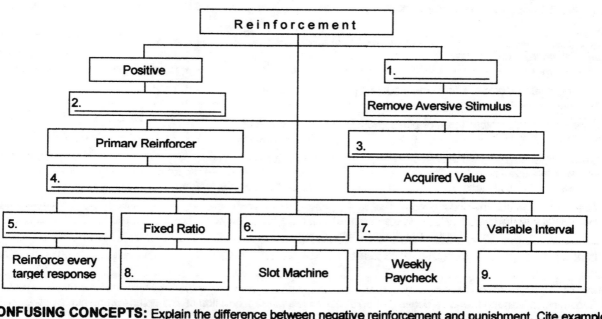

CONFUSING CONCEPTS: Explain the difference between negative reinforcement and punishment. Cite examples of each.

_____

_____

_____

_____

_____

_____

_____

PREPARE A LECTURE: This activity is designed to offer you an opportunity to take advantage of a valuable mode of learning, elaborate rehearsal. Once you have finished the OMSE section, write a lecture using the instructional guide provided below. After your lecture is prepared, you can enhance your learning by writing a quiz covering the material. Now it is time to find some willing and inquisitive audience members. Your roommates or family may be a great place to start. Present them the lecture as if you are teaching a class. Remember to ask for questions and give your students the quiz following the lecture. This exercise can also serve to turn a *study-buddy* group into a very productive way to prepare for the test. Each member of the group can take different OMSE sections for their lecture/teacher role while the rest of the group serves as the class.

I. Key Terms, Names, Dates, and Concepts you will include in this lecture:

1. _____   5. _____   9. _____
2. _____   6. _____   10. _____
3. _____   7. _____   11. _____
4. _____   8. _____   12. _____

II. Learning Objectives (what do you want the student to know and be able to do as a result of your lecture):

1. _____
2. _____
3. _____
4. _____
5. _____

III. Lecture Notes (notes should be brief cues and serve as a guide).

Major topic #1: _____
    Sub-topics and notes: _____
    _____
    _____
    _____

Major topic #2: _____
    Sub-topics and notes: _____
    _____
    _____
    _____

Major topic #3: _____
    Sub-topics and notes: _____
    _____
    _____
    _____

OMSE # 3: COGNITIVE LEARNING

LEARNING OBJECTIVES

1. What is insight, and how does it affect learning?
2. What is latent learning?
3. What is observational learning?
4. What is Bandura's major contribution to psychology?

If all learning were reflexive and mechanistic, school should be a great deal different than what we know it to be. Certainly, cognition is a central component of the learning equation.

LEARNING MASTERY SCORECARD: Update your score card as you work through the various sections of the chapter. First, find and define key terms and concepts included in each section and note the page number(s) from the text that contain important references to the material. Next, gain a practical understanding of the concepts by considering the Laboratory to Life scenarios and thinking of at least one original example of how the concept might apply in real life. Complete the *Objective-Mastery Self-Evaluation* (OMSE) exercises for this section and record your scores. Revisit the exercises, recording your score and the date completed until you have attained mastery (100%). Finally, decide how you would prepare a lecture on each objective using the template provided.

Key Terms	Page #	Key Terms	Page #	Key Terms	Page #	Key Terms	Page #
Cognitive Processes	_____	Insight	_____	Latent Learning	_____	Cognitive Map	_____
Observational Learning	_____	Modeling	_____	Model	_____		

QUICK QUIZ

Date	Score	Date	Score	Date	Score
__/__/__	_____	__/__/__	_____	__/__/__	_____
__/__/__	_____	__/__/__	_____	__/__/__	100%

ELABORATE REHEARSAL

Lecture Preparation	Completion Date
Key Terms, Persons, & Concepts	__/__/__
Learning Objectives	__/__/__
Lecture Notes	__/__/__

A. QUICK QUIZ

1. While learning theory was originally rooted in a foundation of mechanistic processes and reflexive responses, many behavioral psychologists have more recently expressed interest in _____ _____ such as memory, problem solving, and thinking.

2. According to Tolman, _____ is defined as learning that occurs without apparent reinforcement, but is not demonstrated until the organism is motivated to do so.
   a) classical conditioning   c) latent learning
   b) modeling   d) cognitive mapping

3. Bandura's research with children and "Bobo Dolls" indicated that parents really do not need to worry about how much or what type of television violence their children are viewing.
   a) True   b) False

4. Little Suzie goes to the grocery store with her mother. While mom pushes the shopping cart, picking up groceries, little Suzie has her own toy shopping cart. When mom puts a loaf of bread in her cart, Suzie puts a loaf of bread in her cart. In this case, mom is the _____ for Suzie's behavior.

5. Jack has recently begun a new hobby—woodworking. He has been wrestling with a corner joint for a picture frame all morning. Suddenly, as if out of the blue, he realizes he can cut one corner, lay it upside-down on the new board and use it as the template for the new cut. This would be identified as an example of:
   a) observational learning   c) modeling
   b) operant conditioning   d) insight

6. I found myself lost one day in a mid-size city near my hometown. I finally had to stop for directions, and I was informed that I was in a completely wrong part of the town. With good directions, I finally arrived at my destination. Three months later I returned to the city and this time I needed to find an address in the part of town that I had been lost in before. I was surprised that I found my destination so easily. This could be an example of what Tolman would call the result of a _____ _____.

7. My 17-year-old son had never changed a car tire, although he must have seen me change one in the past. He called me at work one day and informed me that he had a flat tire and that he was excited about a date with his new girlfriend and did not want to be late. He explained that he was clueless as to how to change a tire. I told him I was too busy, but I decided to stop and check on his progress. When I arrived, he was tightening the last lug nut. It seems that he really did have a clue. Cognitive learning theorists might attribute his ability to change that tire when properly motivated as a case of _____ _____.

B. MATCHING

_____	1. Learning by imitation	a) insight
_____	2. Mental representation of an area	b) latent learning
_____	3. Sudden realization of a solution	c) cognitive processes
_____	4. Learning without apparent reinforcement	d) observational learning
_____	5. Thinking, knowing, remembering	e) cognitive map

C. COMPLETE THE DIAGRAM: After reading each vignette, determine which concept and theorist best fit.

1. I had just quit playing fetch with my dog and put away her ball, when she went to the apple tree and brought me a mushy apple from the ground. I made the mistake of throwing it. Unfortunately, the apple exploded into bits when it hit the ground. The dog was not pleased. Then, as if she had a kind of "aha" experience, she jumped up and grabbed an apple off a low branch of the tree. When I threw the fresh apple it did not break apart and we both enjoyed more of the fetch game.

Concept [   ]   Theorist [   ]

2. A typical source of anxiety for psychology majors is the fact that they will have to take statistics classes in pursuit of their degree. I was no exception, and I remember the uneasy feeling as my time for this seemingly dreadful experience approached. One day I found myself in the psychology department, watching and listening to some current statistics students trying to reason through and understand concepts like variance, standard deviations, and confidence levels. It was all pretty strange stuff to me, but I listened as they searched for answers. When my time came, I was surprised at my curious ability to understand the concepts.

Concept [   ]   Theorist [   ]

3. A friend was remodeling his family room and asked me to help. While I refinished the oak mantel, he was busy nailing new paneling to the wall. We had to be careful of the new wood floor he had just installed. His son, Jason, was about four years old and enjoyed watching the work and all the exciting tools. We had just started back to work after a break and my friend began nailing another panel to the wall. Jason found a hammer on the floor and began to also pound nails—into the new wooden floor!

Concept [   ]   Theorist [   ]

PREPARE A LECTURE: This activity is designed to offer you an opportunity to take advantage of a valuable mode of learning, elaborate rehearsal. Once you have finished the OMSE section, write a lecture using the instructional guide provided below. After your lecture is prepared, you can enhance your learning by writing a quiz covering the material. Now it is time to find some willing and inquisitive audience members. Your roommates or family may be a great place to start. Present them the lecture as if you are teaching a class. Remember to ask for questions and give your students the quiz following the lecture. This exercise can also serve to turn a *study-buddy* group into a very productive way to prepare for the test. Each member of the group can take different OMSE sections for their lecture/teacher role while the rest of the group serves as the class.

I. Key Terms, Names, Dates, and Concepts you will include in this lecture:

1. _____	5. _____	9. _____
2. _____	6. _____	10. _____
3. _____	7. _____	11. _____
4. _____	8. _____	12. _____

II. Learning Objectives (what do you want the student to know and be able to do as a result of your lecture):

1. _____
2. _____
3. _____
4. _____
5. _____

III. Lecture Notes (notes should be brief cues and serve as a guide).

Major topic #1: _____

    Sub-topics and notes: _____

    _____

    _____

    _____

Major topic #2: _____

    Sub-topics and notes: _____

    _____

    _____

    _____

Major topic #3: _____

    Sub-topics and notes: _____

    _____

    _____

    _____

KEY TERMS AND CONCEPTS EXCERCISE

The key terms and concepts are presented in the order of their appearance in the text. Space is provided for you to include a personalized definition or example of each term or concept. As you encounter each term in the text, make a note of its meaning and context. Next, conceptualize the meaning of the term in a way that makes the most sense to you. You can also think about examples of the term from your own life. Write your definition and/or example in the space provided next to the word in this book. This exercise utilizes a modified *T-note* design so that you can self-evaluate your mastery of the definitions. First lay a sheet of paper over the terms and concepts side of the page so that you only see the definitions. Read the definition and try to recall the term or concept. Mark all those you are unable to answer so you can restudy them. When you have learned all of the terms and concepts in this way, move the paper to the definition side so that you can see only the term or concept, try to recall both the textbook definition and your personal version. Repeat this until you know all of the terms and concepts by definition and personal understanding.

Stimulus	Any event or object in the environment to which an organism responds; plural is stimuli. Pavlov's original hypothesis included the belief that food was the stimulus needed to produce salivation in the dogs. _____ _____ _____
Learning	A relatively permanent change in behavior, capability, or attitude that is acquired through experience and cannot be attributed to illness, injury, or maturation. Hopefully, you've learned through experience that the more you study, the higher you will score on tests. _____ _____ _____ _____

Classical Conditioning	A process through which a response previously made only to a specific stimulus is made to another stimulus that has been paired repeatedly with the original stimulus. Pavlov's dogs were classically conditioned to respond to simple sounds in the same manner in which they responded reflexively to food. _____ _____ _____
Reflex	An involuntary response to a particular stimulus, like the eyeblink response to a puff of air or salivation to food placed in the mouth. Pavlov did not have to train his dogs to salivate to the food. The salivation response was reflexive. _____ _____ _____
Conditioned Reflex	A learned reflex rather than a naturally occurring one. Pavlov noticed that his dogs began to salivate at the sound of clinking dishes prior to the food being placed in their mouths. He understood this phenomenon as a conditioned reflex. _____ _____ _____
Unconditioned Response (UR)	A response that is invariably elicited by the unconditioned stimulus without prior learning. What happens when you hear a car backfire or any other loud, unexpected noise? Most likely you jump, flinch, or startle in some way. Your response to the loud noise is unconditioned. No learning was required. _____ _____ _____
Unconditioned Stimulus (US)	A stimulus that elicits a specific response without prior learning. In the above example, the sound of the car backfiring is the US. _____ _____ _____
Conditioned Stimulus (CS)	A neutral stimulus that after repeated pairings with an unconditioned stimulus becomes associated with it and elicits a conditioned response. In Pavlov's study, the tone, after repeated pairings with the meat powder, elicited the salivation response in the dogs even when presented without the food. _____ _____ _____
Extinction	The weakening and often eventual disappearance of a learned response. In Pavlov's research, if the tone were presented to the dogs repeatedly without the food being presented, the dogs would eventually unlearn or be unconditioned to associate the tone with the food. _____ _____ _____
Spontaneous Recovery	The reappearance of an extinguished response (in a weaker form) when an organism is exposed to the original conditioned stimulus following a rest period. Pavlov gave his dog a break and then returned it to the lab only to discover that the response he thought had been extinguished had returned in a weaker form. The dog salivated to the sound of the tone (CS), but to a lesser degree than before the extinction process. _____ _____ _____
Generalization	In classical conditioning, the tendency to make a conditioned response to a stimulus similar to the original conditioned stimulus. Pavlov found that the dogs would respond similarly when presented with the original CS, the tone, as well as when presented with similar tones and sounds. In operant conditioning, generalization is the tendency to make the learned response to a stimulus similar to the one for which it was originally reinforced. _____ _____ _____

Discrimination	The learned ability to distinguish between similar stimuli so that the conditioned response occurs only to the original conditioned stimulus but not to similar stimuli. This is the opposite of generalization. If Pavlov paired only the original tone (CS) with the food US), and repeatedly sounded similar tones without presenting food, the dog would eventually learn to discriminate between tones and would salivate only to the original conditioned stimulus. _____ _____ _____ _____
Higher-Order Conditioning	Occurs when a neutral stimulus is paired with an existing conditioned stimulus, becomes associated with it, and gains the power to elicit the same conditioned response. Had Pavlov paired a light with the tone (CS) after the dogs had become conditioned to the tone, the dog would have associated the light with the tone (CS) with the food (US) and eventually the light alone would have been enough of a stimulus to initiate the saliva response. _____ _____ _____ _____
Drug Tolerance	A condition in which the user becomes progressively less affected by a drug so that larger and larger doses are necessary to maintain the same effect. Environmental cues, such as persons, places, and things that the drug user associates with the use and effect of the drug can become triggers that evoke drug cravings. _____ _____ _____
Taste Aversion	The dislike and/or avoidance of a particular food that has been associated with nausea or discomfort. A friend recently refused a butterscotch candy. He explained that when he was a child, he had become very ill with the flu shortly after dining on his grandmother's famous butterscotch pudding. He went on to say that he cannot tolerate the smell or taste of butterscotch to this day. Obviously, he has associated butterscotch with becoming ill. _____ _____ _____
Trial-and-Error Learning	Learning that occurs when a response is associated with a successful solution to a problem after a number of unsuccessful responses. "If at first you don't succeed, try, try again" is a fairly well known and oft heard adage that applies well to trial-and-error learning. Thorndike discovered that this is one method by which we learn. _____ _____ _____
Law of Effect	Thorndike's law of learning states that connections between a stimulus and a response will be strengthened if followed by a satisfying consequence and weakened if followed by discomfort. Let's say you were used to receiving a grade of "C" on tests after studying 6 hours per week. However, you earned an "A" on your last test after increasing your study time to 9 hours per week. You would probably be more likely to repeat the longer study time behavior before the next test if your goal was to improve your GPA. The "A" would be a satisfying consequence. _____ _____ _____ _____
Operant Conditioning	A type of learning in which the consequences of behavior tend to increase or decrease that behavior in the future. For example, if you work for a living then you get paid. Having money is rewarding and thereby reinforces your behavior of working. Would you continue to work if you did not get paid? _____ _____ _____ _____

Reinforcer	Anything that strengthens a response or increases the probability that it will occur. In the above scenario, work for pay, the pay is the reinforcer. The pay increases the probability that you will continue to perform work behavior. Imagine the following scenario in which your manager is speaking to you, "You are doing a good job at work. You're well liked by management, and we want you to continue to do a good job here. Oh, by the way, you are no longer being financially compensated for services rendered." What would you do next? _____ _____ _____
Shaping	Gradually molding a desired behavior by reinforcing responses that become progressively closer to it; reinforcing successive approximations of the desired response. You may have had the opportunity to train a dog. If so, you probably used shaping to accomplish the task by rewarding the dog with a biscuit for coming close to the target behavior. _____ _____ _____
Skinner Box	A soundproof operant conditioning chamber with a device for delivering food and either a bar for rats to press or a disk for pigeons to peck. In the box, a rat would be reinforced for lever pressing behavior by the delivery of a food pellet. Thus, the rat would be more likely to continue pressing. _____ _____ _____
Successive Approximations	A series of gradual training steps with each step becoming more like the final desired response. The process of forming a novel or new behavior often involves several small steps, each of which must be reinforced in order to motivate the trainee toward the final step—the new behavior. _____ _____ _____
Extinction	The weakening and often eventual disappearance of a learned response (in operant conditioning, the conditioned response is weakened by withholding reinforcement). Consider the rat in the Skinner box. It has become conditioned to expect a food pellet each time it presses the lever. If the pellets stop coming, the rat will eventually discontinue the lever pressing. _____ _____ _____
Discriminative Stimulus	A stimulus that signals whether a certain response or behavior is likely to be followed by reward or punishment. A rat in a Skinner box can learn that pressing the lever only pays off when the light is on. The light is the discriminative stimulus in the sense that it discriminates between the reinforced condition and the nonreinforced condition. _____ _____ _____
Reinforcement	An event that follows a response and increases the strength of the response and/or the likelihood that it will be repeated. The grading system is a form of reinforcement; high grades are a reward for your hard work and encourage continued hard work. On the other hand, if you are placed on academic probation for poor grades, you may work harder to have the aversive consequences removed. _____ _____ _____
Positive Reinforcement	A reward or pleasant consequence that follows a response and increases the probability that the response will be repeated. The high grades in the above scenario are meant to be positive reinforcement. _____ _____ _____ _____

Negative Reinforcement	The termination of an unpleasant stimulus after a response in order to increase the probability that the response will be repeated. Let's say you are a grade conscious individual who excelled in high school. You find yourself on academic probation after your first semester of college. You realize that if you want to remove this aversive condition from your life you will have to study more than you have. The probation has served as a negative reinforcer, and the target behavior, studying, has been increased. _____
Primary Reinforcer	A reinforcer that fulfills a basic physical need for survival and does not need reinforcing. We all know what it is like to miss a meal. The stomach growls as a pain begins to grow down in its pit. When this happens, we eat something. Hunger is a physically aversive state and food is a primary reinforcer. _____
Secondary Reinforcer	A neutral stimulus that becomes reinforcing after repeated pairings with other reinforcers. Money is a secondary reinforcer that is paired repeatedly with primary reinforcers. For example, without money we may not have shelter and food. Money is therefore paired with the obtaining of primary reinforcers and becomes, of itself, a reinforcer. _____
Continuous Reinforcement	Reinforcement that is delivered after every desired or correct response; the most effective method of conditioning a new response. To condition the lever-pressing response in rats, a food pellet is delivered after every lever press. However, if the rat continued to receive one pellet per press, the behavior would decline as the rat became satiated. Once conditioned, continuous reinforcement is not the most effective way to maintain the learned response.
Partial Reinforcement	A pattern of reinforcement in which some portion, rather than 100 percent, of the correct responses are reinforced. For example, maybe you earn an hourly wage for services rendered, but you don't get paid at the end of every hour. Instead, you take home a check every week or two. _____
Schedule of Reinforcement	A systematic program for administering reinforcements that has a predictable effect on behavior. For example, many commissioned salespeople will work harder to reach an objective toward the end of the month or quarter in order to insure a greater reward in the form of a commission or bonus check. _____
Fixed-Ratio Schedule	A schedule in which a reinforcer is given after a fixed number of correct responses. For example, some painters are paid according to how many square feet of coverage they successfully complete. _____
Variable-Ratio Schedule	A schedule in which a reinforcer is given after a varying number of nonreinforced responses based on an average ratio. In other words, with a variable ratio of 10, you might be reinforced the first time after 2 responses, the next time after 10 responses, and the next after 18 responses. You won't know exactly which responses will be reinforced, but you would know that reinforcement would average 1 in 10. _____

Fixed-Interval Schedule	A schedule in which a reinforcer is given following the first correct response after a fixed period of time has elapsed. A rat might be reinforced with a food pellet for the first lever press after a two-minute interval has elapsed and then must wait two minutes before receiving the next reinforcement.. If you work on a salary, you are on a fixed-interval schedule. Maybe you get paid twice a month like many people. If so, you probably do not show up for work only on payday expecting a check. _____ _____ _____
Variable-Interval Schedule	A schedule in which a reinforcer is given after the first correct response, following a varying time of nonreinforcement based on an average time. In the military, surprise inspections are common. Therefore, military personnel generally keep themselves and their barracks in top shape and ready for inspection. _____ _____ _____
Partial-Reinforcement Effect	The greater resistance to extinction that occurs when a portion, rather than all, of the correct responses are reinforced. When a rat learns that a food pellet will be delivered with every lever press, the rat will only press when hungry. However, when a rat learns that food will be delivered eventually if it continues to press, the rat will press until a pellet is delivered. The rat may even learn how many presses it takes to bring about the delivery of the food. _____ _____ _____
Punishment	The removal of a pleasant stimulus or the presence of an unpleasant stimulus, which tends to suppress a response. Some parents punish their children by administering a scolding or spanking. Other parents take away the child's privileges such as playing video games, watching television, or going out with friends on a Friday night. The hopeful outcome of each of these methods of punishment is to reduce a negative or unwanted target behavior. _____ _____ _____
Avoidance Learning	Learning to avoid events or conditions associated with dreaded or aversive outcomes. Some adolescents may attend their first high school dance, be rejected the first two or three times they ask a prospective partner to dance, and experience a sense of defeat and humiliation for their perceived failure. The pain of that rejection may lead the person to leave early in an effort to avoid further rejection at that dance and to avoid going to future coed functions altogether. _____ _____ _____
Learned Helplessness	The learned response of resigning oneself passively to aversive conditions, rather than taking action to change, escape, or avoid them; learned through repeated exposure to inescapable or unavoidable aversive events. Consider the case of a woman physically abused by her husband repeatedly and over a long period of time. Every time she attempts to escape the situation, he threatens to take the children. She stays because she fears for the safety of herself and her children. Eventually, the woman may give up all hope of escaping and resigns herself to the abusive lifestyle. _____ _____ _____
Biofeedback	The use of sensitive equipment to give people precise feedback about internal physiological processes so that they can learn, with practice, to exercise control over them. For example, people who suffer from tension headaches may learn to regulate their physiological responses to stressful situations, thereby averting another headache. _____ _____ _____

Behavior Modification	The systematic application of the learning principles of operant conditioning, classical conditioning, or observational learning to individuals or groups in order to eliminate undesirable behavior and/or encourage desirable behavior. Consider the practice of some smokers when trying to quit. They wear a stiff rubber band around one wrist and when they think of lighting up, they snap the rubber band inflicting an aversive condition—pain. The idea is that they will begin to associate the pain with smoking, and cravings will decrease. _____ _____ _____ _____
Token Economy	A program that motivates and reinforces socially acceptable behaviors with tokens that can be exchanged for desired items or privileges. This behavior modification technique is used successfully in mental hospitals. Patients who perform desired behaviors are rewarded with tokens. When they save enough tokens, they may use them to purchase special privileges. _____ _____ _____
Cognitive Processes	Mental processes such as thinking, knowing, problem solving, and remembering. According to many theorists, cognitive processes are critically important in a more comprehensive view of learning. _____ _____ _____
Insight	The sudden realization of the relationship between elements in a problem situation, which makes the solution apparent. Did you ever have an "aha" experience? In the course of solving a problem, did you ever work at finding a solution until you gave up on the project and as you were walking away, the crucial solution just seemed to pop into your head? If so, then you know first hand what insight is all about. _____ _____ _____
Latent Learning	Learning that occurs without apparent reinforcement but that is not demonstrated until sufficient reinforcement is provided. Tolman discovered that rats could make a cognitive map of a maze (in effect, learn the maze) but not demonstrate their learning until motivated to do so by a food reward. _____ _____ _____
Cognitive Map	A mental representation of an area. Consider the last time you were asked for directions. Did you pull a street map out of your pocket, or did you mentally picture the directions and relate that cognitive map to the asker? Think now. How would you tell a fellow student to get from your Psychology class to the library? _____ _____ _____
Observational Learning	Learning by observing the behavior of others and the consequences of that behavior; learning by imitation. Over the past few decades, controversy has arisen as to the imitative nature of young people who watch violence on television. This concern stems from the fear that observational learning takes place, or can take place, via the TV. _____ _____ _____
Modeling	Another name for observational learning. Think about way some children grow up. In poverty-stricken neighborhoods, the drug dealers with the fancy cars, and perceived respect may be a more salient role model for children than the mother or father who works hard all week. _____ _____ _____

Model	The individual who demonstrates a behavior or serves as an example in observational learning. The model from the above scenario is the drug dealer, and the learning that may take place is that crime does pay. _____ _____ _____

FROM THE LABORATORY TO REAL LIFE

Small Car Phobia

One of the authors of this study guide was seriously injured in a car accident when he was 15-years-old. One night, he and a couple of friends decided to attend a concert in a nearby town. Dan was riding in the back seat of his friend's small, two-door car. On the way to the concert the driver lost control of the car and came to rest in a 12-foot culvert. Dan awoke from a coma 14 days later and discovered he had broken his back in three places, had a broken collarbone, and had received 180 stitches in his head. He would spend the best part of the next few months flat on his back and did not regain complete mobility for almost a year. One day, a year later, Dan was walking along the road when some friends drove up in a small, two-door car. "Hey Dan, jump in, we'll give you a ride," one of them shouted. As Dan gazed at the car and noticed that the only available space was in the back seat, he felt a sudden rush of anxiety. He realized he wanted no part of that small car and insisted that he was walking for the exercise. As the car pulled away Dan noticed his anxiety begin to diminish. Dan's small car phobia would last for years. Still today Dan drives a pickup truck and prefers to not ride in small cars when it can be avoided.

It has been suggested that phobias have their origin in *Classical Conditioning* and are strengthened and/or maintained through *Operant Conditioning*. From the above example:

1. What is the *unconditioned stimulus*? _____

2. What is the *unconditioned response*? _____

3. What was the *neutral stimulus*? _____

4. What was the *conditioned stimulus*? _____

5. What was the *conditioned response*? _____

6. Describe how *extinction* could be used to help reduce Dan's anxiety in response to small cars.

_____

_____

_____

_____

7. Dan noticed the anxiety begin to diminish as the car moved away. The next time he was confronted with a similar situation it became more likely he would perform a similar escape/avoidance strategy. When the consequence of a behavior increases the likelihood of repeating that behavior in future, similar situations, the consequence is known as a reinforcer. In this case, is this a positive or a negative reinforcer? _____.

SHEEP NO MORE

The text presents an example where classical conditioning is used to solve a problem for sheep ranchers. Coyotes were killing the rancher's sheep, and eating up their profits. One solution would be to kill the coyotes. Another solution might save the sheep and the coyotes. The coyotes were tricked into eating poisoned sheep and became very sick. The acquired taste aversion resulted in the experienced coyotes no longer eating sheep. The classical conditioning issues of *generalization* and *discrimination* will be important if the ultimate goal is preserving both animals.

1. While we hope the coyote will _____ the aversion to other sheep, we also hope the coyote will _____ between sheep and other sources of food.

2. Sometimes we think of short-term solutions and sometimes we are looking for long-term solutions. Can you think of any problem that the ranchers may have, given the above strategy, regarding a long-term solution to protect the sheep from coyotes?

_____

_____

_____

SEYMORE LOVES ATTENTION

I have a big white furry cat named Seymour. I'm not sure who trained whom, but Seymour one day licked my hand and, having gotten my attention, received a petting on his head. When I stopped petting him, he licked my hand again, which resulted in me petting him again. Now, every time Seymour wants to be petted, he licks my hand.

1.   Depending on your perspective (who trained whom), the fact that a behavior resulted in a satisfactory consequence and a tendency to repeat the behavior would indicate that at least one of us was receiving
_____   _____.

WHAT A WAY TO START A DAY

Upon awakening one morning I found myself running late. As I showered and dressed, I thought about several things. First, I had stressed to my students the importance of arriving to class on time. What kind of message would I send to the students if I were late for class? Then, I began to think about the various routes from my home to school and the fastest path from the parking lot to the classroom. Also, there were stoplights to deal with, but a little luck and a little extra gas peddle if the light turned yellow would save me time. I wished I had stopped for gas the day before. I was low and anxious that I may not have enough. On the way out the door I remembered I needed to let the dogs out. Penny wanted to play beyond the time I was able to let her that day, and when I called her she did not come. After several attempts I decided to rattle the box that contained her puppy treats. On hearing that sound, Penny came running to the house. I gave her a treat and finally got on my way.

1.   According to Tolman, when I rehearsed various ways to get from one place to another, I was probably using
_____.

2.   My concern for "practicing what I preach" regarding being to class on time would be a good example of what Bandura calls _____.

3.   If, on the way to school, I encounter a light turning yellow and respond by speeding up a little in order to avoid losing a couple of minutes stopped at that light, the light served as a _____ stimulus.

4.   If I discover that I need to stop at the gas station on the way to school I will probably not make it to class on time. The next time I am driving home with plenty of time and a low gas gauge, I will not just drive by the gas station. In this case, the consequence of driving past the gas station yesterday afternoon resulted in anxiety and a reduction in a particular behavior. I am experiencing the effects of a _____.

5.   When I stop at the gas station in the afternoon, the anxiety related to an insufficient fuel supply the next morning is removed. This is an example of _____ reinforcement.

6.   Although she has never told me, I assume that the sound of the treats rattling in the box have been associated with food enough times that the sound alone now sparks a physiological change in Penny that we humans would call hunger. In this case, we would call the sound of the treats rattling in the box a
_____ stimulus.

7.   When Penny finally answered my calls I gave her one of the treats. She really likes those treats. Eventually, Penny got to the point where she made such a response each time I called her. In this case, receiving the treat became a _____ reinforcer.

FROM THEORY TO PRACTICE

Comparative Psychology

Learning theory has been evolving for centuries. It began to mature as an individual discipline in psychology at a time when the great thinkers of the world were debating the essence of being human. Could it be true that we evolved from the apes, as many interpreted Darwin to be suggesting? This was, at the time, a very difficult concept to consider. It challenged the very essence of our special place in nature. Learning theory, having a heritage of animal research, became a part of that controversy. How could we know something about human beings by studying dogs? A common reaction to learning theory was, "We humans are much more than other animals and we should not be reduced to such a place in nature." What do you think? Can we learn about human learning by studying dogs, rats and pigeons, or is science taking too much of an inferential leap? Consider this issue and write your thoughts in the space below.

_____
_____
_____
_____
_____

Does Learning Theory Take Away Our Minds?

Another criticism put forth by opponents of learning theory is that it is too mechanistic. It is as if learning theory not only thinks of humans as just another of the lower animals, but it thinks of our behavior as mindlessly vulnerable to the whims of the environment. Watson suggested he could "build to order" an infant's future avocation if he had control of that infant's environment. Skinner suggested we could create a utopian society if we could have control over the social environment. Many took offense to such a loss of control over one's own destiny. Behavior therapy (behavioral modification) has been criticized in light of the same basic issue. Behavior therapy would suggest that we can effect important changes in pathology simply by adjusting the patient's environment, and that we really do not need to waste time trying to understand emotions or other mind-based aspects of behavior. Can we really treat a human problem as if we are training a dog to fetch a ball? What do you think, and why?

_____
_____
_____
_____
_____
_____
_____

Ready for a Change?

Do you smoke cigarettes, chew your fingernails, or have some other behavior you would like to change? Could Learning Theory help you? The following exercise will help you to solidify your knowledge of Learning Theory concepts by giving you the opportunity to apply the concepts to your life. In addition to enhancing your knowledge, you may even finally take control of a behavior that you have wanted to change for a long time. Follow the steps listed in this exercise as you design your personal *Behavior Modification Program*. Your text may serve as an important resource as you do this exercise. The chapter on therapy will talk more about behavior modification while the chapters on Motivation and Emotion, States of Consciousness, and Biology and Behavior may help you understand some of the ways we respond to changes in our behavior. If you are planning to address a problem such as weight control or even cigarette smoking, you should talk to your doctor first.

I.   Write the behavior you want to change. Describe the behavior in objective and measurable terms.

_____
_____

II.   List your behavioral goals; what will your behavior look like when the behavior modification program is successfully completed. Again, make your descriptions objective and measurable.

a)   _____
_____
_____

b) _____

_____

_____

c) _____

_____

_____

III Functional Analysis

a) List the events that occur in your environment and that precede your problem behavior:

_____

_____

_____

_____

b) List the consequences you experience as a function of your problem behavior. Some of these consequences may be classified as reinforcers and some may be classified as punishers. However, the reinforcers must currently be stronger than the punishers. Otherwise, by definition, you would already have reduced or stopped your behavior.

_____

_____

_____

_____

IV. Behavior Change Plan: Based on your knowledge of learning theory (positive reinforcement, negative reinforcement, extinction, punishment, stimulus, response, etc.), design a behavior change program that will help you meet the goals you set forth in Section II above. Define your actions in behavioral terms while you set daily change goals and determine consequences for your behavior change efforts.

_____

_____

_____

_____

_____

_____

_____

_____

_____

_____

_____

_____

COMPREHENSIVE PRACTICE TEST

1. Learning is defined as a relatively permanent change in behavior, capability, or attitude as a result of _____, while not attributable to illness, injury, or maturation.
    a) cognition
    b) experience
    c) internal factors
    d) emotions

2. Classical conditioning is to _____ as operant conditioning is to _____:
   a) stimulus associations; unconscious motivation
   b) behavior/consequence associations; stimulus associations
   c) unconscious motivation; reflex responses
   d) stimulus associations; behavior/consequence associations

3. Pavlov would be most associated with:
   a) classical conditioning
   b) operant conditioning
   c) cognitive conditioning
   d) law of effect

4. Which of the following offered parenting advice that may be considered today to be rather unemotional or cold?
   a) Bandura
   b) Pavlov
   c) Skinner
   d) Watson

5. This theorist is famous in learning theory although he seemed to cause a lot of controversy. He believed freedom was a myth and that we could create a better society if we systematically shaped the behavior of its members. His name is:
   a) Bandura
   b) Watson
   c) Tolman
   d) Skinner

6. Which of the following theorists talked about the concepts of latent learning and cognitive mapping?
   a) Pavlov
   b) Kohler
   c) Tolman
   d) Skinner

7. This theorist researched observational learning and the effects of modeling on behavior.
   a) Kohler
   b) Pavlov
   c) Bandura
   d) Skinner

8. Which of the following would be most associated with research on reinforcement theory?
   a) Pavlov
   b) Bandura
   c) Tolman
   d) Skinner

9. An unconditioned response (UR) is one that will occur:
   a) without a stimulus
   b) without previous learning
   c) only after the presentation of the CS
   d) only after a number of conditioning trials

10. The concept below that is associated with cognitive learning is:
    a) negative reinforcement
    b) positive reinforcement
    c) latent learning
    d) none of these are used to support cognitive learning

11. If we were doing research in classical conditioning (e.g., Pavlov's dogs), the dependent variable would be:
    a) the conditioned stimulus
    b) whether or not the unconditioned stimulus is presented
    c) the strength of the conditioned stimulus
    d) the number of unreinforced trials before extinction occurs

12. Jim has been "clean and sober" since he completed an alcohol treatment program. He was told to stay away from all of his old drinking places. The danger is that he may start drinking again as a function of the conditioned stimuli in that environment. This sounds like a good practical example of _____ in classical conditioning.
    a) stimulus generalization
    b) observational learning
    c) spontaneous recovery
    d) extinction

13. The seductive nature of a slot machine in a gambling casino may best be explained by:
    a) negative reinforcement
    b) the fixed interval schedule of reinforcement
    c) continuous reinforcement
    d) the variable ratio schedule of reinforcement

14. For Little Albert, the conditioned stimulus was:
    a) the white rat
    b) a loud noise
    c) Watson
    d) based on negative reinforcement

15. Positive reinforcement increases behavior while negative reinforcement:
    a) decreases behavior
    b) has no effect on behavior
    c) removes a behavior
    d) also increases behavior

16. In avoidance learning, it appears that the fear stimulus is initiated through _____ conditioning and maintained or strengthened through _____ conditioning.
   a) classical; operant
   b) operant; operant
   c) operant; classical
   d) classical; classical

17. A good example of the fixed interval schedule of reinforcement is:
   a) factory piece work
   b) a child's weekly allowance
   c) a slot machine
   d) turning on a light switch

18. A consequence that decreases the likelihood of the behavior that preceded it is called:
   a) negative reinforcement
   b) a latent consequence
   c) punishment
   d) a learned helplessness stimulus

19. In classical conditioning, extinction refers to:
   a) removing a reinforcer
   b) continuing to present the conditioned stimulus without the unconditioned stimulus
   c) presenting a punisher
   d) repeatedly presenting the unconditioned stimulus without the conditioned stimulus

20. In operant conditioning, extinction refers to:
   a) removing the reinforcer
   b) continuing to present the conditioned stimulus without the unconditioned stimulus
   c) presenting a punisher
   d) presenting the unconditioned stimulus without the conditioned stimulus

21. In classical conditioning, discrimination refers to:
   a) responding to a similar but different stimulus
   b) not responding to the conditioned stimulus
   c) not responding to a similar but different stimulus
   d) responding only to the unconditioned stimulus

22. The number of pairings of the unconditioned and the conditioned stimulus, and the intensity of the unconditioned stimulus are two factors that influence:
   a) operant conditioning
   b) observational learning
   c) classical conditioning
   d) cognitive maps

23. The magnitude of reinforcement and the immediacy of reinforcement are two factors that influence:
   a) operant conditioning
   b) observational learning
   c) classical conditioning
   d) cognitive maps

24. In _____ learning, a response which _____ a negative reinforcer is learned.
   a) escape; prevents the occurrence of
   b) escape; terminates
   c) avoidance; terminates
   d) avoidance; initiates

25. The nice thing about continuous reinforcement is that it leaves a behavior very resistant to extinction.
   a) True
   b) False

26. A good example of primary reinforcement would be _____, while a good example of secondary reinforcement would be _____.
   a) money; cashier's check
   b) food; water
   c) food; money
   d) money; food

27. Ms. Doe is a new teacher and is having a difficult time with her misbehaving second graders. When the principal enters the room, the children behave like perfect angels. In this case, the principal may be thought of as a(n):
   a) positive reinforcer
   b) unconditioned stimulus
   c) shaping reinforcer
   d) discriminative stimulus

28. The idea that the connection between a stimulus and a response will be strengthened if followed by a satisfying consequence, and weakened if followed by discomfort became known as:
   a) Skinner's Law of Consequences
   b) Bandura's Law of Modeling
   c) Pavlov's Law of Association
   d) Thorndike's Law of Effect

29. The real life examples of drug tolerance and taste aversion were described in the book in reference to:
   a) operant conditioning
   b) classical conditioning
   c) observational learning
   d) cognitive mapping

30. If you train a dog to respond to Middle C on the piano and discover that the dog also responds to D, you might assume that _____ has occurred.
    a) discrimination
    b) latent learning
    c) generalization
    d) extinction

31. My cat quickly learned the association between the sound of a can opener and his favorite food. One day I noticed that the cat started making his hungry noises not in response to the can opener, but to the sound the cat food cabinet door makes when I open it. It appears as if _____ has taken place.
    a) discrimination
    b) higher-order conditioning
    c) spontaneous recovery
    d) an unconditioned response

32. A baseball player accidentally laced his right shoe incorrectly prior to a big game. He took the field to pitch the best game of his career. From that day forward, he maintained the belief that he must lace his right shoe in the same incorrect manner before each game because doing so would help him to pitch better. This is an example of:
    a) generalization
    b) latent learning
    c) superstition
    d) spontaneous recovery

ANSWER KEY

OMSE # 1: CLASSICAL CONDITIONING

A. Quick Quiz		B. Matching
1. d	9. c	1. d
2. drug tolerance	10. discrimination	2. e
3. neutral	11. a. faithful master; b. sound of car; c. excitement	3. f
4. unconditioned	12. c	4. g
5. conditioned	13. spontaneous recovery	5. c
6. a	14. c	6. a
7. c	15. a	7. b
8. c		

C. Complete The Diagram

1. Before Conditioning	2. During Conditioning	3. After Conditioning	4. Process Summary:
NS = music	NS = music	CS = music	CS = music
US = passion	US = passion	CR = floating on air sensation	US = passion
UR = floating on air sensation	UR = floating on air sensation		CR/UR = floating on air sensation

OMSE # 2: OPERANT CONDITIONING

A. Quick Quiz		B. Matching		C. Complete the Diagram
1. false	9. variable ratio	1. f	6. i	1. negative
2. c	10. false	2. j	7. d	2. reward
3. biofeedback	11. punishment	3. a	8. e	3. negative reinforcer
4. true	12. d	4. b	9. g	4. biological drive
5. c	13. a	5. c	10. h	5. continuous
6. continuous	14. d			6. variable-ratio
7. false	15. immediacy			7. fixed-interval
8. b				8. set number of behaviors
				9. variable passage of time

OMSE # 3: COGNITIVE LEARNING

A. QUICK QUIZ	B. MATCHING	C. COMPLETE THE DIAGRAM
1. cognitive processes	1. d	1. insight; Kohler
2. c	2. e	2. latent learning; Tolman
3. b	3. a	3. modeling; Bandura
4. model	4. b	
5. d	5. c	
6. cognitive map		
7. latent learning		

FROM THE LABORATORY TO REAL LIFE

Small Car Phobia

1. the car accident/dangerous situation
2. anxiety
3. the car
4. the car
5. anxiety
6. ride in a small car and do not get injured
7. negative

Sheep No More

1. generalize; discriminate
2. Since coyotes can not communicate to one another the way people do, the ranchers will need to ensure that every coyote gets a taste of the tainted sheep (unconditioned stimulus). Also, since coyotes do not have history books, the ranchers will need to reintroduce the poisoned sheep (US) to every successive generation.

Seymour Loves Attention

1. positive reinforcement

What a Way to Start a Day

1. cognitive maps
2. modeling
3. discriminative stimulus
4. punishment
5. negative
6. conditioned
7. positive

Comprehensive Practice Exam

1. b	5. d	9. b	13. d	17. b	21. c	25. false	29. b
2. d	6. c	10. c	14. a	18. c	22. c	26. c	30. c
3. a	7. c	11. c	15. d	19. b	23. a	27. d	31. b
4. d	8. d	12. c	16. a	20. a	24. b	28. d	32. c

MEMORY

Memory is defined as the storehouse of everything we know. It is the mental diary of all of our experiences and all that we have learned.

CHAPTER OVERVIEW

My earliest memory is not a particularly good one. I was about three years old and was being bitten by a dog. I also remember that during my first day of preschool, some bully took away my crayons. I remember that in the second grade I had an enormous crush on a girl named Nancy. I can still see her face as I write this passage. I remember as if it were yesterday the day John F. Kennedy was shot. Our teacher had tears in her eyes as she told us the news. Soon after the announcement school was let out for that and the following day. I remember it was a long, sad weekend. When I was in high school, I could recite from memory all of the lyrics to all of the Beatles songs, but I could not remember how to do my algebra problems! One time I studied for a history test by turning the information into a song—it worked! I have vivid memories of childhood and adolescence, but I cannot remember where I left my car keys last night! I can talk for a couple of hours straight about the central nervous system without relying on notes, and then forget to make a simple phone call! I have often been fascinated, and sometimes frustrated with memory—how does it work and where does it live in the brain? Why do we remember some things and not others? The answers to these questions and more are contained in Chapter 6. By understanding the nature and processes of memory, you will have the opportunity to improve your ability to retain and recall information. If you take advantage of this opportunity, you will find that school, and life after school, will be more rewarding.

This chapter will help you gain a more practiced and functional understanding of memory as it is presented in the text. The materials are divided into three OMSE sections: 1) remembering and forgetting, 2) the nature of remembering and forgetting, and retrieval factors, and 3) biology and memory improvement. You will discover the complex processes involved with memory and how it will probably prove to be a whole-brain process. You will also discover some ways to improve your memory.

By completing the exercises provided, you should gain a thorough understanding of the information provided in your text. In other words, you should be better prepared for tests, quizzes, class participation, and life itself.

TIMELINE

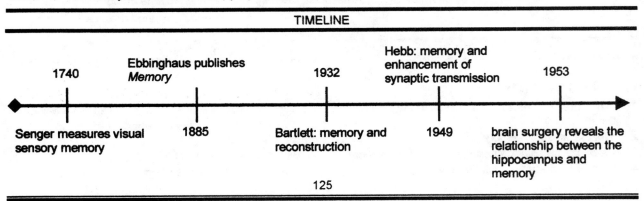

CHAPTER OUTLINE

Remembering

The Three Processes in Memory: Encoding, Storage, and Retrieval

The Three Memory Systems: The Long and the Short of It

The Levels-of-Processing Model: Another View of Memory

Measuring Memory

Three Methods of Measuring Memory

Hermann Ebbinghaus and the First Experimental Studies on Learning and Memory

Forgetting

The Causes of Forgetting

Prospective Forgetting: Forgetting to Remember

The Nature of Remembering and Forgetting

Memory as a Permanent Record: The Videocassette Recorder Analogy

Memory as a Reconstruction: Partly Fact and Partly Fiction

Eyewitness Testimony: Is It Accurate?

Recovering Repressed Memories: A Controversy

Unusual Memory Phenomena

Memory and Culture

Factors Influencing Retrieval

The Serial Position Effect: To Be Remembered, Be First or Last, But Not in the Middle

Environmental Context and Memory

The State-Dependent Memory Effect

Stress, Anxiety, and Memory: Relax and Remember

Biology and Memory

Brain Damage: A Clue to Memory Formation

Neuronal Changes in Memory: Brain Work

Hormones and Memory

Improving Memory

Study Habits That Aid Memory

Apply It! Improving Memory with Mnemonic Devices

Thinking Critically

Chapter Summary and Review

KEY TERMS

Remembering
encoding
storage
consolidation
retrieval
sensory memory
short-term memory
displacement
rehearsal
long-term memory
elaborate rehearsal
priming
episodic memory

semantic memory
nondeclarative memory
declarative memory
levels-of-processing model
Measuring Memory
recall
retrieval cue
recognition
relearning method
savings score
nonsense syllable
Forgetting
encoding failure

consolidation failure
retrograde amnesia
decay theory
interference
motivated forgetting
repression
amnesia
prospective forgetting
The Nature of Remembering and Forgetting
reconstruction
schemas
infantile amnesia
flashbulb memory

eidetic imagery
Factors Influencing Retrieval
serial position effect
primacy effect
recency effect
state-dependent memory effect
Biology and Memory
anterograde amnesia
hippocampus
long-term potentiation
Improving Memory
overlearning
massed practice

OMSE # 1: REMEMBERING AND FORGETTING

LEARNING OBJECTIVES

1. What three processes are involved in the act of remembering?
2. What is sensory memory?
3. What are the characteristics of short-term memory?
4. What is long-term memory, and what are its subsystems?

5. What are the three methods of measuring retention?
6. What was Ebbinghaus's major contribution to psychology?
7. What are six causes of forgetting?
8. What is interference, and how can it be minimized?

LEARNING MASTERY SCORECARD: Update your score card as you work through the various sections of the chapter. First, find and define key terms and concepts included in each section and note the page number(s) from the text that contain important references to the material. Next, gain a practical understanding of the concepts by considering the Laboratory to Life scenarios and thinking of at least one original example of how the concept might apply in real life. Complete the *Objective-Mastery Self-Evaluation* (OMSE) exercises for this section and record your scores. Revisit the exercises, recording your score and the date completed until you have attained mastery (100%). Finally, decide how you would prepare a lecture on each objective using the template provided, outline the lecture, and practice presenting it. Keep an honest tally of your achievements and, when finished, you will have developed learning mastery through elaborate rehearsal.

Key Term	Page #	Key Term	Page #	Key Term	Page #
encoding	_____	episodic memory	_____	nonsense syllable	_____
storage	_____	semantic memory	_____	encoding failure	_____
consolidation	_____	nondeclarative memory	_____	consolidation failure	_____
retrieval	_____	declarative memory	_____	retrograde amnesia	_____
sensory memory	_____	levels-of-processing model	_____	decay theory	_____
short-term memory	_____	recall	_____	interference	_____
displacement	_____	retrieval cue	_____	motivated forgetting	_____
rehearsal	_____	recognition	_____	repression	_____
long-term memory	_____	relearning method	_____	amnesia	_____
elaborate rehearsal	_____	savings score	_____	prospective forgetting	_____
priming	_____				

Quick Quiz

Date	Score	Date	Score	Date	Score
_/_/_	_____	_/_/_	_____	_/_/_	_____
_/_/_	_____	_/_/_	_____	_/_/_	100%

Elaborate Rehearsal

Lecture Preparation	Completion Date
Key Terms, Persons, & Concepts	_/_/_
Learning Objectives	_/_/_
Lecture Notes	_/_/_

A. QUICK QUIZ

1. The first step in the memory process is:
    a) storage
    b) encoding
    c) retrieval
    d) rehearsal

2. The storage capacity of our sensory memory seems to be very small, which is why we forget this information very quickly.
    a) True
    b) False

3. Short-term memory seems to have a limited life span – less than 30 seconds. If you want to keep a phone number in short-term memory you will need to use _____, such as repeating the number several times.

4. Long-term memory has a(n) _____ storage capacity.
    a) limited
    b) restricted
    c) intermediate
    d) unlimited

5. Another name for short-term memory is working memory.
    a) True
    b) False

6. Usually when people talk about memory they are talking about _____ term memory.

7. A good example of _____ memory would be Jim thinking back with fond memories of his first kiss.
   a) episodic
   b) implicit
   c) semantic
   d) nondeclarative

8. Jan took dance lessons when she was a young girl. One day she surprised herself and everyone else with her skills on the dance floor. This was probably due to her explicit memory.
   a) True
   b) False

9. When you take a test in your psychology class, you may be asked to list the names of famous psychologists and their major contributions to psychology. For this task you would be using _____ memory.

10. A fill-in the blank test question would require _____ while a multiple-choice question would rely on _____.
   a) recognition; sensory cues
   b) recall; recognition
   c) recall; semantic cues
   d) recognition; recall

11. Jim found himself in trouble as he sat for his physics test. He could not remember the formulas presented in class. As he pondered his dilemma he realized that he should have been paying more attention to the teacher that day instead of trying to write his English paper. His current memory problem is probably due to _____.
   a) consolidation failure
   b) decay
   c) encoding failure
   d) motivated forgetting

12. According to the book, it appears that decay is most responsible for the loss of long-term memory.
   a) True
   b) False

13. When April moved to a new town she had problems for a long time remembering her new zip code. Every time she tried to think of her new zip code, her prior zip code seemed to interfere with her recall. This is probably an example of _____ interference.

14. The patient cannot remember the period of his life ranging from ages five through seven. When examined by a doctor there was no physical cause identified for this amnesia. There was also no history of injury or other trauma at that or any other age. Freud would probably call this a case of _____.

15. Alice seems to find herself with a lot of personal stress related to forgetting to carry out basic tasks such as paying bills or filling her gas tank. The book would say these were good examples of prospective forgetting.
   a) True
   b) False

B. MATCHING

_____	1. also called implicit memory	a) sensory memory
_____	2. the day you got your driver's license	b) short-term memory
_____	3. also called working memory	c) long-term memory
_____	4. an orange is a kind of a fruit	d) nondeclarative memory
_____	5. sensory information	e) declarative memory
_____	6. also called explicit memory	f) episodic memory
_____	7. loss through consolidation failure	g) semantic memory

Now what was that I was supposed to remember?
Your memory cannot serve you well if you don't treat it well. For example, marijuana can interfere with the ability to form new memories. Alcohol and other drugs can lead to the loss of old memories and interfere with the ability to form new memories. Take care of your memories—they define you and your life.

C. COMPLETE THE DIAGRAM

Rehearsal

Sensory Input

a.

c.

d.

g.

e.

f.

b.

Forgetting

Forgetting

a. _____
b. _____
c. _____
d. _____
e. _____
f. _____
g. _____

PREPARE A LECTURE: This activity is designed to offer you an opportunity to take advantage of a valuable mode of learning, elaborate rehearsal. Once you have finished the OMSE section, write a lecture using the instructional guide provided below. After your lecture is prepared, you can enhance your learning by writing a quiz covering the material. Now it is time to find some willing and inquisitive audience members. Your roommates or family may be a great place to start. Present them the lecture as if you are teaching a class. Remember to ask for questions and give your students the quiz following the lecture. This exercise can also serve to turn a *study-buddy* group into a very productive way to prepare for the test. Each member of the group can take different OMSE sections for their lecture/teacher role while the rest of the group serves as the class.

I. Key Terms, Names, Dates, and Concepts you will include in this lecture:

1. _____
2. _____
3. _____
4. _____
5. _____
6. _____
7. _____
8. _____
9. _____
10. _____
11. _____
12. _____

II. Learning Objectives (what do you want the student to know and be able to do as a result of your lecture):

1. _____
2. _____
3. _____
4. _____
5. _____

III. Lecture Notes (notes should be brief cues and serve as a guide).

Major topic #1: _____
   Sub-topics and notes: _____
   _____
   _____
   _____

Major topic #2: _____
   Sub-topics and notes: _____
   _____
   _____
   _____

Major topic #3: _____
   Sub-topics and notes: _____
   _____
   _____
   _____

OMSE # 2: THE NATURE OF REMEMBERING AND FORGETTING, AND FACTORS OF RETRIEVAL

LEARNING OBJECTIVES

1. What is meant by the statement, "Memory is reconstructive in nature"?
2. What is Bartlett's contribution to our understanding of memory?
3. What are schemas, and how do they affect memory?
4. What conditions reduce the reliability of eyewitness memory?
5. Does hypnosis improve the memory of eyewitnesses?
6. What is the controversy over the therapy used to recover repressed memories of childhood sexual abuse?
7. What is the serial position effect?
8. How does environmental context affect memory?
9. What is the state-dependent memory effect?

LEARNING MASTERY SCORECARD: Update your score card as you work through the various sections of the chapter. First, find and define key terms and concepts included in each section and note the page number(s) from the text that contain important references to the material. Next, gain a practical understanding of the concepts by considering the Laboratory to Life scenarios and thinking of at least one original example of how the concept might apply in real life. Complete the *Objective-Mastery Self-Evaluation* (OMSE) exercises for this section and record your scores. Revisit the exercises, recording your score and the date completed until you have attained mastery (100%). Finally, decide how you would prepare a lecture on each objective using the template provided, outline the lecture, and practice presenting it. Keep an honest tally of your achievements and, when finished, you will have developed learning mastery through elaborate rehearsal.

Key Term	Page #	Key Term	Page #	Key Term	Page #
reconstruction	_____	flashbulb memory	_____	primacy effect	_____
schemas		eidetic imagery		recency effect	
infantile amnesia	_____	serial position effect	_____	state-dependent memory effect	_____

Quick Quiz

Date	Score	Date	Score	Date	Score
_/_/_	_____	_/_/_	_____	_/_/_	_____
_/_/_	_____	_/_/_	_____	_/_/_	100%

Elaborate Rehearsal

Lecture Preparation	Completion Date
Key Terms, Persons, & Concepts	_/_/_
Learning Objectives	_/_/_
Lecture Notes	_/_/_

A. QUICK QUIZ

1. Several studies have provided solid proof that human memory works exactly like a videocassette recorder.
   a) True
   b) False

2. According to researcher, Elizabeth Loftus, memory is pieced together, partly from truth and partly from fiction.
   a) True
   b) False

3. When a memory is pieced together from a few highlights using information that may or may not be accurate, the process is called:
   a) partial memory
   b) schematic memory
   c) retrograde memory
   d) reconstruction

4. You have developed certain frameworks of knowledge and assumptions about people, places, and events through which you assimilate new information and experience. Bartlett called these integrated frameworks:
   a) reconstructive processes
   b) schemas
   c) memory accommodations
   d) consolidation frames

5. When we recount an event from memory, we all leave out some factual details and provide other details from our imaginations.
   a) True   b) False

6. Eyewitness testimony is highly subject to error.
   a) True   b) False

7. Eyewitnesses are more likely to identify the wrong person if the person is of a different race. Misidentifications are approximately _____ percent higher in cross-race than in same-race identifications.
   a) 20   c) 15
   b) 62   d) 45

8. Hypnotized eyewitnesses recall particulars of the event more accurately than eyewitnesses who have not been hypnotized.
   a) True   b) False

9. A patient referred for psychotherapy is found to be suffering from depression, low self-esteem, and perfectionistic tendencies. The therapist concludes that the patient was a victim of childhood sexual abuse, yet the patient has no recollection of any such abuse. After several sessions, the therapist finally helps the patient remember that she was repeatedly molested by her parents from the age of six months until she was two years old. Critics of repressed-memory therapy might suggest that this scenario is extremely unlikely based on _____ .
   a) flashbulb memory   c) infantile amnesia
   b) eidetic imagery   d) anterograde amnesia

10. In a list of items, at which position are the items most easily remembered?
    a) the beginning   c) the middle
    b) the end   d) there is no difference

11. While I was attending to my full-time graduate studies, I was also working full-time and trying to help my wife raise our two sons. My schedule was such that I averaged approximately four hours of sleep per night. I did most of my studying between wake-up at 4:30 A.M., and when I left for work at 7:30 A.M. I hate to admit it but I survived those years by drinking gallons of strong coffee. According to your text, I probably should have showed up for exams tired, full of caffeine and carrying a thermos of strong coffee to get me through. Actually, that is how I showed up for exams and I normally had good retention and recall. This is probably due to _____ .
    a) state-dependent memory   c) context-dependent memory
    b) the primacy effect   d) the recency effect

12. A person who has just suffered a tragedy, such as the loss of a loved one, is likely to perform less well on memory tests than are people who are not suffering from acute stress or general anxiety.
    a) True   b) False

B. MATCHING

_____	1. pieced together from highlights	a)	recency effect
_____	2. integrated frameworks of knowledge and assumptions	b)	state-dependent memory
_____	3. more information given more confidently with more inaccuracy	c)	primacy effect
_____	4. inability to recall events from early years	d)	flashbulb memory
_____	5. memory of a shocking, emotionally charged event	e)	reconstruction
_____	6. image remains for minutes after object is removed from view	f)	schemas
_____	7. I can more easily remember the beginning of the list	g)	hypnosis
_____	8. I can more easily remember the end of the list	h)	infantile amnesia
_____	9. same psychological and pharmacological conditions	i)	eidetic imagery

C. COMPLETE THE DIAGRAM: Write the name of the theorist or researcher in the space provided.

Theory/Research Finding	Theorist/Researcher
1. All memories are permanently preserved—some lying deep in the unconscious.	_____
2. Memory works like a tape recorder, leaving a permanent imprint.	_____
3. Memory is pieced together from highlights and may be accurate or not.	_____
4. Inaccuracies in memory reflect our schemas.	_____

PREPARE A LECTURE: This activity is designed to offer you an opportunity to take advantage of a valuable mode of learning, elaborate rehearsal. Once you have finished the OMSE section, write a lecture using the instructional guide provided below. After your lecture is prepared, you can enhance your learning by writing a quiz covering the material. Now it is time to find some willing and inquisitive audience members. Your roommates or family may be a great place to start. Present them the lecture as if you are teaching a class. Remember to ask for questions and give your students the quiz following the lecture. This exercise can also serve to turn a *study-buddy* group into a very productive way to prepare for the test. Each member of the group can take different OMSE sections for their lecture/teacher role while the rest of the group serves as the class.

I. Key Terms, Names, Dates, and Concepts you will include in this lecture:

1. _____
2. _____
3. _____
4. _____

5. _____
6. _____
7. _____
8. _____

9. _____
10. _____
11. _____
12. _____

II. Learning Objectives (what do you want the student to know and be able to do as a result of your lecture):

1. _____
2. _____
3. _____
4. _____
5. _____

III. Lecture Notes (notes should be brief cues and serve as a guide).

Major topic #1: _____

Sub-topics and notes: _____

_____

_____

Major topic #2: _____

Sub-topics and notes: _____

_____

_____

Major topic #3: _____

Sub-topics and notes: _____

_____

_____

_____

OMSE # 3: BIOLOGY AND MEMORY IMPROVEMENT

LEARNING OBJECTIVES

1. What role does the hippocampus and the rest of the hippocampal region play in episodic and semantic memory?
2. What is long-term potentiation, and why is it important?
3. How do memories of threatening situations, which elicit the "fight-or-flight response" compare with ordinary memories?
4. What are four study habits that can aid memory?
5. What is overlearning, and why is it important?

LEARNING MASTERY SCORECARD: Update your score card as you work through the various sections of the chapter. First, find and define key terms and concepts included in each section and note the page number(s) from the text that contain important references to the material. Next, gain a practical understanding of the concepts by considering the Laboratory to Life scenarios and thinking of at least one original example of how the concept might apply in real life. Complete the *Objective-Mastery Self-Evaluation* (OMSE) exercises for this section and record your scores. Revisit the exercises, recording your score and the date completed until you have attained mastery (100%). Finally, decide how you would prepare a lecture on each objective using the template provided, outline the lecture, and practice presenting it. Keep an honest tally of your achievements and, when finished, you will have developed learning mastery through elaborate rehearsal.

Key Term	Page #	Key Term	Page #	Key Term	Page #
hippocampal region	_____	hippocampus	_____	overlearning	_____
anterograde amnesia	_____	long-term potentiation	_____	massed practice	_____

Quick Quiz

Date	Score	Date	Score	Date	Score
_/_/_	_____	_/_/_	_____	_/_/_	_____
_/_/_	_____	_/_/_	_____	_/_/_	100%

Elaborate Rehearsal

Lecture Preparation	Completion Date
Key Terms, Persons, & Concepts	_/_/_
Learning Objectives	_/_/_
Lecture Notes	_/_/_

QUICK QUIZ

1. There is a story about a fencing accident where the opponent's foil (sword) entered the patient's nose and continued into the brain. From that point on, the patient could no longer form long-term memories of events that occurred following the accident. The patient is suffering from _____ amnesia.

2. The _____ appears to be very important in the formation of long-term memory. However, once memories are stored, this brain structure does not appear to be important for recall.
   a) amygdala
   b) frontal love
   c) hippocampus
   d) cerebellum

3. The study of brain injury patients has indicated there seems to be no difference between semantic and episodic memory, and memory loss.
   a) True
   b) False

4. One theory of memory suggests that neural transmission becomes more efficient along certain paths in the learning process. This increase in transmission efficiency is known as long-term _____.

5. When you study for your next psychology test, it is suggested that you study beyond the point that you think you pretty well know the material. In the same way that you still know the words of you favorite song from childhood, if you repeat or rehearse the material over and over you will probably remember it better. This is identified in the book as _____.

6. Pete started studying for his psychology test six nights ago, spending about 45 minutes per night each night. Jason studied for his test all in one night. He did a non-stop, six-hour study session. Pete ended up getting a better grade on the test than Jason. This is probably due to the fact that while Pete spaced his study over time, Jason did what is called _____ practice, a strategy that is usually not as effective as spaced study.
    a) crammed   c) massed
    b) elaborate   d) benign

7. Which has been shown to be a more effective study method, recitation or rereading?
    a) recitation   b) rereading

8. What did the book call strategies or memory devices used to help memory when other aids such as lists are not available? _____

9. The patient survived the delicate brain surgery and displayed no signs of personality change or loss of intelligence. It was days after the surgery when his doctors realized that he was unable to form long-term memories. He was, however, able to remember everything from before the surgery. After running several tests to confirm their suspicions, the neurosurgeons finally diagnosed their patient with _____ .
    a) anterograde amnesia   c) long-term potentiation
    b) retrograde amnesia   d) dissociative amnesia

B. MATCHING

_____	1. everything in its place	a)	rhyme
_____	2. one, two, buckle my shoe	b)	first letter technique
_____	3. i before e except after c	c)	method of loci
_____	4. 1 goes with 2, 2 goes with 3, 3 goes with 4...	d)	pegword
_____	5. every good boy deserves favors	e)	link method

C. COMPLETE THE DIAGRAM: Memory Enhancement Practice

Use the map of the United States below to help you memorize the following list. By using the method of loci, you will place each item in a different state. After a period of time see if you can remember the list.

List to Remember

encoding	repression
storage	reconstruction
retrieval	overlearning
sensory	primacy
rehearsal	recency
recognition	hippocampus
consolidation	anterograde

Did the method of loci work for you? _____

Can you think of a better mnemonic device for remembering the list? _____

Can you think of a practical First-Letter mnemonic for the list? _____

_____

_____

_____ .

PREPARE A LECTURE: This activity is designed to offer you an opportunity to take advantage of a valuable mode of learning, elaborate rehearsal. Once you have finished the OMSE section, write a lecture using the instructional guide provided below. After your lecture is prepared, you can enhance your learning by writing a quiz covering the material. Now it is time to find some willing and inquisitive audience members. Your roommates or family may be a great place to start. Present them the lecture as if you are teaching a class. Remember to ask for questions and give your students the quiz following the lecture. This exercise can also serve to turn a *study-buddy* group into a very productive way to prepare for the test. Each member of the group can take different OMSE sections for their lecture/teacher role while the rest of the group serves as the class.

I. Key Terms, Names, Dates, and Concepts you will include in this lecture:

1. _____
2. _____
3. _____
4. _____

5. _____
6. _____
7. _____
8. _____

9. _____
10. _____
11. _____
12. _____

II. Learning Objectives (what do you want the student to know and be able to do as a result of your lecture):

1. _____
2. _____
3. _____
4. _____
5. _____

III. Lecture Notes (notes should be brief cues and serve as a guide).

Major topic #1: _____
   Sub-topics and notes: _____
   _____
   _____
   _____

Major topic #2: _____
   Sub-topics and notes: _____
   _____
   _____
   _____

Major topic #3: _____
   Sub-topics and notes: _____
   _____
   _____
   _____

WHAT GRADE ARE YOU HOPING FOR? WHAT GRADE ARE YOU WORKING FOR?

The experts suggest that you study 3 hours per week for every lecture hour of class if you really want an "A."

Don't let your studying stack up. Prepare and follow a schedule. Study for a while every day for every class—keep up with your classes. Waiting until the last week or the last night before a test is called cramming, or massed practice. It is not effective and it is stressful.

Remember that stress adversely affects your ability to recall information.

KEY TERMS AND CONCEPTS EXERCISE

The key terms and concepts are presented in the order of their appearance in the text. Space is provided for you to include a personalized definition or example of each term or concept. As you encounter each term in the text, make a note of its meaning and context. Next, conceptualize the meaning of the term in a way that makes the most sense to you. You can also think about examples of the term from your own life. Write your definition and/or example in the space provided next to the word in this book. The KEY TERMS exercise utilizes a modified *T-note* design so that you can self-evaluate your mastery of the definitions. First lay a sheet of paper over the terms and concepts side of the page so that you only see the definitions. Read the definition and try to recall the term or concept. Mark all those you are unable to answer so you can restudy them. When you have learned all of the terms and concepts in this way, move the paper to the definition side so that you can see only the term or concept, try to recall both the textbook definition and your personal version. Repeat this until you know all of the terms and concepts by definition and personal understanding.

Encoding	Transforming information into a form that can be stored in short-term or long-term memory. Information that is not properly encoded may be difficult to retrieve, like forgetting a computer password makes it difficult to get to the data that is stored on the hard drive. _____
Storage	The act of maintaining information in memory. Understanding human memory is made simple by utilizing the analogous relationship to a computer. RAM (random access memory) is the working memory of a computer. Everything that is on the screen and quickly and easily available to you during a task is stored in RAM while you are working. Everything you are mentally attuned to while working on a cognitive task is stored in short-term memory. _____
Consolidation	A physiological change in the brain that must take place for encoded information to be stored in the brain. _____
Retrieval	The act of bringing to mind material that has been stored in memory. The retrieval process is not vastly different from that of calling up a file on your computer. As long as you encoded the information properly for storage, you should be able to retrieve it. _____
Sensory Memory	The memory system that holds information coming in through the senses for a period ranging from a fraction of a second to several seconds. _____
Short-Term Memory	The second stage of memory which holds about seven (a range of five to nine) items for less than 30 seconds without rehearsal; working memory; the mental workspace we use to keep in mind tasks we are thinking about at any given moment. _____
Displacement	The event that occurs when short-term memory is holding its maximum and each new item entering short-term memory pushes out an existing item. _____
Rehearsal	The act of purposely repeating information to maintain it in short-term memory or to transfer it to long-term memory. When you run into a friend and want to be sure to remember her or his phone number, you probably use rehearsal if you are without a pen or pencil. _____

Long-Term Memory	The relatively permanent memory system with a virtually unlimited capacity. Long-term memory might be likened to the hard drive on your computer. You can keep information stored there for the life of your computer. When you need to use that information, you bring it forward into RAM (like short-term or working memory) where you can use it for the task at hand.
Elaborate Rehearsal	A technique used to encode information into long-term memory by considering its meaning and associating it with other information already stored in long-term memory. _____
Priming	A situation in which an earlier encounter with a stimulus (a word, a picture, etc.) increases the speed or accuracy of naming that stimulus or a related stimulus at a later time. _____
Episodic Memory	The subpart of declarative memory that contains memories of personally experienced events.
Semantic Memory	The subpart of declarative memory that stores general knowledge; our mental encyclopedia or dictionary. _____
Nondeclarative Memory	The subsystem within long-term memory that consists of skills acquired through repetitive practice, habits, and simple classically conditioned responses; also called *implicit memory*.
Declarative Memory	The subsystem within long-term memory that stores facts, information, and personal life experiences; also called *explicit memory*. _____
Levels-Of-Processing Model	A single memory system model in which retention depends on how deeply information is processed. Deeper processing results in better retention. _____
Recall	A measure of retention that requires one to remember material with few or no retrieval cues, as in an essay test. _____
Retrieval Cue	Any stimulus or bit of information that aids in the retrieval of particular information from long-term memory. _____
Recognition	A measure of retention that requires one to identify material as familiar, or as having been encountered before. _____
Relearning Method	Measuring retention in terms of the percentage of time or learning trials saved in relearning material compared with the time required to learn it originally; also called the savings method.

Savings Score	The percentage of time or learning trials saved in relearning material over the amount of time or number of learning trials required for the original learning. _____
Nonsense Syllable	A consonant-vowel-consonant combination that does not spell a word; used to control for the meaningfulness of the material. _____
Encoding Failure	A cause of forgetting resulting from material never having been put into long-term memory. _____
Consolidation Failure	Any disruption in the consolidation process that prevents a permanent memory from forming. _____
Retrograde Amnesia	A loss of memory for events occurring for a period of time preceding a brain trauma that caused a loss of consciousness. _____
Decay Theory	A theory of forgetting that holds that the memory trace, if not used, disappears with the passage of time. _____
Interference	Memory loss that occurs because information or associations stored either before or after a given memory hinder our ability to remember it. _____
Motivated Forgetting	Forgetting through suppression or repression in order to protect oneself from material that is too painful, anxiety or guilt-producing, or otherwise unpleasant. _____
Repression	Removing from one's consciousness disturbing, guilt-provoking, or otherwise unpleasant memories so that one is no longer aware that a painful event occurred. _____
Amnesia	A partial or complete loss of memory resulting from brain trauma or psychological trauma. _____
Prospective Forgetting	Forgetting to carry out some action, such as mailing a letter. _____
Reconstruction	A memory that is not an exact replica of an event but has been pieced together from a few highlights using information that may or may not be accurate. _____
Schemas	The integrated frameworks of knowledge and assumptions we have about people, objects, and events, which affect how we encode and recall information. _____

Infantile Amnesia	The relative inability of older children and adults to recall events from the first few years of life.
Flashbulb Memory	An extremely vivid memory of the conditions surrounding one's first hearing the news of a surprising, shocking, or highly emotional event.
Eidetic Imagery	The ability to retain the image of a visual stimulus several minutes after it has been removed from view.
Serial Position Effect	Upon presentation of a list of items, the tendency to remember the beginning and ending items better than the middle items.
Primacy Effect	The tendency to recall the first items on a list more readily than the middle items.
Recency Effect	The tendency to recall the last items on a list more readily than those in the middle of the list.
State-Dependent Memory Effect	The tendency to recall information better if one is in the same pharmacological or psychological (mood) state as when the information was encoded.
Hippocampal Region	A part of the limbic system, which includes the hippocampus itself (primarily involved in the formation of episodic memories), and its underlying cortical areas (involved in the formation of semantic memories).
Anterograde Amnesia	The inability to form long-term memories of events occurring after a brain injury or brain surgery, although memories formed before the trauma are usually intact.
Hippocampus	The brain structure in the limbic system involved in the formation of memories of facts, information, and personal experiences.
Long-Term Potentiation	A long-lasting increase in the efficiency of neural transmission at the synapses.
Overlearning	Practicing or studying material beyond the point where it can be repeated once without error.
Massed Practice	One long learning practice session as opposed to spacing the learning in shorter practice sessions over an extended period.

FROM THE LABORATORY TO LIFE

I REMEMBER

I, like probably most people, sometimes reminisce, and writing the overview for this chapter sparked a stream of memories. I sure did have a crush on that girl that sat in front of me in the second grade! I remember being in Cub Scouts and selling candy bars. The pack had a deal where the scout who sold the most candy bars would win an official Cub Scout knife and I wanted that knife! I ended up selling more candy bars than all the other scouts combined. The first thing I did with the knife was cut my finger! I also remember when, in grade school, we were first taught to write instead of print. I thought it was pretty cool to be able to write and practiced my letters all the time. To this day my writing style reflects the same good and bad habits I acquired at that time. I also remember first learning to do the multiplication tables. We all had to go to the front of the class and repeat a series of products. I often tell my statistics students to relax—It really is simply a matter of adding, subtracting, multiplying, and dividing, just like you learned in grade school! I remember the day John F. Kennedy was shot as if it were yesterday—vivid memories of my friends and I as we pondered the implications of this event. Yet, try as I have, I can remember nothing about the last half-hour or so before the car accident I was involved in at sixteen. I took quite a hit on my head in that accident and have found myself suffering some strange memory problems since. I can talk for hours about psychology or other topics of interest, yet I probably go through a dozen pairs of sunglasses a year because I forget them when I take them off in a restaurant. In college, I discovered greater success when I spaced my study over time as opposed to cramming for an exam. I also seemed to have more success when I continued study beyond the point of having learned the material. One thing I did was to talk to myself about the information I needed for a test. Hearing myself say the information seemed to make it more available at test time. This seemed especially helpful when I had to take an essay or short answer test. One more thing, when I had to learn about memory in my psychology class, I realized that thinking about my own memories helped me remember more about memory!

1. When I remember things like the girl that sat in front of me in second grade or my experience in Cub Scouts, I am drawing on what the book identifies as _____ memory.

2. Writing and other well-practiced habits are examples of _____ memory.

3. My ability to do math or remember historical facts would be an example of _____ memory.

4. My vivid recollection of the Kennedy assassination is an example of _____ memory.

5. The loss of memory of the events just before my accident is an example of _____ amnesia.

6. When I assert that cramming does not work well for me when seeking to learn material, I am suggesting that _____ practice is better than _____ practice.

7. When I study material beyond the point of knowing it, I am practicing what is known as _____.

8. When I talk to myself about the material I am trying to learn I am practicing _____, a strategy that seems to be more effective than just rereading.

9. I have always seemed to like essay or short answer tests more than multiple-choice tests. In other words, I seem to be more comfortable with _____ questions than _____ questions.

10. If I decide to try hypnosis to recover the moments just before my accident, would the results of controlled experimentation with hypnosis be very encouraging for me? _____

FROM THEORY TO PRACTICE

HERE WE GO AGAIN!

Throughout this study guide, you are being exposed (perhaps to you it feels more like bombarded) to opportunities to practice elaborate rehearsal techniques. Your text identifies elaborate rehearsal as a technique used to encode information into long-term memory by considering its meaning and associating it with other information already stored in long-term memory. You have probably noticed that many of the *Quick Quiz* and *Practice Test* questions contain a sort of real-life flavor. Surely you have picked up on the effort put forward in the *Key Terms and Concepts* exercise to persuade you to include a personal example, definition, and/or meaning after the textbook definition. The *Lab to Life* and *Theory to Practice* sections contained in each chapter require a deeper understanding of the content and context of the materials contained therein. Finally, you are asked to prepare a lecture for every OMSE section contained in the study guide. Have you ever had a professor or teacher who seems to be reading the textbook to you? Pretty boring isn't it? Hopefully, you have had many other professors who include personal examples and interesting insights as they present the material in a way that you think, "Oh yeah, I get it." Those teachers have a genuine, deep understanding of the material that comes from elaborate rehearsal.

Using this chapter as your guide, record the theories, concepts, terms, and personal benefits of each section contained herein. Follow the example provided.

Section	Theories	Concepts	Terms	Benefits
Example	*3 memory system*	*semantic memory*	*relearning method*	*savings score*
Learning Objectives				
Score Card				
Quick Quiz				
Matching				
Diagram				
Lecture Prep				
Terms & Concepts				
Lab to Life				
Theory to Practice				

COMPREHENSIVE PRACTICE TEST

1. The first step in the memory process is known as _____ where information is transformed in a manner to be stored in short-term memory.
   a) retrieval
   b) storage
   c) encoding
   d) rehearsal

2. The process where information is stored in permanent memory involves a change in the brain's physiology. This is known as _____.
   a) consolidation
   b) transformation
   c) hippocampal transformation
   d) recalcitration

3. Who was the 16th president of the United States? In order to answer this question you must bring the needed information to your mind. This process is called _____.
   a) consolidation
   b) retrieval
   c) encoding
   d) transfer

4. You are at a party and meet someone you are really interested in. You get that person's phone number but have no way to write it down so you use the process of _____ in order to get it into memory.
   a) encoding
   b) latent retrieval
   c) storage
   d) recalcitration

5. The type of memory that seems to have unlimited storage capacity and duration is:
   a) sensory memory
   b) long-term memory
   c) short-term memory
   d) permanent memory

6. Remember that phone number you wanted to remember from question four? In order to keep it available in short-term memory you probably repeated it several times. This is known as _____.
   a) encoding
   b) transfer
   c) retrieval
   d) rehearsal

7. The kind of memory that seems to have a large capacity but a very short duration is known as _____ memory.
   a) short-term
   b) sensory
   c) long-term
   d) temporary

8. I was listening to the radio one day. The station had a contest to name a song and I knew the song! All I had to do was call in with the title. As I was listening to the number being announced someone called my name. I lost the number and who knows what kind of great prize! The loss of the number was probably due to a process called _____.
   a) displacement
   b) decay
   c) repression
   d) encoding

9. When I talk about short-term memory in class, I report it is also known as _____ memory.
   a) retrieval
   b) rehearsal
   c) working
   d) short-span

10. Long-term memory can hold only about 5 to 9 items at a time but seems to have unlimited duration.
    a) true
    b) false
    c) false, but is true if you change long-term to short-term

11. A friend is amazed at all the things I have to do all at the same time when I ride a motorcycle. He doesn't think he could remember all the necessary actions. My ability to do this is due to repetitive practice, to the point it is almost reflexive now. This is known as _____ memory.
    a) episodic
    b) explicit
    c) declarative
    d) nondeclarative

12. Implicit is to explicit as _____ is to _____:
    a) motor skills; facts and information
    b) episodic; semantic
    c) semantic; episodic
    d) facts and information; motor skills

13. My friends and I were talking about the times we had in high school. There were some great times, and some not so great times. At any rate we recounted those times as if they had happened yesterday. We were using what is identified in the book as _____ memory.
    a) semantic
    b) implicit
    c) personal
    d) episodic

14. _____ memory is used when you answer questions such as what is the capitol of California.
    a) episodic
    b) semantic
    c) geographic
    d) flashbulb

15. A good example of recall would be your ability to do well on a multiple-choice test.
    a) True
    b) False

16. A good example of recognition would be your ability to do well on a multiple-choice test.
    a) True
    c) False

17. Jim briefly scanned the assigned chapter but did not really study the material. He did very poorly on the test. One explanation for the poor test performance would be:
    a) encoding failure
    b) proactive failure
    c) retroactive failure
    d) test anxiety

18. Sigmund Freud did extensive research with memory. He used nonsense syllables to determine forgetting curves.
    a) True
    b) False
    c) false, but is true if you change Freud to Ebbinghaus

19. When I was 16-years-old, I was severely injured in a car accident and was unconscious for 14 days. I can remember nothing immediately preceding the accident. This is known as _____ amnesia.
    a) trauma
    b) retroactive
    c) proactive
    d) retrograde

20. Today, the most agreed upon theory of loss of long-term memory is the decay theory.
    a) True
    b) False

21. Proactive interference is to retroactive interference as _____ is to _____:
    a) new interferes with old; old interferes with new
    b) old interferes with new; new interferes with old

22. Freud talked about _____ where a person removes an unpleasant memory from consciousness.
    a) regression
    b) traumatic amnesia
    c) repression
    d) degeneration

23. According to the book, it has been proven that psychological amnesia does not exist.
    a) True
    b) False

24. While Penfield believed the reports of patients with temporal lobe stimulation were vivid memories, Neisser suggested that these reports were more like the contents of _____.
    a) flashbulb memories
    b) repression recall
    c) dreams
    d) desires

25. The idea of infantile amnesia is used to dispute the validity of our ability to recover repressed memories from early childhood.
    a) True
    b) False

26. The vivid memory I have of the day John Lennon was shot is known as _____ memory.
    a) historic
    b) flashbulb
    c) semantic
    d) retroactive

27. I remember my friends and I were so jealous of Alice in high school. It seems she could read a book once and remember every thing she read. It was like she had a photographic memory. The book called this _____.
    a) flashbulb memory
    b) eidetic imagery
    c) exact recall
    d) reflection

28. Godden and Baddeley have done research that suggests that context is important for _____ but not for _____.
    a) recognition; recall
    b) semantic information; episodic information
    c) recall; recognition
    d) episodic information; semantic information

29. People tend to remember the first and last items in a list more than the middle. This is called the_____.
    a) recency effect
    b) state dependent effect
    c) primary effect
    d) serial position effect

30. It appears that the _____ is important in the formation of declarative memory.
    a) hippocampus
    b) cerebellum
    c) amygdala
    d) temporal lobe

31. The patient suffered a serious brain injury that left him unable to form new memories. However, he can still remember events prior to the injury. He is suffering from _____ amnesia.
    a) retrograde
    b) state dependent
    c) anterograde
    d) retroactive

32. According to the book, overlearning is basically a waste of time. After you have gone over the material once, you will not experience increased benefit from further study.
    a) True   b) False

ANSWER KEYS

OMSE # 1 ANSWER KEY: REMEMBERING AND FORGETTING

A. Quick Quiz	B. Matching	C. Diagram
1. b	1. d	a) sensory memory
2. false	2. f	b) information loss
3. rehearsal	3. b	c) transfer
4. d	4. g	d) short-term memory
5. true	5. a	e) transfer
6. long	6. e	f) long-term memory
7. a	7. c	g) retrieval
8. false		
9. semantic		
10. b		
11. c		
12. false		
13. proactive		
14. repression		
15. true		

ANSWER KEY: OMSE # 2: THE NATURE OF REMEMBERING AND FORGETTING, AND FACTORS OF RETRIEVAL

A. Quick Quiz	B. Matching	C. Diagram
1. false	1. e	1. Freud
2. true	2. f	2. Penfield
3. d	3. g	3. Loftus
4. b	4. h	4. Bartlett
5. true	5. d	
6. true	6. i	
7. c	7. c	
8. false	8. a	
9. c	9. b	
10. b		
11. a		
12. true		

ANSWER KEY: OMSE # 3: BIOLOGY AND MEMORY IMPROVEMENT

A. Quick Quiz	B. Matching
1. anterograde	1. c
2. c	2. d
3. false	3. a
4. potentiation	4. e
5. overlearning	5. b
6. c	
7. a	
8. mnemonics	
9. a	

ANSWER KEY: LABORATORY TO REAL LIFE

1. episodic
2. implicit or nondeclarative
3. semantic
4. flashbulb
5. retrograde
6. spaced; massed
7. overlearning
8. recitation
9. recall; recognition
10. no

ANSWER KEY: COMPREHENSIVE PRACTICE EXAM

1) c	9) c	17) a	25) true
2) a	10) c	18) c	26) b
3) b	11) d	19) d	27) b
4) c	12) a	20) b	28) c
5) b	13) d	21) b	29) d
6) d	14) b	22) c	30) a
7) b	15) false	23) false	31) c
8) a	16) true	24) c	32) false

7

COGNITION AND LANGUAGE

Language is the mother of thought, not its handmaiden.
–Karl Kraus (1909)

CHAPTER OVERVIEW

As I write this overview, the regional lottery has risen to over 60 million dollars. I try to imagine winning that amount of money. I picture my new house on a private lake. Timber surrounds the property, which features a private road leading to the center of my 50 acre pasture surrounded by horse barns. The house is exactly how I want it—a large library and office fill the lower level of a log cabin design. Tall pine trees frame the yard and line a circular driveway. What an image! Unfortunately, it's only an image unless I win the 60 million dollars. How will I do that? What can I do to increase my chances? What numbers should I select for my ticket? Should I buy my ticket from a place that seems to have a lot of winners, or should I buy it from a place where there have been no winners in the hope that they are due for a winner. I could write numbers on scraps of paper and keep drawing samples to see which numbers come up most often. I could list a variety of special numbers—birth dates, anniversaries, or special events—and use those number combinations. I could check the latest winning numbers and avoid those numbers. I could decide that there is no real chance of winning and use the proposed ticket money to have a nice dinner. Decisions—decisions!

Everyday we are faced with problems and decisions. Everyday we use concepts and imagery to think through problems and make decisions in life. This chapter will help you gain a more practiced and functional understanding of the cognitive processes involved in such activities. In addition, we use language not only to communicate with others, but also to carry out thinking processes like the one discussed above (try to imagine my dream house without using language). This chapter will also help you understand the important role of language in thought and behavior. The materials are divided into two OMSE sections: 1) cognition, and 2) language. You will examine the many important ways we combine thought and language to produce the decisions and behaviors that shape our lives.

By completing the exercises provided, you should gain a thorough understanding of the information provided in your text. In other words, you should be better prepared for tests, quizzes, class participation, and life itself.

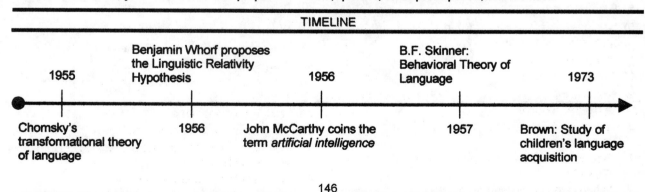

TIMELINE

| | Benjamin Whorf proposes the Linguistic Relativity Hypothesis | | B.F. Skinner: Behavioral Theory of Language | |
| 1955 | | 1956 | | 1973 |

Chomsky's transformational theory of language — 1956 — John McCarthy coins the term *artificial intelligence* — 1957 — Brown: Study of children's language acquisition

CHAPTER OUTLINE

Imagery and Concepts: Tools of Thinking

Imagery: Picture This—Elephants with Purple Polka Dots

Concepts: Our Mental Classification System (Is a Penguin a Bird?)

Deductive and Inductive Reasoning: Logical Thinking

Decision Making: Making Choices in Life

The Additive Strategy

Elimination by Aspects

Heuristics and Decision Making

Framing Alternatives to Influence Decisions

Problem Solving: Beyond Decision Making

Approaches to Problem Solving: Helpful Basic Techniques

Impediments to Problem Solving: Mental Stumbling Blocks

Artificial Intelligence

Language

The Structure of Language

Animal Language

Language and Thinking

Bilingualism

Apply It! Avoiding Bad Decisions

Thinking Critically

Chapter Summary and Review

KEY TERMS

Cognition and Language

cognition

Imagery and Concepts: Tools of Thinking

imagery

concept

formal concept

natural concept

prototype

exemplars

Deductive and Inductive Reasoning: Logical Thinking

reasoning

deductive reasoning

syllogism

inductive reasoning

Decision Making: Making Choices in Life

decision making

additive strategy heuristic

availability heuristic

representativeness heuristic

framing

Problem Solving: Beyond Decision Making

problem solving

trial and error

algorithm

working backwards

means–end analysis

analogy heuristic

functional fixedness

mental set

artificial intelligence

neural networks

Language

language

psycholinguistics

phonemes

morphemes

syntax

semantics

surface structure

deep structure

linguistic relativity hypothesis

OMSE # 1: COGNITION

LEARNING OBJECTIVES

1. What is meant by cognition, and what specific processes does it include?
2. What is imagery?
3. What is a concept?
4. What is the difference between a formal concept and a natural concept?
5. What is the difference between deductive and inductive reasoning?
6. How is the additive strategy used in decision making?
7. When is the elimination-by-aspects strategy most useful?

7. What is the availability heuristic?
8. What is the representativeness heuristic?
9. What is framing?
10. What are three basic approaches to problem solving?
11. What is an algorithm?
12. What are three heuristics used in problem solving?
13. How do functional fixedness and mental set impede problem solving?
14. What is artificial intelligence?

LEARNING MASTERY SCORECARD: Update your score card as you work through the various sections of the chapter. First, find and define key terms and concepts included in each section and note the page number(s) from the text that contain important references to the material. Next, gain a practical understanding of the concepts by considering the Laboratory to Life scenarios and thinking of at least one original example of how the concept might apply in real life. Complete the OMSE exercises for this section and record your scores. Revisit the exercises, recording your score and the date completed until you have attained mastery (100%). Finally, prepare a lecture on each objective using the template provided, outline the lecture, and practice presenting it. Keep an honest tally of your achievements and, when finished, you will have developed learning mastery through elaborate rehearsal.

Key Term	page #	Key Term	page #	Key Term	page #
cognition	_____	syllogism	_____	trial and error	_____
imagery	_____	inductive reasoning	_____	algorithm	_____
concept	_____	decision making	_____	working backwards	_____
formal concept	_____	additive strategy	_____	means–end analysis	_____
natural concept	_____	heuristic	_____	analogy heuristic	_____
prototype	_____	availability heuristic	_____	functional fixedness	_____
exemplars	_____	representativeness heuristic	_____	mental set	_____
reasoning	_____	framing	_____	artificial intelligence	_____
deductive reasoning	_____	problem solving	_____	neural networks	_____

Quick Quiz

Date	Score	Date	Score	Date	Score
__/__/__	_____	__/__/__	_____	__/__/__	_____
__/__/__	_____	__/__/__	_____	__/__/__	100%

Elaborate Rehearsal

Lecture Preparation	Completion Date
Key Terms, Persons, & Concepts	__/__/__
Learning Objectives	__/__/__
Lecture Notes	__/__/__

A. QUICK QUIZ

1. When the text talks about the mental processes involved in the acquisition, storage, retrieval, and use of knowledge, it is talking about _____.
   a) intelligence
   b) cognition
   c) thinking
   d) imagination

2. Processes such as concept formation, reasoning, decision making, and language are all aspects of what is known as _____.

3. _____ is defined as the representation of sensory experience in the mind.

4. Research would suggest that there are similar mental processes in imaging and perception.
   a) True
   b) False

5. Types of furniture, kinds of dairy products, types of transportation, and types of relationships are all examples of:
   a) images
   b) intelligences
   c) concepts
   d) perceptions

6. An elevator would be a good example of a prototype for transportation.
   a) True
   b) False

7. An example of the use of _____ may be in reference to our eating preferences. When I think of the concept of food I think of roast beef, fish, potatoes, green beans, and the like. If someone asks me to try something I have never heard of, I will probably use my concept of food to determine if the new offering will fit.
    a) an image
    b) a formal concept
    c) a framework
    d) an exemplar

8. My understanding of the use and rules of statistical analysis would be a good example of an artificial concept.
    a) True
    b) False

9. Which of the following was exemplified in the text by the use of a syllogism?
    a) deductive reasoning
    b) inductive reasoning

10. All dogs are mammals. My animal is a mammal. Therefore, my animal is a dog. The previous statements represent:
    a) deductive reasoning
    b) a syllogism
    c) cognitive representation
    d) verbal imagery

11. Would the text say that the first two statements in item 10 above lead to a valid conclusion?
    a) yes
    b) no

12. Duane is considering alternatives in preparing to choose which car he wants to buy. The text would say he is engaging in:
    a) cognitive operations
    b) syllogistic reasoning
    c) decision making
    d) deductive cognition

13. Duane decides to list the most important factors involved in selecting his car. He rates his alternatives based on color, price, gas mileage, and safety. He then selects the car that rated highest on these factors. He is using the _____ strategy in decision making.

14. Joann is attempting to make a decision that has many alternatives and involves many factors. She decides to rank the factors from most important to least important. She then starts to eliminate alternatives as they fail to meet the highest ranked factors. This is an example of the _____ strategy of decision making.

15. The decision making strategy described in question # 14 is an example of a compensatory decision strategy.
    a) True
    b) False

B. Matching: Place the appropriate letter in the space provided.

	Description	Term
_____	1. from the general to the specific	a. trial and error
_____	2. start with the solution and work back	b. deductive reasoning
_____	3. rules of thumb derived from experience	c. inductive reasoning
_____	4. try one after another until a solution is found	d. additive strategy
_____	5. apply a familiar strategy without consideration of the specific requirements of the problem	e. elimination by aspects
		f. availability heuristic
_____	6. the highest overall rating is chosen	g. heuristic
_____	7. does it resemble or match an existing prototype?	h. representativeness heuristic
_____	8. a step by step procedure can guarantee a solution	i. framing
_____	9. the probability of an event is based on that event's availability in memory	j. algorithm
		k. working backward
_____	10. the current position is compared with a desired goal	l. means-end analysis
_____	11. is the focus based on a potential gain or loss?	m. functional fixedness
_____	12. factors are ordered from the most important to the least important	n. mental set
_____	13. general conclusions are drawn from particular facts	
_____	14. failure to use familiar objects in novel ways	

C. COMPLETE THE DIAGRAM: For each concept, decide if it is a formal concept or a natural concept. If you think it is a formal concept, place the letter "F" in the space provided. If you think it is a natural concept, place the letter "N" in the space provided.

Concept	Formal or Natural (F or N)
1. quadratic equation	_____
2. pasta	_____
3. bird	_____
4. verb	_____
5. vegetable	_____
6. chair	_____
7. theory	_____
8. punctuation	_____
9. mother	

PREPARE A LECTURE: This activity is designed to offer you an opportunity to take advantage of a valuable mode of learning, elaborate rehearsal. Once you have finished the OMSE section, write a lecture using the instructional guide provided below. After your lecture is prepared, you can enhance your learning by writing a quiz covering the material. Now it is time to find some willing and inquisitive audience members. Your roommates or family may be a great place to start. Present them the lecture as if you are teaching a class. Remember to ask for questions and give your students the quiz following the lecture. This exercise can also serve to turn a *study-buddy* group into a very productive way to prepare for the test. Each member of the group can take different OMSE sections for their lecture/teacher role while the rest of the group serves as the class.

I. Key Terms, Names, Dates, and Concepts you will include in this lecture:

1. _____   5. _____   9. _____
2. _____   6. _____   10. _____
3. _____   7. _____   11. _____
4. _____   8. _____   12. _____

II. Learning Objectives (what do you want the student to know and be able to do as a result of your lecture):

1. _____
2. _____
3. _____
4. _____
5. _____

III. Lecture Notes (notes should be brief cues and serve as a guide).

Major topic #1: _____

   Sub-topics and notes: _____

   _____

   _____

   _____

Major topic #2: _____

   Sub-topics and notes: _____

   _____

   _____

   _____

Major topic #3: _____

   Sub-topics and notes: _____

   _____

   _____

   _____

OMSE # 2: LANGUAGE

LEARNING OBJECTIVES

1. What are the four important components of language?

2. How does language in trained chimpanzees differ from human language?

3. In general, does thought influence language more, or does language influence thought more?

4. What is the best time in life to learn a second language and why?

LEARNING MASTERY SCORECARD: Update your score card as you work through the various sections of the chapter. First, find and define key terms and concepts included in each section and note the page number(s) from the text that contain important references to the material. Next, gain a practical understanding of the concepts by considering the Laboratory to Life scenarios and thinking of at least one original example of how the concept might apply in real life. Complete the *Objective-Mastery Self-Evaluation* (OMSE) exercises for this section and record your scores. Revisit the exercises, recording your score and the date completed until you have attained mastery (100%). Finally, decide how you would prepare a lecture on each objective using the template provided, outline the lecture, and practice presenting it. Keep an honest tally of your achievements and, when finished, you will have developed learning mastery through elaborate rehearsal.

Key Term	Page #	Key Term	Page #	Key Term	Page #
language	_____	morphemes	_____	surface structure	_____
psycholinguistics	_____	syntax	_____	deep structure	_____
phonemes	_____	semantics	_____	linguistic relativity hypothesis	_____

Quick Quiz

Date	Score	Date	Score	Date	Score
_/_/_	_____	_/_/_	_____	_/_/_	_____
_/_/_	_____	_/_/_	_____	_/_/_	100%

Elaborate Rehearsal

Lecture Preparation	Completion Date
Key Terms, Persons, & Concepts	_/_/_
Learning Objectives	_/_/_
Lecture Notes	_/_/_

A. QUICK QUIZ

1. The study of how language is acquired, produced, and used, and how sounds and symbols of language are translated into meaning is known as _____.

2. The smallest units of sound in a spoken language are known as _____.

   a) morphemes
   b) syntax
   c) semantics
   d) phonemes

3. Which of the following would be best matched with syntax?
   a) style
   b) prose
   c) rules
   d) meaning

4. The concepts of surface structure and deep structure would be best matched with:
   a) syntax
   b) semantics
   c) morphemes
   d) linguistic expression

5. Jan was telling her friend Susan what Jack had said to her last night in their telephone conversation. Susan replied "I wonder what he meant by that?" Susan was talking about the _____ structure of Jack's statement.
    a) surface   c) deep
    b) semantic   d) syntaxic

6. Research has shown that chimps, unique among the non-human language acquisition research subjects, have demonstrated the ability to conceptualize language almost as well as humans. If chimps had the appropriate speech apparatus they could converse with humans quite effectively.
    a) True   b) False

7. Frank asserts that what you say—the language you use—determines the nature of your thoughts. Frank would be seen as a proponent of the _____ _____ _____.

8. Studies such as those by Rosch (1973) and Berlin and Kay (1969) have indicated that language does seem to determine thought. This was especially true for words related to colors.

    a) True   b) False

9. The ability to speak more than one language is known as _____.

10. Of the households that speak English as a second language in the United States, the most common first language spoken in the home is:

    a) French   c) German
    b) Chinese   d) Spanish

11. Who seems to have the advantage when it comes to learning a second language?
    a) younger people   b) older people

12. The area in the brain that controls speech production is known as Broca's area.
    a) True   b) False

13. According to the text, Americans are far behind other technologically advanced nations when it comes to speaking a language other than their own native tongue.
    a) True   b) False

14. Is there a difference in the way the speech center in the brain processes the acquisition of a second language between those who learn the second language early and those who learn the second language when they are older?
    a) yes   b) no

B. MATCHING: Place the appropriate letter in the space provided.

	Definition	Term
_____	1. smallest unit of meaning in a language	a. phoneme
_____	2. literal words that are spoken or written in a sentence	b. morpheme
_____	3. underlying meaning of the sentence	c. syntax
_____	4. smallest units of sound in spoken language	d. semantics
_____	5. rules for arranging and combining words	e. surface structure
_____	6. meaning derived from morphemes, words, sentences	f. deep structure

C. COMPLETE THE DIAGRAM: Decide if each of the following is a phoneme (P) or a morpheme (M). Place the corresponding letter (P or M) in the space provided.

1. c ____	3. boot ____	5. who ____	7. o ____	9. oh ____
2. d ____	4. a ____	6. I ____	8. m ____	10. be ____

PREPARE A LECTURE: This activity is designed to offer you an opportunity to take advantage of a valuable mode of learning, elaborate rehearsal. Once you have finished the OMSE section, write a lecture using the instructional guide provided below. After your lecture is prepared, you can enhance your learning by writing a quiz covering the material. Now it is time to find some willing and inquisitive audience members. Your roommates or family may be a great place to start. Present them the lecture as if you are teaching a class. Remember to ask for questions and give your students the quiz following the lecture. This exercise can also serve to turn a *study-buddy* group into a very productive way to prepare for the test. Each member of the group can take different OMSE sections for their lecture/teacher role while the rest of the group serves as the class.

I. Key Terms, Names, Dates, and Concepts you will include in this lecture:

1. _____	5. _____	9. _____
2. _____	6. _____	10. _____
3. _____	7. _____	11. _____
4. _____	8. _____	12. _____

II. Learning Objectives (what do you want the student to know and be able to do as a result of your lecture):
1. _____
2. _____
3. _____
4. _____
5. _____

III. Lecture Notes (notes should be brief cues and serve as a guide).
Major topic #1: _____
    Sub-topics and notes: _____
    _____
    _____
    _____
    _____

Major topic #2: _____
    Sub-topics and notes: _____
    _____
    _____
    _____
    _____

Major topic #3: _____
    Sub-topics and notes: _____
    _____
    _____
    _____
    _____

KEY TERMS AND CONCEPTS EXERCISE

The key terms and concepts are presented in order of their appearance in the text. Space is provided for you to include a personalized definition or example of each term or concept. As you encounter each term in the text, make a note of its meaning and context. Next, conceptualize the meaning of the term in a way that makes the most sense to you. Also, think about examples of the term from your own life. Write your definition and/or example in the space provided next to the word. The KEY TERMS exercise utilizes a modified *T-note* design so that you can self-evaluate your mastery of the definitions. First lay a sheet of paper over the terms and concepts side of the page so that you only see the definitions. Read the definition and try to recall the term or concept. Mark all those you are unable to answer so you can restudy them. When you have learned all of the terms and concepts in this way, move the paper to the definition side so that you can see only the term or concept, try to recall both the textbook definition and your personal version. Repeat this until you know all of the terms and concepts by definition and personal understanding.

Cognition	The mental processes involved in acquiring, storing, retrieving, and using information, which include sensation, perception, imaging, concept formation, reasoning, decision making, problem solving, and language. _____
Imagery	The representation in the mind of a sensory experience—visual, auditory, gustatory, motor, olfactory, or tactile. _____
Concept	A mental category used to represent a class or group of objects, events, people, or relations that share common characteristics or attributes. _____
Formal Concept	A concept that is clearly defined by a set of rules, a formal definition, or a classification system; an artificial concept. _____
Natural Concept	A concept acquired not from a definition but through everyday perceptions and experiences; a fuzzy concept. _____
Prototype	The example that embodies the most common and typical features of a concept. _____
Exemplars	The individual instances of a concept that we have stored in memory from our own experience. _____
Reasoning	A form of thinking in which a conclusion is drawn from a set of facts. _____
Deductive Reasoning	Reasoning from the general to the specific or reasoning in which particular conclusions are drawn from general principles. _____
Syllogism	A form of reasoning in which two statements or propositions known as premises are followed by a valid, logical conclusion. _____
Inductive Reasoning	A form of reasoning in which general conclusions are drawn from particular facts or individual cases. _____
Decision Making	The process of considering alternatives and choosing among them. _____

Additive Strategy	One in which the most important factors in making a decision are listed, and each alternative is rated on each of the factors. The alternative with the highest overall rating is chosen.
Heuristic	A rule of thumb that is derived from experience and used in decision making and problem solving, although it does not guarantee success.
Availability Heuristic	A cognitive rule of thumb that the probability of an event and the importance we assign to information is based on availability—the ease with which the information comes to mind.
Representativeness Heuristic	A thinking strategy based on how closely a new situation is judged to resemble or match an existing prototype of that situation.
Framing	The way information is presented or evaluated based on whether the focus is on a potential gain or loss outcome.
Problem Solving	Thoughts and actions required to achieve a desired goal that is not readily attainable.
Trial And Error	An approach to problem solving in which one solution after another is tried in no particular order until a workable solution is found.
Algorithm	A systematic, step-by-step procedure, such as a mathematical formula, that guarantees a solution to a problem of a certain type if the algorithm is appropriate and executed properly.
Working Backwards	A heuristic strategy in which a person discovers the steps needed to solve a problem by defining the desired goal and working backwards to the current condition.
Means–End Analysis	A heuristic problem-solving strategy in which the current position is compared with the desired goal, and a series of steps are formulated and taken to close the gap between them.
Analogy Heuristic	A rule of thumb that applies a solution that solved a problem in the past to a current problem that shares many similar features.
Functional Fixedness	The failure to use familiar objects in novel ways to solve problems because of a tendency to view objects only in terms of their customary functions.

Mental Set	The tendency to apply a familiar strategy to the solution of a problem without carefully considering the special requirements of that problem. _____
Artificial Intelligence	Computer systems that simulate human thinking in solving problems and making judgements and decisions. _____
Neural Networks	Computer systems that are intended to mimic the human brain. _____
Language	A means of communicating thoughts and feelings, using a system of socially shared but arbitrary symbols (sounds, signs, or written symbols) arranged according to rules of grammar.
Psycholinguistics	The study of how language is acquired, produced, and used, and how the sounds and symbols of language are translated into meaning. _____
Phonemes	The smallest units of sound in a spoken language. _____
Morphemes	The smallest units of meaning in a language. _____
Syntax	The aspect of grammar that specifies the rules for arranging and combining words to form phrases and sentences. _____
Semantics	The meaning or the study of meaning derived from morphemes, words, and sentences. _____
Surface Structure	The literal words that are actually spoken or written (or signed) in a sentence. _____
Deep Structure	The underlying meaning of a sentence. _____
Linguistic Relativity Hypothesis	The notion that the language a person speaks largely determines the nature of that person's thoughts. _____

FROM THE LABORATORY TO LIFE

Shylock and Witless

Famous detective, Shylock Holmes, and his faithful sidekick, Dr. Witless, are fast on the case of the stolen jewels. Holmes reaches a conclusion based on a careful inspection of the facts of the case. He tells Scotland Yard that Moriarty is the thief and assures them his conclusion is accurate by stating it thusly: "Only three people knew the whereabouts of the jewels and had access to them—myself, Madame, and Moriarty. Of the three people, only Moriarty was unaccounted for when the theft occurred. Therefore, Moriarty must be the thief."

1. What type of reasoning has Shylock used to solve the case? _____

2. What is the major premise? _____

3. What is the minor premise? _____

Meanwhile, unaware that the case has been solved, Dr. Witless arrives on the scene with his conclusion that the thief cannot be Moriarty. "You see," said Witless, "Moriarty is a man, and the stolen jewelry is that of a woman. Since he would not wear that jewelry, there would be no reason to steal it."

4. What type of reasoning has Witless used? _____

5. What is the weakness in Witless's logic? _____

_____

_____

_____

FROM THEORY TO PRACTICE

Declaring a Major

A. Paula is finishing her third semester of college and must decide on a major. She is torn between computer engineering and teaching literature. Paula sees her advisor who recommends that she make a list of all of the important factors that will be affected by her decision. Paula lists the following factors: earn a lot of money, live and work just about anywhere, work with people, and have job security. She then rates her two options against each factor and decides on computer engineering.

B. Excited at having made her choice she runs to tell her roommate who asks her which of the factors are really most important to her. Paula considers this query and decides that computer engineering will not give her the opportunity to work directly with people, and working with people is her most important factor. Based on that outcome, she decides to major in literature.

C. Paula is once again relieved and excited and she runs to tell her boyfriend the news. Her boyfriend listens to Paula's decision, and then asks why she has ruled out computer engineering on the basis of not being able to work directly with people. "After all", he states, "You love computer engineering and you love the idea of teaching—so why not teach computer engineering?"

1. In Paragraph A, what decision-making strategy did Paula use? _____

2. In paragraph B, what decision-making strategy did Paula use? _____

3. In paragraph C, Paula's boyfriend gives Paula a new way to think about using the computer and a computer engineering degree—a way that had not occurred to her previously. What is the term for Paula's way of viewing the computer as merely a tool on which to perform computer functions? _____

_____.

COMPREHENSIVE PRACTICE TEST

1. The mental processes involved in acquiring, storing, retrieving, and using knowledge are known collectively as:
   a) conceptualization
   b) cognition
   c) imagery
   d) thinking

2. Which of the following is reported in the text as the most common type of imagery?
   a) auditory
   b) tactile
   c) visual
   d) olfactory

3. In most people, visual images are exclusively a right hemisphere function.
   a) True
   b) False

4. Dog, car, honesty, and trees—these are all examples of:
   a) images
   b) concepts
   c) verbal images
   d) typographs

5. Evidence suggests that the same mental and brain processes are active in both a visual image and in the perception of a visual stimulus.
   a) True
   b) False

6. Of the following: rock, branch, fork, and gun, gun would probably be identified by most people as a _____ of the concept of a weapon.
   a) syntaxic example
   b) syntaxic image
   c) fuzzy concept
   d) prototype

7. Jeffrey went to an antique sale and found a very strange looking object. He searched his own memory for an item that may be a modern incarnation of the object. He finally decided that the antique he was holding was an early version of the calculator he uses each day at his office. He decided the strange object was a kind of adding machine. In this case, Jeffrey's calculator was a(n) _____ for helping him classify the antique.
   a) prototype
   b) visual image
   c) exemplar
   d) fuzzy concept

8. Natural concepts are sometimes called fuzzy concepts.
   a) True
   b) False

9. Artificial concepts are also known as fuzzy concepts.
   a) True
   b) False

10. A good example of a formal concept is:
    a) the table of elements
    b) social display rules
    c) ethical guidelines
    d) established table manners

11. Jim's concept of a great car is one that is bright red and has a high performance engine. This is an example of a(n) _____ concept.
    a) artificial
    b) natural
    c) formal
    d) cognitive

12. The syllogism is an example of _____ reasoning.
    a) deductive
    b) inductive

13. In the early days of personal computers I once forgot the DOS command to load a certain program. I then tried all the commands I could remember until I came upon the one that worked. This would be an example of:
    a) a syllogism
    b) the additive heuristic
    c) inductive reasoning
    d) trial and error

14. Jackie was bitten by a dog when she was younger. She now believes that all dogs are basically mean. This is an example of _____ reasoning.
    a) prototypical
    b) inductive
    c) deductive
    d) heuristic

15. I am trying to decide if I should go west or south for my summer vacation this year. I list the most important factors in this decision, such as historic attractions, highway conditions, and local prices. I then rate these factors for each possible destination. It turns out that going west has the highest rating. I am heading west this summer. I have just used the _____ strategy for making this decision.
    a) elimination by aspects
    b) prototypical
    c) additive
    d) availability

16. A few years ago, I was assigned to attend a conference several hundred miles away. I had to choose the manner of transportation I would use to get to the conference. One night, as I was thinking about the trip, I saw two reports of airplane accidents on the nightly news. I determined that flying was too dangerous and decided to take the train instead. In this example I used the _____ heuristic to make my decision.
    a) elimination by aspects
    b) representativeness
    c) prototypical
    d) availability

17. Pat is asked to predict the likelihood of the next roll of a die being a six. After observing that a six has occurred one time in the last 15 rolls, she says it is about time for a six. This is a good example of framing.
    a) True   b) False

18. My students are taught systematic, step-by-step procedures to solve their statistics problems. This is an example of _____.
    a) algorithms   c) elimination by aspects
    b) trial and error   d) means-end analysis

19. I once amazed my classmates and myself by solving a very complicated algebra problem by starting with the answer and working backwards. In doing so, I discovered the missing step that was keeping us from arriving at a correct solution. This would be identified in the book as an example of an algorithm.
    a) True   b) False

20. My colleagues and I were once charged with the task of designing a new mental health program that would still serve the patients under the current service plan. It seemed like a pretty complicated task, so we decided to make the following statements: "where are we now – where do we want to be, and what are the steps we need to take to get there." This would be a good example of the heuristic known as _____.
    a) framing   c) working backwards
    b) means-end analysis   d) functional fixedness

21. I have learned a lot about problem solving by working in my wood shop. Designing and building cabinets seemed to sharpen my ability to examine possibilities toward goals and solutions. One important step forward was when I learned to see new ways of using tools and other objects in making my projects. I was able to be much more creative and solved many practical problems in my shop. In other words, I seemed to conquer the impediment to problem solving known as:
    a) algorithmic fixedness   c) functional fixedness
    b) heuristic fixedness   d) mental fixedness

22. I was working in my shop one day and could not get the door to a new cabinet to hang and close right. I thought about the problem and remembered a similar problem when I had cut the angles for a picture frame a little off. The frame was not square and would not fit the picture. I considered this example and decided to check the angles on the door I had just assembled. It turned out that they were also cut a little off the required 45 degree angle—problem solved. This is an example of the analogy heuristic of problem solving.
    a) True   b) False

23. Mental set is a term used to describe the problem-solving technique of examining all the possible solutions and selecting the one that best fits the prototype solution.
    a) True   b) False

24. A neural network is a computer system that is designed to mimic:
    a) artificial intelligence   c) human heuristics
    b) animal intelligence   d) the human brain

25. Has research in artificial intelligence led to computers that can replace humans in complex decision making situations?
    a) yes   b) no

26. _____ are defined as the smallest units of sound in a spoken language.
    a) Phonemes   c) Morphemes
    b) Semantics   d) Consonants

27. _____ are defined as the smallest units of meaning in a language.
    a) Phonemes   c) Morphemes
    b) Semantics   d) Consonants

28. Which of the following refer to the rules for arranging and combining words to form phrases and sentences?
    a) psycholinguistics   c) semantics
    b) syntax   d) morphology

29. Joe gave Allen a stern look and said, "thanks a lot"! Allen took this as a sarcastic statement and thought Joe really meant that he was not happy with the decision Allen had just offered. Allen was giving meaning to Joe's statement based on the _____ of that statement.
    a) surface structure
    b) deep structure

30. The above question deals with what the text referred to as:
    a) semantics
    b) neurolinguistics
    c) morphology
    d) syntax

31. After reading the text it becomes obvious that other animals have no real language or communication abilities at all. Any apparent display of such abilities has been shown to be simply a matter of operant conditioning.
    a) True
    b) False

32. The linguistic relativity hypothesis asserts that:
    a) the language a person speaks largely determines the nature of that persons thoughts
    b) the way a person thinks largely determines the way a person uses language

33. Did the study performed by Rosch support the linguistic relativity hypothesis?
    a) yes
    b) no

34. Has research suggested that gender specific pronouns such as "he" influence interpretation between males and females?
    a) yes
    b) no

ANSWER KEYS

Answer Key: OMSE # 1

A. Quick Quiz	B. Matching	C. Complete the Diagram
1. b	1. b	1. F
2. cognition	2. k	2. N
3. imagery	3. g	3. N
4. true	4. a	4. F
5. c	5. n	5. N
6. false	6. d	6. N
7. d	7. h	7. F
8. true	8. j	8. F
9. a	9. f	9. N
10. b	10. l	
11. b	11. i	
12. c	12. e	
13. additive	13. c	
14. elimination by aspects	14. m	
15. false		

Answer Key: OMSE # 2

A. Quick Quiz	B. Matching	C. Complete the Diagram
1. psycholinguistics	1. b	1. P
2. d	2. e	2. P
3. c	3. f	3. M
4. b	4. a	4. P or M
5. c	5. c	5. M
6. false	6. d	6. P or M
7. linguistic relativity hypothesis		7. P
8. false		8. P
9. bilingualism		9. M
10. d		10. M
11. a		
12. true		
13. true		
14. yes		

Answer Key: Laboratory to Life

1. Deductive reasoning
2. Only three people knew . . .
3. Of the three people, only Moriarty . . .
4. Inductive reasoning
5. Witless drew his conclusion from a particular fact—as he understood it. Since he was stuck in his functional fixedness, he did not recognize that Moriarty might be planning to sell the stolen jewels.

Answer Key: Theory to Practice

1. Additive strategy
2. Elimination by aspects strategy
3. Functional fixedness

Answer Key: Comprehensive Practice Test

1. b	10. a	19. false	27. c
2. c	11. b	20. b	28. b
3. false	12. a	21. c	29. b
4. b	13. d	22. true	30. a
5. true	14. b	23. false	31. false
6. d	15. c	24. d	32. a
7. c	16. d	25. b	33. b
8. true	17. false	26. a	34. a
9. false	18. a		

INTELLIGENCE & CREATIVITY

Intelligence is defined variously as an individual's ability to acquire, understand, and use information and complex ideas, and an individual's ability to adapt to situations and the environment, to benefit from experience, and to think through and creatively solve problems.

CHAPTER OVERVIEW

There is a story of three blind men attempting to describe an elephant. Each man touched a different part of the animal and each arrived at a different conclusion regarding the animal's appearance. I am reminded of this story as I consider the construct, intelligence. Intelligence is one of the most controversial topics in psychology. As with the elephant, we seem to define this elusive construct based on our experience and perception, as well as our preconceptions. A subsequent problem is measurement—if we cannot define the construct, how can we possibly quantify it? Still, we continue to make many important decisions about people's lives based on this fuzzy concept (see Chapter Seven). I often pose the following to my students: We meet two people, a calculus professor from a major university who scores in the 99th percentile on a standardized intelligence test, and an individual who has survived the last 40 years in the cold tundra but has never had a formal math class. The tundra survivor scores well below the average on the standardized intelligence test. Now, one day the calculus professor gets lost in the tundra and dies within 24 hours. Who was the most intelligent? I suggest to my students that the answer to this question depends upon the setting. While our tundra survivor would not fare well on campus, the calculus professor could not eat his IQ score, or use it to keep warm in a strange and hostile environment. However we choose to define and use the concept of intelligence, in the long run, if we do not have the where-with-all to adapt and survive, we are not intelligent enough with respect to our current needs.

This chapter will help you gain a more practiced and functional understanding of intelligence and creativity as it is presented in the text. The materials are divided into two OMSE sections: 1) intelligence, and 2) creativity. You will discover the variety of ways we have attempted to define, understand, and measure intelligence in the past century. In addition, you will examine that product of intelligence known as creativity.

By completing the exercises provided, you should gain a thorough understanding of the information presented in your text. In other words, you should be better prepared for tests, quizzes, class participation, and life itself.

TIMELINE

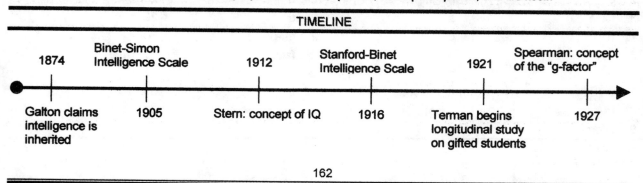

CHAPTER OUTLINE

The Nature of Intelligence

The Search for Factors Underlying Intelligence

Intelligence: More Than One Type?

Measuring Intelligence

Alfred Binet and the First Successful Intelligence Test

Intelligence Testing in the United States

Requirements of Good Tests: Reliability, Validity, and Standardization

The Range of Intelligence

Intelligence and Neural Speed and Efficiency

The IQ Controversy: Brainy Dispute

The Uses and Abuses of Intelligence Tests

The Nature–Nurture Controversy: Battle of the Centuries

Intelligence: Is It Fixed or Changeable?

Expectations, Effort, and Academic Achievement—A Cross-Cultural Comparison

Emotional Intelligence

Personal Components of Emotional Intelligence

Interpersonal Components of Emotional Intelligence

Creativity: Unique and Useful Productions

The Creative Process

The Nature of Creative Thinking

Measuring Creativity: Are There Reliable Measures?

Characteristics of the Creative Person

Savant Syndrome: A Special Form of Creativity

Apply It! Stimulating Creativity

Thinking Critically

Chapter Summary and Review

KEY TERMS

The Nature of Intelligence

g factor

primary mental abilities

triarchic theory of intelligence

Measuring Intelligence

intelligence quotient

norms

Stanford–Binet Intelligence Scale

deviation score

Wechsler Adult Intelligence Scale (WAIS-R)

reliability

validity

aptitude test

standardization

mental retardation

The IQ Controversy: Brainy Dispute

culture-fair intelligence test

nature–nurture controversy

behavioral genetics

twin study method

identical twins

fraternal twins

heritability

adoption method

Emotional Intelligence

emotional intelligence

Creativity: Unique and Useful Productions

creativity

divergent thinking

savant syndrome

TIMELINE

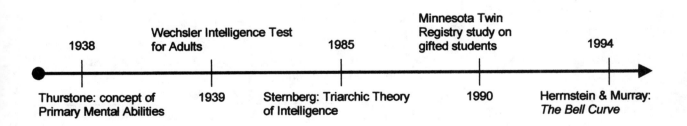

1938

Wechsler Intelligence Test for Adults

1985

Minnesota Twin Registry study on gifted students

1994

Thurstone: concept of Primary Mental Abilities

1939

Sternberg: Triarchic Theory of Intelligence

1990

Herrnstein & Murray: *The Bell Curve*

OMSE # 1: INTELLIGENCE

LEARNING OBJECTIVES

1. What factors underlie intelligence according to Spearman and Thurstone?
2. What types of intelligence did Gardner and Sternberg identify?
3. What is Binet's major contribution to psychology?
4. What is the Stanford–Binet Intelligence Scale?
5. What does IQ mean, and how has the method for calculating it changed over time?
6. What did Wechsler's test provide that the Stanford–Binet did not?
7. What do the terms reliability, validity, and standardization mean?
8. What are the ranges of IQ scores considered average, superior, and in the range of mental retardation?
9. According to the Terman study, how do the gifted differ from the general population?
10. What two criteria must one meet to be classified as mentally retarded?
11. What is the relationship between intelligence and neural speed and efficiency?
12. Of what are intelligence tests good predictors?
13. What are some of the abuses of intelligence tests?
14. How does the nature–nurture controversy apply to intelligence?
15. What is behavioral genetics, and what are the primary methods used in the field today?
16. How do twin studies support the view that intelligence is inherited?
17. What are Jensen's and Herrnstein and Murray's controversial views on race and IQ?
18. What kinds of evidence suggest that IQ is changeable rather than fixed?
19. What are the personal components of emotional intelligence?
20. What are the interpersonal components of emotional intelligence?

LEARNING MASTERY SCORECARD: Update your score card as you work through the various sections of the chapter. First, find and define key terms and concepts included in each section and note the page number(s) from the text that contain important references to the material. Next, gain a practical understanding of the concepts by considering the Laboratory to Life scenarios and thinking of at least one original example of how the concept might apply in real life. Complete the OMSE exercises for this section and record your scores. Revisit the exercises, recording your score and the date completed until you have attained mastery (100%). Finally, prepare a lecture on each objective using the template provided, outline the lecture, and practice presenting it. Keep an honest tally of your achievements and, when finished, you will have developed learning mastery through elaborate rehearsal.

Key Term	page #	Key Term	page #	Key Term	page #
g factor	____	reliability	____	behavioral genetics	____
primary mental abilities	____	validity	____	twin study method	____
triarchic theory of intelligence	____	aptitude test	____	identical twins	____
intelligence quotient	____	standardization	____	fraternal twins	____
norms	____	mental retardation	____	heritability	____
Stanford–Binet Intelligence Scale	____	culture-fair intelligence test	____	adoption method	____
deviation score	____	nature–nurture controversy	____	emotional intelligence	____
Wechsler Adult Intelligence Scale (WAIS-R)	____				

Quick Quiz

Date	Score	Date	Score	Date	Score
_/_/_	____	_/_/_	____	_/_/_	____
_/_/_	____	_/_/_	____	_/_/_	100%

Elaborate Rehearsal

Lecture Preparation	Completion Date
Key Terms, Persons, & Concepts	_/_/_
Learning Objectives	_/_/_
Lecture Notes	_/_/_

A. QUICK QUIZ

1. Charles Spearman developed his "g-theory" after observing that people who are bright in one area tend to be bright in other areas as well.
   a) True   b) False

2. The concept of Primary Mental Abilities was developed by:
   a) Spearman   c) Sternberg
   b) Thurstone   d) Binet

3. The theory that proposed seven different kinds of intelligence including linguistic intelligence and intrapersonal intelligence was developed by Howard _____.

4. Jack is the kind of person that seems to be able to make the world work for him. He knows how to fit in a situation or change the situation to his needs and is very successful in business due to this talent. Sternberg would say he is gifted in terms of _____ intelligence.
   a) componential   c) contextual
   b) experiential   d) general

5. Which of the following developed the concept of the IQ score?
   a) Stern   c) Sternberg
   b) Binet   d) Terman

6. According to the IQ formula, if a child had a mental age of 11 and a chronological age of 12, the child would have an IQ of:
   a) 90   c) 112
   b) 111   d) 91.6

7. Louis Terman, working for the French educational system, developed the first intelligence test as a way to differentiate between average or brighter children and those who would not benefit from regular classes.
   a) True   c) False

8. David _____ is credited with developing the idea of the deviation score, a score that defines a person's IQ by comparing that person to other people of the same age who were used to norm the test.

9. James takes a test and is given an IQ score based on the results of the test. A day later he takes the same test again and gets a much higher score. We might be concerned that the test did not have very good
   _____.
   a) validity   c) componentiality
   b) reliability   d) standardization

10. If Sally scores very low on an IQ test and then is found to be at the top of her class in academic performance, we may be concerned that the IQ test did not have very good _____.
    a) validity   c) standardization
    b) reliability   d) componentiality

11. According to the text, what percent of the population would be classified as mentally retarded?
    a) 5   c) 2
    b) 10   d) 12

12. Research with PET scans has indicated that people of higher intelligence tend to use _____ energy when performing mental tasks than those who are less gifted.
    a) more   b) less

13. A(n) _____ _____ intelligence test is designed to present questions that will not penalize persons whose culture differs from that of the middle or upper classes.

14. Fraternal twins are to _____ as identical twins are to _____.
    a) monozygotic; dizygotic   b) dizygotic; monozygotic

15. In twin studies it has been found that identical twins reared together are no more alike as adults than identical twins reared apart.
    a) True   b) False

16. Research has indicated that, despite the intensity of environment enrichment programs available, IQ seems to be pretty well fixed by our genetic code.
    a) True   b) False

B. MATCHING: Place the appropriate letter in the space provided.

_____	1. g-factor	a.	Gardner
_____	2. primary mental abilities	b.	Stern
_____	3. multiple intelligences	c.	Terman
_____	4. triarchic theory	d.	Spearman
_____	5. IQ score	e.	Wechsler
_____	6. first intelligence test	f.	Galton
_____	7. Stanford-Binet Intelligence Test	g.	Thurstone
_____	8. deviation scores	h.	Jensen
_____	9. nature-nurture controversy	i.	Binet
_____	10. Minnesota twin studies	j.	Sternberg
_____	11. genetic differences in IQ	k.	Bouchard

C. COMPLETE THE DIAGRAM: Show the formula and calculate the IQ Scores

1. What was Stern's formula for the IQ Score? _____

2. If Jack has a mental age of 15 and a chronological age of 13, what is his IQ score?   _____

3. If Helen has a mental age of 12 and a chronological age of 12, what is her IQ score?   _____

4. If Derrick has a mental age of 13 and a chronological age of 14, what is his IQ score?   _____

5. If Paula scores two standard deviations above the mean, what IQ score would she have   _____
   according to Wechsler's scale?

6. If Harold scores one standard deviation below the mean, what IQ score would he have according   _____
   to Wechsler's scale?

PREPARE A LECTURE:
This activity is designed to offer you an opportunity to take advantage of a valuable mode of learning, elaborate rehearsal. Once you have finished the OMSE section, write a lecture using the instructional guide provided below. After your lecture is prepared, you can enhance your learning by writing a quiz covering the material. Now it is time to find some willing and inquisitive audience members. Your roommates or family may be a great place to start. Present them the lecture as if you are teaching a class. Remember to ask for questions and give your students the quiz following the lecture. This exercise can also serve to turn a *study-buddy* group into a very productive way to prepare for the test. Each member of the group can take different OMSE sections for their lecture/teacher role while the rest of the group serves as the class.

I. Key Terms, Names, Dates, and Concepts you will include in this lecture:

1. _____	5. _____	9. _____
2. _____	6. _____	10. _____
3. _____	7. _____	11. _____
4. _____	8. _____	12. _____

II. Learning Objectives (what do you want the student to know and be able to do as a result of your lecture):

1. _____
2. _____
3. _____
4. _____
5. _____

III. Lecture Notes (notes should be brief cues and serve as a guide).

Major topic #1: _____
   Sub-topics and notes: _____
_____
_____
_____

Major topic #2: _____
   Sub-topics and notes: _____
_____
_____
_____

Major topic #3: _____
   Sub-topics and notes: _____
_____
_____
_____

OMSE # 2: CREATIVITY

LEARNING OBJECTIVES

1. What is creativity, and what tests have been designed to measure it?

2. What are the four stages in the creative process?

3. What kinds of tests have been used to measure creativity? Are they good predictors of creativity?

4. What are some characteristics of the creative person?

LEARNING MASTERY SCORECARD: Update your score card as you work through the various sections of the chapter. First, find and define key terms and concepts included in each section and note the page number(s) from the text that contain important references to the material. Next, gain a practical understanding of the concepts by considering the Laboratory to Life scenarios and thinking of at least one original example of how the concept might apply in real life. Complete the *Objective-Mastery Self-Evaluation* (OMSE) exercises for this section and record your scores. Revisit the exercises, recording your score and the date completed until you have attained mastery (100%). Finally, decide how you would prepare a lecture on each objective using the template provided, outline the lecture, and practice presenting it. Keep an honest tally of your achievements and, when finished, you will have developed learning mastery through elaborate rehearsal.

Key Term	Page #	Key Term	Page #	Key Term	Page #
creativity	_____	divergent thinking	_____	savant syndrome	_____

Quick Quiz

Date	Score	Date	Score	Date	Score
_/_/_	_____	_/_/_	_____	_/_/_	_____
_/_/_	_____	_/_/_	_____	_/_/_	100%

Elaborate Rehearsal

Lecture Preparation	Completion Date
Key Terms, Persons, & Concepts	_/_/_
Learning Objectives	_/_/_
Lecture Notes	_/_/_

A. QUICK QUIZ

1. The ability to produce original, appropriate, and valuable ideas and/or solutions to problems is known as
   _____.

2. Which of the following is **NOT** identified as one of the four basic stages in the creative problem-solving process?
   a) preparation
   b) incubation
   c) cognition
   d) translation

3. _____ thinking refers to the mental activity measured by IQ and achievement tests.
   a) Divergent
   b) Convergent
   c) Cognitive
   d) Formal

4. _____ thinking refers to the ability to produce multiple ideas, answers or solutions to a problem for which there is not an agreed upon solution.
   a) Divergent
   b) Convergent
   c) Cognitive
   d) Formal

5. While _____ thinking alone is not enough, it must be developed in order to be creative.

6. The *Unusual Uses Test* and the *Consequences Test* are both used to measure convergent thinking.
   a) True
   b) False

7. The text presented the amazing stories of Arthur, Alonzo, and Arnold. These stories were presented as an illustration of _____ syndrome.

8. The text suggested that one way to stimulate creativity is to relax with activities such as taking a walk or taking a shower.
   a) True
   b) False

9. James and Susan are trying to figure a way to build the kind of home they really want, while keeping within their present budget. The are currently generating a number of ideas. However, they will not evaluate the ideas until they have listed all such ideas. They are engaging in an activity called _____.

B. EXPLAIN EACH OF THE FOLLOWING CHARACTERISTICS OF THE CREATIVE PERSON:

1. Expertise: _____
   _____

2. Openness to Experience: _____
   _____

3. Independence of Mind: _____
   _____

4. Intrinsic Motivation: _____
   _____

5. Perseverance: _____
   _____

C. EXPLAIN EACH OF THE BASIC STEPS IN THE CREATIVE PROBLEM-SOLVING PROCESS.

1. Preparation: _____

_____

2. Incubation: _____

_____

3. Illumination: _____

_____

4. Translation: _____

_____

PREPARE A LECTURE: This activity is designed to offer you an opportunity to take advantage of a valuable mode of learning, elaborate rehearsal. Once you have finished the OMSE section, write a lecture using the instructional guide provided below. After your lecture is prepared, you can enhance your learning by writing a quiz covering the material. Now it is time to find some willing and inquisitive audience members. Your roommates or family may be a great place to start. Present them the lecture as if you are teaching a class. Remember to ask for questions and give your students the quiz following the lecture. This exercise can also serve to turn a *study-buddy* group into a very productive way to prepare for the test. Each member of the group can take different OMSE sections for their lecture/teacher role while the rest of the group serves as the class.

I. Key Terms, Names, Dates, and Concepts you will include in this lecture:

1. _____   5. _____   9. _____
2. _____   6. _____   10. _____
3. _____   7. _____   11. _____
4. _____   8. _____   12. _____

II. Learning Objectives (what do you want the student to know and be able to do as a result of your lecture):

1. _____
2. _____
3. _____
4. _____
5. _____

III. Lecture Notes (notes should be brief cues and serve as a guide).

Major topic #1: _____

   Sub-topics and notes: _____

_____

_____

_____

Major topic #2: _____

   Sub-topics and notes: _____

_____

_____

_____

Major topic #3: _____

   Sub-topics and notes: _____

_____

_____

_____

_____

KEY TERMS AND CONCEPTS EXERCISE

The key terms and concepts are presented in order of their appearance in the text. Space is provided for you to include a personalized definition or example of each term or concept. As you encounter each term in the text, make a note of its meaning and context. Next, conceptualize the meaning of the term in a way that makes the most sense to you. Also, think about examples of the term from your own life. Write your definition and/or example in the space provided next to the word. The KEY TERMS exercise utilizes a modified *T-note* design so that you can self-evaluate your mastery of the definitions. First lay a sheet of paper over the terms and concepts side of the page so that you only see the definitions. Read the definition and try to recall the term or concept. Mark all those you are unable to answer so you can restudy them. When you have learned all of the terms and concepts in this way, move the paper to the definition side so that you can see only the term or concept, try to recall both the textbook definition and your personal version. Repeat this until you know all of the terms and concepts by definition and personal understanding.

g Factor	Spearman's term for a general intellectual ability that underlies all mental operations to some degree.
Primary Mental Abilities	According to Thurstone, seven relatively distinct abilities that singularly or in combination are involved in all intellectual activities.
Triarchic Theory Of Intelligence	Sternberg's theory that intelligence consists of three parts—the componential, the contextual, and the experiential.
Intelligence Quotient (IQ)	An index of intelligence originally derived by dividing mental age by chronological age then multiplying by 100; now derived by comparing an individual's score to the scores of others of the same age.
Norms	Standards based on the range of test scores of a large group of people who are selected to provide the bases of comparison for those who take the test later.
Stanford–Binet Intelligence Scale	An individually administered IQ test for those aged 2 to 23; Terman's adaptation of the Binet–Simon Scale.
Deviation Score	A test score calculated by comparing an individual's score to the scores of others of the same age.
Wechsler Adult Intelligence Scale (WAIS-R)	An individual intelligence test for adults that yields separate verbal and performance (nonverbal) IQ scores as well as an overall IQ score.

Reliability	The ability of a test to yield nearly the same score when the same people are tested and then retested on the same test or an alternative form of the test. _____
Validity	The ability of a test to measure what it is intended to measure. _____
Aptitude Test	A test designed to predict a person's achievement or performance at some future time. _____
Standardization	Establishing norms for comparing the scores of people who will take a test in the future; administering tests using a prescribed procedure. _____
Mental Retardation	Abnormal intelligence reflected by an IQ below 70 and by adaptive functioning severely deficient for one's age. _____
Mainstreaming	Educating mentally retarded students in regular rather than special schools by placing them in regular classes for part of the day or having special classrooms in regular schools. _____
Culture-Fair Intelligence Test	An intelligence test that uses questions that will not penalize those whose culture differs from that of the middle or upper classes. _____
Nature–Nurture Controversy	The debate over whether intelligence and other traits are primarily the result of heredity or environment. _____
Behavioral Genetics	A field of research that investigates the relative effects of heredity and environment on behavior and ability. _____
Twin Study Method	Studying identical and fraternal twins to determine the relative effects of heredity and environment on a variety of characteristics. _____
Identical Twins	Twins with identical genes; monozygotic twins. _____
Fraternal Twins	Twins who are no more alike genetically than ordinary brothers and sisters; dizygotic twins.
Heritability	An index of the degree to which a characteristic is estimated to be influenced by heredity.

Adoption Method	A method researchers use to study the relative effects of heredity and environment on behavior and ability in children adopted shortly after birth, by comparing them to their biological and adoptive parents. _____ _____
Emotional Intelligence	A type of intelligence which includes the awareness of and the ability to manage one's own emotions, the ability to motivate oneself, to have empathy, and to handle relationships successfully. _____ _____
Creativity	The ability to produce original, appropriate, and valuable ideas and/or solutions to problems. _____ _____
Divergent Thinking	The ability to produce multiple ideas, answers, or solutions to a problem for which there is no agreed upon solution. _____ _____
Savant Syndrome	A condition in which an otherwise mentally retarded individual can perform an amazing mental feat or possesses a remarkable specific skill (e.g., computation, music, or art). _____ _____

FROM THE LABORATORY TO LIFE

The _____ Intelligence Test
Your name here

Imagine that you have been asked to develop a new intelligence test. You have decided to create a test that incorporates a variety of different concepts of intelligence. In order to do this, you have read about the current and past attempts to understand and measure intelligence.

1. What if you decided to incorporate Stern's derivation of IQ scores—how would you calculate your test taker's IQ score? _____

2. Your colleague asks you to consider Wechsler's concept of IQ instead. If you did this you would use _____ scores to calculate the IQ score.

3. If you wanted to include questions that were related to Sternberg's concept of contextual intelligence you would compose items that measured the subject's level of common sense or "_____ smarts."

4. If you also wanted to include questions that were related to Sternberg's concept of experiential intelligence you would compose items that measured the subject's level of _____ and _____.

5. You have read about Spearman's "g-factor" and the fact that a test needs to test specific intellectual abilities that are like sub-types of the "g-factor." In this case you may want to compose items that measure what Spearman called _____ factors.

6. Further research has introduced you to Thurstone's idea of Primary Mental Abilities. You are impressed with his identification of seven important sub-types of intelligence and you decide to include at least three of these in your test. List three of Thurstone's Primary Mental Abilities.
   a) _____
   b) _____
   c) _____

7. You also discover that Gardner talked about seven sub-types of intelligence. You decide to include measurements on three of these sub-types – list the three you would include.

    a) _____

    b) _____

    c) _____

8. Once you have written your test you need to check it out in terms of the standards of a good psychological test. First you check its _____ by giving the test to subject's on repeated occasions to see if the subjects score about the same each time they take the test.

9. Next you compare your measure of intelligence to other ways to measure intelligence. You are interested in the _____ of the test—the issue of whether it measures intelligence in the first place.

10. Finally you give your test to a large number of people called the _____ group. This way, when someone takes the test at a later date, you can compare the score to the group. In order to do this you must also compose a set of specific instructions for giving the test, again in order to accurately compare the scores of later test takers with the original group. This procedure is known as _____.

FROM THEORY TO PRACTICE

It's Nature–Nurture Time . . . Again!

That's right—and nowhere in the field of psychology has the nature–nurture issue fueled more controversy. There is a sensitivity of subject matter regarding the controversy swirling around such works as *The Bell Curve*. Researchers have discovered a disparity in the average IQ scores of different groups of people. Even in the US, where equality is a goal if not a reality, we find a significant difference in the IQ scores of different races. Your text presents strong evidence as to why this gap exists. It does not, however, offer a definitive answer. That is your task. In the space below, provide as many pros and cons as you can find for each side of the debate. Based on your findings, decide whether you believe the controversy can be settled one way or another. If not, estimate the percentage of nature and the percentage of nurture that come together to form IQ. Finally, list some factors that might assist you in increasing **your** academic performance, or improving **your** success in life.

NATURE	NURTURE
1.	1.
2.	2.
3.	3.
4.	4.
5.	5.
6.	6.
7.	7.
8.	8.
9.	9.
10.	10.

My Vote (Nature or Nurture): _____ Nature: _____ %. Nurture: _____ %

How can I increase my school performance, or improve my chances for success in life?

_____

_____

_____

COMPREHENSIVE PRACTICE TEST

1. Spearman spoke of the _____ factor, a subtype of the general intelligence he called "g-factor".
   a) s
   b) contextual
   c) l
   d) cognitive

2. Thurstone believed that the single IQ score method of measuring and describing intelligence was the most effective manner of measuring intelligence.
   a) True
   b) False

3. _____ spoke of independent forms of intelligence including musical ability, spatial skills, and interpersonal intelligence.
   a) Sternberg
   b) Binet
   c) Gardner
   d) Terman

4. Sternberg's triarchic theory of intelligence "big three" included contextual intelligence, experiential intelligence, and _____ intelligence.
   a) visio-spatial
   b) componential
   c) cognitive
   d) content

5. Gardner's theory has been criticized for his lack of supporting empirical evidence.
   a) True
   b) False

6. Sternberg's experiential intelligence included:
   a) the ability to learn from past events
   b) the ability to manipulate people's opinions
   c) creative solving and problem solving
   d) basic academic skills

7. Tacit knowledge is to _____ as practical knowledge is to _____.
   a) knowing what; knowing how
   b) knowing who; knowing when
   c) knowing when; knowing who
   d) knowing how; knowing what

8. Which of the following is the correct formula for Stern's IQ score?
   a) Chronological age / Mental age x 100
   b) Mental age / Chronological Age x 100
   c) plot deviation scores from the mean
   d) (Mental Age x 100) / Chronological Age

9. The text identified the Simon-Wechsler Intelligence Scale as the first formal intelligence test.
   a) True
   b) False

10. Who developed the intelligence test that became known as the Stanford-Binet Scale?
    a) Paul Simon
    b) Frederic Stanford
    c) Louis Terman
    d) David Wechsler

11. The WAIS-R intelligence test actually provides two different sub-scale scores, in addition to an overall IQ score. These two sub-scales are:
    a) verbal and mathematical
    b) contextual and componential
    c) performance and musical
    d) verbal and performance

12. One problem with popular intelligence tests such as the Stanford-Binet and the Wechsler test is the fact that they have to be given on an individual basis.
    a) True
    b) False

13. James takes a test that indicates he is shy and introverted. Later, he is observed on several occasions as the "life of the party." In this case, we may wonder if the test was _____.
    a) reliable
    b) valid
    c) contextual
    d) standardized

14. Mike has just taken a test that is designed to predict future achievement or performance. Mike took a(n) _____ test.
    a) aptitude
    b) projective
    c) intelligence
    d) creativity

15. Do you remember taking a test where everybody had to start at the same time and you could not open the book until you were instructed to do so? The test giver probably read the instructions exactly as they were given in the test manual. Everyone also had the same amount of time to take the test. This is an example of _____.
    a) reliability testing
    b) culture-fair testing
    c) standardization
    d) the WAIS-R test

16. I am going to interpret your test score by comparing it to the scores of a large group of people who also took the test. We would hope that this _____ group is representative of you.
    a) reliability
    b) comparability
    c) validity
    d) norm

17. About what percentage of scores fall between −1 and +1 standard deviations under the normal curve?
    a) 34
    b) 68
    c) 50
    d) 13

18. Terman did research that seemed to support the idea that the intellectually gifted pay for their superior intelligence with mental health problems such as depression.
    a) True
    b) False

19. In order for a person to be classified as mentally retarded that person must either have an IQ score below 70 or demonstrate a severe deficiency in everyday functioning.
    a) This statement is true.
    b) This statement is false but could be made true if you change the IQ score to 50.
    c) This statement is false but could be made true if you change "or" to "and."

20. In the 1960s there was a movement to integrate mentally retarded students with their nonhandicapped peers in the schools. This was called:
    a) mainlining
    b) mainstreaming
    c) culture-fairness
    d) mental integration

21. Which of the following groups seem to indicate less brain energy when performing mental tasks?
    a) those who are intellectually gifted
    b) those who are less gifted

22. What did the text report was the correlation between school grades and IQ score?
    a) .75
    b) .63
    c) .50
    d) .95

23. Culture fair intelligence tests were designed to represent different cultural values equally on the same test.
    a) True
    b) False

24. Behavioral genetics is a field of inquiry where scientists study:
    a) how our behavior affects our genes
    b) how our genes affect our behavior and ability
    c) how our genes affect our biology
    d) how our behavior affects our ability

25. Who are more closely related in terms of their genetic makeup?
    a) monozygotic twins
    b) dizygotic twins

26. The adoption method of investigating genetic effects:
    a) studies adopted children as adults to see how the adoptive family influenced their development
    b) compares adopted children with non-adopted children to see who is most like their real parents
    c) studies adopted children shortly after birth – comparing them to both adoptive and biological parents
    d) studies children before they are adopted out to see how they change once they join their new family

27. The Minnesota researchers (Bouchard, et-al) reported a correlation of .60 - .70 between genetics and intelligence. This study has been recognized as important but some dispute the strength of the relationship and assert that environment is more important than the study would indicate.
    a) True
    b) False

28. According to research, the influence of heritability on intelligence seems to _____ with age.
    a) decrease
    b) increase
    c) remain constant
    d) reverse

29. Herrnstein and Murray, in their book *The Bell Curve*, assert that:
    a) genes influence intelligence but the environment can have a major impact on the genetic influence
    b) the environment fixes very early on an individual's intelligence and behavior
    c) the major problems in current society can be attributed to the environment in which kids are raised
    d) one's IQ is set by their genes and will differentiate between those who succeed and those who will not

30. Most research has strongly supported the ultimate importance of the unique effect of genetics on intelligence.
    a) True
    b) False

31. Is intelligence fixed at birth or is there evidence that improved environmental factors can increase IQ scores?
    a) it appears to be fixed at birth
    b) there is evidence that IQ scores can increase with improved environmental factors

32. The concept of emotional intelligence refers to:
    a) the extent to which one's IQ can influence how they respond to their interpersonal environment
    b) the extent to which one's IQ is influenced by their interpersonal relationships
    c) capabilities not necessarily captured by IQ but important for success in life
    d) the correlation between IQ and personal emotional control

33. An "awareness of our own emotions" refers to:
    a) the extent to which we are self-absorbed
    b) the extent to which others can read our emotions
    c) the extent to which others can influence our emotions
    d) the extent to which we are aware of our emotions/moods and our thoughts about those moods

34. It appears that, of all the aspects of emotional intelligence, the ability to _____ is the one most related to future success.
    a) control anger
    b) stay focused on a goal
    c) delay gratification
    d) get along with others

35. Empathy refers to:
    a) ones sense of personal sympathy
    b) the ability to recognize emotions in others
    c) unconditional sympathy for others
    d) the ability to make others understand your emotions

36. According to the text, while intelligence may be necessary for creativity, it is not sufficient.
    a) True
    b) False

37. Which of the following was not identified as a stage in the creative problem-solving process?
    a) research options
    b) illumination
    c) preparation
    d) translation

38. _____ thinking requires fluency, the ability to formulate an abundant quantity of ideas.
    a) convergent
    b) creative
    c) divergent
    d) logical

39. _____ thinking is the type of mental activity usually measured by IQ and achievement tests.
    a) divergent
    b) analytical
    c) emotional
    d) convergent

40. When you attempt to solve a problem by generating a number of possible solutions but do not evaluate any of the solutions until you have finished generating the list of possibilities you are engaging in what the text identified as:
    a) convergent thinking
    b) brain storming
    c) emotional intelligence
    d) creativity

ANSWER KEYS

Answer Key: OMSE # 1

A. Quick Quiz	B. Matching	C. Calculate IQ Scores
1. True	1. d	1. $\dfrac{\text{mental age}}{\text{chronological age}} \times 100$
2. b	2. g	
3. Gardner	3. a	2. 115 (rounded)
4. c	4. j	3. 100
5. a	5. b	4. 93 (rounded)
6. d	6. i	5. 130
7. False	7. c	6. 85
8. Wechsler	8. e	
9. b	9. f	
10. a	10. k	
11. c	11. h	
12. b		
13. culture-fair		
14. b		
15. True		
16. False		

Answer Key: OMSE # 2

A. Quick Quiz	B. Characteristics of a Creative Person	C. Steps in the Creative Process
1. creativity	1. Expertise: the person has developed expertise in a specific area through years of disciplined practice.	1. Preparation: the search for information that may help solve the problem.
2. c		2. Incubation: letting the problem "sit" while the relevant information is digested.
3. b	2. Openness to Experience: creative people have a mind that is open to experience and are able to be in touch with their feelings and fantasies. They are also inherently curious and inquisitive.	
4. a		3. Illumination: the stage where the answer seems to suddenly appear.
5. divergent		4. Translation: the stage where the new insight is transformed into useful action.
6. False	3. Independence of Mind: creative people are independent minded and value this independence, especially in their area of expertise. The creative person can be a kind of intellectual loner.	
7. savant		
8. True		
9. brain-storming	4. Intrinsic Motivation: creative people are intrinsically motivated and become excited about their work. The reward in creativity is the creativity itself.	
	5. Perseverance: creative people are hard workers and will stay focused on their goals.	

Answer Key: Laboratory to Life

1. Mental Age/Chronological Age x 100
2. deviation
3. street
4. creative thinking; problem solving
5. s
6. any three of: verbal comprehension, numerical ability, spatial relations, perceptual speed, word fluency memory, or reasoning
7. any three of: linguistic, logical/mathematical, musical, spatial, bodily kinesthetic, interpersonal, or intrapersonal
8. reliability
9. validity
10. norm; standardization

Answer Key: Comprehensive Practice Test

1. a	11. d	21. a	31. b
2. False	12. True	22. c	32. c
3. c	13. b	23. False	33. d
4. b	14. a	24. b	34. c
5. True	15. c	25. a	35. b
6. c	16. d	26. c	36. True
7. d	17. b	27. True	37. a
8. b	18. False	28. b	38. c
9. False	19. c	29. d	39. d
10. c	20. b	30. False	40. b

9

CHILD DEVELOPMENT

What might be taken for a precocious genius is the genius of childhood. When the child grows up, it disappears without a trace. It may happen that this boy will become a real painter some day, or even a great painter. But then he will have to begin everything again, from zero.

–Pablo Picasso, 1964

CHAPTER OVERVIEW

Such a special time, childhood! Many of my fondest memories are also my earliest memories. I was fortunate to have been granted a childhood free of the dangers and pitfalls faced by so many young people. Actually, not that long ago, childhood was a very dangerous time, and a large percentage of children never reached adolescence, let alone adulthood. We have learned a lot in the last 100 years and childhood is not the hazard it used to be. Many fatal and debilitating illnesses of earlier times have been eradicated in our day. In the 1990s, however, there are still many dangers imposed upon children. Alcohol and drugs threaten the health and even the lives of infants while they are still forming in the womb. Many people are unaware of the serious threat that habits like cigarette smoking and casual drinking can cause in the prenatal environment. The information is out there, but many of us never take time to seek it out. Developmental psychology has served to build a base of theory and knowledge that has provided us with ways to protect infants from many of the difficulties of previous generations. Not only do we know more about how to provide a healthier prenatal environment, but we have also learned much about the process of guiding children through the potentially difficult times in their lives and bringing them healthy and well-balanced into adulthood.

Developmental psychology has spawned many of the most important and well-known theories in psychology. This chapter will introduce some of the most famous names in the history of psychology. Sigmund Freud said that the child was the parent of the adult. I can think of few statements that are more profound in terms of understanding the importance of childhood, both as an event and in terms of how it shapes the rest of our lives.

This chapter will help you gain a more practiced and functional understanding of child development and the ways we seek to learn about this very special time in our lives. The materials are divided into three OMSE sections: 1) Basic issues and prenatal development, 2) physical and cognitive development, and 3) language and socialization. By completing the exercises provided, you should gain a thorough understanding of the information presented in your text. In other words, you should be better prepared for tests, quizzes, class participation, and life itself.

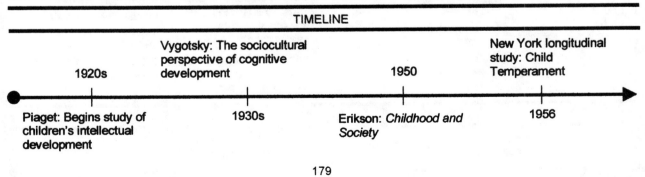

TIMELINE

| 1920s | Vygotsky: The sociocultural perspective of cognitive development | | 1950 | New York longitudinal study: Child Temperament |

Piaget: Begins study of children's intellectual development   1930s   Erikson: *Childhood and Society*   1956

CHAPTER OUTLINE

Developmental Psychology: Basic Issues and Methodology

Controversial Issues in Developmental Psychology

Approaches to Studying Developmental Change

Heredity and Prenatal Development

The Mechanism of Heredity: Genes and Chromosomes

The Stages of Prenatal Development: Unfolding According to Plan

Negative Influences on Prenatal Development: Sabotaging Nature's Plan

Physical Development and Learning in Infancy

The Neonate: Seven Pounds of Beauty?

Perceptual Development in Infancy

Learning in Infancy

Motor Development in Infancy

Emotional Development in Infancy

Temperament: How and When Does it Develop?

The Formation of Attachment

The Father-Child Relationship

Piaget's Theory of Cognitive Development

The Cognitive Stages of Development: Climbing the Steps to Cognitive Maturity

Pioneers: Jean Piaget

An Evaluation of Piaget's Contribution

Vygotsky's Sociocultural View of Cognitive Development

Cognitive Development: The Information-Processing Approach

Language Development

The Stages of Language Development: The Orderly Progression of Language

Theories of Language: How Do We Acquire It?

Socialization of the Child

Erikson's Theory of Psychosocial Development

The Parent's Role in the Socialization Process

Peer Relationships

Television as a Socializing Agent: Does it Help or Hinder?

Apply It! What Kind of Care is Best for Your Child?

Thinking Critically

Chapter Summary and Review

KEY TERMS

Developmental Psychology: Basic Issues and Methodology

Heredity and Prenatal Development

developmental psychology
nature-nurture controversy
longitudinal study
cross-sectional study
genes
chromosomes
sex chromosomes
dominant gene
recessive gene
period of the zygote
prenatal
embryo
fetus
identical (monozygotic) twins

fraternal (dizygotic) twins
teratogens
critical period
fetal alcohol syndrome
low-birth-weight baby
preterm infant

Perceptual Development and Learning in Infancy

neonate
reflexes
visual cliff
habituation
maturation

Emotional Development in Infancy

temperament
attachment
surrogate
separation anxiety

stranger anxiety

Piaget's Theory of Cognitive Development

schemas
assimilation
accommodation
sensorimotor stage
object permanence
preoperational stage
conservation
centration
reversibility
concrete operations stage
formal operations stage

Vygotsky's Sociocultural View of Cognitive Development

Cognitive Development: The Information-Processing Approach

Language Development

babbling
phonemes
overextension
underextension
telegraphic speech
overregularization

Socialization of the Child

socialization
psychosocial stages
basic trust versus basic mistrust
autonomy versus shame and doubt
initiative versus guilt
industry versus inferiority
authoritarian parents
authoritative parents
permissive parents

TIMELINE

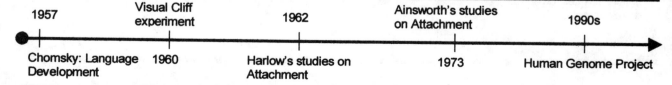

1957	Visual Cliff experiment	1962	Ainsworth's studies on Attachment	1990s
Chomsky: Language Development	1960	Harlow's studies on Attachment	1973	Human Genome Project

OMSE # 1: BASIC ISSUES AND PRENATAL DEVELOPMENT

LEARNING OBJECTIVES

1. What are two types of studies developmental psychologists use to investigate age-related changes?
2. How are hereditary traits transmitted?
3. When are dominant or recessive genes expressed in a person?
4. What are the three stages of prenatal development?
5. What are some negative influences on prenatal development, and during what time is their impact the greatest?

LEARNING MASTERY SCORECARD: Update your score card as you work through the various sections of the chapter. First, find and define key terms and concepts included in each section and note the page number(s) from the text that contain important references to the material. Next, gain a practical understanding of the concepts by considering the Laboratory to Life scenarios and thinking of at least one original example of how the concept might apply in real life. Complete the *Objective-Mastery Self-Evaluation* (OMSE) exercises for this section and record your scores. Revisit the exercises, recording your score and the date completed until you have attained mastery (100%). Finally, decide how you would prepare a lecture on each objective using the template provided, outline the lecture, and practice presenting it. Keep an honest tally of your achievements and, when finished, you will have developed learning mastery through elaborate rehearsal.

Key Term	page #	Key Term	page #	Key Term	page #
developmental psychology	____	dominant gene	____	fraternal (dizygotic) twins	____
nature-nurture controversy	____	recessive gene	____	teratogens	____
longitudinal study	____	period of the zygote	____	critical period	____
cross-sectional study	____	prenatal	____	fetal alcohol syndrome	____
genes	____	embryo	____	low-birth-weight baby	____
chromosomes	____	fetus	____	preterm infant	____
sex chromosomes	____	identical (monozygotic) twins	____		

Quick Quiz

Date	Score	Date	Score	Date	Score
_/_/_	____	_/_/_	____	_/_/_	____
_/_/_	____	_/_/_	____	_/_/_	100%

Elaborate Rehearsal

Lecture Preparation	Completion Date
Key Terms, Persons, & Concepts	_/_/_
Learning Objectives	_/_/_
Lecture Notes	_/_/_

A. QUICK QUIZ

1. The study of how humans grow, develop, and change throughout the life span is known as:
   a) human factors psychology
   b) human growth psychology
   c) developmental psychology
   d) longitudinal psychology

2. In this type of study, the same group of participants is followed and measured at different ages.
   a) longitudinal
   b) ABA baseline
   c) cross-sectional
   d) cross-age

3. When a recessive gene is paired with a dominant gene, the trait for the recessive gene will only be expressed if both parents have the recessive gene.
   a) True
   b) False

4. During this first stage of prenatal development, rapid cell division occurs.
   a) period of the embryo
   b) period of the zygote
   c) period of the fetus
   d) monozygotic period

5. Teratogens:
   a) are substances causing birth defects
   b) are not a factor in moderate drinking
   c) do not include diseases of the mother
   d) affect only physical structure, not mental

6. Everybody knows that hard drugs can have disastrous effects on the unborn child, but moderate drinking and cigarette smoking are considered safe.
   a) True
   b) False

7. Obviously, cocaine use by an expectant mother can lead to severe developmental complications for the unborn child, but it is also a fact that cocaine use by the father at the time of conception can be harmful as well.
   a) True
   b) False

8. Children exposed to alcohol in the prenatal environment might have abnormally small heads with wide-set eyes and a short nose. These features along with extreme hyperactivity and mental retardation are most commonly associated with:
   a) teratogenic abnormality syndrome
   b) fetal alcohol effects
   c) fetal alcohol syndrome
   d) embryonic alcohol deformity

9. The number of newborns in the United States who are born seriously undernourished is estimated at between _____ annually.
   a) 15,000 and 30,000
   b) 80,000 and 100,000
   c) 30,000 and 60,000
   d) 120,000 and 150,000

10. Prenatal exposure to this teratogen increases the likelihood of babies being born prematurely or of low birth weight. It also increases the probability of spontaneous abortion, sudden infant death syndrome, stillbirth, infant mortality, and reduced IQ.
    a) cigarette smoke
    b) heroin
    c) cocaine
    d) x-rays

11. While the jury is still out on the teratogenic effects of this substance, some researchers have reported that heavy use of caffeine is related to low birth weight and miscarriage.
    a) True
    b) False

12. Most teratogens bring about the most severe consequences during critical periods of the _____ trimester, affecting physiological structures or body parts.

13. Prenatal malnutrition can have particularly severe effects on the brain development during the _____ trimester.

14. Exposure to risks during the _____ trimester can result in various types of intellectual and social impairments.

15. Okay, okay! We know better than to take psychoactive drugs during pregnancy. Still, it's okay to take an aspirin if we get a headache, or antibiotics if we have an infection—isn't it?
    a) Yes
    b) Maybe, but only with a doctor's consent
    c) No
    d) Maybe, but only in moderation

B. MATCHING

_____	1. controversial debate that centers on innate & environmental growth	a.	teratogens
_____	2. the first two weeks of prenatal development	b.	preterm babies
_____	3. compare groups of different ages to study age-related changes	c.	nature–nurture
_____	4. research that follows the same individuals over a period of time	d.	period of the zygote
_____	5. major systems, organs, and body structures develop	e.	chromosomes
_____	6. this final stage is a time of rapid growth	f.	cross-sectional research
_____	7. women who smoke or drink during pregnancy are exposing their baby to	g.	period of the embryo
_____	8. newborn infant up to 1 month old	h.	period of the fetus
_____	9. contain the genes and carry hereditary information	i.	longitudinal research
_____	10. birth weight less than 5.5 pounds at or before the 37th week	j.	neonate

C. COMPLETE THE DIAGRAM: Fill in the prenatal period of greatest risk and the potential effects of each teratogen and dangerous condition.

TERATOGEN/DANGER	GREATEST PERIOD OF RISK	POTENTIAL EFFECT
Heroin, cocaine, & crack		
Alcohol		
Cigarettes		
Malnutrition		

PREPARE A LECTURE: This activity is designed to offer you an opportunity to take advantage of a valuable mode of learning, elaborate rehearsal. Once you have finished the OMSE section, write a lecture using the instructional guide provided below. After your lecture is prepared, you can enhance your learning by writing a quiz covering the material. Now it is time to find some willing and inquisitive audience members. Your roommates or family may be a great place to start. Present them the lecture as if you are teaching a class. Remember to ask for questions and give your students the quiz following the lecture. This exercise can also serve to turn a *study-buddy* group into a very productive way to prepare for the test. Each member of the group can take different OMSE sections for their lecture/teacher role while the rest of the group serves as the class.

I. Key Terms, Names, Dates, and Concepts you will include in this lecture:

1. _____
2. _____
3. _____
4. _____

5. _____
6. _____
7. _____
8. _____

9. _____
10. _____
11. _____
12. _____

II. Learning Objectives (what do you want the student to know and be able to do as a result of your lecture):

1. _____
2. _____
3. _____
4. _____
5. _____

III. Lecture Notes (notes should be brief cues and serve as a guide).

Major topic #1: _____

   Sub-topics and notes: _____

_____

_____

_____

Major topic #2: _____

   Sub-topics and notes: _____

_____

_____

_____

Major topic #3: _____

   Sub-topics and notes: _____

_____

_____

_____

OMSE # 2: PHYSICAL AND COGNITIVE DEVELOPMENT

LEARNING OBJECTIVES

1. What are the perceptual abilities of the newborn?
2. What types of learning occur in the first few days of life?
3. What is the primary factor influencing attainment of the major motor milestones?
4. What is temperament, and what are the three temperament types identified by Thomas, Chess, and Birch?
5. What did Harlow's studies reveal about maternal deprivation and attachment in infant monkeys?
6. According to Bowlby, when does the infant have a strong attachment to the mother?
7. What are the four attachment patterns identified in infants?

7. What are the typical differences in the ways mothers and fathers interact with their children?
8. What were Piaget's claims regarding his stages of cognitive development?
9. What is Piaget's sensorimotor stage?
10. What cognitive limitations characterize a child's thinking during the preoperational stage?
11. What cognitive abilities do children acquire during the concrete operations stage?
12. What new capability characterizes the formal operations stage?
13. In Vygotsky's view, how do private speech and scaffolding contribute to cognitive development?

LEARNING MASTERY SCORECARD: Update your score card as you work through the chapter. First, find and define key terms and concepts included in each section and note the page number(s) from the text that contain important references to the material. Next, gain a practical understanding of the concepts by considering the Laboratory to Life scenarios. Complete the *Objective-Mastery Self-Evaluation* (OMSE) exercises for this section and record your scores. Revisit the exercises, recording your score and the date completed until you have attained mastery (100%). Finally, prepare a lecture on each objective using the template provided, and practice presenting it. Keep an honest tally of your achievements and, when finished, you will have developed learning mastery.

Key Term	page #	Key Term	page #	Key Term	page #
neonate	_____	surrogate	_____	object permanence	_____
reflexes	_____	separation anxiety	_____	preoperational stage	_____
visual cliff	_____	stranger anxiety	_____	conservation	_____
habituation	_____	schemas	_____	centration	_____
maturation	_____	assimilation	_____	reversibility	_____
temperament	_____	accommodation	_____	concrete operations stage	_____
attachment	_____	sensorimotor stage	_____	formal operations stage	_____

Quick Quiz

Date	Score	Date	Score	Date	Score
_/_/_	___	_/_/_	___	_/_/_	___
_/_/_	___	_/_/_	___	_/_/_	100%

Elaborate Rehearsal

Lecture Preparation	Completion Date
Key Terms, Persons, & Concepts	_/_/_
Learning Objectives	_/_/_
Lecture Notes	_/_/_

A QUICK QUIZ

1. The visual cliff experiment demonstrated that babies are able to perceive depth about one year after they begin to crawl.
   - a) True
   - b) False

2. Little Joey was given a new teddy bear and it was obvious the toy caught his interest. After a period of time though, Joey lost interest in the teddy bear. Researchers would attribute this loss of interest to _____.
   - a) preference
   - b) extinction
   - c) habituation
   - d) interest span deterioration

3. When Sandra began to crawl, the pediatrician said this was due in part to _____. He explained that this was an example of her genetically programmed, biological timetable of development.

4. In her psychology class, Jennifer's teacher was talking about an infant's individual style of behavior and responding to the environment. Jennifer's teacher was talking about _____.
   - a) infant personality
   - b) temperament
   - c) maturation
   - d) schema

5. Harlow's research on attachment found that children deprived of mothering can suffer negative psychological and physical development effects.
   - a) This statement is false. Harlow found that there were no serious effects resulting from such deprivation.
   - b) This statement is true. In fact, one study found that such deprivation can even contribute to early death.

6. The book identified four different patterns of attachment. When a child does not seem to be responsive to his/her mother and does not seem to be troubled when she is gone, Ainesworth and others would say this represents _____ attachment.

7. Little Johnny's father brought home a new puppy. Johnny learned very quickly that his new best friend was a dog. One day, while playing outside with his mother, Johnny saw the neighbor's cat. He pointed to the cat and said "doggie." According to Piaget this is an example of:
   - a) attraction
   - b) assimilation
   - c) accommodation
   - d) animism

8. Laura was playing with the house keys while her mother was trying to read a book. Her mother finally took the keys and placed them in her purse. Laura surprised her mother this time by going to the purse and searching for the keys. This new development indicated that Laura has graduated from the preoperational stage to the concrete operational stage of cognitive development.
   - a) True
   - b) False

9. Piaget talked about an individual's cognitive structure or concept that is used to make sense of information. This was referred to in the book as a _____.

10. When Jennifer had her second birthday party the cake was cut into 10 equal slices. One of the other children accidentally smashed down her slice of cake. Jennifer was convinced that her friend now had less cake than she did. Piaget would say that Jennifer has not yet mastered the concept of _____.
    - a) conservation
    - b) assimilation
    - c) fair play
    - d) centration

11. Daniel has demonstrated cognitive understanding related to conservation and reversibility. Daniel is in which stage of cognitive development?
   a) sensorimotor
   b) preoperational
   c) concrete operations
   d) formal operations

12. When Amy enters the formal operations stage of cognitive development she will be able to imagine hypothetical situations and future possibilities.
   a) True
   B) False

13. _____ refers to the tendency to focus on only one dimension of a stimulus and ignore other dimensions. The book used this as one explanation for a child's failure to demonstrate the cognitive quality of conservation.

14. Piaget's theory of cognitive development is rare among theories in psychology. This is because it is for the most part as widely accepted today as it was when originally proposed by Piaget.
   a) True
   b) False

15. Vygotsky asserted that the ability to use language to represent things like objects, people, and relationships, is a key component in a child's cognitive development. He called this _____ _____.

16. At what age do children tend to demonstrate the knowledge that thinking is an invisible activity?
   a) six months
   b) five years
   c) two years
   d) three years

B. MATCHING

_____ 1. 7 – 11 years of age	a. sensorimotor
_____ 2. abstract thought	b. preoperational
_____ 3. object permanence	c. concrete operations
_____ 4. egocentric thinking	d. formal operations
_____ 5. understand conservation	
_____ 6. birth to two years of age	
_____ 7. formulate theories	
_____ 8. reversibility	
_____ 9. centration	

C. COMPLETE THE TABLE:
Complete the following table on the progression of motor development by placing the letter corresponding to the description in the appropriate age box.

2 months ____	2½ months ____	3 months ____	6 months ____	6½ months ____	9 months ____
10 months ____	11 months ____	12 months ____	14 months ____	17 months ____	20 months ____

a) stands alone
b) rolls over
c) kicks ball forward
d) walks backward
e) lifts head up
f) sits propped up
g) walks holding on
h) stands holding on
i) stands momentarily
j) sits without support
k) walks up steps
l) walks alone

As infants mature through the sensorimotor stage and begin to be able to explore their surroundings, they find many new and exciting things in their environments. The key is to ensure that they are allowed to assimilate and accommodate new information in safe ways. We do not want a baby to discover electricity, poison, or gravity the hard way.

PREPARE A LECTURE: This activity is designed to offer you an opportunity to take advantage of a valuable mode of learning, elaborate rehearsal. Once you have finished the OMSE section, write a lecture using the instructional guide provided below. After your lecture is prepared, you can enhance your learning by writing a quiz covering the material. Now it is time to find some willing and inquisitive audience members. Your roommates or family may be a great place to start. Present them the lecture as if you are teaching a class. Remember to ask for questions and give your students the quiz following the lecture. This exercise can also serve to turn a *study-buddy* group into a very productive way to prepare for the test. Each member of the group can take different OMSE sections for their lecture/teacher role while the rest of the group serves as the class.

I. Key Terms, Names, Dates, and Concepts you will include in this lecture:

1. _____
2. _____
3. _____
4. _____

5. _____
6. _____
7. _____
8. _____

9. _____
10. _____
11. _____
12. _____

II. Learning Objectives (what do you want the student to know and be able to do as a result of your lecture):

1. _____
2. _____
3. _____
4. _____
5. _____

III. Lecture Notes (notes should be brief cues and serve as a guide).

Major topic #1: _____

   Sub-topics and notes: _____

_____

_____

_____

Major topic #2: _____

   Sub-topics and notes: _____

_____

_____

_____

Major topic #3: _____

   Sub-topics and notes: _____

_____

_____

_____

OMSE # 3: LANGUAGE AND SOCIALIZATION

LEARNING OBJECTIVES

1. What three aspects of cognitive development have information-processing researchers studied extensively?

2. What are the stages of language development from cooing through acquisition of grammatical rules?

3. How do learning theory and the nativist position explain the acquisition of language?

4. What is Erikson's theory of psychosocial development?

5. What are the three parenting styles discussed by Baumrind, and which did she find most effective?

6. How do peers contribute to the socialization process?

7. What are some of the positive and negative effects of television?

LEARNING MASTERY SCORECARD: Update your score card as you work through the various sections of the chapter. First, find and define key terms and concepts included in each section and note the page number(s) from the text that contain important references to the material. Next, gain a practical understanding of the concepts by considering the Laboratory to Life scenarios and thinking of at least one original example of how the concept might apply in real life. Complete the *Objective-Mastery Self-Evaluation* (OMSE) exercises for this section and record your scores. Revisit the exercises, recording your score and the date completed until you have attained mastery (100%). Finally, decide how you would prepare a lecture on each objective using the template provided, outline the lecture, and practice presenting it. Keep an honest tally of your achievements and, when finished, you will have developed learning mastery through elaborate rehearsal.

Key Term	page #	Key Term	page #	Key Term	page #
babbling	___	overregularization	___	initiative versus guilt	___
phonemes	___	socialization	___	industry versus inferiority	___
overextension	___	psychosocial stages	___	authoritarian parents	___
underextension	___	basic trust versus basic mistrust	___	authoritative parents	___
telegraphic speech	___	autonomy versus shame and doubt	___	permissive parents	___

Quick Quiz

Date	Score	Date	Score	Date	Score
_/_/_	___	_/_/_	___	_/_/_	___
_/_/_	___	_/_/_	___	_/_/_	100%

Elaborate Rehearsal

Lecture Preparation	Completion Date
Key Terms, Persons, & Concepts	_/_/_
Learning Objectives	_/_/_
Lecture Notes	_/_/_

A QUICK QUIZ

1. Which of the following is defined by statements such as, "baby's first speech," "biologically determined," and "common to all children?"
   a) one-word stage
   b) telegraphic speech
   c) babbling
   d) suffixes

2. Sometimes young children use the same one-word phrase to mean several different things. The book called this holophrases.
   a) True
   b) False

3. When Peg was a very young child she loved to spend time with her favorite pets, her two dogs. One of the family pets, Tasha, would often sleep on the couch right next to her. Peg would then say, "doggie sleep." This is an example of _____ speech.

4. One day, her mother asked Peg where Tasha was. Peg responded, "Tasha goed outside." This is an example of
   _____.
   a) overregularization
   b) underextension
   c) overextension
   d) telegraphic speech

5. One day, Peg's mother pointed out the neighbor's Poodle. Peg looked at her big black lab, and then asked her mother what kind of animal the poodle was. This is an example of overextension in language development.
   a) True
   b) False

6. When Peg got a little older, she couldn't believe her young brother insisted on calling not only Tasha a doggie, but also the cat, and even a horse they saw at their uncle's farm. Her brother was demonstrating what is known in language development as _____.

7. A phoneme is:
   a) a basic step in speech development
   b) a basic concept that leads to complex thought
   c) a basic step in cognitive development
   d) a basic sound that can lead to words

8. That language is acquired through the processes of reinforcement and imitation is a tenet of the
   _____ theory of language development.

9. Noam Chomsky proposed that the brain contained a language acquisition device and that language ability was innate. This became known as the nativist position in language development.
   a) True
   b) False
   c) yes, but Skinner proposed this, not Chomsky

10. Katie is four years old and she has a special baby doll named Hold-Me Hannah. She talks to her Hannah doll just like her mother talks to her baby brother – with simple, short phrases and an exaggerated intonation combined with repetition. This type of speech is known as _____.

11. Stephen is at that age where he is asking all kinds of questions and seems to be engaging in new motor and play behaviors. According to Erikson's stage theory, if the appropriate behaviors are encouraged, he will develop a sense of _____. If his parents react in a way that makes the questions seem silly or his activity is responded to as a nuisance, Stephen may develop a sense of _____.

12. There was a time when the most important thing in Stephanie's life was the extent to which her parents provided a nurturing environment. In other words, were her basic needs met and were they met in a loving and affectionate manner? Erikson referred to this as the stage of _____ versus _____.

13. Erikson's second stage of psychosocial development is:
    a) basic trust versus mistrust
    b) industry versus inferiority
    c) autonomy versus shame
    d) initiative versus guilt

14. Parenting style seems to play an important role in the development of the child. A child who appears immature, impulsive, and dependent was probably raised by _____ parents. One subtype of this parenting style can result in children who display behavior problems including drinking and promiscuous sex.
    a) permissive
    b) authoritative
    c) authoritarian
    d) foster

15. According to the book, popular children tend to have parents who use a(n) _____ parenting style.

16. According to the information presented in the text, it appears that, in the long run, television viewing does not have an important effect on the behavior or attitudes of children.
    a) True
    b) False

B. MATCHING

_____	1. initiative versus guilt	a.	adolescence
_____	2. ego integrity versus despair	b.	level of care is important
_____	3. basic trust versus basic mistrust	c.	late adulthood
_____	4. identity versus role confusion	d.	independence and choices
_____	5. intimacy versus isolation	e.	middle adulthood
_____	6. autonomy versus shame and doubt	f.	initiate activities
_____	7. generativity versus stagnation	g.	young adulthood
_____	8. industry versus inferiority	h.	accomplishments

C. COMPLETE THE TABLE: Place the letter of the corresponding description in the correct age box.

2 – 3 months _____	8 months _____	24 months _____
20 weeks _____	12 months _____	30 months _____
6 months _____	18 – 20 months _____	36 months _____

a) focus on phonemes, rhythm, and intonation of native tongue

b) telegraphic speech

c) cooing sounds and smiles when talked to

d) single words

e) babbling and phonemes of all languages

f) grammar rules and overregularization

g) vowel and consonant sounds mixed with cooing

h) vocabulary of about 270 words

i) two-word sentences

Fortunately, babies have ways of communicating their needs long before they develop language skills. Unfortunately, this early communication method is often most active at 2:00 AM. Also, it can be difficult to differentiate between the, "I want food," communication and the, "You'd better change my diaper," communication.

PREPARE A LECTURE: This activity is designed to offer you an opportunity to take advantage of a valuable mode of learning, elaborate rehearsal. Once you have finished the OMSE section, write a lecture using the instructional guide provided below. After your lecture is prepared, you can enhance your learning by writing a quiz covering the material. Now it is time to find some willing and inquisitive audience members. Your roommates or family may be a great place to start. Present them the lecture as if you are teaching a class. Remember to ask for questions and give your students the quiz following the lecture. This exercise can also serve to turn a *study-buddy* group into a very productive way to prepare for the test. Each member of the group can take different OMSE sections for their lecture/teacher role while the rest of the group serves as the class.

I. Key Terms, Names, Dates, and Concepts you will include in this lecture:

1. _____
2. _____
3. _____
4. _____

5. _____
6. _____
7. _____
8. _____

9. _____
10. _____
11. _____
12. _____

II. Learning Objectives (what do you want the student to know and be able to do as a result of your lecture):

1. _____
2. _____
3. _____
4. _____
5. _____

III. Lecture Notes (notes should be brief cues and serve as a guide).

Major topic #1: _____

　　Sub-topics and notes: _____

_____

_____

_____

Major topic #2: _____

　　Sub-topics and notes: _____

_____

_____

_____

Major topic #3: _____

　　Sub-topics and notes: _____

_____

_____

_____

KEY TERMS AND CONCEPTS EXERCISE

The key terms and concepts are presented in the order of their appearance in the text. Space is provided for you to include a personalized definition or example of each term or concept. As you encounter each term in the text, make a note of its meaning and context. Next, conceptualize the meaning of the term in a way that makes the most sense to you. You can also think about examples of the term from your own life. Write your definition and/or example in the space provided next to the word in this book. The KEY TERMS exercise utilizes a modified *T-note* design so that you can self-evaluate your mastery of the definitions. First lay a sheet of paper over the terms and concepts side of the page so that you only see the definitions. Read the definition and try to recall the term or concept. Mark all those you are unable to answer so you can restudy them. When you have learned all of the terms and concepts in this way, move the paper to the definition side so that you can see only the term or concept, try to recall both the textbook definition and your personal version. Repeat this until you know all of the terms and concepts by definition and personal understanding.

Developmental Psychology	The study of how humans grow, develop, and change throughout the life span. _____ _____ _____ _____
Nature-Nurture Controversy	The debate concerning the relative influences of heredity and environment on development. Is everything that you are the result of a genetic blueprint that can never be altered, or have life experiences served to mold and shape you as you have grown? _____ _____ _____ _____
Longitudinal Study	A type of developmental study in which the same group of subjects is followed and measured at different ages. _____ _____
Cross-Sectional Study	A type of developmental study in which researchers compare groups of subjects of different ages on certain characteristics to determine age-related differences. _____ _____ _____ _____
Genes	Within the chromosomes, the segments of DNA that are the basic units for the transmission of hereditary traits. Genes are the biological blueprints of life. _____ _____ _____ _____
Chromosomes	Rod-shaped structures in the nuclei of body cells, which contain all the genes and carry all the hereditary information. With the exception of sperm cells and mature egg cells, all normal body cells contain 23 pairs of chromosomes. _____ _____ _____
Sex Chromosomes	The 23rd pair of chromosomes, which carry the genes that determine one's sex and primary and secondary sex characteristics. _____ _____
Dominant Gene	The gene that is expressed in the individual. In other words, if you have one gene for brown hair and one gene for blond hair, the brown hair gene, being the dominant gene, will be expressed over the blond hair gene, or recessive gene, and you will have brown hair. _____ _____ _____ _____

Recessive Gene	A gene that will not be expressed if paired with a dominant gene but will be expressed if paired with another recessive gene. If you are born with two genes for blond hair, then you will have blond hair—naturally. _____
Period Of The Zygote	Lasting about two weeks, the period from conception to the time the zygote attaches itself to the uterine wall; during this two-week period, the first stage of prenatal development, rapid cell division occurs. _____
Prenatal	Occurring between conception and birth and lasting approximately 38 weeks. _____
Embryo	The developing human organism during the period (week 3 through week 8) when the major systems, organs, and structures of the body develop. _____
Fetus	The developing human organism during the period (week 9 until birth) when rapid growth and further development of the structures, organs, and systems of the body occur. _____
Identical (Monozygotic) Twins	Twins with exactly the same genes, who develop after one egg is fertilized by one sperm, and the zygote splits into two parts. _____
Fraternal (Dizygotic) Twins	Twins, no more alike genetically than ordinary siblings, who develop after two eggs are released during ovulation and are fertilized by two sperm. _____
Teratogens	Harmful agents in the prenatal environment, which can have a negative impact on prenatal development or even cause birth defects. Drugs, including alcohol and cigarettes, illnesses, X rays, and toxic waste are examples of teratogens. _____
Critical Period	A period that is so important to development that a harmful environmental influence can keep a bodily structure or behavior from developing normally. _____
Fetal Alcohol Syndrome	A condition, caused by maternal alcohol intake during pregnancy, in which the baby is born mentally retarded, abnormally small, and with facial, organ, and limb abnormalities. _____
Low-Birth-Weight Baby	A baby weighing less than 5.5 pounds. Poor nutrition, poor prenatal care, cigarette smoking, drug use, and maternal infection all increase the likelihood of having a low-birth-weight baby with complications. _____
Preterm Infant	An infant born before the 37th week and weighing less than 5.5 pounds; a premature infant. _____

Neonate	Newborn infant up to one month old. _____
Reflexes	Inborn, unlearned, automatic responses to certain environmental stimuli (examples: coughing, blinking, sucking, grasping). _____
Visual Cliff	An apparatus used to test depth perception in infants and young animals. _____
Habituation	A decrease in response or attention to a stimulus as an infant becomes accustomed to it.
Maturation	Changes that occur according to one's genetically determined, biological timetable of development. _____
Temperament	A person's behavioral style or characteristic way of responding to the environment. _____
Attachment	The strong, affectionate bond a child forms with the mother or primary caregiver. _____
Surrogate	Substitute; someone or something that stands in place of. _____
Separation Anxiety	The fear and distress shown by toddlers when their parent leaves, occurring from 8 to 24 months and reaching a peak between 12 and 18 months. _____
Stranger Anxiety	A fear of strangers common in infants at about 6 months and increasing in intensity until about 12½ months, and then declining in the second year. _____
Schemas	Piaget's term for a cognitive structure or concept used to identify and interpret information. According to Piaget, cognitive development begins with only a few basic schemas, which are modified while other new schemas develop through a process called accommodation. _____
Assimilation	The process by which new objects, events, experiences, or information are incorporated into existing schemas. _____
Accommodation	The process by which existing schemas are modified and new schemas are created to incorporate new objects, events, experiences, or information. For example, a child who has been exposed to only one type of 4-legged creature, a dog, may think all 4-legged creatures are dogs. The child will eventually develop a new schema for cats, horses, and other animals.

Sensorimotor Stage	Piaget's first stage of cognitive development (ages birth to 2 years), culminating with the development of object permanence and the beginning of representational thought. _____ _____ _____ _____
Object Permanence	The realization that objects continue to exist even when they are no longer perceived. When the ball rolls under the sofa and out of sight, a child who has not developed object permanence assumes that the ball no longer exists. _____ _____
Preoperational Stage	Piaget's second stage of cognitive development (ages 2 to 7 years), characterized by rapid development of language and thinking governed by perception rather than logic. _____ _____ _____
Conservation	The concept that a given quantity of matter remains the same despite the rearrangement or change in its appearance, as long as nothing has been added or taken away. Two balls of clay are perceived as being equal, but when one ball is rolled out into a cigar shape, are they still the same amount or quantity of clay? _____ _____
Centration	A preoperational child's tendency to focus on only one dimension of a stimulus and ignore other dimensions. _____ _____ _____
Reversibility	The realization that any change in the shape, position, or order of matter can be reversed mentally. _____ _____ _____
Concrete Operations Stage	Piaget's third stage of cognitive development (ages 7 to 11 years), during which a child acquires the concepts of reversibility and conservation and is able to apply logical thinking to concrete objects. _____ _____ _____
Formal Operations Stage	Piaget's fourth and final stage, characterized by the ability to apply logical thinking to abstract problems and hypothetical situations. _____ _____ _____
Babbling	Vocalization of the basic speech sounds (phonemes), which begins between 4 and 6 months. _____ _____
Phonemes	The basic speech sounds in any language that, when combined, form words. _____ _____
Overextension	The act of using a word, on the basis of some shared feature, to apply to a broader range of objects than appropriate. _____ _____ _____
Underextension	Restricting the use of a word to only a few, rather than all, members of a class of subjects. _____ _____ _____

Telegraphic Speech	Short sentences that follow a strict word order and contain only essential content elements.
Overregularization	The act of inappropriately applying the grammatical rules for forming plurals and past tenses to irregular nouns and verbs.
Socialization	The process of learning socially acceptable behaviors, attitudes, and values.
Psychosocial Stages	Erikson's eight developmental stages through the life span, each defined by a conflict that must be resolved satisfactorily in order for healthy personality development to occur.
Basic Trust Versus Basic Mistrust	Erikson's first stage (ages birth to 1 year), when infants develop trust or mistrust based on the quality of care, love, and affection provided.
Autonomy Versus Shame And Doubt	Erikson's second stage (ages 1 to 3 years), when infants develop autonomy or shame based on how parents react to their expressions of will and their wish to do things for themselves.
Initiative Versus Guilt	Erikson's third stage (ages 3 to 6 years), when children develop a sense of initiative or guilt depending on how parents react to their initiation of play, their motor activities, and their questions.
Industry Versus Inferiority	Erikson's fourth stage (ages 6 years to puberty), when children develop a sense of industry or inferiority based on how parents and teachers react to their efforts to undertake projects.
Authoritarian Parents	Parents who make arbitrary rules, expect unquestioned obedience from their children, punish transgressions, and value obedience to authority.
Authoritative Parents	Parents who set high but realistic standards, reason with the child, enforce limits, and encourage open communication and independence.
Permissive Parents	Parents who make few rules or demands and allow children to make their own decisions and control their own behavior.

FROM THE LABORATORY TO REAL LIFE

Swallowed a Bullet!

I remember when I was quite young—just old enough to remember my favorite television shows and major events in my life—a friend of my mother's and her son came to visit. He was a few years older than I was, and he had with him a BB gun, a popular item for boys of that age. When I saw that BB gun, all I could think of was my favorite heroes on all the popular television westerns of the time. In those TV shows the good guy always carried a gun with bullets that would explode out of the barrel and leave the bad guys sorry they messed with the law! Anyway, I was just amazed! This guy had a real gun just like my heroes on TV! And, to make it even better, he had the bullets that went in the gun – the BBs. I could not believe my luck! I got hold of one of the BBs and ended up swallowing it! Please don't ask me how it ended up in my mouth. I was terrified. I knew that bullets exploded and left the bad guys dead. I sat there as still as I could, not saying a thing. I was sure that I would explode with a bullet flying out of my stomach if I dared move a muscle! I didn't dare tell anybody either as I was certain to be in big trouble for swallowing a bullet. Finally, after some time, I realized that I was not going to blow up and concluded that there must be a difference between the BBs my new friend had and the real bullets one would fire from a real gun.

1. Piaget would refer to my concept of guns and bullets as a _____.

2. When I believed the BB gun and BBs were just like the real guns I saw on television, I was doing what Piaget would call _____.

3. When I changed my concepts of guns and bullets in terms of a more complex classification system Piaget would suggest that experience resulted in _____.

Drugs and Pre-natal Development

I have spent many years counseling alcohol and drug dependent adults. One of the more tragic problems faced by addiction industry professionals is that of a pregnant woman who uses alcohol or drugs. This can be harmful or even fatal for the developing baby. Often, early in treatment, the mother expresses deep guilt and regret once her head begins to clear and she is able to consider the potential harm that her child may experience due to her chemical abuse. Unfortunately, in many cases, the mother enters treatment after some damage has been done.

1. It has been determined that there are three stages of pre-natal development called trimesters. The first trimester is marked by _____ periods during which body structures develop and environmental factors can interfere with and permanently alter this development.

2. Things such as drugs, alcohol, other toxic chemicals, and even infections suffered by the mother can have a harmful effect on the pre-natal environment. These are all examples of
_____.

3. One serious outcome of maternal drinking is known as _____ _____ syndrome. Babies suffering from this are unusually small and mentally retarded.

Proud Parents

1. I have a friend who has a 19-month-old daughter. He and his wife are very proud of this energetic little girl and they should be – she is a wonderful child. They are especially happy to tell people that their daughter can speak about 50 words already and that this is well beyond what would be expected for a child of that age. Is this assertion correct? _____

2. My friend also likes to point out that his daughter frequently uses two-word sentences and he swears that 19-month-olds rarely use sentences of any kind. Is he right? _____

3. He also gloats over the fact that his little girl already understands that when a ball rolls under the couch, it really is under the couch and has not discontinued to exist. He claims there is a name for this but he cannot remember it. Can you? _____ _____.

FROM THEORY TO PRACTICE

Born to Be Wild

Developmental theory is not the only place in the broad field of psychology where you will run across the nature-nurture controversy. In fact, nature-nurture is a fundamental discussion throughout much of the text and most sub-specialties within psychology. Occasionally, I present workshops and seminars for professionals and paraprofessionals in the field. Invariably, someone always asks a question about what to do with a child who simply will not mind his teachers, nor seems to be troubled by receiving consequences for not minding. Also invariably, I respond with a question about the type of parenting the child is receiving. Unfortunately, I usually already know what the answer will be. In today's society, there are many parents who value their personal interests above raising their children. Of course there are many very good parents, but there are always some parents who need a "time out" more than do their children. Recently, I was speaking before a group of caseworkers who work with troubled children and their families. One audience member stayed after the workshop to ask me about a particular case—that of a 6-year-old boy who seemed to be constantly in trouble at school. The caseworker asked me how to begin to shape the boy's behavior in different ways, explaining that he hits other students and teachers, and uses a great deal of profanity. She reported that he was in detention or suspended much of the time and that these punishments seemed to have a paradoxical effect on the child—in other words, he seemed to feel good about getting in trouble. When asked about the child's parents and their interest in therapy or parenting skills, I was informed that the father had disappeared before the child was born, and the mother was a drug addict who had been in and out of treatment several times. She also told me that the boy had been born with cocaine in his system.

1. How much of this child's behaviors and attitudes is probably the result of heredity or nature? Support your answer with references from the text using the clue provided.   Nature _____%

a) Temperament? _____
_____
_____

2. How much of the child's attitudes and behaviors is probably the result of environmental effects? Use the text, the guide below, your knowledge of substance abuse, and common sense to support your answer.   Nurture _____%

a) Malnutrition? _____

b) Teratogens? _____

c) Attachment? _____

d) Assimilation? _____

e) Accommodation? _____

f) Parenting? _____

3. Describe the child's behaviors and attitudes as they relate to Erikson's theory. _____
_____
_____
_____
_____

COMPREHENSIVE PRACTICE TEST

1. From the evidence presented in the book, it appears that the nature-nurture controversy has been solved – our development is based primarily on our biology.
   a) True
   b) False

2. We are interested in the effects of rock videos on the gender attitudes of children. We show the same videos to five different groups of children. Each group consists of children born in the same year, and the ages range from ten through 15 years. We then ask the members of each group to respond to questions related to gender attitudes. This sounds like a _____ study.
   a) cross-sectional
   b) childhood factors
   c) longitudinal
   d) multi-factors

3. A _____ study follows the same children over a period of time.
   a) cross-sectional
   b) multi-measurement
   c) longitudinal
   d) multi-factors

4. Genes are composed of DNA and are located on chromosomes.
   a) True
   b) False

5. Except for gametes, our body cells contain how many chromosomes?
   a) 23
   b) 23 pairs
   c) 46 pairs
   d) different cells can have different numbers

6. XX _____ as XY is to _____:
   a) healthy; disorder
   b) male; female
   C) disorder; healthy
   d) female; male

7. Some traits are dominant and some traits are recessive. If Kim gets a dominant and a recessive gene for a certain trait, the recessive trait will be expressed since she is has an XX chromosome combination.
   a) True
   b) False

8. After conception is the period of the zygote. This lasts for about _____, and then the fertilized egg attaches to the uterine wall.
   a) 48 hours
   b) three months
   c) two weeks
   d) 48 days

9. The period of time from conception to birth is generally called the period of _____ development.
   a) neonatal
   b) prenatal
   c) post-zygotic
   d) post-fertilization development

10. The second stage of pregnancy is known as the _____ stage.
    a) germination
    b) embryo
    c) fetal
    d) zygote

11. The last stage of pregnancy is known as the _____ stage.
    a) germination
    b) embryo
    c) fetal
    d) zygote

12. Monozygotic is to dizygotic as _____ is to _____.
    a) identical; fraternal
    b) female; male
    c) male; female
    d) fraternal; identical

13. Cocaine, alcohol, certain medicines and environmental chemicals can cause harm to the developing baby. These are known as teratogens.
    a) True
    b) False

14. With alcohol, it will actually take the mother drinking a large quantity on a regular basis before there is a danger of harmful effects to the developing baby.
    a) True
    b) False

15. Low birth weight refers to a baby who weighs less than _____ at birth.
    a) 10 pounds
    b) 5.5 pounds
    c) five pounds
    d) 2 pounds

16. A baby is listed as pre-term if he or she is born:
    a) some place other than in a hospital
    b) prior to the parents paying the doctor's bill
    c) before the 45th week
    d) before the 37th week

17. June is just a few days old. She can see, but she still needs to fine-tune her perceptual abilities. If she is a typical baby she probably has _____ vision.
    a) 20/40
    b) 20/600
    c) 40/20
    d) 10/40

18. Habituation is:
    a) a way to determine if a newborn is addicted to drugs
    b) a way to determine if a newborn has all the proper reflex responses
    c) a child's tendency to decrease attention or responding to an object to which it has become accustomed
    d) a new way to accurately measure learning in infants

19. Maturation is:
    a) genetically determined biological changes that follow a timetable of development
    b) behavioral changes based on the child's interaction with the environment
    c) behavioral changes that take place when the child enters high school
    d) applicable only in terms of physiology and not cognition or psychosocial matters

20. Cindy talks about her new baby's general responses to things that happen in the environment, like how the baby smiles so happily every time she holds him. Cindy is talking about her baby's _____.
    a) response system
    b) temperament
    c) latent personality
    d) infant personification

21. Harlow found that attachment seems to be:
    a) very important for the emotional health of the individual
    b) desirable, but not terribly important in the long run
    c) very important for both emotional and physical health in development
    d) fine for monkeys but with no real benefit for humans

22. In the long run, does there appear to be any difference in the mental health status of children who have been determined to have easy temperaments compared with those who are called difficult?
    a) yes
    b) no

23. Sometimes children can be very energetic! Sometimes they seem uncontrollable. The good news is that most will grow out of this and there is no indication of greater future behavior problems than with other children.
    a) True
    b) False

24. Separation anxiety seems to peak at:
    a) 8 – 12 months
    b) 2 – 3 years
    c) 12 – 18 months
    d) 20 – 30 months

25. A child who is suffering from _____ exhibits a wasted appearance, seemingly due to insufficient attention and lack of affection.
    a) stranger anxiety
    b) attention deficit disorder
    c) failure to thrive
    d) attachment disorder

26. Where would an infant most likely experience stranger anxiety—in a familiar setting or a strange setting?
    a) familiar
    b) strange

27. Piaget talked about _____ differences in the way we think as we progress through four stages of cognitive development.
    a) qualitative
    b) quantitative

28. When I was about two and a half-years-old I was bitten by a dog. Fortunately it did not have much of an effect on me. If I had taken on a conceptual idea of dogs as big, mean animals that want to hurt me, people who have studied Piaget's theory might suggest that my _____ about dogs was a bit scary.
    a) prototype
    b) ideal
    c) schema
    d) conditioned response

29. Assimilation is to accommodation as _____ are to _____:
    a) new schemas; existing schemas
    b) existing schemas; new schemas
    c) positive responses; negative responses
    d) negative responses; positive responses

30. Which is the second stage of Piaget's four stages of cognitive development?
    a) formal operational
    b) preoperational
    c) sensorimotor
    d) autonomy versus shame and doubt

31. Pete tried the conservation experiment described in the book on his little brother Jeremy. Jeremy responded with the fact that the different sized glass still had the same amount of water. Jeremy is at least in the stage of:
    a) autonomy versus shame and doubt
    b) concrete operations
    c) sensorimotor
    d) industry versus inferiority

32. Object permanence generally marks the end of the _____ stage of cognitive development.
    a) fourth
    b) second
    c) third
    d) first

33. Vygotsky talked about the _____ view of cognitive development.
    a) sociocultural
    b) metacognitive
    c) psychosocial
    d) memocognitive

34. Metacognition refers to the cognitive ability to know what other people are thinking.
    a) True
    b) False

35. Little Lisa is using what is known as telegraphic speech. She is in the _____ stage of speech development.
    a) one-word
    b) babbling
    c) two-word
    d) formal

36. The nativist position of speech development would suggest that:
    a) speech is something that seems to be most influenced by our culture
    b) speech can be enhanced by letting our children grow up in an environment most similar to their heritage
    c) language ability is primarily innate
    d) language is primarily learned in the family

37. When Jim's mommy says to him, "look at the good little boy eat his dinner," while speaking in a slow, high pitched voice with exaggerated intonation, she is using what the book identified as _____.
    a) preoperational communication
    b) concrete operational communication
    c) babyese
    d) motherese

38. Larry is at the stage where his parents encourage him to take on special little projects. They give him plenty of encouragement and praise him for a job well done. This sense of industry will become important to his future development and personality. Larry is in the _____ stage of Erikson's psychosocial development.
    a) first
    b) second
    c) third
    d) fourth

39. One of the major oppositions to Erikson's theory is that it only covers through adolescence.
   a) True
   b) False

40. The statement, "because I said so," would most likely come from _____ parents.
   a) permissive
   b) authoritarian
   c) authoritative
   d) punitive

ANSWER KEYS

Answer Key: OMSE # 1

A. Quick Quiz	B. Matching
1. c	1. c
2. a	2. d
3. false	3. f
4. b	4. i
5. a	5. g
6. false	6. h
7. true	7. a
8. c	8. j
9. b	9. e
10. a	10. b
11. true	
12. first	
13. third	
14. second	
15. b	

C. Complete the Diagram

Teratogen/Danger	Trimester	Effects
Heroin, cocaine, and crack	First	miscarriage, premature birth, low birth weight, physical defects, fetal death
Alcohol	All	FAS/FAE, lowered IQ
Cigarettes	All	premature birth, low birth weight, spontaneous abortion, sudden infant death syndrome, still birth
Malnutrition	Third	retardation, blindness, hearing loss, death

Answer Key: OMSE # 2

A. Quick Quiz	B. Matching
1. false	1. c
2. c	2. d
3. maturation	3. a
4. b	4. b
5. b	5. c
6. avoidant	6. a
7. b	7. d
8. false	8. b
9. schema	9. b
10. a	
11. c	
12. true	
13. centration	
14. false	
15. private speech	
16. d	

C. Complete the Table

e	b	f	j	h	g
i	a	l	d	k	c

Answer Key: OMSE # 3

A. Quick Quiz	B. Matching
1. c	1. f
2. true	2. c
3. telegraphic	3. b
4. a	4. a
5. false	5. g
6. overextension	6. d
7. d	7. e
8. learning	8. h
9. a	
10. motherese	
11. initiative; guilt	
12. basic trust; basic mistrust	
13. c	
14. a	
15. authoritative	
16. false	

C. Complete the Table

c	a	h
g	d	b
e	i	f

Answer Key: Lab to Life

Swallow a Bullet	Drugs and Prenatal Development	Proud Parents
1. schema	1. critical	1. no
2. assimilation	2. teratogens	2. no
3. accommodation	3. fetal alcohol	3. object permanence

Answer Key: Comprehensive Practice Test

Comprehensive Practice Exam

1. false	11. c	21. c	31. c
2. a	12. a	22. yes	32. b
3. c	13. true	23. false	33. a
4. true	14. false	24. c	34. false
5. b	15. b	25. c	35. c
6. d	16. d	26. b	36. c
7. false	17. b	27. a	37. d
8. c	18. c	28. c	38. d
9. b	19. a	29. b	39. false
10. b	20. b	30. d	40. b

10

ADOLESCENCE AND ADULTHOOD

The imagination of a boy is healthy, and the mature imagination of a man is healthy, but there is a space of life between, in which the soul is in a ferment, the character undecided, the way of life uncertain, the ambition thick-sighted: thence proceeds mawkishness.

–John Keats (1818)

CHAPTER OVERVIEW

When I was 15 years old, I was in a car accident so serious that by the time I got to the hospital I was basically "gone." Somehow, I became stable enough to endure emergency surgery and fourteen days later I woke from a coma. The reason I relate this at this point is because of the changes that occurred in my life following my recovery. Prior to the accident I was not a great student and had no plans to go to college. I really did not know what I wanted to do with my life. Erikson would say I was in the midst of role confusion. After my recovery, however, I felt as if I had a second chance and I decided to see what I could do if I really tried. When I got back to school, my grades went from consistent Ds and Fs to As and Bs. I seemed to have gained an important insight about myself as I lay in that hospital. In my last year in high school I had the opportunity to take a psychology course and it was then that I discovered my passion, at least in terms of a career. I guess I moved from role confusion to identity. I look back on that time now and realize how important those adolescent years can be in the development of who we become as adults. Everyday I use my own experience of adolescence, that of others I knew, and the theories presented in the text to understand and teach the fascinating process of human development.

This chapter will help you gain a more practiced and functional understanding of the developmental processes of adolescence and adulthood. The materials are divided into two OMSE sections: 1) adolescence, and 2) Erikson and adulthood. You will examine the many challenges and transition events we face as we continue to experience, grow, and change throughout the life cycle.

By completing the exercises provided, you should gain a thorough understanding of the information provided in your text. In other words, you should be better prepared for tests, quizzes, class participation, and life itself.

TIMELINE

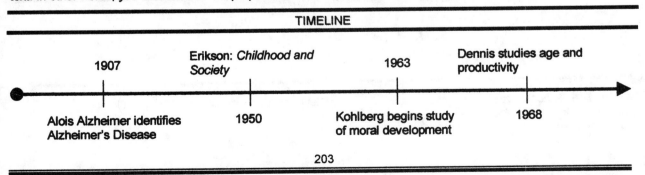

| | | Erikson: *Childhood and Society* | | 1963 | | Dennis studies age and productivity |
| 1907 | | | | | | |

| Alois Alzheimer identifies Alzheimer's Disease | | 1950 | | Kohlberg begins study of moral development | | 1968 |

CHAPTER OUTLINE

Adolescence: Physical and Cognitive Development

Physical Development during Adolescence: Growing, Growing, Grown

Cognitive Development in Adolescence: Piaget's Formal Operations Stage

Adolescence: Moral and Social Development

Kohlberg's Theory of Moral Development

Parental Relationships: Their Quality and Influence

The Peer Group

Sexuality and Adolescence

Teenage Pregnancy: Too Much Too Soon

Part-Time Jobs for Adolescents: A Positive or a Negative

Erikson's Psychosocial Theory: Adolescence through Adulthood

Identity versus Role Confusion: Erikson's Stage for Adolescence

Intimacy versus Isolation: Erikson's Stage for Early Adulthood

Pioneers: Erik Homberger Erikson

Generativity versus Stagnation: Erikson's Stage for Middle Adulthood

Ego Integrity versus Despair: Erikson's Final Stage

Erikson's Theory: Does Research Support It?

Other Theories of Adulthood

Levinson's Seasons of Life

Reinke, Ellicott, and Harris: The Life Course in Women

Life Stages: Fact or Fiction

Early and Middle Adulthood

Physical Changes in Adulthood

Intellectual Capacity During Early and Middle Adulthood

Lifestyle Patterns in Adulthood

Personality and Social Development in Middle Age

Later Adulthood

Physical Changes in Later Adulthood

Cognitive Development in Later Adulthood

Personality and Social Development in Later Adulthood

Culture and Care for the Elderly

Death and Dying

Apply It!

Thinking Critically

Chapter Summary and Review

KEY TERMS

Adolescence: Physical and Cognitive Development

adolescence

puberty

adolescent growth spurt

secondary sex characteristics

menarche

formal operations stage

imaginary audience

personal fable

Adolescence: Moral and Social Development

preconventional level

conventional level

postconventional level

Erikson's Psychosocial Theory: Adolescence through Adulthood

identity versus role confusion

intimacy versus isolation

generativity versus stagnation

ego integrity versus despair

Other Theories of Adulthood

life structure

midlife crisis

Later and Middle Adulthood

presbyopia

menopause

Later Adulthood

crystallized intelligence

fluid intelligence

senile dementia

Alzheimer's disease

TIMELINE

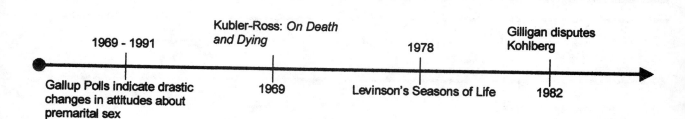

OMSE # 1: ADOLESCENCE

LEARNING OBJECTIVES

1. How difficult is adolescence for most teenagers?
2. What physical changes occur during puberty?
3. What are the psychological effects of early and late maturation for boys and girls?
4. What cognitive abilities develop during the formal operations stage?
5. What are Kohlberg's three levels of moral reasoning?
6. What do cross-cultural studies reveal about the universality of Kohlberg's theory?
7. What outcomes are often associated with the authoritative, authoritarian, and permissive parenting styles?
8. What are some of the useful functions of the adolescent peer group?
9. What are some of the disturbing consequences of teenage pregnancy?
10. In general, what is the impact of adolescents working more than 15 or 20 hours a week during the school year?

LEARNING MASTERY SCORECARD: Update your score card as you work through the various sections of the chapter. First, find and define key terms and concepts included in each section and note the page number(s) from the text that contain important references to the material. Next, gain a practical understanding of the concepts by considering the Laboratory to Life scenarios and thinking of at least one original example of how the concept might apply in real life. Complete the *Objective-Mastery Self-Evaluation* (OMSE) exercises for this section and record your scores. Revisit the exercises, recording your score and the date completed until you have attained mastery (100%). Finally, decide how you would prepare a lecture on each objective using the template provided, outline the lecture, and practice presenting it. Keep an honest tally of your achievements and, when finished, you will have developed learning mastery through elaborate rehearsal.

Key Term	page #	Key Term	page #	Key Term	page #
adolescence	____	menarche	____	preconventional level	____
puberty	____	formal operations stage	____	conventional level	____
adolescent growth spurt	____	imaginary audience	____	postconventional level	____
secondary sex characteristics	____	personal fable	____		

Quick Quiz

Date	Score	Date	Score	Date	Score
__/__/__	____	__/__/__	____	__/__/__	____
__/__/__	____	__/__/__	____	__/__/__	100%

Elaborate Rehearsal

Lecture Preparation	Completion Date
Key Terms, Persons, & Concepts	__/__/__
Learning Objectives	__/__/__
Lecture Notes	__/__/__

A. QUICK QUIZ

1. The text referred to _____ as the most startling change during puberty.
   a) the development of secondary sex characteristics
   b) the adolescent growth spurt
   c) the change in children's voices
   d) the development of primary sex characteristics

2. On the average, puberty starts earlier for girls than for boys.
   a) True
   b) False

3. Menarche is the term used to describe the onset of _____.

4. Which of the following groups seem to enjoy the most initial advantages?
   a) early puberty females
   b) late puberty males
   c) early puberty males
   d) late puberty females

5. Early puberty girls are most likely, in the long run, to enjoy future academic and social success. They are overwhelmingly found at the top of the academic rankings at school.
   a) True
   b) False

6. Jennifer has mastered algebra and is thinking about the future a lot these days. She fascinates her parents with her ability to interpret, and even provide her own revisions to famous philosophical ideas. Jennifer appears to be in the _____ stage of Piaget's theory of cognitive development.

7. Janet faced her current dilemma with fear and the knowledge that tomorrow everybody in school would be talking about her new braces. The text identified Janet's negative anticipation as a kind of egocentrism called:
   a) the personal fable
   b) the adolescent audience
   c) social phobia
   d) the imaginary audience

8. According to the concept of _____, adolescents may take risks such as driving fast, starting cigarette smoking, or engaging in other unsafe activities because they believe they are indestructible.
   a) the fallacy of eternal youth
   b) the adolescent schema
   c) the personal fable
   d) the post conventional fable

9. The above two questions deal with what the text referred to as _____ _____.

10. Kohlberg would suggest that a child who has attained a level of formal operations is probably at the conventional level of moral reasoning.
    a) True
    b) False

11. Tamara believes that pleasing others defines a good person. She is at which stage of moral development?
    a) stage 4
    b) stage 5
    c) stage 2
    d) stage 3

12. Research has found that adolescent conflict with parents is both universal and inevitable.
    a) True
    b) False

13. Which of the following parenting styles seems to result in the most well adjusted adolescents?
    a) authoritative
    b) permissive
    c) authoritarian
    d) unavailable

14. An interesting finding is that, for boys, athletic ability and conformity is an important factor in gaining popularity with girls, as well as with other boys.
    a) True
    b) False

15. The text indicated that _____ percent of adolescent girls who have babies, and choose to raise their babies, will never complete high school.

B. MATCHING: Place the appropriate letter in the space provided.

_____ 1. eventually taller and slimmer than counterparts	a.	early time maturation boys
_____ 2. often teased and treated like kids	b.	late time maturation girls
_____ 3. enhanced peer group status	c.	early time maturation girls
_____ 4. more likely to be unhappy with physical appearance later on	d.	late time maturation boys
_____ 5. receive sexual advances from older members of the opposite sex		
_____ 6. feel confident		
_____ 7. often judged less attractive by peers and adults		
_____ 8. may eventually become shorter and heavier than counterparts		

C. COMPLETE THE DIAGRAM: Place the letter corresponding to the correct stage of Kohlberg's theory in the space provided.

	STAGE			MORAL REASONING
a.	Stage 1	_____	1.	He should not steal the drug because people do not like a thief.
b.	Stage 2	_____	2.	He should steal the drug because his wife's life is more important than the law.
c.	Stage 3	_____	3.	He should not steal the drug because it is against the law.
d.	Stage 4	_____	4.	He should not steal the drug because he will get punished for doing that.
e.	Stage 5	_____	5.	He should not steal the drug because his duty is to maintain social order.
f.	Stage 6	_____	6.	He should steal the drug because his wife will cook and clean for him once she is better.

PREPARE A LECTURE: This activity is designed to offer you an opportunity to take advantage of a valuable mode of learning, elaborate rehearsal. Once you have finished the OMSE section, write a lecture using the instructional guide provided below. After your lecture is prepared, you can enhance your learning by writing a quiz covering the material. Now it is time to find some willing and inquisitive audience members. Your roommates or family may be a great place to start. Present them the lecture as if you are teaching a class. Remember to ask for questions and give your students the quiz following the lecture. This exercise can also serve to turn a *study-buddy* group into a very productive way to prepare for the test. Each member of the group can take different OMSE sections for their lecture/teacher role while the rest of the group serves as the class.

I. Key Terms, Names, Dates, and Concepts you will include in this lecture:

1. _____
2. _____
3. _____
4. _____

5. _____
6. _____
7. _____
8. _____

9. _____
10. _____
11. _____
12. _____

II. Learning Objectives (what do you want the student to know and be able to do as a result of your lecture):

1. _____
2. _____
3. _____
4. _____
5. _____

III. Lecture Notes (notes should be brief cues and serve as a guide).

Major topic #1: _____

   Sub-topics and notes: _____

_____

_____

_____

Major topic #2: _____

   Sub-topics and notes: _____

_____

_____

_____

Major topic #3: _____

   Sub-topics and notes: _____

_____

_____

_____

OMSE # 2: ERIKSON AND ADULTHOOD

LEARNING OBJECTIVES

1. How did Erikson explain the fifth psychosocial stage—identity versus role confusion?
2. What is Erikson's psychosocial task for early adulthood?
3. What changes did Erikson believe are essential for healthy personality development in middle age?
4. What is the key to a positive resolution to Erikson's eighth stage—ego integrity versus despair?
5. How is Levinson's concept of life structure related to his proposed stages of development?
6. What did Reinke, Ellicott, and Harris's study of middle-class women reveal about major transitional periods in the life cycle?
7. What are the physical changes associated with middle age?
8. In general, can adults look forward to an increase or a decrease in intellectual performance from their 20s to their 60s?
9. What are some of the trends in lifestyle patterns in young adulthood?
10. What effect does parenthood have on marital satisfaction?
11. Why is middle age often considered the prime of life?
12. What are some physical changes generally associated with later adulthood?
13. What happens to mental ability in later adulthood?
14. What is Alzheimer's disease?
15. According to Kübler-Ross, what stages are experienced by terminally ill patients as they come to terms with death?
16. What are some benefits of hospice care?

LEARNING MASTERY SCORECARD: Update your score card as you work through the various sections of the chapter. First, find and define key terms and concepts included in each section and note the page number(s) from the text that contain important references to the material. Next, gain a practical understanding of the concepts by considering the Laboratory to Life scenarios and thinking of at least one original example of how the concept might apply in real life. Complete the *Objective-Mastery Self-Evaluation* (OMSE) exercises for this section and record your scores. Revisit the exercises, recording your score and the date completed until you have attained mastery (100%). Finally, decide how you would prepare a lecture on each objective using the template provided, outline the lecture, and practice presenting it. Keep an honest tally of your achievements and, when finished, you will have developed learning mastery through elaborate rehearsal.

Key Term	Page #	Key Term	Page #	Key Term	Page #
identity versus role confusion	____	life structure	____	crystallized intelligence	____
intimacy versus isolation	____	midlife crisis	____	fluid intelligence	____
generativity versus stagnation	____	presbyopia	____	senile dementia	____
ego integrity versus despair	____	menopause	____	Alzheimer's disease	____

Quick Quiz

Date	Score	Date	Score	Date	Score
_/_/_	____	_/_/_	____	_/_/_	____
_/_/_	____	_/_/_	____	_/_/_	100%

Elaborate Rehearsal

Lecture Preparation	Completion Date
Key Terms, Persons, & Concepts	_/_/_
Learning Objectives	_/_/_
Lecture Notes	_/_/_

A. QUICK QUIZ

1. Charlene is at a point in her life where she is wrestling with a sense of who she is and where she will go from here. She would be considered to be in Erikson's _____ stage of psychosocial development.
   a) second
   b) third
   c) fourth
   d) fifth

2. Would Erikson say that a strong self-identity is important for an intimate relationship?
    a) yes   b) no

3. Has subsequent research supported Erikson's theory?
    a) yes, unconditionally   c) yes, with some qualifications
    b) no, not at all   d) only 1 or 2 stages

4. According to the text, the physical "prime of life" occurs for most people during the _____.
    a) teens   c) 30s
    b) 20s   d) 40s

5. The most common symptom associated with menopause is _____.
    a) depression   c) weight gain
    b) hot flashes   d) weight loss

6. Has the "conventional wisdom" that intellectual ability reaches its peak in the 20s been shown to be true?
    a) yes   c) yes for males but not for females
    b) yes for females but not for males   d) no

7. Dennis (1968) found that the decade of the _____ was the most productive for the 738 persons he studied.
    a) 20s   c) 40s
    b) 30s   d) 50s

8. The birth of the first child, for most couples, begins a time of increased marital satisfaction.
    a) True   b) False

9. According to the text, how many young adults will change jobs or occupational fields in the course of their life?
    a) 10 percent   c) 25 percent
    b) 33 percent   d) 45 percent

10. What did Levinson call the basic pattern of one's life at any given time? _____ _____

11. Does research support the idea of the mid-life crisis?
    a) yes   c) yes for white males only
    b) no   d) yes for lower socioeconomic males

12. In the aging brain, the apparent shrinkage of the cortex seems to be due to a breakdown of myelin sheath.
    a) True   b) False

13. Walter is a very active and content 93-year-old man. The text suggested that his childhood personality trait of _____ would predict his current status.

14. _____ intelligence is to verbal ability as _____ intelligence is to abstract reasoning.

15. Which of the following would be listed as the third stage in the Kubler-Ross theory of grieving?
    a) denial   c) anger
    b) bargaining   d) depression

Those who start eating right and exercising regularly when they are young can maintain solid physical and mental functioning throughout their lives. Later adulthood can offer exciting and enjoyable rewards for those who continue to practice good health habits and exercise their mental capacities.

B. MATCHING: Match the appropriate age range with Levinson's transitional period description.

	TRANSITIONAL PERIOD DESCRIPTION	AGE RANGE
_____	1. choices of occupation and love relationships	a. 17 - 22
_____	2. mid-life crisis	b. 22 - 28
_____	3. climbing the ladder of success	c. 28 - 33
_____	4. psychological separation from parents	d. 33 - 40
_____	5. looking to the retirement years	e. 40 - 45
_____	6. modification of the first adult life structure	f. 45 - 60
_____	7. similar to Erikson's seventh stage	g. 60 - 65

C. COMPLETE THE DIAGRAM—ERIKSON'S PSYCHOSOCIAL THEORY: Complete the following table by placing the letter indicating the name of the stage next to the corresponding age range, and the letter which describes the stage next to the corresponding stage name.

Age Range	Stage Name	Stage Description
1. Birth to 1	1.	1.
2. 1 – 3	2.	2.
3. 3 – 6	3.	3.
4. 6 to puberty	4.	4.
5. adolescence	5.	5.
6. young adult	6.	6.
7. middle adult	7.	7.
8. late adult	8.	8.

Stage Name		Stage Description	
a. initiative vs. guilt		i. plan and undertake tasks, enjoy developing motor and other abilities	
b. identity vs. role confusion		j. develop the ability to share with, care for, and commit self to another	
c. generativity vs. stagnation		k. status depends on the degree and regularity of care, love, and affection	
d. trust vs. mistrust		l. the individual reviews his/her life	
e. intimacy vs. isolation		m. children attempt to accomplish tasks – making and doing things	
f. ego integrity vs. despair		n. children learn to express their will and independence	
g. autonomy vs. shame and doubt		o. transition from childhood to adulthood	
h. industry vs. inferiority		p. contribute to the development of the next generation	

PREPARE A LECTURE: This activity is designed to offer you an opportunity to take advantage of a valuable mode of learning, elaborate rehearsal. Once you have finished the OMSE section, write a lecture using the instructional guide provided below. After your lecture is prepared, you can enhance your learning by writing a quiz covering the material. Now it is time to find some willing and inquisitive audience members. Your roommates or family may be a great place to start. Present them the lecture as if you are teaching a class. Remember to ask for questions and give your students the quiz following the lecture. This exercise can also serve to turn a *study-buddy* group into a very productive way to prepare for the test. Each member of the group can take different OMSE sections for their lecture/teacher role while the rest of the group serves as the class.

I. Key Terms, Names, Dates, and Concepts you will include in this lecture:

1. _____	5. _____	9. _____
2. _____	6. _____	10. _____
3. _____	7. _____	11. _____
4. _____	8. _____	12. _____

II. Learning Objectives (what do you want the student to know and be able to do as a result of your lecture):

1. _____
2. _____
3. _____
4. _____
5. _____

III. Lecture Notes (notes should be brief cues and serve as a guide).

Major topic #1: _____

    Sub-topics and notes: _____
_____
_____
_____
_____

Major topic #2: _____

    Sub-topics and notes: _____
_____
_____
_____
_____

Major topic #3: _____

    Sub-topics and notes: _____
_____
_____
_____
_____

KEY TERMS AND CONCEPTS EXERCISE

The key terms and concepts are presented in order of their appearance in the text. Space is provided for you to include a personalized definition or example of each term or concept. As you encounter each term in the text, make a note of its meaning and context. Next, conceptualize the meaning of the term in a way that makes the most sense to you. Also, think about examples of the term from your own life. Write your definition and/or example in the space provided next to the word. The KEY TERMS exercise utilizes a modified *T-note* design so that you can self-evaluate your mastery of the definitions. First lay a sheet of paper over the terms and concepts side of the page so that you only see the definitions. Read the definition and try to recall the term or concept. Mark all those you are unable to answer so you can restudy them. When you have learned all of the terms and concepts in this way, move the paper to the definition side so that you can see only the term or concept, try to recall both the textbook definition and your personal version. Repeat this until you know all of the terms and concepts by definition and personal understanding.

Adolescence	The developmental stage that begins at puberty and encompasses the period from the end of childhood to the beginning of adulthood. _____ _____
Puberty	A period of rapid physical growth and change that culminates in sexual maturity. _____ _____
Adolescent Growth Spurt	A period of rapid physical growth that peaks in girls at about age 12 and in boys at about age 14. _____ _____
Secondary Sex Characteristics	Those physical characteristics that are not directly involved in reproduction but distinguish the mature male from the mature female. _____ _____

Menarche	The onset of menstruation, menarche marks the advent of puberty for girls, and generally occurs between the ages of 10 and 15 ½.
Formal Operations Stage	Piaget's final stage of cognitive development, characterized by the ability to use logical reasoning in abstract situations.
Imaginary Audience	The belief of adolescents that they are or will be the focus of attention in social situations and that others are or will be as critical or approving as they are of themselves.
Personal Fable	An exaggerated sense of personal uniqueness and indestructibility, which may be basis of risk taking common during adolescence.
Preconventional Level	Kohlberg's lowest level of moral reasoning, based on the physical consequences of the act; "right" is whatever avoids punishment or gains a reward.
Conventional Level	Kohlberg's second level of moral reasoning, in which right and wrong are based on the internalized standards of others; "right" is whatever helps or is approved of by others, or whatever is consistent with the laws of society.
Postconventional Level	Kohlberg's highest level of moral reasoning, in which moral reasoning involves weighing moral alternatives; "right" is whatever furthers basic human rights.
Identity Versus Role Confusion	Erikson's fifth psychosocial stage, when adolescents need to establish their own identity and to form values to live by; failure can lead to an identity crisis.
Intimacy Versus Isolation	Erikson's sixth psychosocial stage, when the young adult must establish intimacy in a relationship in order to avoid feeling a sense of isolation and loneliness.
Generativity Versus Stagnation	Erikson's stage for middle age, when people become increasingly concerned with guiding the next generation rather than stagnating.
Ego Integrity Versus Despair	Erikson's stage for old age, when people look back on their lives with satisfaction or with major regrets.
Life Structure	Levinson's term for the basic pattern of one's life at any given time, including one's relationships and activities and the significance they have for the individual.

Midlife Crisis	A period of turmoil usually occurring in a person's 40s and brought on by an awareness of one's mortality; characterized by a reassessment of one's life and a decision to make changes, either drastic or moderate, in order to make the remaining years better. _____
Presbyopia	A condition occurring in the late to mid 40s in which the eyes' lenses no longer accommodate adequately for near vision, and reading glasses or bifocals are required for reading. _____
Menopause	The cessation of menstruation, occurring between ages 45 or 55 and signifying the end of reproductive capacity. _____
Crystallized Intelligence	Aspects of intelligence, including verbal ability and accumulated knowledge, that tend to increase over the life span. _____
Fluid Intelligence	Aspects of intelligence involving abstract reasoning and mental flexibility, which peak in the early 20's and decline slowly as people age. _____
Senile Dementia	A state of mental deterioration caused by physical deterioration of the brain and characterized by impaired memory and intellect and by altered personality and behavior; senility. _____
Alzheimer's Disease	An incurable form of dementia characterized by progressive deterioration of intellect and personality, resulting from widespread degeneration of brain cells. _____

FROM THE LABORATORY TO LIFE

ADOLESCENCE: FROM THE OUTSIDE LOOKING IN

Barb is 14, slender and shows no signs of physical maturity. She seems bright and, despite her lack of physical maturity, appears competent and confident in social situations. Barb enjoys reasoning through story problems in algebra class. She displays a deep respect for the rights of others, values society's rules, and expresses concern for the welfare of others. Barb recently asked her parents for their opinion on her future plans to attend medical school. Sandra is 13, and much more outgoing than Barb. She thinks her parents are square and argues with her mother a great deal. She is just beginning to mature and she feels inferior to other people her age. She talks of becoming wealthy, but has no plans for future education. Sandra spends most of her time with a certain group of kids and has recently picked up cigarette smoking and swearing. Sandra smokes in front of her mother, but is careful not to smoke around teachers because she fears being suspended. Sandra is failing algebra and science and skips school often. Aaron, also 13, is quite physically mature for his age. He excels in sports, and enjoys popularity with his classmates. His favorite class is algebra and he maintains an "A" average. He is interested in computers and is planning to major in computer science. He relies heavily on his parents' advice in important matters. Aaron appears very responsible and demonstrates respect for authority. Jessica, at 12 years old, is more physically mature than other girls her age. She has already developed secondary sex characteristics, and feels out of place in school because she is taller than her peers. She does not understand the concepts presented in algebra class. Jessica goes out of her way to try and please other people, yet feels that she can never please her parents. Jessica, who lacks self-confidence and self-reliance, has not considered her future and has made no plans for college or a career.

Following the guide provided, describe each of these young people in terms of stages and levels.

NAME	PIAGET'S STAGE	KOHLBERG'S LEVEL & STAGE	ERIKSON'S STAGE
Barb			
Sandra			
Aaron			
Jessica			

What type of parenting styles might the parents of each young person practice, and why?

NAME	PARENTING STYLE	WHY
Barb		
Sandra		
Aaron		
Jessica		

FROM THEORY TO PRACTICE

What an ego!

When I was in the fourth grade, my younger brother had a good friend who died of a brain tumor. I was dumbfounded – how could a young person just die like that? As I entered my early teens and full-fledged adolescence, I entertained Piaget's personal fable in earnest. One day, my brother and I had walked across the frozen Illinois River! We were always doing crazy things. As I look back, I often wonder, "what could I have been thinking?" As this chapter overview relates, my personal fable came to a screeching halt one night when I was fifteen years old. I also remember the day I returned to school from that accident – I had been gone for a whole year. What a big shot I felt like! I figured I would be the center of attraction as everyone gathered around me—me, the one who had come back from the brink. I think I have learned some important lessons from my own experience of adolescent egocentrism, and I use these lessons to this day. Think back on your own life. Can you identify examples of the personal fable and the imaginary audience? Use the following spaces to relate the more interesting examples of these.

_____

_____

_____

_____

_____

_____

_____

_____

_____

_____

Golden curls and puppy dog tails

I had a teacher who once said to me that men create and engage in war while women wait behind the lines to heal us so that we may fight another day. I don't know if this was an original or an obscure quote, but as I think of gender and morality I sometimes wonder—have males really evolved to be more morally sophisticated than females as Kohlberg has asserted? Kohlberg maintained that most women reach and remain at stage three of his moral development theory, while most men reach stage four. What do you think of this? Was this ever true? Is it true today? Where do you fit into this classification of moral reasoning?

_____
_____
_____
_____
_____
_____
_____
_____
_____

COMPREHENSIVE PRACTICE TEST

1. Adolescence is identified as the developmental stage that begins at puberty and covers the period from the end of childhood to the middle teenage years.
   a) True
   b) False

2. Which of the following is not an example of secondary sex characteristics?
   a) development of breasts in females
   b) differentiation of internal reproductive organs
   c) male voice deepens
   d) female hips round

3. The onset of menarche has been found to occur earlier for girls who experience certain environmental stresses.
   a) True
   b) False

4. According to research, the majority of adolescents report they are:
   a) very confused
   b) somewhat stressed and unhappy
   c) usually stressed and unhappy
   d) happy and self-confident

5. In general, early maturation in boys:
   a) results in favorable peer and adult appraisals
   b) results in poor peer and adult appraisals
   c) results in poor academic performance
   d) results in poor athletic performance

6. In general, while late maturation girls do not seem to experience much stress at first, they will tend to be shorter and heavier than their early maturation counterparts as they grow older.
   a) True
   b) False

7. Piaget's final stage of cognitive development is known as the _____ stage.
   a) concrete operations
   b) cognitive integrity
   b) generativity
   d) formal operations

8. One example of adolescent egocentrism is the _____, wherein the individual believes he or she is the center of a group's admiration or criticism.
   a) peer audience
   b) imaginary peer group
   c) imaginary audience
   d) personal audience

9. Peter is sure that no one else has ever felt his kind of emotional pain. He has just split with his girlfriend of six weeks, and he is sure he will never recover from this terrible loss. While his best friend has tried to comfort him, he knows nobody could ever understand his pain. This is an example of what the text identified as the _____.
   a) imaginary audience
   b) personal fable
   c) adolescent loss syndrome
   d) adolescent bereavement syndrome

10. In Kohlberg's _____ level of moral reasoning, the child is governed by the standards of others rather than his or her internalized ideas of right and wrong. An act is judged based on its physical consequences.
   a) trust vs. mistrust
   b) conventional
   c) preconventional
   d) preadolescence

11. An individual in Kohlberg's second level of moral reasoning would see an act as good if it meets with the approval of others or if it is consistent with the laws of society.
   a) True
   b) False

12. It is generally thought that a person needs to be at the level of formal operations in order to attain Kohlberg's _____ level of moral reasoning.
   a) conventional
   b) formal conventional
   c) postconventional
   d) ego integrity

13. If I told you that I have read your text and have discovered that research indicates that all people will eventually reach Kohlberg's fifth stage of moral reasoning, should you believe I have really read the text?
   a) yes
   b) no

14. Would the text suggest that the *generation gap* is a common problem in most families today?
   a) yes
   b) no

15. While females tend to lean more toward care and compassion, males tend to stress _____, or both this and care in equal measure.
   a) romance
   b) aggression
   c) justice
   d) morality

16. According to the text, which of the following parenting styles seems to result in adolescents developing alcohol and drug problems, along with reduced school involvement?
   a) authoritarian
   b) permissive
   c) authoritative
   d) unconventional

17. According to the text, teenage pregnancy in the United States is higher than in any other developed country. About what percent of these pregnancies result in live births, and of these live births, what percentage of the babies are put up for adoption?
   a) 75; 20
   b) 53; 5
   c) 50; 20
   d) 53; 15

18. According to the text, do the children of teenage mothers tend to display academic or behavioral difficulties?
   a) yes
   b) only if the mothers used drugs during pregnancy
   c) no
   d) actually, they tend to score higher on tests

19. The good news about working teenagers is the fact that the self-discipline necessary to hold a job usually flows over to result in enhanced academic performance.
   a) True
   b) False

20. This stage of psychosocial development finds the individual facing the task of forming intimate relationships?
   a) the fifth stage
   b) the fourth stage
   c) the seventh stage
   d) the sixth stage

21. The crisis faced by individuals in middle adulthood is related to generativity vs. stagnation.
   a) True
   b) False

22. The most obvious changes as an individual gets older are usually:
    a) cognitive
    b) physical
    c) social
    d) sexual

23. The only intellectual ability found to show a continuous decline from the mid-twenties to the eighties was:
    a) deductive reasoning
    b) math ability
    c) perceptual speed
    d) reading comprehension

24. The text reports that about _____ of the households in the United States are headed by a married couple.
    a) two thirds
    b) one third
    c) one half
    d) thirty percent

25. Since 1970, has the average age of first marriage increased or decreased?
    a) decreased
    b) increased

26. Studies have shown that, in dual-earner households, husbands who help with child care benefit in several important ways, including improved mental health.
    a) True for all socioeconomic households
    b) True for upper socioeconomic households
    c) False
    d) True for lower socioeconomic households

27. Job satisfaction is higher for _____ persons than for _____ persons.
    a) middle aged; young adult
    b) young adult; middle aged

28. It appears that women go to work mainly because of:
    a) financial need
    b) marital conflict
    c) personal fulfillment
    d) increased recreational opportunities

29. Levinson described transitional stages in life. The stage where adults build a second life structure and anchor themselves more firmly in family or community is identified as the _____ stage.
    a) age 30 transition
    b) midlife transition
    c) middle adult era
    d) settling down

30. According to the research of Reinke, et-al, women in the launching phase became more _____.
    a) concerned about the empty nest syndrome
    b) depressed
    c) introspective and assertive
    d) likely to experience divorce

31. What appears to be the factor that differentiates the "oldest old" from those who die younger?
    a) an active life-style
    b) a genetic advantage
    c) improved health care
    d) more recreational time

32. Contrary to popular belief, the elderly who exercise do not seem to reap many benefits. In fact, the text presented a quote from Horn & Meer, 1987, "People wear out from overuse faster than they rust out from disuse."
    a) This statement is true
    b) This statement is false

33. A test that measures verbal ability and accumulated knowledge is measuring _____ intelligence, while a test that measures abstract reasoning and mental flexibility is measuring _____ intelligence.
    a) crystallized; fluid
    b) formal; concrete
    c) concrete; formal
    d) fluid; crystallized

34. About _____ percent of all cases of senility result from Alzheimer's disease.
    a) 20 - 30
    b) 75
    c) 40 - 50
    d) 50 - 60

35. The results of current research seem to indicate that older adults are _____ younger adults.
    a) less happy and satisfied with life than
    b) as satisfied with life as
    c) as dissatisfied with life as
    d) less satisfied but more secure than

36. According to the text, for the majority of those who stop working, retirement is not as stressful as popularly believed
   a) True   b) False

37. According to the text, what seems to be the most stressful event faced by people in their lifetimes?
   a) retirement   c) children leaving home
   b) losing a spouse   d) restricted physical ability due to age

38. The text presents a discussion on the end of life and the controversies involved with a person's right to determine their time of death, especially when facing a painful terminal illness. Dr. Jack Kevorkian is identified as one who would dispute the current laws against the right to assist a terminally ill person with their own suicide. He has been called "Dr. Death" due to the fact that he has defied the laws prohibiting assisted suicide. Kohlberg would probably say that Dr. Kevorkian has reached the _____ stage of moral reasoning.
   a) second   c) third
   b) fourth   d) fifth

ANSWER KEYS

ANSWER KEY: OMSE # 1

A. Quick Quiz	B. Matching	C. Complete the Diagram
1. b	1. b	1. c
2. True	2. d	2. f
3. menstruation	3. a	3. e
4. c	4. c	4. a
5. False	5. c	5. d
6. formal	6. a	6. b
7. d	7. d	
8. c	8. c	
9. adolescent egocentrism		
10. False		
11. d		
12. False		
13. a		
14. True		
15. 50		

ANSWER KEY: OMSE # 2

A. Quick Quiz		B. Matching
1. d	9. b	1. b
2. a	10. life structure	2. e
3. c	11. b	3. d
4. b	12. True	4. a
5. b	13. conscientiousness	5. g
6. d	14. crystallized; fluid	6. c
7. c	15. b	7. f
8. False		

C. Complete the Diagram—Erikson's Psychosocial Theory

Age Range	Stage Name	Stage Description
1. Birth to 1	1. d	1. k
2. 1 – 3	2. g	2. n
3. 3 – 6	3. a	3. i
4. 6 to puberty	4. h	4. m
5. adolescence	5. b	5. o
6. young adult	6. e	6. j
7. middle adult	7. c	7. p
8. late adult	8. f	8. l

ANSWER KEY: LABORATORY TO LIFE

Following the guide provided, describe each of these young people using the correct concepts from the text.

NAME	PIAGET'S STAGE	KOHLBERG'S LEVEL & STAGE	ERIKSON'S STAGE
Barb	Formal Operations Stage	Level III: Postconventional Level Stage 5	Identity versus Role Confusion
Sandra	Concrete Operations Stage	Level I: Preconventional Level Stage 1	Industry versus Inferiority
Aaron	Formal Operations Stage	Level II: Conventional Level Stage 4	Identity versus Role Confusion
Jessica	Concrete Operations Stage	Level II: Conventional Level Stage 3	Industry versus Inferiority

What type of parenting styles might the parents of each young person practice, and why?

NAME	PARENTING STYLE	WHY
Barb	Authoritative	Psychosocial competence and reliance on parents' opinions
Sandra	Permissive	Smoking, conduct problems, not engaged in school
Aaron	Authoritative	Psychosocial competence and reliance on parents' opinions
Jessica	Authoritarian	Cannot please her parents, lacks self-confidence and self-reliance

ANSWER KEY: COMPREHENSIVE PRACTICE EXAM

1. false	11. true	21. true	30. c
2. b	12. c	22. b	31. b
3. true	13. no	23. c	32. b
4. d	14. no	24. a	33. a
5. a	15. c	25. b	34. d
6. false	16. b	26. c	35. b
7. d	17. b	27. a	36. true
8. c	18. a	28. a	37. b
9. b	19. false	29. d	38. d
10. c	20. d		

11

MOTIVATION AND EMOTION

From his cradle to his grave a man never does a single thing which has any *first and foremost* object but one—to secure peace of mind, spiritual comfort, for *himself*.

–Mark Twain

CHAPTER OVERVIEW

Motivation and emotion are actively guiding each of us at any given time in our everyday lives. Teachers ponder that which will motivate their students to want to study and learn. Parents hope to motivate their children to make the right decisions and are concerned about their emotional welfare. Our emotions can direct our personal behaviors and influence our interactions with others. Emotional states can affect how we respond to such basic motivational states as hunger and sleep. In fact, the manner in which our physiological motivations are being expressed can be important in understanding complex emotional problems such as depression. Did you ever wonder what it is that motivates people to do things when their behavior results in serious problems for themselves or others? What would motivate a person to become so angry that he or she would shoot someone else just for failure to use a turn signal when changing lanes? What can I do to motivate my customer to buy my product? What motivates people to act in ways that seem to be so contrary to their own best interests? How can a person seem so happy one moment, and so sad or angry the next? Motivation and emotion is at the heart of human behavior. These are complex processes but our understanding of human behavior demands an understanding of motivation and emotion.

This chapter will help you gain a more practiced and functional understanding of motivation and emotion as it is presented in the text. The materials are divided into two OMSE sections: 1) motivation, and 2) emotion. You will discover the variety of ways we currently seek to understand the physiological and psychological states that motivate behavior along with the most accepted theories of motivation and emotion. You will also discover how important issues such as human relationships and eating disorders can be better understood through the study of motivation and emotion.

By completing the exercises provided, you should gain a thorough understanding of the information provided in your text. In other words, you should be better prepared for tests, quizzes, class participation, and life itself.

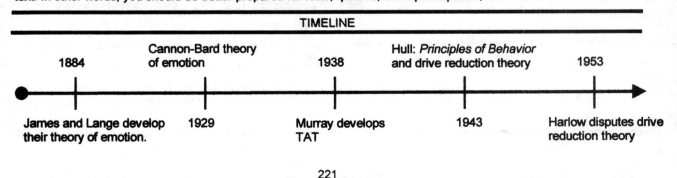

| | | | TIMELINE | | | |

| 1884 | Cannon-Bard theory of emotion | 1938 | Hull: *Principles of Behavior* and drive reduction theory | 1953 |

| James and Lange develop their theory of emotion. | 1929 | Murray develops TAT | 1943 | Harlow disputes drive reduction theory |

221

CHAPTER OUTLINE

Introduction to Motivation

Theories of Motivation

Instinct Theories of Motivation
Drive Reduction Theory: Striving to
Keep a Balanced Internal State
Arousal Theory: Striving for an
Optimal Level of Arousal
Maslow's Hierarchy of Needs: Putting
our Needs in Order

The Primary Drives: Hunger and Thirst

Thirst: We All Have Two Kinds
The Biological Basis of Hunger:
Internal Hunger Cues
Other Factors Influencing Hunger:
External Eating Cues
Understanding Body Weight: Why
We Weigh What We Weigh
Dieting: A National Obsession
Eating Disorders: Tyranny of the
Scale

Social Motives

The Need for Achievement: The
Drive to Excel
Fear of Success
Work Motivation

The What and Why of Emotions

Motivation and Emotion: What is the
Connection?
The Components of Emotions: The
Physical, the Cognitive, and the
Behavioral
Theories of Emotion: Which Comes
First, the Thought or the Feeling?
The Polygraph: Lie Detector or
Emotion Detector?

The Expression of Emotion

The Range of Emotion: How Wide is
It?
The Development of Facial
Expressions in Infants: Smiles and
Frowns Come Naturally

Facial Expressions for the Basic
Emotions—A Universal Language
Cultural Rules for Displaying Emotion
Emotion as a Form of
Communication

Experiencing Emotion

The Facial-Feedback Hypothesis:
Does the Face Cause the Feeling?
Emotion and Rational Thinking
Gender Differences in Experiencing
Emotion
Love: The Strongest Emotional Bond

Apply It! The Quest for Happiness

Thinking Critically

Chapter Summary and Review

KEY TERMS

Introduction to Motivation
motivation
motives
incentive
intrinsic motivation
extrinsic motivation
Theories of Motivation
instinct
instinct theory
drive-reduction theory
drive
homeostasis
arousal

arousal theory
stimulus motives
Yerkes–Dodson law
sensory deprivation
hierarchy of needs
self-actualization
**The Primary Drives:
Hunger and Thirst**
primary drive
lateral hypothalamus
ventromedial hypothalamus
metabolic rate

fat cells
set point
anorexia nervosa
bulimia nervosa
Social Motives
social motives
Thematic Apperception Test
(TAT)
need for achievement (n Ach)
industrial/organizational
psychologist (I/O)
work motivation
**The What and Why of
Emotions**

emotion
James-Lange theory
Cannon-Bard theory
Schachter-Singer theory
Lazarus' theory
polygraph
The Expression of Emotion
basic emotions
display rules
Experiencing Emotion
facial-feedback hypothesis
triangular theory of love
consummate love

TIMELINE

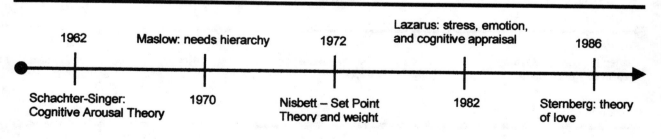

1962   Maslow: needs hierarchy   1972   Lazarus: stress, emotion,   1986
                                                                               and cognitive appraisal

Schachter-Singer: 1970   Nisbett – Set Point   1982   Sternberg: theory
Cognitive Arousal Theory   Theory and weight   of love

OMSE # 1: MOTIVATION

1. What is the difference between intrinsic and extrinsic motivation?
2. How do instinct theories explain motivation?
3. What is the drive-reduction theory of motivation?
4. How does arousal theory explain motivation?
5. How does Maslow's hierarchy of needs account for human motivation?
6. Under what types of conditions do the two types of thirst occur?
7. What are the roles of the lateral hypothalamus and the ventromedial hypothalamus in the regulation of eating behavior?
8. What are some of the body's hunger and satiety signals?
9. What are some nonbiological factors that influence what and how much we eat?
10. What are some factors that account for variations in body weight?
11. How does set point affect body weight?
12. Why is it almost impossible to maintain weight loss by cutting calories alone?
13. What are the symptoms of anorexia nervosa?
14. What are the symptoms of bulimia nervosa?
15. What is Murray's contribution to the study of motivation?
16. What is the need for achievement?
17. What are some characteristics that are shared by people who are high in achievement motivation?
18. What is work motivation, and what are two effective techniques for increasing it?

LEARNING MASTERY SCORECARD: Update your score card as you work through the various sections of the chapter. First, find and define key terms and concepts included in each section and note the page number(s) from the text that contain important references to the material. Next, gain a practical understanding of the concepts by considering the Laboratory to Life scenarios and thinking of at least one original example of how the concept might apply in real life. Complete the *Objective-Mastery Self-Evaluation* (OMSE) exercises for this section and record your scores. Revisit the exercises, recording your score and the date completed until you have attained mastery (100%). Finally, decide how you would prepare a lecture on each objective using the template provided, outline the lecture, and practice presenting it. Keep an honest tally of your achievements and, when finished, you will have developed learning mastery through elaborate rehearsal.

Key Terms	page #	Key Terms	page #	Key Terms	page #
motivation	_____	arousal	_____	metabolic rate	_____
motives	_____	arousal theory	_____	fat cells	_____
incentive	_____	stimulus motives	_____	set point	_____
intrinsic motivation	_____	Yerkes–Dodson law	_____	anorexia nervosa	_____
extrinsic motivation	_____	sensory deprivation	_____	bulimia nervosa	_____
instinct	_____	hierarchy of needs	_____	social motives	_____
instinct theory	_____	self-actualization	_____	Thematic Apperception Test (TAT)	_____
drive-reduction theory	_____	primary drive	_____	need for achievement (*n* Ach)	_____
drive	_____	lateral hypothalamus	_____	industrial/organizational psychologist (I/O)	_____
homeostasis	_____	ventromedial hypothalamus	_____	work motivation	_____

Quick Quiz

Date	Score	Date	Score	Date	Score
__/__/__	_____	__/__/__	_____	__/__/__	_____
__/__/__	_____	__/__/__	_____	__/__/__	100%

Elaborate Rehearsal

Lecture Preparation	Completion Date
Key Terms, Persons, & Concepts	__/__/__
Learning Objectives	__/__/__
Lecture Notes	__/__/__

A. QUICK QUIZ

1. _____ were defined as needs or desires that energize and direct behavior towards a goal.

2. Jeffrey mows his parent's lawn and, in the winter, cleans snow off his sidewalk and his elderly neighbor's sidewalk. He does this because he enjoys the feeling he gets from being a good boy and helping others. This would be an example of _____ motivation.

3. Fred, on the other hand, will only help around the house if he receives a financial reward or special privilege. This would be an example of _____ motivation.

4. When Fred's parents offer to allow him a later weekend curfew if he keeps his room clean, they are hoping to encourage his behavior through the use of a(n) _____.
   a) reward
   b) incentive
   c) extrinsic motivator
   d) internal motivator

5. _____ refers to the faithful and continued efforts to keep working at a task until a goal is achieved or a project is finished.
   a) persistence
   b) activation
   c) intensity
   d) constitution

6. My dog walks around her bed three times before she lies down. Other dog owners tell me similar stories about their pets. This behavior seems to be inborn, unlearned, and fixed. This behavior is probably a good example of an _____.

7. A good example of homeostasis would be a person choosing to balance his or her life between work and recreation.
   a) True
   b) False

8. Jack always seems to want to ride the wildest rides at the amusement park. He also seems to get bored very easily and then has a tendency to act out in a way that creates action in his environment. His behavior would probably best be explained by the _____ theory of motivation.
   a) incentive
   b) instinct
   c) arousal
   d) homeostasis

9. Franklin, who is taking his first chemistry test and finds the material very difficult, has a surprisingly low level of anxiety. The Yerkes-Dodson Law would predict that he will:
   a) do well on the test
   b) not perform at optimal levels on the test
   c) experience more anxiety after the test is completed
   d) achieve the highest grade in the class

10. Which of the following would **NOT** be a good example of a primary drive?
    a) hunger
    b) sex
    c) thirst
    d) peer approval

11. The _____ hypothalamus acts as the feeding center, and the _____ hypothalamus acts as the satiety center.
    a) ventromedial; lateral
    b) lateral; ventromedial

12. Hunger is experienced when _____ is low and _____ is high.
    a) insulin; glucose
    b) internal motivation; external motivation
    c) glucose; insulin
    d) external motivation; internal motivation

13. It seems that the most important factor in a successful long-term weight loss program is _____.

14. _____ nervosa involves rigid restriction of calorie intake while _____ nervosa involves a cycle of bingeing and purging.

15. Needs for affiliation, power, or achievement were identified as _____ motives.
    a) personal
    b) interpersonal
    c) social
    d) vanity

16. A person with a high need for achievement will most likely set goals of _____ difficulty.
   a) low
   b) moderate
   c) high
   d) mediocre

B. MATCHING

_____	1. initiates, sustains, and directs behavior	a. Yerkes–Dodson law
_____	2. she did it because she wanted to	b. metabolism
_____	3. he will—if you pay him	c. social motives
_____	4. human behavior is motivated by innate tendencies	d. Thematic Apperception test
_____	5. derived largely from the concept of homeostasis	e. motivation
_____	6. internal state of tension or arousal	f. need for achievement
_____	7. a state of alertness	g. drive-reduction theory
_____	8. performance is best when arousal level is optimal	h. intrinsic motivation
_____	9. the development of one's full potential	i. extrinsic motivation
_____	10. normally maintained body weight	j. drive
_____	11. acquired through experience and interaction with others	k. instinct theory
_____	12. describe the picture and project your motives	l. arousal
_____	13. this class is tough, but I need to earn an "A"	m. self-actualization
_____	14. the rate at which we burn calories to produce energy	n. set point

C. COMPLETE THE DIAGRAM: Place the appropriate need in each segment of Maslow's hierarchy.

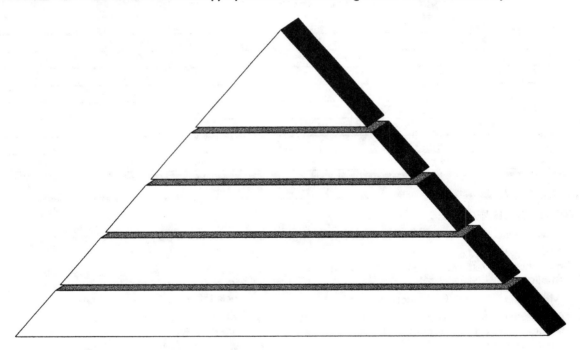

PREPARE A LECTURE: This activity is designed to offer you an opportunity to take advantage of a valuable mode of learning, elaborate rehearsal. Once you have finished the OMSE section, write a lecture using the instructional guide provided below. After your lecture is prepared, you can enhance your learning by writing a quiz covering the material. Now it is time to find some willing and inquisitive audience members. Your roommates or family may be a great place to start. Present them the lecture as if you are teaching a class. Remember to ask for questions and give your students the quiz following the lecture. This exercise can also serve to turn a *study-buddy* group into a very productive way to prepare for the test. Each member of the group can take different OMSE sections for their lecture/teacher role while the rest of the group serves as the class.

I. Key Terms, Names, Dates, and Concepts you will include in this lecture:

1. _____
2. _____
3. _____
4. _____

5. _____
6. _____
7. _____
8. _____

9. _____
10. _____
11. _____
12. _____

II. Learning Objectives (what do you want the student to know and be able to do as a result of your lecture):

1. _____
2. _____
3. _____
4. _____
5. _____

III. Lecture Notes (notes should be brief cues and serve as a guide).

Major topic #1: _____

Sub-topics and notes: _____
_____
_____
_____

Major topic #2: _____

Sub-topics and notes: _____
_____
_____
_____

Major topic #3: _____

Sub-topics and notes: _____
_____
_____
_____

OMSE # 2: EMOTION

LEARNING OBJECTIVES

1. What are the three components of emotions?
2. According to the James–Lange theory, what sequence of events occurs when we experience an emotion?
3. What is the Cannon–Bard theory of emotion?
4. According to the Schachter–Singer theory, what two factors must occur in order for us to experience an emotion?
5. According to Lazarus, what sequence of events occur when we feel an emotion?

6. What does a polygraph measure?
7. What are basic emotions?
8. How does the development of facial expressions of different emotions in infants suggest a biological basis for emotional expression?
9. Why is emotion considered a form of communication?
10. What is the facial-feedback hypothesis?
11. How does Sternberg's triangular theory of love account for the different kinds of love?

LEARNING MASTERY SCORECARD: Update your score card as you work through the various sections of the chapter. First, find and define key terms and concepts included in each section and note the page number(s) from the text that contain important references to the material. Next, gain a practical understanding of the concepts by considering the Laboratory to Life scenarios and thinking of at least one original example of how the concept might apply in real life. Complete the *Objective-Mastery Self-Evaluation* (OMSE) exercises for this section and record your scores. Revisit the exercises, recording your score and the date completed until you have attained mastery (100%). Finally, decide how you would prepare a lecture on each objective using the template provided, outline the lecture, and practice presenting it. Keep an honest tally of your achievements and, when finished, you will have developed learning mastery through elaborate rehearsal.

Key Term	Page #	Key Term	Page #	Key Term	Page #
emotion	____	Lazarus' theory	____	facial-feedback hypothesis	____
James-Lange theory	____	polygraph	____	triangular theory of love	____
Cannon-Bard theory	____	basic emotions	____	consummate love	____
Schacter-Singer theory	____	display rules	____		

Quick Quiz

Date	Score	Date	Score	Date	Score
_/_/_	____	_/_/_	____	_/_/_	____
_/_/_	____	_/_/_	____	_/_/_	100%

Elaborate Rehearsal

Lecture Preparation	Completion Date
Key Terms, Persons, & Concepts	_/_/_
Learning Objectives	_/_/_
Lecture Notes	_/_/_

A. QUICK QUIZ

1. We experience emotion as a result of becoming aware of our physical response to a situation. This statement would be best matched with:
   a) the Cannon-Bard theory
   b) the Schachter-Singer theory
   c) the James-Lange theory
   d) Lazarus' theory

2. Our physical response and our emotional response occur at the same time. This statement would be best matched with:
   a) the James-Lange theory
   b) the Cannon-Bard theory
   c) the Schachter-Singer theory
   d) Lazarus' theory

3. We experience the physical response and then give it meaning. From this comes our emotional response. This statement would be best matched with:
   a) Lazarus' theory
   b) the Cannon-Bard theory
   c) the James-Lange theory
   d) the Schachter-Singer theory

4. Which of the following is best matched with the idea of appraisal?
   a) the Schachter-Singer theory
   b) Lazarus' theory
   c) the James-Lange theory
   d) the Cannon-Bard theory

5. Feelings of fear, anger, disgust, surprise, joy, or happiness were identified in the text as _____ emotions.

6. Research suggests that people have stronger reactions to positive stimuli than to negative stimuli.
   a) True
   b) False

7. Amber understood the risks involved in blind dating but was excited about the possibility of meeting a potential soul mate. When she met John she was somewhat disappointed. He seemed nice but he was just not her type. Amber treated her date politely and they had a nice dinner. Afterward, Amber shook his hand, and said she was pleased to meet him. According to the text, Amber was probably following _____ rules – rules that dictate how emotions should be expressed in her cultural environment.

8. The facial-feedback hypothesis states that the muscular movements involved in facial expressions of emotional responses actually produce subjective emotions.
   a) True
   b) False

9. The triangular theory of love was developed by:
   a) Sternberg
   b) Schachter
   c) Lazarus
   d) Maslow

10. According to the triangular theory of love, the most complete form of love is:
    a) romantic love
    b) companionate love
    c) consummate love
    d) infatuated love

B. MATCHING: Place the corresponding letter in the space provided.

_____	1. decision/commitment without intimacy or passion	a. liking
_____	2. includes intimacy, decision/commitment, and passion	b. infatuated love
_____	3. includes passion and decision/commitment but not intimacy	c. empty love
_____	4. a strong bond including intimacy but not passion or decision/commitment	d. romantic love
_____	5. consists of intimacy and commitment but the passion is gone	e. fatuous love
_____	6. the common "love at first sight"—passion only	f. companionate love
_____	7. a combination of intimacy and passion	g. consummate love

C. COMPLETE THE DIAGRAM: Place the letter corresponding to the correct icon in the order they occur according to the various theories of emotion. In some cases, a box may contain more than one correct response.

	1st	2nd	3rd
1. James-Lange theory			
2. Cannon-Bard theory			
3. Schachter-Singer theory			
4. Lazarus' theory			

a) stimulus event

b) physiological response

c) cognitive response

d) emotional response

PREPARE A LECTURE: This activity is designed to offer you an opportunity to take advantage of a valuable mode of learning, elaborate rehearsal. Once you have finished the OMSE section, write a lecture using the instructional guide provided below. After your lecture is prepared, you can enhance your learning by writing a quiz covering the material. Now it is time to find some willing and inquisitive audience members. Your roommates or family may be a great place to start. Present them the lecture as if you are teaching a class. Remember to ask for questions and give your students the quiz following the lecture. This exercise can also serve to turn a *study-buddy* group into a very productive way to prepare for the test. Each member of the group can take different OMSE sections for their lecture/teacher role while the rest of the group serves as the class.

I. Key Terms, Names, Dates, and Concepts you will include in this lecture:

1. _____   5. _____   9. _____
2. _____   6. _____   10. _____
3. _____   7. _____   11. _____
4. _____   8. _____   12. _____

II. Learning Objectives (what do you want the student to know and be able to do as a result of your lecture):

1. _____
2. _____
3. _____
4. _____
5. _____

III. Lecture Notes (notes should be brief cues and serve as a guide).

Major topic #1: _____

  Sub-topics and notes: _____
  _____
  _____
  _____
  _____

Major topic #2: _____

  Sub-topics and notes: _____
  _____
  _____
  _____
  _____

Major topic #3: _____

  Sub-topics and notes: _____
  _____
  _____
  _____
  _____

KEY TERMS AND CONCEPTS EXERCISE

The key terms and concepts are presented in order of their appearance in the text. Space is provided for you to include a personalized definition or example of each term or concept. As you encounter each term in the text, make a note of its meaning and context. Next, conceptualize the meaning of the term in a way that makes the most sense to you. Also, think about examples of the term from your own life. Write your definition and/or example in the space provided next to the word. The KEY TERMS exercise utilizes a modified *T-note* design so that you can self-evaluate your mastery of the definitions. First lay a sheet of paper over the terms and concepts side of the page so that you only see the definitions. Read the definition and try to recall the term or concept. Mark all those you are unable to answer so you can restudy them. When you have learned all of the terms and concepts in this way, move the paper to the definition side so that you can see only the term or concept, try to recall both the textbook definition and your personal version. Repeat this until you know all of the terms and concepts by definition and personal understanding.

Motivation	The process that initiates, directs, and sustains behavior to satisfy physiological or psychological needs or wants. _____
Motives	Needs or desires that energize and direct behavior toward a goal. _____
Incentive	An external stimulus that motivates behavior (examples: money, fame). _____
Intrinsic Motivation	The desire to perform an act because it is satisfying or pleasurable in and of itself. _____

Extrinsic Motivation	The desire to perform an act to gain a reward or to avoid an undesirable consequence. _____ _____ _____
Instinct	An inborn, unlearned, fixed pattern of behavior that is characteristic of an entire species. _____ _____
Instinct Theory	The notion that human behavior is motivated by certain innate tendencies, or instincts, shared by all individuals. _____ _____ _____
Drive-Reduction Theory	A theory of motivation suggesting that a need creates an unpleasant state of arousal or tension called a drive, which impels the organism to engage in behavior that will satisfy the need and reduce tension. _____ _____ _____
Drive	A state of tension or arousal brought about by an underlying need, which motivates one to engage in behavior that will satisfy the need and reduce the tension. For example, if you do not eat for a period of time, you experience a need state and are motivated to find food and eat in order to reduce the tension. _____ _____ _____
Homeostasis	The tendency of the body to maintain a balanced internal state with regard to oxygen level, body temperature, blood sugar, water balance, and so forth. _____ _____ _____
Arousal	A state of alertness and mental and physical activation. _____ _____ _____
Arousal Theory	A theory suggesting that the aim of motivation is to maintain an optimal level of arousal. _____ _____ _____ _____
Stimulus Motives	Motives that cause us to increase stimulation and that appear to be unlearned (examples: curiosity and the need to explore, manipulate objects, and play). _____ _____ _____
Yerkes–Dodson Law	The principle that performance on tasks is best when the arousal level is appropriate to the difficulty of the task—higher arousal for simple tasks, moderate arousal for tasks of moderate difficulty, and lower arousal for complex tasks. _____ _____ _____
Sensory Deprivation	A condition in which sensory stimulation is reduced to a minimum or eliminated. _____ _____
Hierarchy of Needs	Maslow's theory of motivation, in which needs are arranged in order of urgency ranging from physical needs to security needs, belonging needs, esteem needs, and finally the need for self-actualization. _____ _____ _____
Self-Actualization	The development of one's full potential; the highest need on Maslow's hierarchy. _____ _____ _____

Primary Drive	A state of tension or arousal arising from a biological need; one not based on learning. _____
Lateral Hypothalamus (LH)	The part of the hypothalamus that supposedly acts as a feeding center and, when activated, signals an animal to eat; when the LH is destroyed, the animal refuses to eat. _____
Ventromedial Hypothalamus (VMH)	The part of the hypothalamus that presumably acts as a satiety center and, when activated, signals an animal to stop eating; when the area is destroyed, the animal overeats, becoming obese. _____
Metabolic Rate	The rate at which the body burns calories to produce energy. _____
Fat Cells	Numbering 30 to 40 billion, cells that serve as storehouses for liquefied fat in the body; with weight loss, they decrease in size but not number. _____
Set Point	The weight the body normally maintains when one is trying neither to gain nor to lose weight (if weight falls below the normal level, appetite increases and metabolic rate decreases; if weight is gained, appetite decreases and metabolic rate increases so that the original rate is restored). _____
Anorexia Nervosa	An eating disorder characterized by an overwhelming, irrational fear of being fat, compulsive dieting to the point of self-starvation, and excessive weight loss. _____
Bulimia Nervosa	An eating disorder characterized by repeated and uncontrolled episodes of binge eating, frequently followed by purging—self-induced vomiting and/or the use of large quantities of laxatives and diuretics. _____
Social Motives	Motives acquired through experience and interaction with others. _____
Thematic Apperception Test (Tat)	A projective test consisting of drawings of ambiguous human situations, which the subject describes; thought to reveal inner feelings, conflicts, and motives. _____
Need For Achievement (n Ach)	The need to accomplish something difficult and to perform at a high standard of excellence.
Industrial/ Organizational Psychologist (I/O)	The specialty that focuses on the relationship between the workplace or work organization and the worker. _____

Work Motivation	The conditions and processes responsible for the arousal, direction, magnitude, and maintenance of effort one puts forth in one's job.
Emotion	A feeling state involving physiological arousal, a cognitive appraisal of the situation arousing the state, and an outward expression of the state.
James-Lange Theory	The theory that emotional feelings result when we become aware of our physiological response to an emotion-provoking stimulus (for example, we are afraid because we tremble).
Cannon-Bard Theory	An emotion-provoking stimulus is transmitted simultaneously to the cortex, providing the feeling of emotion, and to the sympathetic nervous system, causing physiological arousal.
Schachter-Singer Theory	A two-stage theory stating that for an emotion to occur, there must be (1) physiological arousal and (2) an explanation for the arousal.
Lazarus' Theory	An emotion-provoking stimulus triggers a cognitive appraisal, from which follow the emotion and the physiological arousal.
Polygraph	A device designed to pick up changes in heart rate, blood pressure, respiration rate, and galvanic skin response that typically accompany the anxiety that occurs when a person lies.
Basic Emotions	Emotions that are found in all cultures, that are reflected in the same facial expressions across cultures, and that emerge in children according to their biological timetable (examples: anger, disgust, happiness, sadness, distress).
Display Rules	Cultural rules that dictate how emotions should be expressed, and when and where their expression is appropriate.
Facial-Feedback Hypothesis	The idea that the muscular movements involved in certain facial expressions trigger the corresponding emotions (for example, smiling makes us happy).
Triangular Theory Of Love	Sternberg's theory that three components—intimacy, passion, and decision/commitment—singly and in various combinations produce seven different kinds of love.
Consummate Love	According to Sternberg's theory, the most complete form of love, consisting of three components—intimacy, passion, and decision/commitment.

FROM THE LABORATORY TO LIFE

Why Do They Do That?

It is the first really warm day of the spring and the sun has finally found its way from behind the clouds. Frank decides to get out to the garden and get it ready for planting. He is an old fashioned gardener and does all the work by hand and hoe. He really doesn't need the food from the garden and takes great pride in giving his prize vegetables to his neighbors. After a few hours working hard in the sun, Frank wipes his forehead and realizes that he is really thirsty. His neighbor watches as Frank goes to get a glass of ice water and wonders why Frank works so hard this way. Frank has said that he just loves working in his garden.

1. What kind of motivation drives Frank's hard work in the garden? _____

2. Which theory of motivation would best explain Frank's desire to get a glass of water? _____
    _____

Charlene has always been a hard worker in school. She ranked in the top ten of her high school class and is currently on the Dean's list at college. She does this because she has always been motivated to live up to her full potential and be the best student she can be. Her parents want her to go to medical school and she thinks that is a good idea. The problem is that while her parents are thinking of all the money she could make as a doctor, Charlene has visions of working in a not-for-profit community clinic.

3. What kind of motivation drives Charlene's hard work as a student? _____

4. Charlene's parents are hoping that the potential earning power of being a doctor will serve as a good
    _____ for her to pursue that profession.

5. What would Maslow say is motivating Charlene's drive to be the best student she can be?
    _____

Charles is the least popular foreman on the construction crew. He sees everything as a challenge and knows that the harder he and his crew work, the more money they will all make. He is also a very aggressive competitor when it comes to getting jobs in the first place. His aggressive nature seems to be the way he responds to all aspects of his life. When he feels threatened he will lash out in a very intimidating manner. He chose his line of work, building construction, because he loves the thrill of being high above the street, the danger seems to invigorate him.

6. What kind of motivation drives Charles' drive to work hard and get the jobs? _____

7. What theory of motivation would best explain Charles' aggressive nature? _____

8. What motivation theory would best explain Charles' attraction for his type of work? _____

Why Did They Feel That?

Jeffrey is walking up to the front of the class to present his first speech in his college speech class. He suddenly realizes that he is feeling a knot in his stomach and that his palms are wet. He now feels terrified at the thought that he is about to give the speech.

1. Which theory of emotion best explains Jeffrey's emotional reaction? _____

Sandra is regretting the fact that she was running late this morning now that she has to walk to the far reaches of the parking lot all by herself at night. As she proceeds to her car, she notices that there is another person following her and there is no other car in the vicinity. Sandra then begins to think of the possible reasons for this person following her and becomes convinced that she is about to be attacked. She feels a surge of fear as she also begins to tremble.

2. Which theory of emotion best explains Sandra's reaction? _____

Jimmy is on his newspaper route when he becomes aware that a very angry sounding dog is quickly headed his way. He immediately feels a sense of fear and begins to tremble.

3.   Which theory of emotion best explains Jimmy's reaction? _____

Barbara hears the phone ring and her heart begins to pound. She figures it is James calling to break another date. She is feeling angry as she picks up the phone.

4.   Which theory of emotion best explains Barbara's reaction? _____

FROM THEORY TO PRACTICE

What is Your Motivation? An Exercise in Discovery

By now you have read about several different theories of motivation. They all seem to make sense given a specific situation, but is there one particular theory that best applies to you and your education? Answer the following questions and then assign the concept, theorist, or theory of motivation that best fits.

Why are you taking this psychology class?   _____

- Does your answer reveal extrinsic or intrinsic motivation?   _____

What grade do you want to earn in this class, and why? _____

- Which theorist best explains the reason behind your answer?   _____

What will you do with the information you learn in this class? _____

- Which of Maslow's needs does your answer reveal? _____

How does this class fit into your career goals?   _____

Do you find it easier to learn and retain knowledge in your major field of study than in other courses? _____

- Why?   _____

When you sit down to take an exam, do you usually experience a low, medium, or high level of arousal?   _____

Does the amount of preparation time affect your arousal level on exams?   _____

- According to Atkinson, why might that be?   _____

_____

_____

Emotion: An Exercise in Discovery

You are hiking through the woods, enjoying nature and feeling calm and relaxed. Suddenly, as you round a bend, there in front of you stands a huge grizzly bear—and he's looking right at you. Close your eyes and envision this scene as if it were really taking place. Order the following events as they would occur.

Physiological arousal   _____   Cognitive Appraisal   _____   Emotional Response   _____

Okay, now imagine that walking with you is a first time visitor to the planet Earth. She knows nothing about the planet or the creatures of Earth. In what ways might her reaction be different from yours? _____

_____

Which theory of emotion makes the most sense to you in light of this exercise?   _____

Why?   _____

_____

_____

_____

_____

COMPREHENSIVE PRACTICE TEST

1. When we study _____, we are interested in the underlying processes that initiate, direct, and sustain behavior.
    a) emotion
    b) motivation
    c) stimuli
    d) biological bases

2. If James is responding to an incentive, he is responding to an _____ stimulus.
    a) external
    b) internal

3. I read research and statistics books because these subjects fascinate me. I really enjoy spending time learning about new approaches to research, and the results of major research projects. It appears that I am most driven by _____ motivation.
    a) intrinsic
    b) intellectual
    c) academic
    d) extrinsic

4. Jill reads her chemistry book every night because she wants to excel in this topic. She believes she will make a great deal of money if she becomes a chemist. We would say Jill is being driven mainly by _____ motivation.
    a) career
    b) intrinsic
    c) extrinsic
    d) academic

5. The primary characteristics of motivation are:
    a) activation, persistence, and goal
    b) activation, persistence, and reward
    c) activation, persistence, and focus
    d) activation, persistence, and intensity

6. A good example of the instinct theory of motivation would be Jim wanting to ride the roller coaster instead of the water rides because he has a natural desire for greater thrills.
    a) True
    b) False

7. Franklin has been working in his garden all morning and the sun is getting high and hot. He wipes his head and decides to go to the corner store for a cold drink. He is hoping this will quench his intense thirst. This is an example of the _____ theory of motivation.
    a) instinct
    b) arousal
    c) drive-reduction
    d) balance

8. The text defines a _____ as a state of tension or arousal brought about by an underlying need, which motivates one to engage in behavior that will satisfy the need and reduce the tension.
    a) drive
    b) balance stimulus
    c) stimuli
    d) homeostimulus

9. A good example of the effect of the process of homeostasis would be when Franklin's body detects a reduced level of fluids due to sweating in the sun and he has the subjective experience of thirst.
    a) True
    b) False

10. Angel has interests that sometimes scare his friends. He drives his motorcycle fast, he loves bungee jumping, and he can't wait for his first parachute jump. We would probably explain these interests with the _____ theory of motivation.
    a) instinct
    b) risky shift
    c) arousal
    d) homeostasis

11. Janet loves math. She seems to have a natural understanding of concepts that leave others confused. However, she hates history and can't seem to grasp the social and political implications of major events in human behavior. The Yerkes-Dodson law predicts that she will do best on her upcoming math and history tests if she has _____ arousal for the math test and _____ arousal for the history test.
    a) lower; higher
    b) higher; lower

12. According to Maslow, the needs for love and affiliation are _____ from the bottom in his hierarchy of needs pyramid.
    a) second
    b) fifth
    c) fourth
    d) third

13. Jim realizes that the goals he has set for himself are going to take too much time and effort so he decides to compromise and go for what he considers less difficult but more rational goals. This is a good example of self-actualization.
    a) True
    b) False

14. Which is the best example of a primary drive?
    a) Jack prefers red cars over other colored cars because he believes girls will like him better with a red car.
    b) Charlene wants to be an executive because she wants to go beyond the gender restrictions in the work force.
    c) Francis, a long-haul truck driver, stops for dinner because he has not eaten in several hours.
    d) Arlene wants to have one son and one daughter.

15. When I am hungry I am experiencing the effects of the _____ hypothalamus and when I have eaten and feel full, I am experiencing the effects of the _____ hypothalamus.
    a) ventromedial; lateral
    b) lateral; ventromedial

16. If my _____ is low and my _____ is high, I will probably experience hunger.
    a) insulin; glucose
    b) lateral hypothalamus; ventromedial hypothalamus
    c) glucose; insulin
    d) ventromedial hypothalamus; lateral hypothalamus

17. According to the text, genes appear to be an important factor in body size and obesity.
    a) True
    b) False

18. When a person loses weight their fat cell status changes in terms of decreased _____, but not decreased _____.
    a) number; size
    b) inner structures; outer structures
    c) size; number
    d) outer structures; inner structures

19. An important concept in weight control is the idea of _____. This states that appetite will increase and metabolic rate decrease when weight falls below the normal level. If weight increases beyond the normal level, the appetite will decrease and the metabolic rate will increase.
    a) genetic weight
    b) set point
    c) metabolic homeostasis
    d) metiastasis

20. Donald was known for his extracurricular activities in high school. He appeared in just about every group photo in the yearbook. He loved being with people and doing things in groups. The problem was that he often alienated other group members because he always wanted to be in charge, and he seemed to push himself and others toward greater levels of achievement in whatever project they were attempting. The text would say Donald was being driven by _____ motives.
    a) dictatorial
    b) social
    c) organizational
    d) interpersonal

21. People who suffer from anorexia nervosa probably displayed behavior problems and the symptoms of attention deficit disorder when they were children.
    a) True
    b) False

22. Murray developed the Thematic Apperception Test as a way to measure _____.
    a) anger
    b) personal perception of success
    c) personal needs
    d) social needs

23. A person with a _____ n Ach will likely set either very low goals or impossibly high goals.
    a) high
    b) moderate
    c) low
    d) borderline

24. The Balkin (1987) study found that college women with friends who also attended college suffered
_____ from a fear of success than those who had few or no close friends attending college.
   a) less
   b) more

25. Jim is an I/O psychologist. According to the text he is most interested in _____ and _____.
   a) employee satisfaction; job performance
   b) job safety; work motivation
   c) work motivation; job performance
   d) employee satisfaction; work motivation

26. According to the expectancy theory of work motivation, instrumentality refers to the belief that:
   a) more effort will result in improved performance
   b) a well done job will be noticed and rewarded
   c) the rewards for one's efforts are worth the effort
   d) the work effort will result in a better life

27. Helen walked to the front of the class to give her speech. She did not realize how nervous she really was until she
felt a knot in her stomach and noticed her hands shaking as she held her note cards. Helen's experience would
be best explained by the _____ theory of emotion.
   a) Cannon-Bard
   b) James-Lange
   c) Schachter-Singer
   d) Lazarus

28. Which of the following theories assert that, when presented with an emotion-producing stimulus, we feel the
physiological effects and the subjective experience of emotion at about the same time.
   a) James-Lange
   b) Lazarus
   c) Cannon-Bard
   d) Schachter-Singer

29. Which of the following theories emphasizes the importance of making a cognitive appraisal of an event in the
determination of one's emotional response to the event?
   a) Lazarus
   b) Schachter-Singer
   c) James-Lange
   d) Cannon-Bard

30. Which of the following theories asserts that we must attribute a reason for our physiological arousal in response
to a situation in order to label the emotional response we have to the situation?
   a) Cannon-Bard
   b) Schachter-Singer
   c) Lazarus
   d) James-Lange

31. All researchers who are doing work in the physiology of emotions agree upon the idea of basic emotions and
instinctual responses such as fear, rage, and joy.
   a) True
   b) False

32. According to the text, children need to be at least _____ months old before they will show emotions
such as empathy, envy, or embarrassment.
   a) three
   b) seven
   c) eighteen
   d) twelve

33. Diane has learned the _____ of her culture. This was evidenced by the fact that she smiled and
thanked her friend for the birthday gift that she really did not like. She also acted happy to see her aunt at the
birthday party even though she does not really like her aunt.
   a) social rules
   b) interpersonal rules
   c) display rules
   d) expressive rules

34. According to the text, we can perceive the emotions of others as early as our first year of life.
   a) True
   b) False

35. The facial-feedback hypothesis has been well supported through research. This hypothesis states that our facial
expression is directly influenced by our subjective experience of emotion.
   a) the first sentence above is true but the second sentence is incorrect.
   b) both the first and the second sentences are true
   c) both sentences are false
   d) the first sentence is false but the second sentence accurately describes the facial-feedback hypothesis

36. Empty love is characterized as the "love at first sight" kind of love that two people may experience when they first meet
    a) True   b) False

ANSWER KEYS

ANSWER KEY: OMSE # 1

A. Quick Quiz	B. Matching	C. Figure Completion (from top to bottom)
1. motives	1. e	Need for self-actualization
2. intrinsic	2. h	Esteem needs
3. extrinsic	3. i	Belonging and love needs
4. b	4. k	Safety needs
5. a	5. g	Physiological needs
6. instinct	6. j	
7. False	7. l	
8. c	8. a	
9. b	9. m	
10. d	10. n	
11. b	11. c	
12. c	12. d	
13. exercise	13. f	
14. anorexia; bulimia	14. b	
15. c		
16. b		

ANSWER KEY: OMSE # 2

A. Quick Quiz	B. Matching
1. c	1. c
2. b	2. g
3. d	3. e
4. b	4. a
5. basic	5. f
6. False	6. b
7. display	7. d
8. True	
9. a	
10. c	

C. Complete the Diagram

	1st	2nd	3rd
James-Lange theory	a	c	d
Cannon-Bard theory	a	b/c	d
Schachter-Singer theory	a	b	c/d
Lazarus' theory	a	c	b/d

ANSWER KEY: LAB TO LIFE
Why Did They Do That?

Frank	Charlene	Charles
1. intrinsic	3. intrinsic	6. extrinsic
2. drive reduction theory	4. incentive	7. instinct theory
	5. self-actualization	8. arousal theory

Why Did They Feel That?

Jeffry:	1. James-Lange Theory
Sandra:	2. Lazarus Theory of Emotion
Jimmy:	3. Cannon-Bard Theory
Barbara:	4. Schachter-Singer Theory

ANSWER KEY: COMPREHENSIVE PRACTICE TEST

1. b	7. c	13. false	19. b	25. c	31. false
2. a	8. a	14. c	20. b	26. b	32. c
3. a	9. true	15. b	21. b	27. b	33. c
4. c	10. c	16. c	22. d	28. c	34. true
5. d	11. b	17. true	23. c	29. a	35. a
6. false	12. d	18. c	24. a	30. b	36. false

12

HUMAN SEXUALITY AND GENDER

Sexual love is undoubtedly one of the chief things in life, and the union of mental and bodily satisfaction in the enjoyment of love is one of its culminating peaks.

-Sigmund Freud

CHAPTER OVERVIEW

Human Sexuality and Gender has emerged as a distinct and legitimate area of study over the past several decades. There is often confusion as to what this field of study represents—a confusion that may translate to diverse interpretations in the minds of college students preparing to take a class on the subject. At one time, students giggled as they signed up to take a class in a subject that they believed was already among their areas of expertise. Many students entered these classes expecting a free ride and an easy "A." It rarely took more than one or two class meetings before they began to wake up to their unfortunate misinterpretation. Those students that stuck around after the rude awakening soon learned that human sexuality was a fascinating review of everything from human physiology to interpersonal relations. That was true even before research, fueled by curiosity and controversy, gave us the kind of reliable information that we have seen emerge on the subject in just the past decade.

Sigmund Freud believed that human sexuality was the driving force behind most of what we do, think, say, feel, and wish. While that may not be the case, we know that human sexuality and gender motivate much of our behavior and shape much of our culture. A quick look at the past century in the U.S. is all that is needed to find numerous examples of a culture changing in the face of greater understanding and awareness. Beginning with the women's movement and moving through the Kinsey surveys, females in combat positions in the military, gay rights, the AIDS epidemic, fathers staying home to care for infants, and a general increase of women in the workforce we see many examples of the cultural productivity of gender studies. This chapter provides a cursory view of the attitudes and behaviors, advances, trends, and understanding of what we term, "Human Sexuality and Gender."

This chapter will help you gain a more practiced and functional understanding of human sexuality as it is presented in the text. The materials are divided into two OMSE sections, 1) gender issues, and 2) sexual orientation and sexual health. You will discover the multifaceted nature of the human sexual behavior and relationships. By completing the exercises provided, you should gain a thorough understanding of the information provided in you text. In other words, you should be better prepared for tests, quizzes, class participation, and life itself.

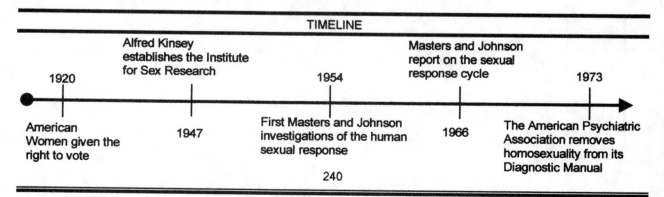

TIMELINE

Alfred Kinsey establishes the Institute for Sex Research

Masters and Johnson report on the sexual response cycle

1920
1954
1973

American Women given the right to vote
1947
First Masters and Johnson investigations of the human sexual response
1966
The American Psychiatric Association removes homosexuality from its Diagnostic Manual

CHAPTER OUTLINE

What Makes a Male, a Male and a Female, a Female?

The Sex Chromosomes: X's and Y's

The Sex Hormones: Contributing to Maleness and Femaleness

Gender-Role Development

Environmental Influences on Gender Typing

Psychological Theories of Gender-Role Development

Gender Differences: Fact or Myth?

Gender Differences in Cognitive Abilities

Gender Differences in Social Behavior and Personality

Adjustment and Gender Typing: Feminine, Masculine, or Androgynous

Gender Stereotyping—Who Wins? Who Loses?

Sexual Attitudes and Behavior

The Kinsey Surveys: The First In-Depth look at Sexual Behaviors

Sexual Attitudes and Behavior Today: The New Sexual Revolution

Sexual Desire and Arousal: Driving the Sex Drive

Child Sex Abuse

Sexual Orientation

What Determines Sexual Orientation? The Physiological or the Psychological

Research Findings on the Developmental Experiences of Gay Men and Lesbians

Social Attitudes toward Gays: From Celebration to Condemnation

Sexual Dysfunctions

Sexual Desire Disorders: From Disinterest to Aversion

Sexual Arousal Disorders

Orgasmic Disorders

Sexual Pain Disorders

Sexually Transmitted Diseases: The Price of Casual Sex

The Bacterial Infections

The Viral Infections.

Acquired Immune Deficiency Syndrome (AIDS)

Protection against Sexually Transmitted Diseases: Minimizing Risk

Apply It! Protecting Yourself From Rape

Thinking Critically

Chapter Summary and Review

KEY TERMS

What Makes a Male, a Male and a Female, a Female?

sex

sex chromosomes

gonads

androgens

genitals

primary sex characteristics

secondary sex characteristics

Gender-Role Development

gender

gender roles

gender typing

social learning theory

cognitive developmental theory

gender identity

gender-schema theory

androgyny

Sexual Attitudes and Behavior

coitus

sexual response cycle

excitement phase

plateau phase

orgasm phase

resolution phase

estrogen

progesterone

testosterone

Sexual Orientation

sexual orientation

homophobia

Sexual Dysfunctions

sexual dysfunction

hypoactive sexual desire control

sexual aversion disorder

female sexual arousal disorder

male erectile disorder

female orgasmic disorder

male orgasmic disorder

premature ejaculation

dispareunia

vaginismus

Sexually Transmitted Diseases: The Price of Casual Sex

sexually transmitted diseases

chlamydia

pelvic inflammatory disease

gonorrhea

syphilis

genital warts

genital herpes

acquired immune deficiency syndrome (AIDS)

HIV (human immunodeficiency virus)

TIMELINE

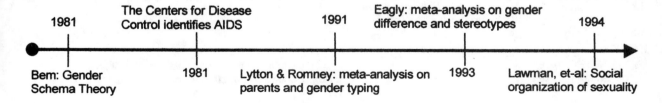

1981

The Centers for Disease Control identifies AIDS

1991

Eagly: meta-analysis on gender difference and stereotypes

1994

Bem: Gender Schema Theory

1981

Lytton & Romney: meta-analysis on parents and gender typing

1993

Lawman, et-al: Social organization of sexuality

OMSE # 1: GENDER ISSUES

LEARNING OBJECTIVES

1. What are the biological factors that determine whether a person is male or female?
2. What role do biological influences play in gender typing?
3. What is gender typing, and what are the environmental factors that contribute to it?
4. What are three theories of gender-role development?
5. Do good adjustment and high self-esteem seem to be related to masculine traits, feminine traits, or androgyny?
6. For what cognitive abilities are there proven gender differences?

7. What gender differences are found in social behavior and personality?
8. What were the famous Kinsey surveys?
9. According to Masters and Johnson, what are the four phases of the human sexual response cycle?
10. What are the male and female sex hormones, and how do they affect sexual desire and activity in males and females?
11. What psychological and cultural factors influence sexual arousal?

LEARNING MASTERY SCORECARD: Update your score card as you work through the various sections of the chapter. First, find and define key terms and concepts included in each section and note the page number(s) from the text that contain important references to the material. Next, gain a practical understanding of the concepts by considering the Laboratory to Life scenarios and thinking of at least one original example of how the concept might apply in real life. Complete the *Objective-Mastery Self-Evaluation* (OMSE) exercises for this section and record your scores. Revisit the exercises, recording your score and the date completed until you have attained mastery (100%). Finally, decide how you would prepare a lecture on each objective using the template provided, outline the lecture, and practice presenting it. Keep an honest tally of your achievements and, when finished, you will have developed learning mastery through elaborate rehearsal.

Key Term	page #	Key Term	page #	Key Term	page #
sex	____	gender roles	____	sexual response cycle	____
sex chromosomes	____	gender typing	____	excitement phase	____
gonads	____	social learning theory	____	plateau phase	____
androgens	____	cognitive developmental theory	____	orgasm phase	____
genitals	____	gender identity	____	resolution phase	____
primary sex characteristics	____	gender-schema theory	____	estrogen	____
secondary sex characteristics	____	androgyny	____	progesterone	____
gender	____	coitus	____	testosterone	____

Quick Quiz

Date	Score	Date	Score	Date	Score
_/_/_	____	_/_/_	____	_/_/_	____
_/_/_	____	_/_/_	____	_/_/_	100%

Elaborate Rehearsal

Lecture Preparation	Completion Date
Key Terms, Persons, & Concepts	_/_/_
Learning Objectives	_/_/_
Lecture Notes	_/_/_

A. QUICK QUIZ

1. XX is to _____ as XY is to _____:
   - a) female; male
   - b) male: female
   - c) genetically healthy; genetic dysfunction
   - d) genetic dysfunction; genetically healthy

2. Prenatal androgens will increase aggression in males but do not seem to have an effect on female gender-based behavior.
    a) True   b) False

3. If androgen is present the result will be male genitals and if androgen is absent the result will be female genitals. In other words, androgen determines _____ sex characteristics.

4. _____ sex characteristics become apparent at the onset of puberty.
    a) Primary   c) Secondary
    b) Male   d) Female

5. It appears that middle-class parents are more likely than lower-class parents to encourage daughters to pursue careers in traditionally male-dominated fields.
    a) True   b) False

6. Judy, at about age 2 to 3 years, acquired her sense of gender _____, her sense of being female. At about age five, Judy realized that she would be female for her entire life. This realization is known as gender _____.

7. _____ refers to a combination of desirable male and female characteristics in one person.
    a) Gender stereotype   c) Gender schema
    b) Androgyny   d) Dualism

8. While males are more aggressive in general, females will also show aggression. One striking observation has been that women tend to be more willing than men to act aggressively in the absence of provocation.
    a) True   b) False

9. Hedges and Nowell (1995) found that females seemed to do better in _____ and _____ while males did better in _____ and _____.

10. Evidence suggests that females tend to be more oriented toward _____ and males tend to be more oriented toward _____.
    a) people; feelings   c) objects; people
    b) feelings; people   d) people; objects

11. Based on the text discussion of gender differences, it is apparent that gender differences are mostly genetic and are not likely to be changed by factors such as the environment.
    a) True   c) this is True for males but not for females
    b) False   d) this is True for females but not males

12. Which is the correct sequence of phases in the sexual response cycle?
    a) excitement; plateau; resolution; orgasm   c) excitement; plateau; orgasm; resolution
    b) resolution; orgasm; plateau; excitement   d) plateau; excitement; orgasm; resolution

13. Which hormone was found to be most associated with male aggressiveness and sexual motivation?

    _____

14. Which hormone is associated with secondary sex characteristics, and control of the menstrual cycle in females?

    _____

15. While there is little question about the negative effects of viewing violent pornography (e.g., the rape myth) there does seem to be disagreement as to the effects of viewing nonviolent pornography.
    a) True   b) False

B. MATCHING

_____	1. The sex glands	a. androgyny
_____	2. Internal and external reproductive organs	b. sexual orientation
_____	3. Sex characteristics developed at puberty	c. estrogen
_____	4. Expectations for gender-appropriate behavior	d. gonads
_____	5. Sense of being male or female	e. testosterone
_____	6. Combination of male and female characteristics	f. progesterone
_____	7. Promotes secondary female sex characteristics	g. primary sex characteristics
_____	8. Prepares uterus for pregnancy	h. gender identity
_____	9. Associated with male aggressiveness	i. gender roles
_____	10. Direction of one's sexual preference	j. secondary sex characteristics

C. COMPLETE THE DIAGRAM: Fill in each blank with the best match, either male (M) or female (F).

Statement or Term	M or F	Statement or Term	M or F
1. physical aggression	_____	10. people oriented	_____
2. verbal abilities	_____	11. cooperation	_____
3. spatial abilities	_____	12. competition	_____
4. reading comprehension	_____	13. physical sex	_____
5. nurturing	_____	14. relationships	_____
6. assertive	_____	15. pride regarding virginity	_____
7. sensitive	_____	16. embarrassed about virginity	_____
8. independent	_____	17. estrogen	_____
9. object oriented	_____	18. testosterone	_____

PREPARE A LECTURE: This activity is designed to offer you an opportunity to take advantage of a valuable mode of learning, elaborate rehearsal. Once you have finished the OMSE section, write a lecture using the instructional guide provided below. After your lecture is prepared, you can enhance your learning by writing a quiz covering the material. Now it is time to find some willing and inquisitive audience members. Your roommates or family may be a great place to start. Present them the lecture as if you are teaching a class. Remember to ask for questions and give your students the quiz following the lecture. This exercise can also serve to turn a *study-buddy* group into a very productive way to prepare for the test. Each member of the group can take different OMSE sections for their lecture/teacher role while the rest of the group serves as the class.

I. Key Terms, Names, Dates, and Concepts you will include in this lecture:

1. _____   5. _____   9. _____
2. _____   6. _____   10. _____
3. _____   7. _____   11. _____
4. _____   8. _____   12. _____

II. Learning Objectives (what do you want the student to know and be able to do as a result of your lecture):

1. _____
2. _____
3. _____
4. _____
5. _____

III. Lecture Notes (notes should be brief cues and serve as a guide).

Major topic #1: _____

   Sub-topics and notes: _____

_____
_____
_____

Major topic #2: _____

    Sub-topics and notes: _____

_____

_____

_____

Major topic #3: _____

    Sub-topics and notes: _____

_____

_____

_____

OMSE # 2: SEXUAL ORIENTATION AND SEXUAL HEALTH

LEARNING OBJECTIVES

1. What is meant by sexual orientation?
2. What are the various biological factors that have been suggested as possible determinants of a gay or lesbian sexual orientation?
3. What does the study by Bell, Weinberg, and Hammersmith reveal about the developmental experiences of gay men and lesbians?
4. What are two sexual desire disorders and their defining features?
5. What are the sexual arousal disorders and their defining features?
6. What are the three orgasmic disorders and the defining features of each?
7. What are the major bacterial and viral infections known s sexually transmitted diseases?
8. Why do chlamydia and gonorrhea pose a greater threat to women than to men?
9. Why is genital herpes particularly upsetting to those who have it?
10. What happens to a person from the time of infection with HIV to the development of full-blown AIDS?
11. What happens to a person from the time of infection with HIV to the development of full-blown AIDS?
12. How is AIDS transmitted?
13. What are the most effective methods of protection against sexually transmitted diseases?

LEARNING MASTERY SCORECARD: Update your score card as you work through the various sections of the chapter. First, find and define key terms and concepts included in each section and note the page number(s) from the text that contain important references to the material. Next, gain a practical understanding of the concepts by considering the Laboratory to Life scenarios and thinking of at least one original example of how the concept might apply in real life. Complete the *Objective-Mastery Self-Evaluation* (OMSE) exercises for this section and record your scores. Revisit the exercises, recording your score and the date completed until you have attained mastery (100%). Finally, decide how you would prepare a lecture on each objective using the template provided, outline the lecture, and practice presenting it. Keep an honest tally of your achievements and, when finished, you will have developed learning mastery through elaborate rehearsal.

Key Term	Page #	Key Term	Page #	Key Term	Page #
sexual orientation	_____	female orgasmic disorder	_____	pelvic inflammatory disease (PID)	_____
homophobia	_____	male orgasmic disorder	_____	gonorrhea	_____
sexual dysfunction	_____	premature ejaculation	_____	syphilis	_____
hypoactive sexual desire control	_____	dispareunia	_____	genital warts	_____
sexual aversion disorder	_____	vaginismus	_____	genital herpes	_____
female sexual arousal disorder	_____	sexually transmitted diseases	_____	AIDS	_____
male erectile disorder	_____	chlamydia	_____	HIV	_____

Quick Quiz

Date	Score	Date	Score	Date	Score
__/__/__	_____	__/__/__	_____	__/__/__	_____
__/__/__	_____	__/__/__	_____	__/__/__	100%

Elaborate Rehearsal

Lecture Preparation	Completion Date
Key Terms, Persons, & Concepts	__/__/__
Learning Objectives	__/__/__
Lecture Notes	__/__/__

A. QUICK QUIZ

1. Sexual orientation refers to one's sexual _____.
    a) understanding
    b) preference
    c) stereotypes
    d) condition

2. While once considered a learned behavior, more recent research suggests that homosexual orientation is probably the result of biological processes.
    a) True
    b) False

3. It has been reported that, in an area of the brain structure known as the _____, size differences exist between homosexual and heterosexual men.

4. There have been studies to determine the influence of genetics on sexual orientation. However, without evidence of identical twins _____, the influence of the environment cannot be ruled out.
    a) raised together
    b) who are of the opposite sex
    c) reared apart
    d) who are of the same sex

5. A meta-analysis of sexual orientation and childhood gender based behaviors would certainly indicate that all adult gay males report gender nonconforming behaviors as children.
    a) True
    b) False

6. An individual who exhibits a strong, irrational dislike for homosexual behaviors or individuals would be said to be _____.

7. An individual who has little sexual desire or interest in sexual activity would probably be diagnosed with _____.
    a) hyperactive sexual desire disorder
    b) sexual dyskinesthia
    c) sexual dystonia
    d) hypoactive sexual desire disorder

8. Male erectile disorder has been found to be, for the most part, a physical disorder.
    a) True
    b) False

9. The most common sexual dysfunction as identified in the text is _____.

10. Sexually transmitted diseases such as chlamydia or gonorrhea are caused by a(n) _____ infection.
    a) viral
    b) fungal
    c) bacterial
    d) unknown

11. The good news is that, other than AIDS, sexually transmitted diseases are on a sharp decline.
    a) True
    b) False

12. Sexually transmitted diseases such as genital warts, herpes, and AIDS are caused by a _____ infection.

B. MATCHING

Match the sexual dysfunction with its symptoms by placing the letter of the disorder in the corresponding symptom box.

DISORDERS:

a. hypoactive sexual desire
b. female sexual arousal disorder
c. sexual aversion disorder
d. male erectile disorder

e. female orgasmic disorder
f. male orgasmic disorder
g. dyspareunia
h. vaginismus

SYMPTOMS

1.	persistent inability to reach orgasm or a delay in reaching orgasm with adequate sexual stimulation
2.	aversion to, or a desire to avoid genital contact with a sexual partner
3.	absence of ejaculation or ejaculation occurs only after extreme effort
4.	little or no sexual desire or interest in sexual activity
5.	inability to have or sustain an erection firm enough for coitus
6.	sexual pain in which involuntary muscle contractions create a tightening and closing of the vagina
7.	lack of arousal or inadequate lubrication-swelling in response to sexual stimulation
8.	sexual pain for males and females marked by genital pain associated with sexual intercourse

C. COMPLETE THE DIAGRAM

Match the STD with the symptoms by placing the letter of the STD in the corresponding symptom box. Each STD may have more than one symptom set.

STD

a. chlamydia
b. pelvic inflammatory disease
c. gonorrhea
d. syphilis

e. genital herpes
f. AIDS
g. genital warts

SYMPTOMS

1.	infection in female pelvic organs which can result from other untreated STDs
2.	painful blisters on genitals – incurable and highly contagious
3.	untreated progression in three stages
4.	often resemble cauliflower in appearance
5.	rare forms of cancer or pneumonia
6.	most common form of bacterial STD
7.	male symptom is a puslike discharge from the penis
8.	first and second symptoms often disappear even without treatment
9.	male symptoms, but no adverse reproductive consequences
10.	severe symptoms including serious weight loss and swollen lymph nodes
11.	blisters may be followed by viral movement to base of the spinal cord
12.	HPV

PREPARE A LECTURE: This activity is designed to offer you an opportunity to take advantage of a valuable mode of learning, elaborate rehearsal. Once you have finished the OMSE section, write a lecture using the instructional guide provided below. After your lecture is prepared, you can enhance your learning by writing a quiz covering the material. Now it is time to find some willing and inquisitive audience members. Your roommates or family may be a great place to start. Present them the lecture as if you are teaching a class. Remember to ask for questions and give your students the quiz following the lecture. This exercise can also serve to turn a *study-buddy* group into a very productive way to prepare for the test. Each member of the group can take different OMSE sections for their lecture/teacher role while the rest of the group serves as the class.

I. Key Terms, Names, Dates, and Concepts you will include in this lecture:

1. _____   5. _____   9. _____

2. _____   6. _____   10. _____

3. _____   7. _____   11. _____

4. _____   8. _____   12. _____

II. Learning Objectives (what do you want the student to know and be able to do as a result of your lecture):

1. _____

2. _____

3. _____

4. _____

5. _____

III. Lecture Notes (notes should be brief cues and serve as a guide).

Major topic #1: _____

Sub-topics and notes: _____

_____

_____

_____

Major topic #2: _____

Sub-topics and notes: _____

_____

_____

_____

Major topic #3: _____

Sub-topics and notes: _____

_____

_____

_____

KEY TERMS AND CONCEPTS EXERCISE

The key terms and concepts are presented in the order of their appearance in the text. Space is provided for you to include a personalized definition or example of each term or concept. As you encounter each term in the text, make a note of its meaning and context. Next, conceptualize the meaning of the term in a way that makes the most sense to you. You can also think about examples of the term from your own life. Write your definition and/or example in the space provided next to the word in this book. The KEY TERMS exercise utilizes a modified *T-note* design so that you can self-evaluate your mastery of the definitions. First lay a sheet of paper over the terms and concepts side of the page so that you only see the definitions. Read the definition and try to recall the term or concept. Mark all those you are unable to answer so you can restudy them. When you have learned all of the terms and concepts in this way, move the paper to the definition side so that you can see only the term or concept, try to recall both the textbook definition and your personal version. Repeat this until you know all of the terms and concepts by definition and personal understanding.

Sex	Biological determination of whether one is male or female. _____
Sex Chromosomes	The pair of chromosomes that determines the sex of a person (XX in females and XY in males). _____
Gonads	The sex glands; the ovaries in females and the testes in males. _____
Androgens	Male sex hormones; in the embryo, androgens must be present for male genitals to be formed. _____
Genitals	The internal and external reproductive organs. _____
Primary Sex Characteristics	The internal and external reproductive organs; the genitals. _____
Secondary Sex Characteristics	The physical characteristics that are not directly involved in reproduction but that develop at puberty and are associated with sexual maturity. _____
Gender	Psychological and sociocultural definition of masculinity and femininity based on the expected behaviors for males and females. _____
Gender Roles	Cultural expectations about the behavior appropriate to each gender. _____
Gender Typing	The process by which individuals acquire the traits, behaviors, attitudes, preferences, and interests that the culture considers appropriate for their gender. _____
Social Learning Theory	A theory that explains the process of gender typing in terms of observation, imitation, and reinforcement. _____
Cognitive Developmental Theory	A theory suggesting that when children realize their gender is permanent, they are motivated to seek out same-sex models and learn to act in ways considered appropriate for their gender. _____
Gender Identity	One's sense of being a male or a female. _____
Gender-Schema Theory	A theory suggesting that young people are motivated to attend to and behave in ways consistent with gender-based standards and stereotypes of the culture. _____

Androgyny	A combination of the desirable male and female characteristics in one person. _____ _____ _____
Coitus	Penile-vaginal intercourse. _____ _____ _____
Sexual Response Cycle	The four phases—excitement, plateau, orgasm, and resolution—that Masters and Johnson found are part of the human sexual response in both males and females. _____ _____
Excitement Phase	The first stage in the sexual response cycle, characterized by an erection in males and a swelling of the clitoris and vaginal lubrication in females. _____ _____
Plateau Phase	The second stage of the sexual response cycle, during which muscle tension and blood flow increase in preparation for orgasm. _____ _____
Orgasm Phase	The third phase in the sexual response cycle, marked by rhythmic muscle contractions and a sudden discharge of accumulated sexual tension. _____ _____
Resolution Phase	The final stage of the sexual response cycle, during which the body returns to an unaroused state. _____ _____
Estrogen	A female sex hormone that promotes the secondary sex characteristics in females and controls the menstrual cycle. _____ _____
Progesterone	A female sex hormone that plays a role in the regulation of the menstrual cycle and prepares the lining of the uterus for possible pregnancy. _____ _____
Testosterone	The most powerful androgen secreted by the testes and adrenal glands in males and by the adrenal glands in females; influences the development and maintenance of male sex characteristics and sexual motivation; associated with male aggressiveness. _____ _____
Sexual Orientation	The direction of one's sexual preference—toward members of the opposite sex (heterosexuality), toward one's own sex (homosexuality), or toward both sexes (bisexuality). _____ _____
Homophobia	An intense, irrational hostility toward or fear of homosexuals. _____ _____
Sexual Dysfunction	A persistent or recurrent problem that causes marked distress and interpersonal difficulty and that may involve any or some combination of the following: sexual desire, sexual arousal or the pleasure associated with sex, or orgasm. _____ _____

Hypoactive Sexual Desire Control	A sexual dysfunction marked by little or no desire or interest in sexual activity. _____ _____ _____
Sexual Aversion Disorder	A sexual disorder characterized by an aversion to or a desire to avoid genital contact with a sexual partner. _____ _____ _____
Female Sexual Arousal Disorder	A sexual dysfunction in which a woman may not feel sexually aroused in response to sexual stimulation or may be unable to achieve or sustain "an adequate lubrication-swelling response to sexual excitement." _____ _____ _____
Male Erectile Disorder	The repeated inability to have or sustain an erection firm enough for coitus; erectile dysfunction or impotence. _____ _____ _____
Female Orgasmic Disorder	The persistent inability of a woman to reach orgasm, or a delay in reaching orgasm despite adequate sexual stimulation. _____ _____ _____
Male Orgasmic Disorder	A sexual dysfunction in which there is an absence of ejaculation, or in which ejaculation occurs only after strenuous effort over an extremely prolonged period. _____ _____ _____
Premature Ejaculation	A chronic or recurring condition orgasmic disorder in which orgasm and ejaculation occur with little stimulation, before, at, or shortly after penetration and before the person desires it. _____ _____ _____
Dispareunia	A sexual pain disorder marked by genital pain associated with sexual intercourse, occurring in both males and females. _____ _____ _____
Vaginismus	A sexual pain disorder in which involuntary muscle contractions create a tightening and closing of the vagina, making intercourse painful or impossible. _____ _____ _____
Sexually Transmitted Diseases (STDs)	Infections that are spread primarily through intimate sexual contact. STDs include curable bacteria infections and incurable viral infections including AIDS. _____ _____ _____
Chlamydia	The most common bacterial STD found in both sexes, and one that can cause infertility in females. _____ _____ _____
Pelvic Inflammatory Disease	An infection in the female pelvic organs, which can result from untreated chlamydia or gonorrhea and can cause pain, scarring of tissue, and even infertility or ectopic pregnancy. _____ _____
Gonorrhea	An STD that, in males, causes a puslike discharge from the penis; if untreated, females can develop pelvic inflammatory disease and possible infertility. _____ _____ _____

Syphilis	An STD that progresses through three stages; if left untreated, it can eventually be fatal. Famous Chicago gangster Al Capone lived his last years crippled by tertiary (final stage) syphilis, which eventually took his life. _____ _____ _____
Genital Warts	Caused by human papillomavirus (HPV), these growths often resemble cauliflower in appearance and are found most often in the genital and anal regions. _____ _____ _____
Genital Herpes	An STD caused by the herpes simplex virus (usually type 2) that results in painful blisters on the genitals; presently incurable, and usually recurring. Highly contagious during outbreaks, herpes can be transmitted even when there are no outward signs of contagion. _____ _____
Acquired Immune Deficiency Syndrome (AIDS)	A devastating and incurable illness that is caused by HIV and progressively weakens the body's immune system, leaving the person vulnerable to opportunistic infections that usually cause death. _____ _____ _____
HIV (Human Immunodeficiency Virus)	The virus that causes AIDS. _____ _____ _____

FROM THE LABORATORY TO REAL LIFE

Which One is Which? Read each statement below and place the corresponding letter in the space provided.

A. A 14-year-old male
B. A 14-year-old female
C. A 27-year-old male
D. A 27-year-old female

1. _____ Research shows I will do better on my high-school English papers than my other gender counterparts.
2. _____ I deserve a promotion but they always seem to go to my other gender counterparts instead.
3. _____ I am on several committees at work and I seem to want to dominate the discussions.
4. _____ I am the youngest XY of the group.
5. _____ I love rough and tumble games on weekends when we are not in school.
6. _____ I am more interested in the quality of the relationship than just physical sex with my spouse.
7. _____ My parents are still concerned that I prefer playing sports on non-school days—they call me a tomboy.
8. _____ I am the oldest XY of the group.
9. _____ I remember puberty—my secondary sex characteristics were most influenced by estrogen.
10. _____ As an adult, if I become aggressive, people say I have too much testosterone.
11. _____ I am the youngest XX of the group.
12. _____ I am currently developing secondary sex characteristics—influenced by estrogen.
13. _____ I am embarrassed to tell my school friends that I am still a virgin.
14. _____ I am the oldest XX of the group.
15. _____ I use both hemispheres when I am in English or Composition class in my high school.
16. _____ When my friends and I go on a business trip, sex often dominates our discussions.
17. _____ My child is an XX, just like me.
18. _____ I will probably do better in my high-school math classes than my other gender counterparts.
19. _____ My mother has warned me that I am too young for adult behaviors such as sexual intercourse, and that if I do engage in these behaviors, I could get diseases such as PID.
20. _____ Progesterone is an important hormone in my reproductive capabilities.

FROM THEORY TO PRACTICE

BOYS WILL BE BOYS AND GIRLS WILL BE GIRLS

A few years ago, several parent couples appeared in a documentary about gender-role development. Each couple had elected to raise their children in a totally non-gender based environment. In other words, both boys and girls were raised in neutral colored rooms and were allowed to choose their clothing from an assortment that included traditional male and female attire. No toy guns, soldiers, or other traditionally male toys were present in the homes, and boys were encouraged to play with dolls and other traditionally female toys. The social experiment was a success—sort of. What was discovered was that boys will be boys. One scene at a family's dinner table showed a three-year-old male playing with a doll—he had removed certain appendages and fashioned the doll into a makeshift pistol. The parents denied knowledge of where their son might have picked up the idea. Most couples finally had to admit that their children were taking on either female or male roles respectively, despite their best efforts to avoid gender stereotyping in their homes.

Using the theories and concepts from the text, explain why this social experiment probably turned out the way it did.

_____

_____

_____

_____

_____

_____

_____

_____

_____

_____

_____

_____

_____

_____

SEXUAL ORIENTATION: THE PATH TO PREFERENCE AND THE ATTITUDES THAT FOLLOW

There is still a great deal of controversy over why some people have a same sex preference while others have an opposite sex preference. The text includes research supporting a possible genetic predisposition, as well as a disclaimer that more research is needed before a conclusion may be drawn. Research not included in the text contains references to the idea that boys raised by overbearing, controlling mothers tend to more often become gay. There is much research still to be done on this subject and, as in many other areas of research, we may never have a definitive answer. Perhaps more important than the causes of homosexuality are the attitudes of our society toward men and women who, for whatever reason, have a same sex orientation. Read the following scenarios and address each in terms of your personal attitude as well as the information included in the text. Give reasons for your personal attitude that reflect the research provided.

1. In President Clinton's first term of office, he passed legislation through Congress allowing gays and lesbians to remain in the military provided that they kept their orientation a secret. The policy, known as the "don't ask—don't tell" policy, ensures that the military is not legally allowed to ask questions regarding one's sexual preference. However, if military personnel are discovered to be homosexual, they can be discharged.

_____

_____

_____

2. Only a few years ago, a regional superintendent of schools decided to test the tolerance of teachers, students, and parents by introducing children's books depicting same sex couples as parents in an effort to address alternative lifestyles with children as early as the first grade. Opposition from parents was rampant, and the idea (as well as the administrator) was eventually tossed out.

_____

_____

_____

3. In the past decade, many churches have altered their policies to allow for the inclusion of homosexuals. In many other churches, members and ministers alike are appalled at the idea of embracing "sinners" in the church.

_____

_____

_____

4. Long considered abnormal behavior, homosexuality was included in the Diagnostic and Statistical Manual of the American Psychiatric Association for many years until recently. There are still organizations whose primary or sole purpose is to assist homosexuals to return to the world of heterosexuality.

_____

_____

_____

COMPREHENSIVE PRACTICE TEST

1. If the sperm cell that fertilizes an egg carries a Y chromosome, and the baby is born healthy and normal, the baby will be _____.
   a) female
   b) male

2. In terms of gender typing, females exposed to prenatal androgens show no differences from girls who are not exposed to prenatal androgens.
   a) True
   b) False

3. Males primarily use the _____ hemisphere for language tasks.
   a) right
   c) left
   b) central
   d) lateral

4. Who seems to differentiate between boys and girls more—fathers or mothers?
   a) fathers
   b) mothers

5. The internal and external reproductive organs are called the _____.
   a) secondary sex characteristics
   c) genitals
   b) androgens
   d) gender organs

6. Biological structures such as the penis and the vagina are examples of _____.
   a) primary sex characteristics
   b) secondary sex characteristics

7. Gender typing refers to the process by which boys and girls take on the gender characteristics of their opposite sex parent.
   a) True
   b) False

8. Evidence would suggest that parents would like for John to do best in _____ and Mary to do best in _____.
   a) English; math
   b) math; English

9. Boys raised in father-absent households tend to demonstrate fewer male gender typed behaviors than their father-present counterparts, but this seems to turn around by the time they reach adolescence.
   a) True
   b) False

10. Alice knows she is a girl and her little brother is a boy. This represents the concept of:
    a) gender stereotyping
    b) gender constancy
    c) gender identity
    d) gender stability

11. Iva knows she will be a girl even if she wears a cap and plays baseball. This is because she has developed a sense of _____.
    a) gender stereotyping
    b) gender constancy
    c) gender identity
    d) gender stability

12. Sandra Bem would suggest that, with the onset of gender identity, children use gender as a way to organize and process information. This is known as _____ theory.
    a) social learning
    b) gender specific
    c) cognitive developmental
    d) gender-schema

13. Diane seems to have a good balance of both male and female characteristics. She would be said to be _____.
    a) gender typed
    b) gender balanced
    c) androgynous
    d) gender nonspecific

14. Based on research, who will generally do better on spelling tasks?
    a) females
    b) there is no detected difference in this cognitive ability
    c) males

15. Who, as adults, tend to interrupt others more in conversations?
    a) females
    b) males

16. Females are to _____ as males are to _____:
    a) art; literature
    b) objects; people
    c) people; objects
    d) literature; art

17. The good news is that in today's world, there seems to be no differences between the sexes in terms of professional opportunity or income.
    a) True
    b) False

18. Launann, et-al published <u>The Organization of Sexuality</u>, in which was reported:
    a) people with multiple sexual partners are happier than people with one sexual partner
    b) over a lifetime, women tend to have more sex partners than men
    c) more women than men report being faithful to their spouses
    d) an equal number of men and women report that they masturbate occasionally

19. Recently, males are reporting more pride in their virgin status.
    a) True
    b) False

20. Which list of the phases of the Sex Response Cycle is in the correct order?
    a) resolution; plateau; excitement; orgasm
    b) excitement; plateau; orgasm; resolution
    c) excitement; resolution; orgasm; plateau
    d) plateau; excitement; orgasm; resolution

21. Which of the following is responsible for secondary sex characteristics in females?
    a) estrogen
    b) testosterone
    c) progesterone
    d) androgen

22. Do females have testosterone?
    a) Yes
    b) No

23. Sexual fantasy is most common with people who report a satisfactory sex life.
   a) True   b) False

24. Which was not listed as an enduring problem for children who suffer sexual abuse?
   a) depression   c) unsupported self-confidence
   b) interpersonal problems   d) low self-esteem

25. While there are no final explanations for the findings, it seems there are differences in the _____
   in the brains of homosexual and heterosexual individuals.
   a) amygdala   c) cerebellum
   b) hypothalamus   d) septum

26. There is now no doubt that homosexuality is almost completely the result of genes.
   a) True   b) False

27. If an individual has no sexual desire or interest in sexual activity, he or she would be diagnosed with:
   a) sexual arousal disorder   c) orgasmic disorder
   b) dyspareunia   d) hypoactive sexual disorder

28. Are the orgasmic disorders, *male orgasmic disorder* and *premature ejaculation,* basically different names for the
   same problem?
   a) Yes   b) No

29. Which of the following is the most common bacterial STD?
   a) chlamydia   c) gonorrhea
   b) genital warts   d) syphilis

30. Which of the following can be cured if treated in a timely manner?
   a) AIDS   c) genital herpes
   b) syphilis   d) this is not true for any listed STD

ANSWER KEYS

Answer Key: Gender Issues

A. Quick Quiz	B. Matching	C. Complete the Diagram	
1. a	1. d	1. m	10. f
2. false	2. g	2. f	11. f
3. primary	3. j	3. m	12. m
4. c	4. i	4. f	13. m
5. true	5. h	5. f	14. f
6. identity; stability	6. a	6. m	15. f
7. b	7. c	7. f	16. m
8. false	8. f	8. m	17. f
9. reading; writing; science; math	9. e	9. m	18. m
10. d	10. b		
11. b			
12. c			
13. testosterone			
14. estrogen			
15. true			

Answer Key: Sexual Orientation, Dysfunction, and Sexually Transmitted Disease

A. Quick Quiz	B. Matching	Complete the Diagram
1. b	1. e	1. b
2. true	2. c	2. e
3. hypothalamus	3. f	3. d
4. c	4. a	4. g
5. false	5. d	5. f
6. homophobic	6. h	6. a
7. d	7. b	7. c
8. false	8. g	8. d
9. premature ejaculation		9. a
10. c		10. f
11. false		11. e
12. viral		12. g

Answer Key: Laboratory to Real Life

1. B	5. A	9. D	13. A	17. D
2. D	6. D	10. C	14. D	18. A
3. C	7. B	11. B	15. B	19. B
4. A	8. C	12. B	16. C	20. D

Answer Key: Comprehensive Practice Test

1. b	11. b	21. a
2. false	12. d	22. yes
3. c	13. c	23. false
4. a	14. a	24. c
5. c	15. b	25. b
6. a	16. c	26. false
7. false	17. false	27. d
8. b	18. c	28. no
9. true	19. true	29. a
10. c	20. b	30. b

13

PERSONALITY THEORY AND ASSESSMENT

Man's main task in life is to give birth to himself, to become what he potentially is. The most important product of his effort is his own personality.

–Eric Fromm (1947)

CHAPTER OVERVIEW

You are the world's foremost authority on at least one thing—your own theory of personality. Everyday we operate within our individual social environments. We make decisions about other people and ourselves. We decide whom we like and whom we dislike, and we make judgements and form expectations about other peoples' behaviors. We use the concept of personality so often that we rarely even think about it. "I like his outgoing personality." "Doesn't she have a nice personality?" Our theories of personality come from several sources; most notably our own personalities, the ways we have been taught to view the world and behave in that world, and our personal experiences. You are an expert on your own theory of personality. Still, you probably find it difficult to define and describe this complex aspect of humanness. Well, you are not alone in this dilemma. The text will present a variety of different and often conflicting views on the sources, nature, and implications of personality. One problem with defining personality is the fact that it is a construct—we cannot examine, measure, or dissect it. Our understanding of personality comes from observing the results, or the influence this construct has on human behavior. Even our measurements are based not on the actual construct of personality, but on the products of that personality—our behaviors, attitudes, beliefs, and ways of viewing the world. This ambiguity makes for fascinating reading.

This chapter will help you gain a more practiced and functional understanding of personality as it is presented in the text. The materials are divided into two OMSE sections: 1) personality theories, and 2) personality assessment. You will discover the variety of ways in which theorists have developed their particular theories of personality, how they explain personality and its effects, and how we can use an understanding of personality to better understand human behavior.

By completing the exercises provided, you should gain a thorough understanding of the information presented in your text. In other words, you should be better prepared for tests, quizzes, class participation, and life itself.

TIMELINE

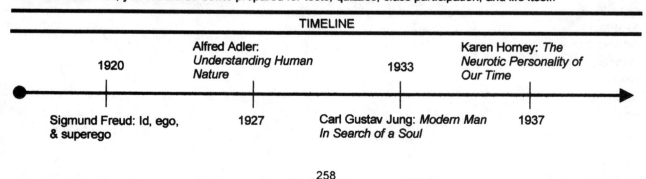

	Alfred Adler: *Understanding Human Nature*		Karen Horney: *The Neurotic Personality of Our Time*
1920		1933	
Sigmund Freud: Id, ego, & superego	1927	Carl Gustav Jung: *Modern Man In Search of a Soul*	1937

CHAPTER OUTLINE

Sigmund Freud and Psychoanalysis

The Conscious, the Preconscious, and the Unconscious: Levels of Awareness

The Id, the Ego, and the Superego: Warring Components of the Personality

Pioneers: Sigmund Freud

Defense Mechanisms: Protecting the Ego

The Psychosexual Stages of Development: Centered on the Erogenous Zones

Freud's Explanation of Personality

Evaluating Freud's Contribution

The Neo-Freudians

Carl Gustav Jung

Alfred Adler: Overcoming Inferiority

Karen Horney: Champion of Feminine Psychology

Trait Theories

Gordon Allport: Personality Traits in the Brain

Raymond Cattell's 16 Personality Factors

Hans Eysenck: Stressing Two Factors

The Five-Factor Theory of Personality: The Big Five

Evaluating the Trait Perspective

Learning Theories and Personality

The Behaviorist View of B. F. Skinner

The Social-Cognitive Theorists: Expanding the Behaviorist View

Humanistic Personality Theories

Abraham Maslow: The Self-Actualizing Person

Carl Rogers: The Fully Functioning Person

Evaluating the Humanistic Perspective

Personality: Is It in the Genes?

The Twin Study Method: Studying Identical and Fraternal Twins

The Shared and Nonshared Environment

The Adoption Method

Personality and Culture

Personality Assessment

Observation, Interviews, and Rating Scales

Personality Inventories: Taking Stock

Projective Tests: Projecting from the Unconscious

Personality Theories: A Final Comment

Apply It! Becoming More Optimistic

Thinking Critically

Chapter Summary and Review

KEY TERMS

Sigmund Freud and Psychoanalysis

personality

psychoanalysis

conscious

preconscious

unconscious

id

pleasure principle

libido

ego

superego

defense mechanism

repression

projection

denial

rationalization

regression

reaction formation

displacement

sublimation

psychosexual stages

fixation

oral stage

anal stage

phallic stage

Oedipus complex

latency period

genital stage

The Neo-Freudians

personal unconscious

collective unconscious

archetype

extroversion

introversion

Trait Theories

trait

trait theories

cardinal trait

central trait

surface traits

source traits

five-factor theory

Learning Theories

reciprocal determinism

self-efficacy

locus of control

The Humanistic Perspective

humanistic psychology

self-actualization

conditions of worth

unconditional positive regard

Personality: Is It in the Genes

behavioral genetics

heritability

Personality Assessment

halo effect

inventory

Minnesota Multiphasic Personality Inventory–2 (MMPI–2)

California Psychological Inventory (CPI)

Myers-Briggs Type Indicator (MBTI)

projective test

Rorschach Inkblot Test

Thematic Apperception Test (TAT)

OMSE # 1: PERSONALITY THEORIES

LEARNING OBJECTIVES

1. To what two aspects of Freud's work does the term psychoanalysis apply?
2. What are the three levels of awareness in consciousness?
3. What are the roles of the id, the ego, and the superego?
4. What is a defense mechanism?
5. What are two ways in which repression operates?
6. What are some other defense mechanisms?
7. What are the psychosexual stages, and why did Freud consider them so important in personality development?
8. What is the Oedipus complex?
9. According to Freud, what are the two primary sources of influence on the personality?
10. According to Jung, what are the three components of personality?
11. What are five archetypes that Jung believed have a major influence on personality?
12. What did Adler consider to be the driving force of the personality?
13. Why is Horney considered a pioneer in psychology?
14. What are trait theories of personality?
15. How did Allport differentiate between cardinal and central traits?
16. How did Cattell differentiate between surface and source traits?
17. What does Eysenck consider to be the two most important dimensions of personality?
18. What are the big five personality dimensions in the five-factor theory as described by McCrae and Costa?
19. How did Skinner account for what most people refer to as personality?
20. What are the components that make up Bandura's concept of reciprocal determinism, and how do they interact?
21. What does Rotter mean by the terms internal and external locus of control?
22. Who were the two pioneers in humanistic psychology, and how did they view human nature?
23. What is self-actualization, and how did Maslow study it?
24. According to Rogers, why don't all people become fully functioning persons?
25. What has research in behavioral genetics revealed about the influence of the genes and the environment on personality?

LEARNING MASTERY SCORECARD:
Update your score card as you work through the chapter. First, find and define key terms and concepts included in each section and note the page number(s) from the text that contain important references to the material. Next, gain a practical understanding of the concepts by considering the Laboratory to Life scenarios. Complete the *Objective-Mastery Self-Evaluation* (OMSE) exercises for this section and record your scores. Revisit the exercises, recording your score and the date completed until you have attained mastery (100%). Finally, prepare a lecture on each objective using the template provided, and practice presenting it. Keep an honest tally of your achievements and, when finished, you will have developed learning mastery.

Key Term	page #	Key Term	page #	Key Term	page #
personality		reaction formation		trait	
psychoanalysis		displacement		trait theories	
conscious		sublimation		cardinal trait	
preconscious		psychosexual stages		central trait	
unconscious		fixation		surface traits	
id		oral stage		source traits	
pleasure principle		anal stage		five-factor theory	
libido		phallic stage		reciprocal determinism	
ego		Oedipus complex		self-efficacy	
superego		latency period		locus of control	
defense mechanism		genital stage		humanistic psychology	
repression		personal unconscious		self-actualization	
projection		collective unconscious		conditions of worth	
denial		archetype		unconditional positive regard	
rationalization		extroversion		behavioral genetics	
regression		introversion		heritability	

Quick Quiz

Date	Score	Date	Score	Date	Score
_/_/_	___	_/_/_	___	_/_/_	___
_/_/_	___	_/_/_	___	_/_/_	100%

Elaborate Rehearsal

Lecture Preparation	Completion Date
Key Terms, Persons, & Concepts	_/_/_
Learning Objectives	_/_/_
Lecture Notes	_/_/_

A. QUICK QUIZ

1. According to Freud, which personality structure is completely unconscious and operates on the pleasure principle?
   a) phallic
   b) id
   c) ego
   d) superego

2. According to Freud, which of the following is the logical and rational part of the personality?
   a) superego
   b) the unconscious
   c) id
   d) ego

3. According to Freud, which of the following is very much like long-term memory?
   a) the conscious
   b) the unconscious
   c) the preconscious
   d) the superego

4. Which of the following presents Freud's stages of psychosexual development in the correct order?
   a) anal, oral, phallic, latency, genital
   b) oral, anal, phallic, latency, genital
   c) oral, anal, phallic, genital, latency
   d) anal, oral, latency, phallic, genital

5. In which of the following stages does Freud's Oedipus complex appear?
   a) phallic
   b) anal
   c) oral
   d) genital

6. Of all the personality theories presented in the text, Freud's theory enjoys the most empirical support.
   a) True
   b) False

7. Which of the following was **NOT** identified as a defense mechanism?
   a) projection
   b) denial
   c) desensitization
   d) sublimation

8. Jung talked about:
   a) the inferiority complex
   b) psychosocial development
   c) archetypes
   d) self actualization

9. According to Jung, what accounted for the similarity of certain myths, dreams, symbols, and religious beliefs in cultures?
   a) the evolved conscious
   b) the cultural unconscious
   c) the personal unconscious
   d) the collective unconscious

10. Adler believed that personality is influenced more by early childhood than by future goals.
    a) True
    b) False

11. Karen Horney believed that indifferent, unaffectionate, or hostile parents could result in a child who experiences basic anxiety. The attempt to cope with this anxiety forms the child's basic attitude toward life.
    a) True
    b) False

12. Mother Teresa would be said to possess the _____ trait of altruism.
   a) central
   b) surface
   c) intrinsic
   d) cardinal

13. According to Cattell, _____ traits are the observable qualities of personality, while _____ traits make up the most basic personality structure and cause behavior.

14. According to Eysenck, _____ is(are) more important in determining personality than are(is) _____.
   a) genes; the environment
   b) the environment; genes

15. Which of the following is **NOT** one of the "big five" factors of personality as they are proposed by Goldberg?
   a) agreeableness
   b) emotionality
   c) neuroticism
   d) conscientiousness

16. Did Walter Mischel (the person-situation debate) agree with the concepts of trait theory?
   a) yes
   b) no

17. According to Skinner, the personality is learned through unconscious behaviors.
   a) True
   b) False

18. Bandura asserted that personal/cognitive factors, our behavior, and external environment all influence each other and are influenced by each other. He called this _____.

19. Concepts such as self-actualization and conditions of worth would be matched with:
   a) the social-cognitive approach
   b) the psychoanalytic approach
   c) the humanistic approach
   d) the trait theory approach

20. Unlike Freud, Rogers views people as basically _____.

B. MATCHING: Place the appropriate letter in the space provided.

	DESCRIPTION OR CONCEPT	PERSONALITY THEORIST
_____	1. psychoanalysis	a. Cattell
_____	2. personal and collective unconscious	b. Rogers
_____	3. inferiority and superiority	c. Bandura
_____	4. feminine psychology	d. Freud
_____	5. central and cardinal traits	e. Skinner
_____	6. surface and source traits	f. Jung
_____	7. personality is determined by the genes	g. Maslow
_____	8. five factor theory of personality	h. Adler
_____	9. personality is a collection of learned behaviors	i. Rotter
_____	10. reciprocal determinism	j. Allport
_____	11. locus of control	k. Horney
_____	12. self-actualization	l. Goldberg
_____	13. fully functioning person	m. Eysenck

TIMELINE

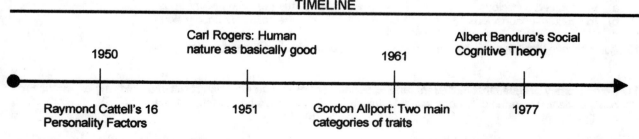

1950	Carl Rogers: Human nature as basically good	1961	Albert Bandura's Social Cognitive Theory
Raymond Cattell's 16 Personality Factors	1951	Gordon Allport: Two main categories of traits	1977

C. COMPLETE THE TABLE: Write in a brief description of each of the following defense mechanisms.

Defense Mechanism	Description
1. Repression	
2. Projection	
3. Denial	
4. Rationalism	
5. Regression	
6. Reaction formation	
7. Displacement	
8. Sublimation	

PREPARE A LECTURE: This activity is designed to offer you an opportunity to take advantage of a valuable mode of learning, elaborate rehearsal. Once you have finished the OMSE section, write a lecture using the instructional guide provided below. After your lecture is prepared, you can enhance your learning by writing a quiz covering the material. Now it is time to find some willing and inquisitive audience members. Your roommates or family may be a great place to start. Present the lecture as if you are teaching a class. Remember to ask for questions and quiz your students. This exercise can also serve to turn a *study-buddy* group into a very productive way to prepare for the test. Each member of the group can take different OMSE sections for their lecture/teacher role while the rest of the group serves as the class.

I. Key Terms, Names, Dates, and Concepts you will include in this lecture:

1. _____
2. _____
3. _____
4. _____

5. _____
6. _____
7. _____
8. _____

9. _____
10. _____
11. _____
12. _____

II. Learning Objectives (what do you want the student to know and be able to do as a result of your lecture):

1. _____
2. _____
3. _____
4. _____
5. _____

III. Lecture Notes (notes should be brief cues and serve as a guide).

Major topic #1: _____

   Sub-topics and notes: _____

_____

_____

_____

Major topic #2: _____

   Sub-topics and notes: _____

_____

_____

_____

Major topic #3: _____

   Sub-topics and notes: _____

_____

_____

_____

_____

OMSE # 2: PERSONALITY ASSESSMENT

LEARNING OBJECTIVES

1. What are the three major methods used in personality assessment?
2. What is an inventory, and what are the MMPI-2 and the CPI designed to reveal?
3. How do projective tests provide insight into personality, and what are several of the most commonly used projective tests?

LEARNING MASTERY SCORECARD: Update your score card as you work through the chapter. First, find and define key terms and concepts included in each section and note the page number(s) from the text that contain important references to the material. Next, gain a practical understanding of the concepts by considering the Laboratory to Life scenarios. Complete the *Objective-Mastery Self-Evaluation* (OMSE) exercises for this section and record your scores. Revisit the exercises, recording your score and the date completed until you have attained mastery (100%). Finally, prepare a lecture on each objective using the template provided, and practice presenting it. Keep an honest tally of your achievements and, when finished, you will have developed learning mastery.

Key Term	page #	Key Term	page #
halo effect	_____	Myers-Briggs Type Indicator (MBTI)	_____
inventory	_____	projective test	_____
Minnesota Multiphasic Personality Inventory-2 (MMPI-2)	_____	Rorschach Inkblot Test	_____
California Psychological Inventory (CPI)	_____	Thematic Apperception Test (TAT)	_____

Quick Quiz

Date	Score	Date	Score	Date	Score
_/_/_	_____	_/_/_	_____	_/_/_	_____
_/_/_	_____	_/_/_	_____	_/_/_	100%

Elaborate Rehearsal

Lecture Preparation	Completion Date
Key Terms, Persons, & Concepts	_/_/_
Learning Objectives	_/_/_
Lecture Notes	_/_/_

A. QUICK QUIZ

1. The research on heritability and personality indicates a relationship that seems to range at approximately:
   a) 25%
   b) 40 – 50%
   c) 90%
   d) 60 – 75%

2. It appears that the *nonshared environment* factors that influence behavior and personality can help us understand the differences in personalities between those siblings raised in the same households.
   a) True
   b) False

3. All of the following were discussed in the text as methods for assessing personality **except:**
   a) observation
   b) neuropsychological testing
   c) inventories
   d) projective tests

4. Behaviorists (those psychologists who follow the behavioral perspective) usually prefer the _____ method to other methods of personality assessment.

5. The unstructured interview, with its freedom of individuality, has the advantage of greater objectivity when compared with the structured interview of personality assessment.
   a) True
   b) False

6. One problem with the personality assessment method of using rating scales is the _____ where a rater can be excessively influenced in his/her overall evaluation by one or a few favorable or unfavorable traits.

7. Of the many different personality inventories in use today in the field of psychology, which of the following is the most widely used.
   a) the California Psychological Inventory
   b) the Thematic Apperception Test
   c) the Rorschach test
   d) the Minnesota Multiphasic Personality Inventory

8. The problem with inventories as a personality assessment instrument is the fact that they are not scored according to standardized procedures. This results in idiosyncratic interpretation.
   a) True
   b) False

9. The CPI is identified in the book as a personality assessment inventory that has been shown to be useful for predicting all of the following **except:**
   a) academic success
   b) leadership and executive success
   c) personality disorders
   d) effectiveness of police and military personnel

10. The Myers-Briggs Type Indicator is a personality assessment instrument that is based on _____ theory of personality.
    a) Freud's
    b) Jung's
    b) Bandura's
    d) Adler's

11. The Rorschach Inkblot method was identified in the text as an example of a _____ test.

12. If you are being given the results of a personality assessment test you have just taken and the psychologist talks to you about your *typology* in terms of four letters such as ENFP, which of the following tests did you most likely take?
    a) MMPI
    b) CPI
    c) Myers-Briggs
    d) Rorschach

13. Although the Rorschach test can be interesting and fun it is rarely used in actual psychological practice or personality research.
    a) True
    b) False

14. The TAT is a test used to measure personality. It is based on the importance of an element or theme in subject responses that recurs _____ in the series of stories.
   a) at least 50% of the time
   b) at least 75% of the time
   c) five or more times
   d) three or more times

B. MATCHING: Place the appropriate letter in the space provided.

	BASIC DESCRIPTION	ASSESSMENT TECHNIQUE
_____	1. often used in behavior modification programs	a. MMPI-2
_____	2. questions are carefully planned ahead of time	b. Rorschach
_____	3. "true," "false," "cannot say"	c. Myers-Briggs
_____	4. an instrument used to assess a normal person	d. observation
_____	5. inkblots probe the unconscious	e. TAT
_____	6. 16 profiles – four bipolar dimensions	f. CPI
_____	7. vague drawings of human figures in situations	g. Sentence Completion Method
_____	8. possible the most valid projective technique	h. structured interview

C. COMPLETE THE TABLE: Complete the following table by filling in the associated theorists and assumptions for each approach to personality.

APPROACH	THEORIST(S)	ASSUMPTION ABOUT BEHAVIOR
1. Psychoanalytic		
2. Trait		
3. Learning-behaviorist		
4. Social-cognitive		
5. Humanistic		

TIMELINE: PERSONALITY ASSESSMENT

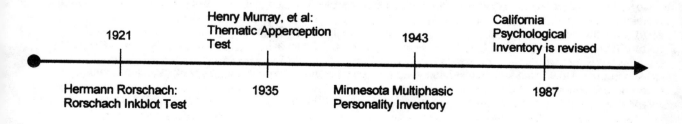

1921 — Hermann Rorschach: Rorschach Inkblot Test

Henry Murray, et al: Thematic Apperception Test — 1935

1943 — Minnesota Multiphasic Personality Inventory

California Psychological Inventory is revised — 1987

PREPARE A LECTURE: This activity is designed to offer you an opportunity to take advantage of a valuable mode of learning, elaborate rehearsal. Once you have finished the OMSE section, write a lecture using the instructional guide provided below. After your lecture is prepared, you can enhance your learning by writing a quiz covering the material. Now it is time to find some willing and inquisitive audience members. Your roommates or family may be a great place to start. Present the lecture as if you are teaching a class. Remember to ask for questions and quiz your students. This exercise can also serve to turn a *study-buddy* group into a very productive way to prepare for the test. Each member of the group can take different OMSE sections for their lecture/teacher role while the rest of the group serves as the class.

I. Key Terms, Names, Dates, and Concepts you will include in this lecture:

1. _____
2. _____
3. _____
4. _____

5. _____
6. _____
7. _____
8. _____

9. _____
10. _____
11. _____
12. _____

II. Learning Objectives (what do you want the student to know and be able to do as a result of your lecture):

1. _____
2. _____
3. _____
4. _____
5. _____

III. Lecture Notes (notes should be brief cues and serve as a guide).

Major topic #1: _____
    Sub-topics and notes: _____
_____
_____
_____

Major topic #2: _____
    Sub-topics and notes: _____
_____
_____
_____

Major topic #3: _____
    Sub-topics and notes: _____
_____
_____
_____

KEY TERMS AND CONCEPTS EXERCISE

The key terms and concepts are presented in order of their appearance in the text. Space is provided for you to include a personalized definition or example of each term or concept. As you encounter each term in the text, make a note of its meaning and context. Next, conceptualize the meaning of the term in a way that makes the most sense to you. Also, think about examples of the term from your own life. Write your definition and/or example in the space provided next to the word. The KEY TERMS exercise utilizes a modified *T-note* design so that you can self-evaluate your mastery of the definitions. First lay a sheet of paper over the terms and concepts side of the page so that you only see the definitions. Read the definition and try to recall the term or concept. Mark all those you are unable to answer so you can restudy them. When you have learned all of the terms and concepts in this way, move the paper to the definition side so that you can see only the term or concept, and try to recall both the textbook definition and your personal version. Repeat this until you know all of the terms by definition and personal understanding.

Personality	A person's unique and stable pattern of characteristics and behaviors. _____ _____ _____
Psychoanalysis	Freud's term for his theory of personality and his therapy for treating psychological disorders. _____ _____
Conscious	The thoughts, feelings, and memories of which we are aware at any given moment. The conscious is sometimes compared to the short-term or working memory. _____ _____ _____
Preconscious	The thoughts, feelings, and memories that we are not consciously aware of at the moment but that may be brought to consciousness. The preconscious has been compared to the long-term memory. _____ _____
Unconscious	For Freud, the primary motivating force of behavior, containing repressed memories as well as instincts and wishes that have never been conscious. _____ _____
Id	The unconscious system of the personality, which contains the life and death instincts and operates on the pleasure principle. _____ _____
Pleasure Principle	The principle by which the id operated to seek pleasure, avoid pain, and obtain immediate gratification. _____ _____
Libido	Freud's name for the psychic or sexual energy that comes from the id and provides the energy for the entire personality. _____ _____
Ego	In Freudian theory, the rational, largely conscious system of personality, which operates according to the reality principle. _____ _____
Superego	The moral system of the personality, which consists of the conscience and the ego ideal. _____ _____
Defense Mechanism	An unconscious, irrational means used by the ego to defend against anxiety; involves self-deception and the distortion of reality. _____ _____
Repression	Involuntarily removing an unpleasant memory or barring disturbing sexual and aggressive impulses from consciousness. _____ _____

Projection	Attributing one's own undesirable thoughts, impulses, traits, or behaviors to others. _____
Denial	Refusing to acknowledge consciously the existence of danger or a threatening condition. _____
Rationalization	Supplying a logical, rational, socially acceptable reason rather than the real reason for the action. _____
Regression	Reverting to a behavior characteristic of an earlier stage of development. _____
Reaction Formation	Denying an unacceptable impulse, usually sexual or aggressive, by giving strong conscious expression to its opposite. _____
Displacement	Substituting a less threatening object for the original object of an impulse. For example, a boss at work reprimands a person and because yelling at the boss could mean getting fired, he or she goes home and kicks the cat. _____
Sublimation	Rechanneling sexual or aggressive energy into pursuits that society considers acceptable or admirable. _____
Psychosexual Stages	A series of stages through which the sexual instinct develops; each stage is defined by an erogenous zone that becomes the center of new pleasures and conflicts. _____
Fixation	Arrested development at a psychosexual stage occurring because of excessive gratification or frustration at that stage. _____
Oral Stage	Freud's first psychosexual stage (birth to 1½ years), in which sensual pleasure is derived mainly through stimulation of the mouth. _____
Anal Stage	Freud's second psychosexual stage (ages 1½ to 3 years), in which the child derives sensual pleasure mainly from expelling and withholding feces. _____
Phallic Stage	Freud's third psychosexual stage (ages 3 to 5 or 6 years), during which sensual pleasure is derived mainly through touching the genitals, and the Oedipus complex arises. _____

Oedipus Complex	Occurring in the phallic stage, a conflict in which the child is attracted to the opposite-sex parent and feels hostility toward the same-sex parent. _____
Latency Period	The period following the phallic stage (ages 5 or 6 to puberty), in which the sex instinct is largely repressed and temporarily sublimated in school and play activities. _____
Genital Stage	Freud's final psychosexual stage (from puberty on), in which for most people the focus of sexual energy gradually shifts to the opposite sex, culminating in the attainment of full adult sexuality. _____
Personal Unconscious	In Jung's theory, the layer of the unconscious containing all of the thoughts and experiences that are accessible to the conscious, as well as repressed memories and impulses. _____
Collective Unconscious	In Jung's theory, the most inaccessible layer of the unconscious, which contains the universal experiences of humankind transmitted to each individual. _____
Archetype	Existing in the collective unconscious, an inherited tendency to respond in particular ways to universal human situations. _____
Extroversion	The tendency to be outgoing, adaptable, and sociable; elements of one of Jung's archetypes, "self." _____
Introversion	The tendency to focus inward; to be reflective, retiring, and nonsocial. _____
Trait	A personal characteristic that is used to describe or explain personality. _____
Trait Theories	Theories that attempt to explain personality and differences between people in terms of their personal characteristics. _____
Cardinal Trait	Allport's name for a personal quality that is so strong a part of a person's personality that he or she may become identified with that trait. _____
Central Trait	Allport's name for the type of trait you would use in writing a letter of recommendation. _____

Surface Traits	Cattell's name for observable qualities of personality, such as those used to describe a friend.
Source Traits	Cattell's name for traits that make up the most basic personality structure and cause behavior.
Five-Factor Theory	A trait theory that attempts to explain personality using five broad dimensions, each of which is composed of a constellation of personality traits.
Reciprocal Determinism	Bandura's concept that behavior, personal/cognitive factors, and environment all influence and are influenced by each other.
Self-Efficacy	A person's belief in his or her ability to perform competently in whatever is attempted.
Locus Of Control	A concept used to explain how people account for what happens in their lives—people with an *internal* locus of control see themselves as primarily in control of their behavior and its consequences; those with an *external* locus of control perceive what happens to be in the hands of fate, luck, or chance.
Humanistic Psychology	An approach to psychology that stresses the uniquely human attributes and a positive view of human nature.
Self-Actualization	Developing to one's fullest potential.
Conditions Of Worth	Conditions upon which the positive regard of others rests.
Unconditional Positive Regard	Unqualified caring and nonjudgmental acceptance of another.
Behavioral Genetics	The field of research that investigates the relative effects of heredity and environment on behavior and ability.
Heritability	An index of the degree to which a characteristic is estimated to be influenced by heredity.
Halo Effect	The tendency of raters to be excessively influenced in their overall evaluation of a person by one or a few favorable or unfavorable traits.

Inventory	A paper-and-pencil test with questions about a person's thoughts, feelings, and behaviors, which can be scored according to a standard procedure. _____ _____ _____
Minnesota Multiphasic Personality Inventory–2	(MMPI–2): A revision of the most extensively researched and widely used personality test; used to screen and diagnose psychiatric problems and disorders. _____ _____
California Psychological Inventory (CPI)	A highly regarded personality test used to assess the normal personality. _____ _____
Myers-Briggs Type Indicator (MBTI)	An inventory for classifying persons on the basis of an adaptation of Jung's theory of personality types. _____ _____
Projective Test	A personality test in which people respond to inkblots, drawings of ambiguous human situations, incomplete sentences, and the like, by projecting their own inner thoughts, feelings, fears, or conflicts onto the test materials. _____ _____ _____
Rorschach Inkblot Test	A projective test composed of ten inkblots to which a subject responds; used to reveal unconscious functioning and the presence of psychiatric disorders. _____ _____
Thematic Apperception Test (TAT)	A projective test consisting of drawings of ambiguous human situations, which the subject describes; thought to reveal inner feelings, conflicts, and motives, which are projected onto the test materials. _____ _____ _____

FROM THE LABORATORY TO LIFE

John, Diane, Shawaunda, and Dave were talking one day after psychology class. Each offered his or her theory of personality. John stated that there really is no sense in the whole debate—that all we are is our behaviors and that we learn our behaviors through classical and operant conditioning. Shawaunda stated that our personalities are based on free will and the fact that we are all basically good people trying to make it in a sometimes-difficult world. She cited her own situation as evidence, relating that she is going to college to be a school counselor and believes that if she can help each student see his or her potential, then those students will be motivated to reach their fullest promise. She also said that she plans to be as nonjudgmental as possible with each student because of her belief that each student will benefit most from unconditional positive regard. Dave said that John and Shawaunda were both wrong, and that unconscious motivation and the way we deal with the world as we progress though early stages of development shape our personalities. Diane responded with her belief that a better understanding of our genes and biology could solve the whole problem. She stated her conviction that environmental or developmental factors are, at best, superficial. Diane has been especially interested lately in concepts such as extroversion and introversion.

If we can assume that each of the above students are being influenced by their readings in psychology, identify the theory and theorist(s) that seem to have had the greatest impact on each.

Student	Theorist(s)	Theory
John		

Shawaunda		
Dave		
Diane		

FROM THEORY TO PRACTICE

AND THE WINNER FOR BEST THEORY IN THE CATEGORY, PERSONALITY, IS . . .

As you read through this chapter, attend lectures, and participate in discussions on personality theory, you might find yourself feeling a bit confused or overwhelmed. After all is said and done, which theory is the right theory? If Freud was right about the unconscious and psychosexual stages, then why bother with all of the other theories. If Jung's collective unconscious is accurate, then Bandura must be wrong about reciprocal determinism. And, if Skinner has the answers, then why do we even need a chapter on personality—why not just cover this information in the chapter on Learning? Well, there is no easy answer to these questions. Personality is a construct, which means that it is an intangible—something that cannot be seen, heard, smelled, tasted, or felt. Consequently, all of the theorists mentioned in this chapter might be wrong—or, they all might be right (at least partially).

Looking at your life in terms of personality, record below one or two thoughts, feelings, or behaviors that seem to fit into each of the categories listed. Can you build your own theory by piecing together bits and pieces of the theories studied? Give it a try in the space provided following this exercise.

Freud's Psychoanalysis	
Pleasure Principle	
Defense Mechanisms	
Fixation	

Jung's Analytical Psychology	
Archetype	
Extroversion/ Introversion	

Adler's Individual Psychology	
Inferiority/Superiority	
Style of Life	

Trait Theories	
Cardinal Trait	

Central/Surface Trait	
Source Trait	
Learning Theories	
Reinforced Behaviors	
Self-Efficacy	
Locus of Control	
Self-Actualization	
Humanistic Theories	
Unconditional Positive Regard	
Heritability (Look at your family—any similarities?)	

Completion of the preceding exercise should have provided you with a better understanding of the various theories, as well as a greater insight into your own personality and the sources of your thoughts, feelings, and behaviors. Armed with this new understanding and insight, piece together a theory of personality that best fits you.

The _____ Personality Theory

_____

_____

_____

_____

_____

_____

_____

_____

_____

_____

_____

_____

_____

_____

_____

_____

_____

COMPREHENSIVE PRACTICE TEST

1. The study of a person's unique and stable pattern of characteristics and behaviors is the description of which of the following?
   - a) motivation
   - b) emotion
   - c) personality
   - d) cognition

2. Freud's theory of personality and his therapy for the treatment of psychological disorders are collectively known as:
   - a) behaviorism
   - b) psychosocialism
   - c) psychoanalysis
   - d) humanism

3. Jackson was telling Allan about Freud's concept of the unconscious. He told Allan that his unconscious included the thoughts, feelings, and memories that he was not consciously aware of at the moment, but that could be brought into consciousness. He said that the unconscious is very much like our long-term memory.
   - a) Jackson's definition of the unconscious is correct.
   - b) Jackson's definition is incorrect—he is actually giving the definition of the ID.
   - c) Jackson's definition is incorrect—he is actually talking about the motivation for self-actualization.
   - d) Jackson's definition is incorrect—he is actually talking about the preconscious.

4. Of Freud's three conceptual structures of personality, the _____ is mainly in the conscious, the _____ is split between the conscious and the unconscious, and the _____ is completely in the unconscious.
   - a) id; ego; superego
   - b) ego; superego; id
   - c) superego; ego; id
   - d) ego; id; superego

5. The libido is Freud's name for the psychic or sexual energy that comes from the superego and provides the energy for the entire personality.
   - a) True
   - b) False

6. The _____ operates on the reality principle while the _____ is guided by the pleasure principle.
   - a) superego; ego
   - b) id; ego
   - c) ego; superego
   - d) ego; id

7. Freud talks about _____, unconscious and irrational means used by the ego to protect oneself from anxiety.
   - a) defense mechanisms
   - b) anxiety complex mechanisms
   - c) phallic responses
   - d) libido responses

8. There was a great cartoon on television when I was growing up. The character (Fred) was often faced with a decision of whether to do the right thing and keep his promise to his wife, or do the more selfish thing and go to the lodge with his friends. As he pondered this dilemma there would appear a little devil on one shoulder that would tell him to go with his friends and a little angel on the other shoulder that would tell him to do the right thing and go with his wife as he had promised. If we were to ascribe Freud's theory to these little decision helpers, the little devil would be Fred's _____ and the little angel would be Fred's _____.
   - a) ego; id
   - b) id; ego
   - c) id; superego
   - d) superego; id

9. Janet had a bad day at work. Her boss was especially critical of her work today and she felt as if her boss was being unfair in her criticisms. However, Janet did not feel comfortable challenging her boss on such criticisms. When she got home from work, she found that the neighbor's child had left his bicycle in her yard. She called the child's mother and scolded her for letting her son run wild. Now Janet sees how her reaction was much stronger than the bicycle incident called for. Freud would probably say Janet was using which defense mechanism?
   - a) projection
   - b) displacement
   - c) reaction formation
   - d) rationalization

10. Anna is about 13 months old and her mouth is her primary area of sensual pleasure. Anna is in Freud's
_____ stage of psychosexual development.
a) anal
b) oral
c) phallic
d) genital

11. Art is suffering the rite of passage that Freud would call the Oedipus complex. Art is in Freud's _____
stage of psychosexual development.
a) anal
b) oral
c) phallic
d) genital

12. One attractive feature of Freud's theory is that it is relatively easy to carry out research designed to test the
theory.
a) True
b) False

13. The _____ unconscious is to one's unique experience as the _____ unconscious is to
the universal experience of humankind.
a) personal; collective
b) collective; personal

14. The persona, the shadow, the anima and animus, and the self are all examples of what Carl Gustav Jung referred
to as:
a) ego identities
b) cardinal traits
c) surface traits
d) archetypes

15. A central theme in Adler's theory is the individual's quest for feelings of _____.
a) superiority
b) the collective unconscious
c) adequacy
d) ego integrity

16. Adler saw birth order as important in personality development.
a) True
b) False

17. Karen Horney disagreed with most of what Freud said about stages of development and the id, ego, and
superego. However, she did agree with Freud regarding the importance of the sexual instinct in shaping
personality.
a) True
b) False

18. A central theme in Karen Horney's theory is the concept of _____.
a) ego integrity
b) penis envy
c) basic anxiety
d) introversion/extroversion

19. Allport and Cattell were presented in the text as important representatives of the _____ theory
approach to understanding personality.
a) stage
b) trait
c) biological
d) humanistic

20. Jim is usually outgoing, energetic, and friendly. Allport would say that this is an example of a description of Jim's
_____ traits.
a) cardinal
b) central
c) surface
d) secondary

21. Has subsequent research on Cattell's 16 factors supported his model?
a) yes
b) no

22. Which of the following "big five" factors has been found to be a virtual requirement for creative accomplishment?
a) extroversion
b) conscientiousness
c) neuroticism
d) openness to experience

23. Based on meta-analysis, Sulloway (1996,1997) would suggest that _____ are more likely to be extroverted and conscientious, but less emotionally stable and less likely to be agreeable and open to experience.
    a) twins raised together
    b) first borns
    c) later borns
    d) twins raised apart

24. Walter Mischel disagreed with the trait theory. He suggested that _____, not traits determined behavior.
    a) unconscious motivation
    b) the motivation for self-actualization
    c) the situation
    d) the surface structure of the personality

25. According to the chapter section, "Personality and Culture," Native Americans value and place more importance on qualities such as a generous nature than they do on property and wealth.
    a) True
    b) False

26. B.F. Skinner would suggest that the concept of personality is a waste of time and that what we call personality is really nothing more than a collection of learned behaviors and habits.
    a) True
    b) False

27. The concept of reciprocal determinism is presented in the text under the heading of:
    a) the behaviorist view of personality
    b) the humanistic view of personality
    c) the social-cognitive view of personality
    d) the biological view of personality

28. Bandura's theory includes a concept that is defined as the belief a person has regarding his/her ability to perform competently whatever is attempted. This concept is:
    a) reciprocal determinism
    b) self-efficacy
    c) extroversion
    d) conditions of worth

29. Rick perceives that what happens to him is based on fate, luck, or chance. He follows a kind of "whatever will be will be" personal philosophy. Rotter would say that he has a(n) _____ locus of control.
    a) internal
    b) unconscious
    c) external
    d) social

30. Eysenck would most likely assert a(n) _____ explanation for behavior.
    a) sociological
    b) interpersonal
    c) unconscious motivation based
    d) biological

31. Humanistic psychology offers a more positive view of human nature and personality.
    a) True
    b) False

32. Rogers talked about conditions of worth—the idea that our parents teach us important values in life and that we as individuals will be motivated to seek out those values.
    a) True
    b) False

33. When Maslow talks about reaching one's fullest potential, he is talking about _____.
    a) humanistic motivation
    b) external locus of control
    c) self-actualization
    d) reciprocal determinism

34. Did the text assert evidence for genetic influences on behavior?
    a) yes
    b) the text cited the research but indicated there was little evidence for genetic influence

35. Ira, an athletic looking, clean-cut young man, arrived for his interview on time and demonstrated excellent social skills in greeting the interviewer. The evaluator immediately believed he knew the kind of person he was talking with and seemed to rate Ira's responses based on his outstanding appearances. The ratings seemed to be inaccurate in the long run due to the rater being unduly influenced by these factors. It would appear that the rater fell prey to the _____ effect.
    a) observation
    b) external factors
    c) halo
    d) recent impressions

36. The MMPI-2 is a good example of a projective personality test.
    a) True   b) False

37. Personality profile scales such as *hysteria, psychasthenia, hypomania, and paranoia* are found on the
    _____.
    a) Rorschach test   c) Myers-Briggs Type Indicator
    b) MMPI-2   d) CPI

38. The California Psychological Inventory was developed to evaluate the personality of _____.
    a) the mentally ill   b) normal people
    b) males   d) females

39. The Myers-Briggs Type Indicator has been shown to be the most accurate assessment test for all types of personalities.
    a) True   b) False

40. You are asked to tell a story about a vague, black and white picture. You are probably responding to
    _____.
    a) the Rorschach   b) the Myers-Briggs
    b) the CPI   d) the TAT

ANSWER KEYS

ANSWER KEY: OMSE#1

A. Quick Quiz	B. Matching
1. b	1. d
2. d	2. f
3. c	3. h
4. b	4. k
5. a	5. j
6. false	6. a
7. c	7. m
8. c	8. l
9. d	9. e
10. false	10. c
11. true	11. i
12. d	12. g
13. surface; source	13. b
14. a	
15. b	
16. b	
17. false	
18. reciprocal determinism	
19. c	
20. good	

C. Complete the Table

Defense Mechanism	Description
1. Repression	Involuntarily remove an unpleasant memory from consciousness or barring disturbing sexual and aggressive impulses from consciousness.
2. Projection	Attribute one's own undesirable traits or impulses to another.
3. Denial	Refuse to acknowledge consciously the existence of danger or a threatening situation.
4. Rationalism	Supply a logical, rational reason rather than the real reason for an action or event.
5. Regression	Revert to a behavior characteristic of an earlier stage of development.
6. Reaction Formation	Express exaggerated ideas and emotions that are the opposite of disturbing, unconscious impulses and desires.
7. Displacement	Substitute a less threatening object for the original object of an impulse.
8. Sublimation	Rechannel sexual and aggressive energy into pursuits that society considers acceptable or even admirable.

ANSWER KEY: OMSE # 2

A. Quick Quiz

1. b
2. true
3. b
4. observation
5. false
6. halo effect
7. d
8. false
9. c
10. b
11. projective
12. c
13. false
14. d

B. Matching

1. d
2. h
3. a
4. f
5. b
6. c
7. e
8. g

C. Complete the Table

APPROACH	THEORIST(S)	ASSUMPTION ABOUT BEHAVIOR
1. Psychoanalytic	Freud	Behavior arises mostly from unconscious conflict between pleasure seeking id and moral-perfectionist superego with the reality-oriented ego serving as mediator.
2. Trait	Allport, Cattell, Eysenck	Behavior springs from personality traits that may be influenced by both heredity and environment.
3. Learning-behaviorist	Skinner	Behavior is determined strictly by environmental influences.
4. Social-cognitive	Bandura, Rotter	Behavior results from an interaction between internal cognitive factors and environmental factors.
5. Humanistic	Maslow, Rogers	Behavior springs from the person's own unique perception of reality and conscious choices.

ANSWER KEY: LAB TO LIFE

Student	Theorist(s)	Theory
John	Skinner	Behaviorist
Shawaunda	Maslow, Rogers	Humanistic
Dave	Freud	Psychoanalytic
Diane	Eysenck	Trait

ANSWER KEY: COMPREHENSIVE PRACTICE TEST

1. c	11. c	21. b	31. true
2. c	12. false	22. d	32. false
3. d	13. a	23. b	33. c
4. b	14. d	24. c	34. a
5. false	15. a	25. true	35. c
6. d	16. true	26. true	36. false
7. a	17. false	27. c	37. b
8. c	18. c	28. b	38. b
9. b	19. b	29. c	39. false
10. b	20. b	30. d	40. d

14

HEALTH AND STRESS

According to the World Health Organization, health is a state of complete physical, mental, and social well being and not merely the absence of disease or infirmity.

CHAPTER OVERVIEW

Imagine for a moment that it is 200,000 years ago and you are going about your daily routine. Your body and brain cooperate to help you through your daily struggle for survival. There are no fast food restaurants or grocery stores, and housing is a matter of finding the safest natural habitat not already taken. The weather is unpredictable, and you never know when or where you will find your next meal. In fact, you are not too certain that you will not be a next meal yourself. Fortunately, you have two capable allies—your sympathetic nervous system and your endocrine system. Together, they help you when you are in stressful situations, like being attacked by a saber-toothed tiger. The fight-or-flight response has gotten you out of some pretty dangerous jams and your body even knows to conserve food when there is a lack of that valuable commodity. Fortunately, you survive.

Stress, although often looked poorly upon, has played an important role in getting us to where we are today. However, our bodies have not fully kept pace with the advances of our world. What served our survival needs well in earlier times appears to be overcorrecting for many of our modern day, non-emergency hassles. Today, most of our problems are not really of the life or death variety. Traffic jams, long lines, and failed exams never directly killed anyone. But, when we exaggerate the nature and intensity of our modern worries, the brain begins to act as if we are once again dealing with daily issues of imminent survival. The cost can be eventual *wear-out*, and vulnerability to a variety of health problems.

This chapter will help you gain a more practiced and functional understanding of the important relationship between stress, stress management, and health. The materials are divided into two OMSE sections, 1) stress, and 2) health and disease. You will gain knowledge about the often-misunderstood concept of stress, and its variety of effects on health and behavior. You will learn ways to consider health and health maintenance. Finally, you will appreciate more than ever the old adage: "an ounce of prevention is worth a pound of cure."

By completing the exercises provided, you should gain a thorough understanding of the information provided in your text. In other words, you should be better prepared for tests, quizzes, class participation, and life itself.

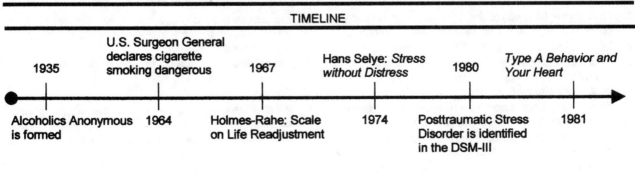

TIMELINE

| 1935 | U.S. Surgeon General declares cigarette smoking dangerous | 1967 | Hans Selye: *Stress without Distress* | 1980 | *Type A Behavior and Your Heart* |

Alcoholics Anonymous is formed   1964   Holmes-Rahe: Scale on Life Readjustment   1974   Posttraumatic Stress Disorder is identified in the DSM-III   1981

CHAPTER OUTLINE

KEY TERMS

OMSE # 1: STRESS

LEARNING OBJECTIVES

1. How do the biomedical and biopsychosocial models differ in their approaches to health and illness?
2. What is the general adaptation syndrome?
3. What are the roles of primary and secondary appraisal when people are confronted with a potentially stressful event?
4. How do approach-approach, avoidance-avoidance, and approach-avoidance conflicts differ?
5. How do the unpredictability of and lack of control over a stressor affect its impact?
6. How do people typically react to catastrophic events?
7. What is posttraumatic stress disorder?
8. For people to function effectively and find satisfaction on the job, what nine variables should fall within their comfort zone?
9. What are some of the psychological and health consequences of job stress?
10. What is burnout?
11. What is the difference between problem-focused and emotion-focused coping?
12. What was the Social Readjustment Rating Scale designed to reveal?
13. What role do hassles and uplifts play in the stress of life according to Lazarus?

LEARNING MASTERY SCORECARD: Update your score card as you work through the chapter. First, find and define key terms and concepts included in each section and note the page number(s) from the text that contain important references to the material. Next, gain a practical understanding of the concepts by considering the *Laboratory to Life* scenarios. Complete the *Objective-Mastery Self-Evaluation* (OMSE) exercises for this section and record your scores. Revisit the exercises, recording your score and the date completed until you have attained mastery (100%). Finally, prepare a lecture on each objective using the template provided, and practice presenting it. Keep an honest tally of your achievements and, when finished, you will have developed learning mastery.

Key Term	page #	Key Term	page #	Key Term	page #
biomedical model	_____	exhaustion stage	_____	burnout	_____
biopsychosocial model	_____	primary appraisal	_____	coping	_____
health psychology	_____	secondary appraisal	_____	problem-focused coping	_____
stress	_____	approach-approach conflict	_____	emotion-focused coping	_____
stressor	_____	avoidance-avoidance conflict	_____	proactive coping	_____
general adaptation syndrome (GAS)	_____	approach avoidance conflict	_____	Social Readjustment Rating Scale	_____
alarm stage	_____	posttraumatic stress disorder (PTSD)	_____	hassles	_____
resistance stage	_____	decision latitude	_____	uplifts	_____

Quick Quiz

Date	Score	Date	Score	Date	Score
_/_/_	_____	_/_/_	_____	_/_/_	_____
_/_/_	_____	_/_/_	_____	_/_/_	100%

Elaborate Rehearsal

Lecture Preparation	Completion Date
Key Terms, Persons, & Concepts	_/_/_
Learning Objectives	_/_/_
Lecture Notes	_/_/_

A. QUICK QUIZ

1. Medicine has been dominated by the _____ model, which focuses on illness over health. However, the _____ model, which asserts that both health and illness are determined by a combination of biological, psychological, and social factors, seems to be gaining acceptance.

2. The field of psychology that is concerned with the psychological factors that contribute to health, illness, and recovery is known as _____.
    a) biopsychology
    b) health psychology
    c) stress psychology
    d) psychobiology

3. A good example of stress is being caught in a traffic jam when you are late for an appointment.
    a) True
    b) False – stress would be your response to the traffic jam

4. The fight-or-flight response is controlled by the _____ and the endocrine glands.
    a) parasympathetic nervous system
    b) central nervous system
    c) reticular activating system
    d) sympathetic nervous system

5. Hans Selye's concept of the General Adaptation Syndrome is credited with bringing to our attention the important relationship between stress and health. However, critics believe he focused too much on the psychological response component in his theory.
    a) True
    b) False

6. The first stage of the General Adaptation Syndrome is the _____ stage.

7. The General Adaptation Syndrome stage during which the adrenal glands release powerful hormones to help the body resist stressors is called the _____ stage.
   a) alarm
   b) resistance
   c) exhaustion
   d) adaptation

8. Angry words spoken by the boss, a dog suddenly charging at you, or a car that suddenly swerves into your lane would all be examples of _____.

9. Lazarus' theory is considered to be a _____ theory of stress and coping.
   a) adaptive
   b) biological
   c) cognitive
   d) psychobiological

10. According to Lazarus, primary appraisal occurs when we evaluate our coping resources in response to a problem and decide how to deal with the situation.
    a) True
    b) False

11. Joe can't decide between the four-wheel drive pickup truck and the minivan. He loves them both but can only buy one of them. He is experiencing an _____ conflict.
    a) approach-approach
    b) avoidance-approach
    c) approach-avoidance
    d) avoidance-avoidance

12. Being a member of a minority group can be stressful in a variety of settings, even when there are no racist attitudes or discrimination-based actions.
    a) True
    b) False

13. Posttraumatic stress disorder can result from:
    a) acute illness
    b) chronic disappointment
    c) a catastrophic event
    d) failed relationships

14. Alice lost her job due to company cost cutting. She considered the situation and decided that this was an opportunity to finally do what she really wanted to do—become a nurse. She enrolled in school and is soon going to graduate as a Registered Nurse. She has supported herself through school loans and a second mortgage on her home. The text would suggest her response to this problem involved both _____ coping and _____ coping.

15. Which of the following workers would probably have the most decision latitude?
    a) machine-paced assembly workers
    b) executives and professionals

16. Religion, while providing a short-term coping mechanism for people suffering stress, has not been shown to be very advantageous in the long run when it comes to helping people survive serious stress situations.
    a) True
    b) False

17. Laura knew the upcoming interview would be difficult so she prepared by doing her research. She discovered in advance the kinds of questions she would be asked. She then considered the best possible responses. The text would suggest that Laura has practiced _____ coping.

18. The Social Readjustment Rating Scale predicts future health problems by measuring:
    a) life change events
    b) negative situations in life
    c) emotional styles
    d) cognitive evaluation styles

Stress can result from both good and bad events in your life. What do you think—would winning a million-dollar lottery be more or less stressful than failing your psychology class?

B. MATCHING: Place the appropriate letter in the space provided.

_____   1. It focuses on illness, rather than health.
_____   2. It focuses on health as well as illness.
_____   3. It is the physiological and psychological response to a threat.
_____   4. A GAS stage: emotional arousal and fight-or-flight.
_____   5. A GAS stage: resist or adapt to the stressor.
_____   6. A GAS stage: occurs if you fail to resist the stressor.
_____   7. He discovered General Adaptation Syndrome.
_____   8. He coined the term primary appraisal.
_____   9. A conflict: choosing between two good options.
_____   10. A conflict: choosing between two bad options.
_____   11. It is a reaction to a catastrophic event.
_____   12. It means dealing with overwhelming demands.
_____   13. They are the little stressors that add up to big trouble.
_____   14. These can neutralize the hassles.

a. coping
b. alarm
c. uplifts
d. hassles
e. stress
f. approach-approach
g. biomedical model
h. resistance
i. PTSD
j. exhaustion
k. Hans Selye
l. biopsychosocial model
m. avoidance-avoidance
n. Richard Lazarus

C. COMPLETE THE DIAGRAM:

Forces Favoring Health and Wellness

Complete the biopsychosocial model by filling in the appropriate factors.

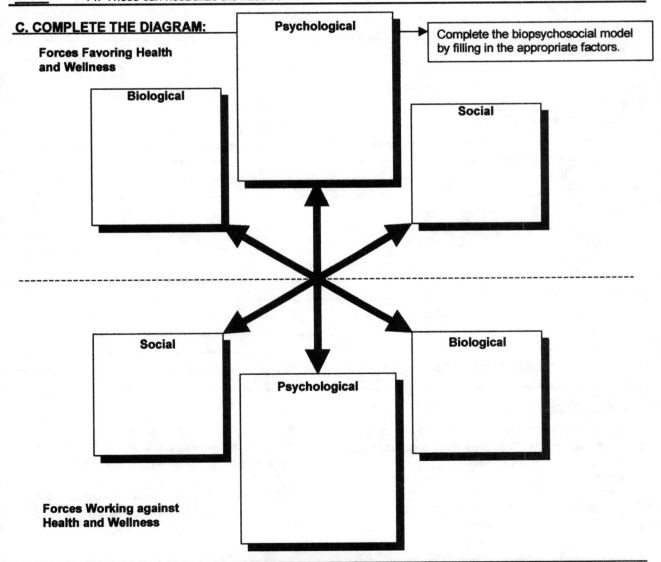

Forces Working against Health and Wellness

PREPARE A LECTURE: This activity is designed to offer you an opportunity to take advantage of a valuable mode of learning, elaborate rehearsal. Once you have finished the OMSE section, write a lecture using the instructional guide provided below. After your lecture is prepared, you can enhance your learning by writing a quiz covering the material. Now it is time to find some willing and inquisitive audience members. Your roommates or family may be a great place to start. Present the lecture as if you are teaching a class. Remember to ask for questions and quiz your students. This exercise can also serve to turn a *study-buddy* group into a very productive way to prepare for the test. Each member of the group can take different OMSE sections for their lecture/teacher role while the rest of the group serves as the class.

I. Key Terms, Names, Dates, and Concepts you will include in this lecture:

1. _____   5. _____   9. _____
2. _____   6. _____   10. _____
3. _____   7. _____   11. _____
4. _____   8. _____   12. _____

II. Learning Objectives (what do you want the student to know and be able to do as a result of your lecture):

1. _____
2. _____
3. _____
4. _____
5. _____

III. Lecture Notes (notes should be brief cues and serve as a guide).

Major topic #1: _____
    Sub-topics and notes: _____
    _____
    _____
    _____

Major topic #2: _____
    Sub-topics and notes: _____
    _____
    _____
    _____

Major topic #3: _____
    Sub-topics and notes: _____
    _____
    _____
    _____

OMSE # 2: HEALTH AND DISEASE

LEARNING OBJECTIVES

1. What are the Type A and Type B behavior patterns?
2. What aspect of the Type A behavior pattern is most clearly linked to heart disease?
3. What are the effects of stress and depression on the immune system?
4. What three personal factors are associated with health and resistance to stress?
5. What constitutes an unhealthy lifestyle, and how serious a factor is lifestyle in illness and health?
6. Why is smoking considered the single most preventable cause of death?
7. What are some health risks of alcohol consumption?
8. What are some benefits of regular aerobic exercise?

LEARNING MASTERY SCORECARD: Update your score card as you work through the chapter. First, find and define key terms and concepts included in each section and note the page number(s) from the text that contain important references to the material. Next, gain a practical understanding of the concepts by considering the Laboratory to Life scenarios. Complete the *Objective-Mastery Self-Evaluation* (OMSE) exercises for this section and record your scores. Revisit the exercises, recording your score and the date completed until you have attained mastery (100%). Finally, prepare a lecture on each objective using the template provided, and practice presenting it. Keep an honest tally of your achievements and, when finished, you will have developed learning mastery.

Key Term	page #	Key Term	page #	Key Term	page #
sedentary lifestyle	____	lymphocytes	____	social support	____
Type A behavior pattern	____	psychoneuroimmunology	____	controlled drinking	____
Type B behavior pattern	____	hardiness	____	aerobic exercise	____

Quick Quiz

Date	Score	Date	Score	Date	Score
_/_/_	____	_/_/_	____	_/_/_	____
_/_/_	____	_/_/_	____	_/_/_	100%

Elaborate Rehearsal

Lecture Preparation	Completion Date
Key Terms, Persons, & Concepts	_/_/_
Learning Objectives	_/_/_
Lecture Notes	_/_/_

A. QUICK QUIZ

1. Ed has discovered certain benefits from being sick. When he is sick he gets sympathy, attention, and concern. He also finds that when he is sick he does not have to fulfill certain responsibilities. He now seems to get sick every time he is confronted with such responsibilities or other demands. The text would say that Ed is taking comfort in the _____ role.
   a) hypochondriac
   b) stressor
   c) sick
   d) disease

2. Who are more likely to seek medical services—men or women?
   a) men
   b) women

3. Which is more likely to result in a healthier lifestyle—Type A or Type B behavior patterns?
   a) Type A
   b) Type B

4. Research has suggested that social-based coping strategies are more effective than escape-based coping strategies when dealing with the stress of cancer.
   a) True
   b) False

5. African Americans have a _____ rate of diabetes than White Americans.
   a) lower
   b) higher

6. Cirrhosis of the liver occurs for Native Americans about _____.
   a) 50% more than other Americans
   b) 25% less than for White Americans
   c) three times as much as the general U.S. population
   d) 25% less than for African Americans

7. Jan is a psychologist. She works with biologists and medical researchers to determine the effects of psychological factors on the immune system. Jan works in the field of _____.

8. B cells come from _____ and T cells come from _____.
   a) the thymus; bone marrow
   b) the adrenal gland; the pituitary gland
   c) the pituitary gland; the adrenal gland
   d) bone marrow; the thymus

9. Poor marital relationships, sleep deprivation, and academic pressure have all been found to be related to
    _____.

10. Pessimists, due to their constant worry, tend to be more likely to take action to prevent illness and to get treatment once illness strikes.
    a) True   b) False

11. Which of the following was **NOT** listed as a characteristic of hardiness?
    a) sense of control over one's life   c) a stubborn refusal to be upset by problems
    b) a commitment to one's personal goals   d) view change as a challenge

12. Research has suggested that the perception of social support can be more important than actual received support.
    a) True   b) False

13. One large study indicated that, at least with nurses, being overweight increased the risk of stroke by _____.
    a) 50%   c) 25%
    b) 2 to 2.5 times   d) 75%

14. What percentage of Americans age 18 and over are smokers?
    a) 25%   c) 27%
    b) 31%   d) 46%

15. Is there an apparent relationship between alcoholism and depression?
    a) a very small relationship   c) yes, quite large
    b) about 50%   d) there is no real evidence to support this

16. One approach to alcoholism treatment is _____ therapy, wherein a therapist meets with the alcoholic and a small group of friends and family at regular intervals.

17. Controlled drinking has been shown to be most successful with older drinkers who have had a serious problem with alcohol for several years.
    a) True   b) False

18. The advantage of aerobic exercise is that it works large muscle groups without making the heart work harder.
    a) True   b) False

B. MATCHING: Place the appropriate letter in the space provided.

_____	1. It is the leading cause of death in the U.S.A.	a. hardiness
_____	2. Exercise less than 20 minutes three times a week.	b. smoking
_____	3. It is marked by impatience, competitiveness, hostility, and anger.	c. optimism
_____	4. It protects us from infection and disease.	d. alcohol
_____	5. These are B cells, T cells, and macrophages.	e. sedentary lifestyle
_____	6. It is the study of psychological factors on the immune system.	f. aerobic exercise
_____	7. A positive attitude that may reduce the risk of illness.	g. lymphocytes
_____	8. People who view change as a challenge have this.	h. Type A behavior pattern
_____	9. It is related to 434,000 deaths annually in the U.S.A.	i. psychoneuroimmunology
_____	10. Some people use this to deal with stress and end up with cirrhosis.	j. coronary heart disease
_____	11. This pays healthful dividends for people of all ages.	k. immune system

C. FILL IN THE BLANKS: Find the correct responses in your text, and complete.

1. Jonathan has learned that he is pampered and does not have to fulfill responsibilities when he is sick. He seems to be sick quite often. Jonathan appears to take comfort in the _____ _____.

2. Harold is a medical student and has been studying pathology. He has noticed that he is experiencing anxiety as a result of his having developed symptoms of the diseases he is learning about. Harold is experiencing what the text called _____ _____ _____.

3. A _____ lifestyle is defined as one that includes less than 20 minutes of exercise three times per week.

4. Alice answered no to most of the questions in a questionnaire that included items such as, "I usually feel guilty when I relax and do nothing," or " When talking to others, I get impatient and try to hurry them along." Alice would be said to have a _____ behavior pattern.

5. _____ seems to be a healthier perspective on life than pessimism.

6. _____ are the white blood cells that are key components of the immune system—B cells, T cells, and macrophages.

7. An important contributing factor to better health is _____ _____, support provided in a time of need by a spouse or other family members, friends, and/or neighbors.

8. Current statistics estimate that approximately _____ deaths annually in the United States are directly related to smoking.

9. While alcohol can damage any organ in the body, it is especially dangerous for the _____.

10. Exercise that uses the large muscle groups in continuous, repetitive action and requires increased oxygen intake with increased breathing and heart rates is good for your health. This kind of exercise is called _____ exercise.

PREPARE A LECTURE: This activity is designed to offer you an opportunity to take advantage of a valuable mode of learning, elaborate rehearsal. Once you have finished the OMSE section, write a lecture using the instructional guide provided below. After your lecture is prepared, you can enhance your learning by writing a quiz covering the material. Now it is time to find some willing and inquisitive audience members. Your roommates or family may be a great place to start. Present the lecture as if you are teaching a class. Remember to ask for questions and quiz your students. This exercise can also serve to turn a *study-buddy* group into a very productive way to prepare for the test. Each member of the group can take different OMSE sections for their lecture/teacher role while the rest of the group serves as the class.

I. Key Terms, Names, Dates, and Concepts you will include in this lecture:

1. _____	5. _____	9. _____
2. _____	6. _____	10. _____
3. _____	7. _____	11. _____
4. _____	8. _____	12. _____

II. Learning Objectives (what do you want the student to know and be able to do as a result of your lecture?):

1. _____
2. _____
3. _____
4. _____
5. _____

III. Lecture Notes (notes should be brief cues and serve as a guide):

Major topic #1: _____

   Sub-topics and notes: _____

_____

_____

_____

Major topic #2: _____

   Sub-topics and notes: _____

_____

_____

_____

Major topic #3: _____

   Sub-topics and notes: _____

_____

_____

_____

KEY TERMS AND CONCEPTS EXERCISE

The key terms and concepts are presented in order of their appearance in the text. Space is provided for you to include a personalized definition or example of each term or concept. As you encounter each term in the text, make a note of its meaning and context. Next, conceptualize the meaning of the term in a way that makes the most sense to you. Also, think about examples of the term from your own life. Write your definition and/or example in the space provided next to the word. The KEY TERMS exercise utilizes a modified *T-note* design so that you can self-evaluate your mastery of the definitions. First lay a sheet of paper over the terms and concepts side of the page so that you only see the definitions. Read the definition and try to recall the term or concept. Mark all those you are unable to answer so you can restudy them. When you have learned all of the terms and concepts in this way, move the paper to the definition side so that you can see only the term or concept, and try to recall both the textbook definition and your personal version. Repeat this until you know all of the terms by definition and personal understanding.

Biomedical Model	A perspective that focuses on illness rather than health, explaining illness in terms of biological factors without regard to psychological and social factors. _____ _____
Biopsychosocial Model	A perspective that focuses on health as well as illness and holds that both are determined by a combination of biological, psychological, and social factors. _____ _____
Health Psychology	The field concerned with the psychological factors that contribute to health, illness, and recovery. _____ _____
Stress	The physiological and psychological response to a condition that threatens or challenges a person and requires some form of adaptation or adjustment. _____ _____ _____
Stressor	Any event capable of producing physical or emotional stress. _____ _____ _____

General Adaptation Syndrome (GAS)	The predictable sequence of reactions (the alarm, resistance, and exhaustion stages) that organisms show in response to stressors. _____
Alarm Stage	The first stage of the general adaptation syndrome, when there is emotional arousal and the defensive forces of the body are prepared for fight or flight. _____
Resistance Stage	The second stage of the general adaptation syndrome, when there are intense physiological efforts to resist or adapt to the stressor. _____
Exhaustion Stage	The final stage of the general adaptation syndrome, occurring if the organism fails in its efforts to resist the stressor. _____
Primary Appraisal	Evaluating the significance of a potentially stressful event according to how it will affect one's well-being—whether it is perceived as irrelevant or as involving harm or loss, threat, or challenge. _____
Secondary Appraisal	Evaluating one's coping resources and deciding how to deal with a stressful event. _____
Approach-Approach Conflict	A conflict arising from having to choose between desirable alternatives. _____
Avoidance-Avoidance Conflict	A conflict arising from having to choose between two undesirable alternatives. _____
Approach Avoidance Conflict	A conflict arising when the same choice has both desirable and undesirable features. _____
Posttraumatic Stress Disorder (PTSD)	A prolonged and severe stress reaction to a catastrophic event or a chronic intense illness. _____
Decision Latitude	The degree to which employees have the opportunity to exercise initiative and use their skills to improve their working conditions. _____
Burnout	The result of intense, unrelieved, and unmanaged job stress; a condition in which an individual becomes pessimistic, dissatisfied, inefficient on the job, and debilitated psychologically. _____
Coping	Efforts through action and thought to deal with demands that are perceived as taxing or overwhelming. _____

Problem-Focused Coping	A response aimed at reducing, modifying, or eliminating a source of stress. _____ _____ _____
Emotion-Focused Coping	A response aimed at reducing the emotional impact of the stressor. _____ _____ _____
Proactive Coping	Efforts or actions taken in advance of a potentially stressful situation to prevent its occurrence or to minimize its consequences. _____ _____ _____
Social Readjustment Rating Scale (SRRS)	Holmes and Rahe's stress scale, which ranks 43 life events from most to least stressful and assigns a point value to each. _____ _____ _____
Hassles	Little stressors that include the irritating demands and troubled relationships that can occur daily and that, according to Lazarus, cause more stress than do major life changes. _____ _____ _____ _____
Uplifts	The positive experiences in life that can neutralize the effects of many of the hassles. _____ _____ _____
Sedentary Lifestyle	A lifestyle in which a person exercises less than 20 minutes three times a week. _____ _____
Type A Behavior Pattern	A behavior pattern marked by a sense of time urgency, impatience, excessive competitiveness, hostility, and anger; considered a risk factor in coronary heart disease. _____ _____ _____
Type B Behavior Pattern	A behavior pattern marked by a relaxed, easygoing approach to life; not associated with coronary heart disease. _____ _____
Lymphocytes	The white blood cells that are key components of the immune system—B cells, T cells, and macrophages. _____ _____
Psychoneuro-immunology	A field in which psychologists, biologists, and medical researchers study the effects of psychological factors on the immune system. _____ _____
Hardiness	A combination of three psychological qualities shared by people who can undergo high levels of stress yet remain healthy; a sense of control over one's life, commitment to one's personal goals, and a tendency to view change as a challenge rather than as a threat. _____ _____
Social Support	Tangible support, information, advice, and/or emotional support provided in time of need by family, friends, and others: the feeling that we are loved, valued, and cared for. _____ _____ _____

Controlled Drinking	A behavioral approach to the treatment of alcoholism, designed to teach the skills necessary so that alcoholics can drink socially without losing control. _____ _____
Aerobic Exercise	Exercise that uses the large muscle groups in continuous, repetitive action and requires increased oxygen intake and increased breathing and heart rates. _____ _____

FROM THE LABORATORY TO LIFE

Oral Examination Blues

I remember all too well the day I was scheduled to take my comprehensive oral examination, the final hurdle in the completion of my graduate degree. There were nine of us in the graduate program and none of us wanted to be the first to endure and possibly fail the oral exam. I considered the dilemma and found myself vacillating between, "do it and get it over," and "yea, but if I let someone else go first I may learn things that can help me pass." I was both drawn to, and repelled from the whole idea of going first. Anyway, I studied to the point that I felt I was as prepared as possible. I finally set the date for the exam. As the day approached I became very nervous. I kept thinking about the potential implications: "If I fail this exam, all the time and work I have invested will be wasted, and I will not get to do what I have wanted to for so long. This exam will be very difficult. Will I be up for the challenge?" When the big day finally arrived, I was a basket case. I was to take the exam at 1:00 PM, and I had the whole morning to worry. I went to a seminar that morning in a failed effort to distract myself from the worry and tension. Instead, I just sat there fidgeting, and worried about the exam. I finally left the seminar to try something else. Eventually, I realized that I was setting myself up for failure by the kinds of things I was saying to myself, and by the way I was behaving. I decided to go to the Psychology Department building where I found a quiet place to relax, and I replaced my thoughts of dread with images of success. I imagined my feeling and reaction as I was informed I had passed the exam. By exam time, I was somewhat more relaxed. The next thing I knew it was over—I passed!

1. Lazarus would suggest that statements such as, "If I fail this exam, all the time and work I have invested will be wasted," are examples of _____ _____.

2. My desire to both "get it over with" while also wondering if waiting may be advantageous would be an example of an _____ conflict.

3. When I finally took action designed to reduce the effects of the stressful event I was about to endure, and hopefully contribute to success in the endeavor, I was partaking in a coping strategy the text referred to as _____ _____.

FROM THEORY TO PRACTICE

Stress-Reduction Worksheet

As a college student, you face many of the hassles referred to by Lazarus on a daily basis. On top of the hassles adding up over time, you may also face some of the larger stressors of life. For example, are student loans starting to stack up? Are you realizing that the major you selected is just not for you and that you are forced to make a change? Are you preparing to move into a Greek house? Do you have a parent or other close relative who has been ill? Are you finding it difficult to juggle a part-time job and make the grade in five classes at once? Have you switched from eating mom's home cooking to eating pizza and tacos? Now that you are on your own, have you taken to drinking alcohol at parties? Are you experiencing problems with your boy or girlfriend? Say, how is your term paper research coming along? Okay, by now you probably get the point. We all face stress in our daily lives, we all respond differently to different stressors, and each of us finds that certain methods of coping with stress are more effective for us than are others. For some people, exercise helps alleviate stress. Others find that a hot bath is a good stress breaker. What works best for you? Following are a list of several stress breakers. Add a few of your own if you like. Assign a ranking to each stress breaker from 1 = most effective, to 9 – 12 = least effective. Use these daily or as needed.

Meditation	____	Progressive Relaxation	____	Deep Breathing	____
Aerobic Exercise	____	Anaerobic Exercise	____	Participating in Sports	____
Taking a Bath	____	Reading	____	Talking with Friends	____
_____	____	_____	____	_____	____

COMPREHENSIVE PRACTICE TEST

1. The _____ model is to illness as the _____ model is to health and illness.
    a) biomedical; biopsychosocial
    b) biopsychosocial; biomedical

2. The text defines stress as the kinds of threats and problems we encounter in life.
    a) True
    b) False

3. Hans Selye developed the _____.
    a) diathesis stress model
    b) General Adaptation Syndrome model
    c) cognitive stress model
    d) conversion reaction model

4. The second stage of Selye's model is the _____ stage, where the body mobilizes its physical energy in a manner to resist the stressor.
    a) alarm
    b) exhaustion
    c) resistance
    d) arousal

5. The fight-or-flight response would be seen in which of the following stages of Selye's model?
    a) alarm
    b) exhaustion
    c) resistance
    d) arousal

6. In the stress response, the hypothalamus signals the pituitary gland to release ACTH which then stimulates the adrenal cortex to release other stress hormones known as glucocorticoids.
    a) True
    b) False

7. Symptoms such as increased blood pressure, suppressed immune system, and damaged muscle tissue would be found in the _____ stage.
    a) alarm
    b) exhaustion
    c) resistance
    d) arousal

8. Which of the following is **NOT** one of the four phases Lazarus talks about regarding the stress response.
    a) a causal agent
    b) the stress reaction
    c) mind/body evaluates the stressor
    d) the outcome evaluation

9. Which of the following is the best example of a primary appraisal?
    a) Joe reviews the coping resources that he has available to respond to his impending surgery.
    b) Janet tells herself that her impending divorce will free her from years of an unhappy life.
    c) Charles views his company's upcoming layoffs as a serious threat to his ability to sustain his lifestyle.
    d) Brenda reviews her response to her doctor's diagnosis and believes she is coping well.

10. Lack of exercise, poor diet, and disease and injury are considered to be _____ forces that work against health and wellness.
    a) environmental
    b) psychological
    c) biological
    d) social

11. James knows he needs the flu shot but at the same time he is terrified of getting shots. He is experiencing an _____ conflict.
    a) approach-approach
    b) approach-avoidance
    c) avoidance-avoidance
    d) avoidance-approach

12. Patricia has been looking for a bedroom set. She has found two that she really likes. She is sitting at home trying to decide which one she will purchase. Patricia is experiencing an _____ conflict.
    a) approach-approach
    b) approach-avoidance
    c) avoidance-avoidance
    d) avoidance-approach

13. Which of the following seem to be less stressful in the long run?
    a) stressors we know are coming because we can then plan for them
    b) unexpected stressors because we do not spend a lot of time worrying about them in advance

14. It appears that our sense of control over a situation can have an important beneficial influence on how a stressor influences us, even if we do not exercise that control.
    a) True
    b) False

15. What percent of Americans meet the diagnostic criteria for Posttraumatic Stress Disorder?
    a) 15%
    b) 5%
    c) 10%
    d) 1-2%

16. In order to be considered a sufferer of racial stress, the individual must be a victim of some form of racially based discrimination or a hate crime.
    a) True
    b) False

17. Does posttraumatic stress leave some people more vulnerable for future mental health problems?
    a) Yes
    b) Yes – for men only
    c) No
    d) Yes – for women only

18. Which of the following is the best example of emotion-focused coping?
    a) Cassandra decides to study harder to raise her grade in psychology.
    b) Roosevelt decides that breaking up with his girlfriend will provide an opportunity to find a better relationship anyway.

19. Which of the following is the best example of problem-focused coping?
    a) Edward decides to get on a strict budget in order to solve his money problems.
    b) Tamara sees her current bad luck as a kind of punishment for past bad behavior.

20. Which of the following was **NOT** identified as a variable in work stress?
    a) workload
    b) clarity of job description
    c) perceived equitability of pay for work
    d) task variety

21. Decision latitude refers to the extent to which an employee can challenge his or her supervisor's orders or decisions.
    a) True
    b) False

22. George has had it. He hates his job and sees it as way too stressful. He has become pessimistic, inefficient, and seems to be tired all the time. He also seems to be getting sick all the time. According to the text, it sounds like George is suffering from _____.
    a) stress inoculation
    b) anhedonic life disorder
    c) posttraumatic stress disorder
    d) burnout

23. Does religious faith help people cope with negative life events?
    a) yes, it appears so
    b) no, the evidence indicates no real benefit
    c) yes, but only when there are medical problems
    d) the research is inconclusive

24. Rachel had been worried about her upcoming surgery. Having realized that all of her worrying had only resulted in headaches, she finally decided to take action. She read about her medical problem and the surgery. She also talked to her doctor about things she could do now that would help her deal with the medical problem and assist in her post-operative recovery. Rachel is practicing what the text would call _____ coping.
    a) optimistic
    b) proactive
    c) positive
    d) cognitive-behavioral

25. Has the Social Readjustment Rating Scale shown itself to be a good predictor of future health problems?
    a) yes   b) no

26. According to Lazarus, life's ongoing hassles can add up to be more stressful than major life changes such as divorce.
    a) True   b) False

27. According to Lazarus, the positive experiences that can serve to cancel out the effects of day-to-day hassles are known as:
    a) stress assets   c) uplifts
    b) coping mechanisms   d) appraisals

28. Can being sick sometimes reinforce sick behaviors?
    a) yes   b) no

29. We do not seem to be well-behaved patients. As a matter of fact, it appears that up to _____ percent of patients fail to follow the doctor's orders.
    a) 25   c) 75
    b) 15   d) 50

30. Jack is always on the go. He seems to be constantly under the clock and always trying to do more than is reasonable. He also seems to have a short temper and finds it difficult to enjoy just relaxing and taking it easy. Jack would be said to have _____.
    a) a Type A behavior pattern   c) Type B behavior pattern
    b) stress hardiness   d) exhaustion stage stress disorder

31. According to your text, Type B behavior patterns seem to be more correlated with heart disease than do Type A behavior patterns.
    a) True   b) False

32. Anger seems to contribute to a reduced risk of heart disease because it helps blow off steam and lessen the chronic effects of stress and resentment.
    a) True   b) False

33. Did you read the section, *Health in the United States*? Which of the following is the accurate listing of minority groups in the United States from the largest to the smallest?
    a) African Americans, Native Americans, Hispanic Americans, Asian Americans
    b) Native Americans, African Americans, Asian Americans, Hispanic Americans
    c) African Americans, Hispanic Americans, Asian Americans, Native Americans
    d) Hispanic Americans, African Americans, Native Americans, Asian Americans

34. B cells produce antibodies that are effective in destroying antigens that _____, while T cells are important in the destruction of antigens that _____.
    a) live outside the body cells; live inside the body cells
    b) live inside the body cells; live outside the body cells

35. According to the text, about _____ percent of us do not engage in enough physical activity to remain healthy.
    a) 25   c) 40
    b) 60   d) 50

36. According to Holly Prigerson, severe bereavement can weaken the immune system of the sufferer for up to two years following a partner's death.
    a) True   b) False

37. A particularly lethal form of pessimism is _____.
    a) anger   c) suspiciousness
    b) low expectations from other people   d) hopelessness

38. Characteristics such as commitment, control, and challenge were listed as components of _____.
    a) healthiness
    b) hardiness
    c) cognitive fluency
    d) preparedness

ANSWER KEYS

ANSWER KEY: OMSE # 1

A. Quick Quiz		B. Matching	
1. biomedical; biopsychosocial	10. false	1. g	8. n
2. b	11. a	2. l	9. f
3. false	12. true	3. e	10. m
4. d	13. c	4. b	11. i
5. false	14. problem; emotion	5. h	12. a
6. alarm	15. b	6. j	13. d
7. b	16. false	7. k	14. c
8. stressors	17. proactive		
9. c	18. a		

C. Complete the Diagram

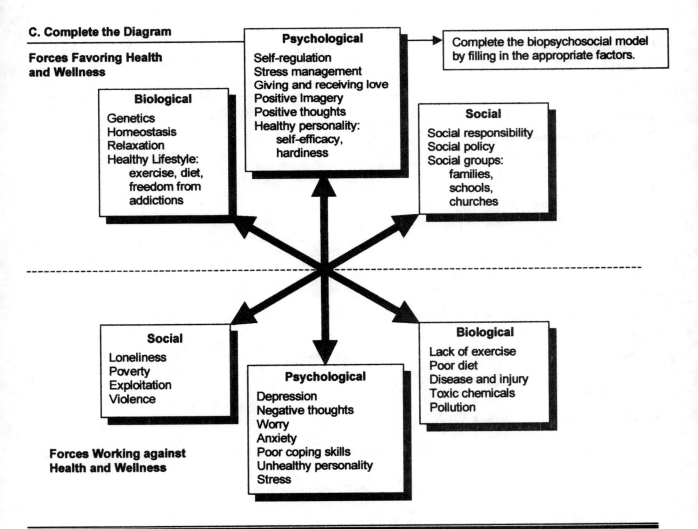

Forces Favoring Health and Wellness

Complete the biopsychosocial model by filling in the appropriate factors.

Psychological
Self-regulation
Stress management
Giving and receiving love
Positive Imagery
Positive thoughts
Healthy personality:
    self-efficacy,
    hardiness

Biological
Genetics
Homeostasis
Relaxation
Healthy Lifestyle:
    exercise, diet,
    freedom from
    addictions

Social
Social responsibility
Social policy
Social groups:
    families,
    schools,
    churches

Social
Loneliness
Poverty
Exploitation
Violence

Psychological
Depression
Negative thoughts
Worry
Anxiety
Poor coping skills
Unhealthy personality
Stress

Biological
Lack of exercise
Poor diet
Disease and injury
Toxic chemicals
Pollution

Forces Working against Health and Wellness

ANSWER KEY: OMSE #2

A. Quick Quiz	B. Matching	C. Fill In The Blanks
1. c	1. j	1. sick role
2. b	2. e	2. medical student disease
3. b	3. h	3. sedentary
4. true	4. k	4. Type B
5. b	5. g	5. Optimism
6. c	6. i	6. Lymphocytes
7. psychoneuroimmunology	7. c	7. social support
8. d	8. a	8. 434,000
9. lowered immune activity	9. b	9. liver
10. false	10. d	10. aerobic
11. c	11. f	
12. a		
13. b		
14. c		
15. c		
16. network		
17. false		
18. false		

Answer Key: Lab to Life

Oral Examination Blues

1. Primary Appraisal
2. Approach-avoidance
3. Proactive coping

Answer Key: Comprehensive Practice Test

1. a	11. b	21. false	31. false
2. b	12. a	22. d	32. false
3. b	13. a	23. a	33. c
4. c	14. true	24. b	34. a
5. a	15. d	25. b	35. b
6. true	16. false	26. true	36. true
7. b	17. a	27. c	37. d
8. d	18. b	28. a	38. b
9. c	19. a	29. d	
10. c	20. c	30. a	

15

PSYCHOLOGICAL DISORDERS

Abnormal psychology is defined as the branch of psychology concerned with the study of mental and emotional disorders including psychosis, personality disorders, organic mental syndromes, psychophysiologic disorders, and mental retardation.

CHAPTER OVERVIEW

The Williamsburg Hospital Annual Report of 1879 indicates causes of insanity. This report includes the following:

Cause	Men	Women
Affliction	3	20
Menstrual disturbance		14
Business affairs	10	
Domestic trouble	7	15
Masturbation	42	
Religious excitement	10	13
Womb disease		22

Our understanding of mental illness is relatively new. It was not that long ago that the mentally ill were seen as possessed by demons. They were punished, and pushed into the back wards of asylums where it was likely they would waste away. A visit to a museum of the treatment of the insane can be an eye-opening experience as you discover the harsh ways the mentally ill were treated not all that long ago. This mistreatment was not necessarily because of a mean spirit or disdain for the mentally ill. We were merely operating based on our best knowledge and technology—we just did not understand mental illness. The table above is evidence of our lack of understanding.

This chapter will help you gain a more practiced and functional understanding of psychological disorders as it is presented in the text. The materials and divided into two OMSE sections: 1) schizophrenia and the mood disorders, and 2) anxiety, somatoform, and other disorders. You will find a diverse variety of theoretical perspectives by which we identify, classify, and understand the problems that can interrupt the lives of those who suffer mental and emotional disorders. You will also discover a new emphasis on the biological components of psychological disorders and how this biological component can combine with the environment to shape behavior.

By completing the exercises provided, you should gain a thorough understanding of the information provided in your text. In other words, you should be better prepared for test, quizzes, class participation, and life itself.

TIMELINE

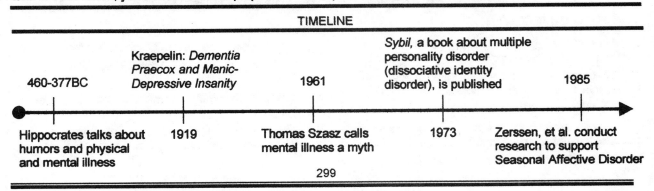

| 460-377BC | Kraepelin: *Dementia Praecox and Manic-Depressive Insanity* | 1961 | *Sybil*, a book about multiple personality disorder (dissociative identity disorder), is published | 1985 |

Hippocrates talks about humors and physical and mental illness

1919

Thomas Szasz calls mental illness a myth

1973

Zerssen, et al. conduct research to support Seasonal Affective Disorder

CHAPTER OUTLINE

What is Abnormal?

Perspectives on the Causes and Treatments of Psychological Disorders

Defining and Classifying Psychological Disorders

Schizophrenia

The Symptoms of Schizophrenia: Many and Varied

Types of Schizophrenia

The Causes of Schizophrenia

Mood Disorders

Depressive Disorders and Bipolar Disorder: Emotional Highs and Lows

Causes of Major Depressive Disorder and Bipolar Disorder

Suicide and Gender, Race, and Age

Anxiety Disorders: When Anxiety is Extreme

Generalized Anxiety Disorder

Panic Disorder

Phobias: Persistent, Irrational Fears

Obsessive-Compulsive Disorder

Somatoform and Dissociative Disorders

Somatoform Disorders: Physical Symptoms with Psychological Causes

Dissociative Disorders: Mental Escapes

Other Psychological Disorders

Sexual and Gender Identity Disorders

Personality Disorders: Troublesome Behavior Patterns

Apply It! Depression—Bad Thoughts, Bad Feelings

Thinking Critically

Chapter Summary and Review

KEY TERMS

What is Abnormal?

DSM-IV

neurosis

psychosis

Schizophrenia

schizophrenia

hallucination

delusion

delusion of grandeur

delusion of persecution

inappropriate affect

catatonic schizophrenia

disorganized schizophrenia

paranoid schizophrenia

diathesis-stress model

Mood Disorders

mood disorders

major depressive disorder

seasonal affective disorder

bipolar disorder

manic episode

first-degree relatives

Anxiety Disorders: When Anxiety is Extreme

anxiety disorder

anxiety

generalized anxiety disorder

panic attack

panic disorder

phobia

agoraphobia

social phobia

specific phobia

obsessive-compulsive disorder

obsession

compulsion

Somatoform and Dissociative Disorders

somatoform disorders

hypochondriasis

conversion disorder

dissociative disorders

dissociative amnesia

dissociative fugue

dissociative identity disorder

Other Psychological Disorders

sexual dysfunction

paraphilia

gender identity disorders

personality disorder

antisocial personality disorder

OMSE # 1: SCHIZOPHRENIA AND THE MOOD DISORDERS

LEARNING OBJECTIVES

1. What criteria might be used to differentiate normal from abnormal behavior?
2. What are five current perspectives that attempt to explain the causes of psychological disorders?
3. What is the DSM-IV?
4. What are some of the major positive and negative symptoms of schizophrenia?
5. What are the four types of schizophrenia?
6. What are some suggested causes of schizophrenia?
7. What are the symptoms of major depressive disorder?
8. What are the extremes of mood suffered in bipolar disorder?
9. What are some suggested causes of major depressive disorder and bipolar disorder?

LEARNING MASTERY SCORECARD: Update your score card as you work through the chapter. First, find and define key terms and concepts included in each section and note the page number(s) from the text that contain important references to the material. Next, gain a practical understanding of the concepts by considering the Laboratory to Life scenarios. Complete the *Objective-Mastery Self-Evaluation* (OMSE) exercises for this section and record your scores. Revisit the exercises, recording your score and the date completed until you have attained mastery (100%). Finally, prepare a lecture on each objective using the template provided, and practice presenting it. Keep an honest tally of your achievements and, when finished, you will have developed learning mastery.

Key Term	page #	Key Term	page #	Key Term	page #
DSM-IV	____	delusion of persecution	____	mood disorders	____
neurosis	____	inappropriate affect	____	major depressive disorder	____
psychosis	____	catatonic schizophrenia	____	seasonal affective disorder	____
schizophrenia	____	disorganized schizophrenia	____	bipolar disorder	____
hallucination	____	paranoid schizophrenia	____	manic episode	____
delusion	____	diathesis-stress model	____	first-degree relatives	____
delusion of grandeur	____				

Quick Quiz

Date	Score	Date	Score	Date	Score
_/_/_	____	_/_/_	____	_/_/_	____
_/_/_	____	_/_/_	____	_/_/_	100%

Elaborate Rehearsal

Lecture Preparation	Completion Date
Key Terms, Persons, & Concepts	_/_/_
Learning Objectives	_/_/_
Lecture Notes	_/_/_

A. QUICK QUIZ

1. The _____ perspective views abnormal behavior as a symptom of an underlying physical disorder.
   a) psychoanalytic
   b) cognitive
   c) biological
   d) psychosocial

2. The DSM-IV is a _____ manual.
   a) treatment
   b) diagnostic
   c) legal
   d) medical

3. Neurosis is the new term used to describe psychological disorders that are not serious enough to be considered psychotic.
   a) True
   b) False

4. The most serious psychological disorder is _____.

5. Symptoms such as hallucinations, delusions, and disorganized speech are considered to be _____ symptoms of schizophrenia.
   a) bizarre
   b) negative
   c) positive
   d) psychotic

6. Fred believes that there are three men who follow him around and whisper messages in his ear, telling him to do bad things. He also believes that these three men say bad things about him to his boss. Fred's false beliefs are called _____.
   a) hallucinations
   b) neologisms
   c) derailment
   d) delusions

7. James will appear to be completely unaware of his environment, as he stands for hours in a rigid posture. He has _____ schizophrenia.
    a) paranoid
    b) disorganized
    c) catatonic
    d) postural

8. Symptoms such as social withdrawal, apathy, slowed movements, and limited speech are examples of the _____ symptoms of schizophrenia.

9. When we study the brain of a schizophrenic patient we often find that the ventricles are _____ than those of the normal, nonschizophrenic brain.
    a) smaller
    b) larger

10. One compelling theory regarding the cause of schizophrenia is the _____ model. This model suggests that a person may have a constitutional predisposition toward the disease and that sufficient environmental stress may then make them vulnerable to experiencing the symptoms of the disease.

11. Johanna is experiencing extreme and unwarranted disturbances in feelings and mood. She would be assessed as suffering from a _____ disorder.
    a) mood
    b) somatic
    c) dissociative
    d) interpersonal

12. SAD refers to a kind of depression knows as _____.

13. The patient presented to his doctor with the following symptoms: psychomotor disturbances, overwhelming sadness, hopelessness, changed appetite and sleep patterns, and a sense of despair. This patient appears to be suffering from _____.

14. Frank called his best friend one night at two-o-clock in the morning. He seemed to be extremely excited about his great idea. He was going to have the Rolling Stones come to his backyard and perform a concert for his birthday party. He knew his idea could not fail and was going to call London to contact the rock band as soon as he got off the phone with his best friend. Frank was probably suffering a _____ episode.

15. Frank (above) appears to be suffering from _____.
    a) self-adulation delusional disorder
    b) bipolar disorder
    c) catatonic schizophrenia
    d) major anxiety disorder

16. Too little norepinephrine is related to mania and too much norepinephrine is related to depression.
    a) True
    b) False

17. The National Task Force on Women and Depression would assert that the higher rate of depression in women is due largely to _____.
    a) genetic factors
    b) environmental factors

18. Most people who say they are going to commit suicide are really just seeking attention. The true suicide risk patient will not display hints about his or her intentions.
    a) True
    b) False

B. MATCHING

	Key Words			Category
_____	1.	major depression, bipolar	a.	Anxiety Disorders
_____	2.	antisocial, histrionic	b.	Somatoform
_____	3.	panic, obsessive-compulsive	c.	Dissociative
_____	4.	autistic, conduct, Tourette's	d.	Schizophrenia & other psychotic disorders
_____	5.	fugue, amnesia	e.	Mood Disorders
_____	6.	abuse, dependence, intoxication	f.	Personality Disorders
_____	7.	anorexia, bulimia	g.	Substance-related Disorders
_____	8.	conversion disorder	h.	First Diagnosed in Infancy, Childhood, or Adolescence
_____	9.	hallucinations, delusions	i.	Eating Disorders

C. Complete the Table: Complete the table by filling in a basic description of how each perspective explains psychological disorders.

Perspective	Explanation
1. Biological	
2. Psychodynamic	
3. Learning	
4. Cognitive	
5. Humanistic	

PREPARE A LECTURE: This activity is designed to offer you an opportunity to take advantage of a valuable mode of learning, elaborate rehearsal. Once you have finished the OMSE section, write a lecture using the instructional guide provided below. After your lecture is prepared, you can enhance your learning by writing a quiz covering the material. Now it is time to find some willing and inquisitive audience members. Your roommates or family may be a great place to start. Present the lecture as if you are teaching a class. Remember to ask for questions and quiz your students. This exercise can also serve to turn a *study-buddy* group into a very productive way to prepare for the test. Each member of the group can take different OMSE sections for their lecture/teacher role while the rest of the group serves as the class.

I. Key Terms, Names, Dates, and Concepts you will include in this lecture:

1. _____   5. _____   9. _____
2. _____   6. _____   10. _____
3. _____   7. _____   11. _____
4. _____   8. _____   12. _____

II. Learning Objectives (what do you want the student to know and be able to do as a result of your lecture):

1. _____
2. _____
3. _____
4. _____
5. _____

III. Lecture Notes (notes should be brief cues and serve as a guide).

Major topic #1: _____

   Sub-topics and notes: _____

_____

_____

_____

Major topic #2: _____

   Sub-topics and notes: _____

_____

_____

_____

Major topic #3: _____

   Sub-topics and notes: _____

_____

_____

_____

OMSE # 2: ANXIETY, SOMATOFORM, AND OTHER DISORDERS

LEARNING OBJECTIVES

1. When is anxiety normal, and when is it abnormal?
2. What are the symptoms of panic disorder?
3. What are the characteristics of the three categories of phobias?
4. What do psychologists believe are some probable causes of phobias?
5. What is obsessive-compulsive disorder?
6. What are two somatoform disorders, and what symptoms do they share?
7. What are dissociative amnesia and dissociative fugue?
8. What are some of the identifying symptoms of dissociative identity disorder?
9. What are the sexual and gender identity disorders?
10. What characteristics are shared by most people with personality disorders?

LEARNING MASTERY SCORECARD:
Update your score card as you work through the chapter. First, find and define key terms and concepts included in each section and note the page number(s) from the text that contain important references to the material. Next, gain a practical understanding of the concepts by considering the Laboratory to Life scenarios. Complete the *Objective-Mastery Self-Evaluation* (OMSE) exercises for this section and record your scores. Revisit the exercises, recording your score and the date completed until you have attained mastery (100%). Finally, prepare a lecture on each objective using the template provided, and practice presenting it. Keep an honest tally of your achievements and, when finished, you will have developed learning mastery.

Key Term	page #	Key Term	page #	Key Term	page #
anxiety disorder	_____	specific phobia	_____	dissociative amnesia	_____
anxiety	_____	obsessive-compulsive disorder	_____	dissociative fugue	_____
generalized anxiety disorder	_____	obsession	_____	dissociative identity disorder	_____
panic attack	_____	compulsion	_____	sexual dysfunction	_____
panic disorder	_____	somatoform disorders	_____	paraphilia	_____
phobia	_____	hypochondriasis	_____	gender identity disorders	_____
agoraphobia	_____	conversion disorder	_____	personality disorder	_____
social phobia	_____	dissociative disorders	_____	antisocial personality disorder	_____

Quick Quiz

Date	Score	Date	Score	Date	Score
_/_/_	____	_/_/_	____	_/_/_	____
_/_/_	____	_/_/_	____	_/_/_	100%

Elaborate Rehearsal

Lecture Preparation	Completion Date
Key Terms, Persons, & Concepts	_/_/_
Learning Objectives	_/_/_
Lecture Notes	_/_/_

A. QUICK QUIZ

1. Hypochondriasis is an example of a(n) _____ disorder.
    a) dissociative
    b) anxiety
    c) mood
    d) somatoform

2. Bipolar disorder is considered to be a mood disorder.
    a) True
    b) False

3. Sarah experiences attacks of sudden and unexplained waves of fear. The attacks seem to come out of nowhere. Sarah is suffering from _____ disorder.

4. While still a psychiatric disorder with its associated suffering, at least people with anxiety disorders have little problem getting an accurate diagnosis and subsequent treatment.
    a) True
    b) False

5. Paula has an intense fear of being in a situation where immediate escape is not possible or help not available in the case of incapacitating anxiety. Paula is suffering from _____.

6. One day, when Jason was about five-years-old, he became terribly embarrassed. While standing in front of the class, he was laughed at because his zipper was down. He now experiences anxiety every time he is in a social situation, especially if he will be the center of attention. Jason is suffering from _____.
    a) social phobia
    b) monophobia
    c) agoraphobia
    d) anthropophobia

7. An obsession is to _____ as a compulsion is to _____.
    a) an urge to behave; involuntary thoughts
    b) psychosis; neurosis
    c) neurosis; psychosis
    d) involuntary thoughts; an urge to behave

8. Obsessive-compulsive disorder is an example of a(n) _____ disorder.
    a) psychotic
    b) mood
    c) anxiety
    d) dissociative

9. Robert's paralysis has defied medical diagnosis. There seems to be no physical reason for his condition. It is likely that he is suffering from what the text calls a _____ disorder.

10. Dissociative Identity Disorder is the newer term for what used to be called multiple schizophrenia.
    a) True
    b) False

11. Some clinicians believe that dissociative identity disorder is a function of patient play-acting, and not a real psychiatric disorder.
    a) True
    b) False

12. Disorders with names such as histrionic, borderline, antisocial, or narcissistic are collectively known as _____ disorders.

13. Sam has been in a lot of trouble lately, both with people close to him and with the law. He demonstrates a callous disregard for the rights and feelings of others. Other characteristics include manipulative, impulsive, aggressive, and reckless behaviors. He reportedly shows no remorse when he breaks the law or hurts others. Sam will likely receive a diagnosis of _____ disorder.
   a) schizophrenic
   b) dissociative fugue
   c) antisocial personality
   d) borderline personality disorder

14. Cheryl has never felt comfortable with her gender and believes she should have been a male. The DSM-IV would list her diagnosis as _____ disorder.
   a) paraphilia
   b) gender identity
   c) dissociative
   d) fetish

15. Is homosexuality considered a sexual disorder by the DSM-IV?
   a) yes
   b) no

B. Matching: Match the symptom with the disorder.

	Symptom	Disorder
_____	1. sexual urges, fantasies, and behaviors involving sexual activity with a child or children	a. paraphilia
		b. fetishism
_____	2. low sexual desire or other sexual performance problems	c. pedophilia
_____	3. sexual urges, fantasies, and behaviors involving nonhuman objects, children, or nonconsenting persons	d. exhibitionism
		e. voyeurism
_____	4. sexual urges, fantasies, and behavior involving being made to suffer	f. sexual masochism
_____	5. sexual urges, fantasies, and behaviors involving an inanimate object	g. sexual sadism
_____	6. sexual urges, fantasies, and behaviors that involve inflicting pain on another	h. other paraphilias
_____	7. sexual urges, fantasies, and behaviors that involve watching unsuspecting people who are naked, undressing, or in sexual activity	i. sexual dysfunctions
_____	8. sexual urges, fantasies, and behaviors that involve exposing one's genitals to an unsuspecting stranger	
_____	9. sexual urges, fantasies, or behaviors that involve things like animals, feces, or corpses	

C. Complete the Table: Complete the following table by filling in a basic description of each of the following personality disorders.

Disorder	Symptoms
1. Paranoid	
2. Antisocial	
3. Histrionic	

4. Narcissistic	
5. Borderline	

PREPARE A LECTURE: This activity is designed to offer you an opportunity to take advantage of a valuable mode of learning, elaborate rehearsal. Once you have finished the OMSE section, write a lecture using the instructional guide provided below. After your lecture is prepared, you can enhance your learning by writing a quiz covering the material. Now it is time to find some willing and inquisitive audience members. Your roommates or family may be a great place to start. Present the lecture as if you are teaching a class. Remember to ask for questions and quiz your students. This exercise can also serve to turn a *study-buddy* group into a very productive way to prepare for the test. Each member of the group can take different OMSE sections for their lecture/teacher role while the rest of the group serves as the class.

I. Key Terms, Names, Dates, and Concepts you will include in this lecture:

1. _____   5. _____   9. _____
2. _____   6. _____   10. _____
3. _____   7. _____   11. _____
4. _____   8. _____   12. _____

II. Learning Objectives (what do you want the student to know and be able to do as a result of your lecture?):

1. _____
2. _____
3. _____
4. _____
5. _____

III. Lecture Notes (notes should be brief cues and serve as a guide):

Major topic #1: _____
   Sub-topics and notes: _____
_____
_____
_____

Major topic #2: _____
   Sub-topics and notes: _____
_____
_____
_____

Major topic #3: _____
   Sub-topics and notes: _____
_____
_____
_____

KEY TERMS AND CONCEPTS EXERCISE

The key terms and concepts are presented in order of their appearance in the text. Space is provided for you to include a personalized definition or example of each term or concept. As you encounter each term in the text, make a note of its meaning and context. Next, conceptualize the meaning of the term in a way that makes the most sense to you. Also, think about examples of the term from your own life. Write your definition and/or example in the space provided next to the word. The KEY TERMS exercise utilizes a modified *T-note* design so that you can self-evaluate your mastery of the definitions. First lay a sheet of paper over the terms and concepts side of the page so that you only see the definitions. Read the definition and try to recall the term or concept. Mark all those you are unable to answer so you can restudy them. When you have learned all of the terms and concepts in this way, move the paper to the definition side so that you can see only the term or concept, and try to recall both the textbook definition and your personal version. Repeat this until you know all of the terms by definition and personal understanding.

DSM-IV	The *Diagnostic and Statistical Manual of Mental Disorders (Fourth Edition)*, a manual published by the American Psychiatric Association, which describes about 290 mental disorders and their symptoms. _____
Neurosis	An obsolete term for a disorder causing personal distress and some impairment in functioning but not causing loss of contact with reality or violation of important social norms. _____
Psychosis	A severe psychological disorder marked by loss of contact with reality and a seriously impaired ability to function. _____
Schizophrenia	A severe psychological disorder characterized by loss of contact with reality, hallucinations, delusions, inappropriate or flat affect, some disturbance in thinking, social withdrawal, and/or other bizarre behavior. _____
Hallucination	A sensory perception in the absence of any external stimulation; an imaginary sensation. _____
Delusion	A false belief, not generally shared by others in the culture, that cannot be changed despite strong evidence to the contrary. _____
Delusion of Grandeur	A false belief that one is a famous person or one who has some great knowledge, ability, and authority. _____
Delusion of Persecution	An individual's false belief that a person or group is trying in some way to harm him or her. _____
Inappropriate Affect	A symptom common in schizophrenia in which a person's behavior (including facial expressions, tone of voice, and gestures) does not reflect the emotion that would be expected under the circumstances; for example, a person laughs at a tragedy, cries at a joke. _____

Catatonic Schizophrenia	A type of schizophrenia characterized by complete stillness or stupor and/or periods of great agitation and excitement; patients may assume an unusual posture and remain in it for long periods.
Disorganized Schizophrenia	The most serious type of schizophrenia, marked by inappropriate affect, silliness, laughter, grotesque mannerisms, and bizarre behavior.
Paranoid Schizophrenia	A type of schizophrenia characterized by delusions of grandeur or persecution.
Diathesis–Stress Model	The idea that people with a constitutional predisposition (diathesis) toward a disorder, such as schizophrenia, may develop the disorder if they are subjected to sufficient environmental stress.
Mood Disorders	Disorders characterized by extreme and unwarranted disturbances in feeling or mood.
Major Depressive Disorder	A mood disorder marked by feelings of great sadness, despair, guilt, worthlessness, and hopelessness.
Seasonal Affective Disorder (SAD)	A mood disorder in which depression comes and goes with the seasons. Winter depression is more prevalent and seems to be triggered by light deficiency.
Bipolar Disorder	A mood disorder in which one has manic episodes alternating with periods of depression, usually with relatively normal periods in between.
Manic Episode	A period of extreme elation, euphoria, and hyperactivity, often accompanied by delusions of grandeur and by hostility if activity is blocked.
First-Degree Relatives	A person's parents, children, or siblings.
Anxiety Disorder	Psychological disorders characterized by severe anxiety (e.g., panic disorder, phobias, general anxiety disorder, obsessive compulsive disorder).
Anxiety	A generalized feeling of apprehension, fear, or tension that may be associated with a particular object or situation or may be free-floating, not associated with anything specific.
Generalized Anxiety Disorder	An anxiety disorder in which people experience excessive anxiety or worry that they find difficult to control.
Panic Attack	An attack of overwhelming anxiety, fear, or terror.

Panic Disorder	An anxiety disorder in which a person experiences recurrent unpredictable attacks of overwhelming anxiety, fear, or terror. _____
Phobia	A persistent, irrational fear of an object, situation, or activity that the person feels compelled to avoid. _____
Agoraphobia	An intense fear of being in a situation where immediate escape is not possible or help is not immediately available in case of incapacitating anxiety. _____
Social Phobia	An irrational fear and avoidance of social situations in which people believe they might embarrass or humiliate themselves by appearing clumsy, foolish, or incompetent. _____
Specific Phobia	A marked fear of a specific objector situation; a catchall category for any phobia other than agoraphobia and social phobia. _____
Obsessive-Compulsive Disorder (OCD)	An anxiety disorder in which a person suffers from obsessions and/or compulsions. _____
Obsession	A persistent, recurring, involuntary thought, image, or impulse that invades consciousness and causes great distress. _____
Compulsion	A persistent, irresistible, irrational urge to perform an act or ritual repeatedly. _____
Somatoform Disorders	Disorders in which physical symptoms are present that are due to psychological rather than physical causes. _____
Hypochondriasis	A somatoform disorder in which persons are preoccupied with their health and convinced they have some serious disorder despite reassurance from doctors to the contrary. _____
Conversion Disorder	A somatoform disorder in which a loss of motor or sensory functioning in some part of the body has no physical cause but solves some psychological problem. _____
Dissociative Disorders	Disorders in which, under stress, one loses the integration of consciousness, identity, and memories of important personal events. _____
Dissociative Amnesia	A dissociative disorder in which there is a loss of memory for limited periods in one's life or for one's entire personal identity. _____
Dissociative Fugue	A dissociative disorder in which one has a complete loss of memory for one's entire identity, travels away from home, and may assume a new identity. _____

Dissociative Identity Disorder	A dissociative disorder in which two or more distinct personalities occur in the same person, each taking over at different times; also called multiple personality. _____ _____
Sexual Dysfunction	A persistent or recurrent problem that causes marked distress and interpersonal difficulty and that may involve any or some combination of the following: sexual desire, sexual arousal or the pleasures associated with sex, or orgasm. _____ _____
Paraphilia	A sexual disorder in which sexual urges, fantasies, and behavior generally involve children, other nonconsenting partners, nonhuman objects, or the suffering and humiliation of one or one's partner. _____ _____
Gender Identity Disorders	Disorders characterized by a problem accepting one's identity as male or female. _____ _____
Personality Disorder	A continuing, inflexible, maladaptive pattern of inner experience and behavior that causes great distress or impaired functioning and differs significantly from the patterns expected in the person's culture. _____ _____
Antisocial Personality Disorder	A disorder marked by lack of feeling for others; selfish, aggressive, irresponsible behavior; and willingness to break the law, lie, cheat, or exploit others for personal gain. _____ _____

FROM THE LABORATORY TO LIFE

HERE'S YOUR CHANCE—YOU BE THE PSYCHOLOGIST (Please, don't try this at home).

In this exercise you are the diagnostician. Read each list of symptoms and then determine and record the correct psychological disorder diagnosis.

1. Major symptoms include:
   a) Markedly diminished interest or pleasure in all or almost all activities most of the day
   b) Psychomotor agitation or retardation
   c) Fatigue or loss of energy
   d) Insomnia or hypersomnia
   e) Feelings of worthlessness or excessive guilt
   f) Recurrent thoughts of death, recurrent suicidal ideation

   Your diagnosis: _____

2. Major symptoms include:
   a) A pattern of unstable and intense interpersonal relationships characterized by extremes of idealization and/or devaluation
   b) Impulsivity in at least two areas that are potentially self-dangerous
   c) Recurrent suicidal behaviors or self-mutilating behaviors
   d) Inappropriate, intense anger or difficulty controlling anger
   e) Markedly and persistently unstable self-image or sense of self
   f) Frantic efforts to avoid real or imagined abandonment

   Your diagnosis: _____

3. Major symptoms include:
    a) Delusions
    b) Hallucinations
    c) Disorganized speech
    d) Grossly disorganized or catatonic behavior
    e) Emotions change often and are not appropriate to the situation
    f) Lack of ability to experience pleasure

    Your diagnosis: _____

4. Major symptoms include:
    a) The presence of two or more distinct identities or personality states, each with its own relatively enduring pattern of thought about the world and the self.
    b) At least two of the above identities recurrently take control of the person's behavior
    c) Inability to recall important personal information that is too extensive to be explained by ordinary forgetfulness
    d) Not due to direct effects of substance use (blackouts or intoxication)

    Your diagnosis: _____

5. Major symptoms include:
    a) Recurrent episodes of binge eating – sense of lack of control over the binge
    b) Self-evaluation is unduly influenced by body shape and weight
    c) Recurrent episodes of self-induced vomiting, use of laxatives

    Your diagnosis: _____

6. Major symptoms include:
    a) Recurrent and persistent thoughts, impulses, or images that are experienced as intrusive and result in marked anxiety or distress
    b) The thoughts are not just excessive about real life problems
    c) Repetitive behaviors that the person feels driven to perform in response to an obsession
    d) The behaviors or mental acts are designed to reduce distress or prevent some dreaded event or situation
    e) Behaviors are time consuming and interfere with daily functioning

    Your diagnosis: _____

FROM THEORY TO PRACTICE

THEORETICAL PERSPECTIVES ON HOW, WHY, AND WHEN

Well, you have now covered 15 chapters of some pretty tough material. You have read and heard about several theorists and their beliefs. You have explored numerous theories that are designed to explain human nature. All of this hard work is supposed to leave you with a better understanding of why we (humans that is) are the way we are and why we do the things we do. Now, on top of all that, we want you to have an idea of why sometimes things go wrong—why we don't quite function as well as we would like. Review each syndrome presented in the Lab to Life exercise one more time. This time, as you read the syndromes, keep in mind the various theories presented in the chapter. In the space provided below, circle the theory that you feel best explains the disorder (you may circle more than one). Then, write in the theoretical causes or conditions leading to the psychological disorder.

DISORDER	PERSPECTIVE	EXPLANATION
1.	Biological	_____
	Psychodynamic	_____
	Learning	_____
	Cognitive	_____
	Humanistic	_____

2.	Biological	_____
	Psychodynamic	_____
	Learning	_____
	Cognitive	_____
	Humanistic	_____
3.	Biological	_____
	Psychodynamic	_____
	Learning	_____
	Cognitive	_____
	Humanistic	_____
4.	Biological	_____
	Psychodynamic	_____
	Learning	_____
	Cognitive	_____
	Humanistic	_____
5.	Biological	_____
	Psychodynamic	_____
	Learning	_____
	Cognitive	_____
	Humanistic	_____
6.	Biological	_____
	Psychodynamic	_____
	Learning	_____
	Cognitive	_____
	Humanistic	_____

COMPREHENSIVE PRACTICE TEST

1. Questions that deal with issues such as personal distress, maladaptive behavior, and dangerousness to self or others are related to the definition of _____.
   - a) schizophrenia
   - b) abnormal
   - c) neurons
   - d) insane

2. The _____ perspective sees abnormal behavior as a symptom of an underlying physical disorder.
   - a) cognitive
   - b) psychoanalytic
   - c) biological
   - d) behavioral

3. The _____ sees abnormal behavior as the result of faulty and negative thinking.
   - a) psychoanalytic
   - b) cognitive
   - c) behavioral
   - d) biological

4. The _____ sees abnormal behavior as the result of early childhood experiences and unconscious sexual and aggressive conflict.
    a) cognitive   c) humanistic
    b) biological   d) psychoanalytic

5. The _____ perspective sees psychological disorders as resulting from a blocking of one's tendency toward self-actualization.
    a) humanistic   c) biological
    b) cognitive   d) psychoanalytic

6. A _____ disorder is diagnosed when physical symptoms have a psychological origin instead of a medical origin.
    a) dissociative   c) somatoform
    b) psychotic   d) mood

7. Psychosis is to neurosis as less serious is to more serious.
    a) True   b) False

8. Histrionic, narcissistic, and borderline are all examples of _____ disorders.
    a) personality   c) psychosis
    b) neurosis   d) dissociative

9. Panic disorder, phobia, and obsessive-compulsive disorder are all examples of _____ disorders.
    a) neurotic   c) personality
    b) anxiety   d) somatoform

10. Which of the following neurotransmitters are not mentioned in the text regarding anxiety?
    a) serotonin   c) norepinephrine
    b) dopamine   d) acetylcholine

11. The definition of _____ is an intense fear of being in a situation where immediate escape is not possible or help is not immediately available in case of incapacitating anxiety.
    a) panic disorder   c) generalized anxiety disorder
    b) multiple phobic disorder   d) agoraphobia

12. Women are _____ times as likely to be diagnosed with agoraphobia.
    a) five   c) four
    b) two   d) six

13. Jim's fear of snakes can be traced to his anxiety related to sexual and aggressive impulses. This statement would most likely come from:
    a) Skinner   c) Rogers
    b) Bandura   d) Freud

14. Jessica's life has been seriously interrupted by her constant worry about germs and disease. She carries with her tissues and cleaning pads so that she can wash things before she touches them. She also washes her hands a few dozen times per day. Jessica 's worry is an example of _____ and her constant cleaning and hand washing is an example of _____.
    a) compulsions; obsessions   c) psychosis; anxiety
    b) anxiety; psychosis   d) obsessions; compulsions

15. Obsessive-compulsive disordered patients who repeatedly check things have been shown to:
    a) have episodic memory impairment   c) lack confidence in their memory
    b) have semantic memory impairment   d) have a fear of Alzheimer's disease

16. Dawn is constantly worried about her health. She is convinced she has a disease and goes from one doctor to another searching for a diagnosis. The problem is that all the doctors have said the same thing; "There is nothing physically wrong with her." Dawn is suffering from _____.
    a) hypochondriasis
    b) seasonal affective disorder
    c) conversion disorder
    d) body dysmorphic disorder

17. A good example of a conversion disorder would be Paul, who is sick all the time even though he suffers a great deal of personal loss due to his illness.
    a) True
    b) False

18. Dissociative amnesia is to _____ as dissociative fugue is to _____:
    a) biological causes; psychological causes
    b) forget; forget and leave/new identity
    c) forget and leave/new identity; forget
    d) psychological causes; biological causes

19. Most patients with dissociative identity disorder are _____.
    a) elderly
    b) women
    c) men
    d) in their early 20s

20. A common early experience for dissociative identity disordered patients is:
    a) drug use by their mother while pregnant
    b) measles or mumps when young
    c) parental divorce
    d) early physical or sexual abuse

21. Jean demonstrates unstable mood, behavior, and self-image, as well as impaired social relationships. Other symptoms noted by her doctor include intense fear of abandonment, impulsive and reckless behavior, and suicidal gestures. Jean is suffering from the _____ disorder known as _____.
    a) personality; histrionic
    b) mood; bipolar
    c) schizophrenic; catatonic
    d) personality; borderline

22. Hallucinations, delusions, and disorganized thinking and speech are characteristic of the _____ symptoms of _____.
    a) negative; schizophrenia
    b) positive; schizophrenia
    c) positive; bipolar disorder
    d) negative; bipolar

23. Hallucinations refer to false perceptions such as seeing things that are not really there.
    a) True
    b) False

24. A typical psychotic symptom picture might include delusions of grandeur.
    a) True
    b) False

25. A good example of a delusion is:
    a) Fred is hearing voices telling him to do bad things
    b) Jackson believes he is a secret agent for the devil
    c) Alice is threatening to commit suicide
    d) Camilla feels bugs crawling under her skin

26. Social withdrawal, apathy, loss of motivation, and limited speech are included in the list of _____ symptoms of _____.
    a) positive; borderline disorder
    b) motivational; catatonia
    c) negative; schizophrenia
    d) psychotic; bipolar disorder

27. The patient sits completely still for hours as if he were in a stupor. This is sometimes followed by periods of great agitation and excitement. The patient is suffering from _____ schizophrenia.
    a) disorganized
    b) undifferentiated
    c) paranoid
    d) catatonic

28. Ira, while being interviewed at the local mental health clinic, laughs while talking about a very sad event in his life. The text would say that Ira is exhibiting _____.
    a) catatonia
    b) disorganized emotional expression
    c) inappropriate affect
    d) anhedonia

29. Which of the following seems to indicate the best chance for recovery?
    a) catatonic schizophrenia
    b) paranoid schizophrenia
    c) disorganized schizophrenia
    d) undifferentiated schizophrenia

30. According to the text, the diathesis-stress model would suggest that we do not actually inherit schizophrenia, but the predisposition to develop schizophrenia given enough stress in a person's life.
    a) True
    b) False

31. Major depression, SAD, bipolar disorder, and dysthymia are all examples of _____ disorders.
    a) personality
    b) psychotic
    c) mood
    d) emotional

32. Dysthymia is _____ serious than major depression.
    a) more
    b) less

33. Depression is diagnosed more often in _____ than in _____.
    a) children; adults
    b) women; men
    c) men; women
    d) adults; children

34. _____ disorder would include periods of inflated self-esteem, wild optimism, and hyperactivity known as manic episodes.
    a) Paranoid schizophrenia
    b) Major depression
    c) Borderline personality
    d) Bipolar

35. Which of the following two neurotransmitters are known to be involved in mood disorders?
    a) dopamine and acetylcholine
    b) GABA and serotonin
    c) serotonin and norepinephrine
    d) norepinephrine and dopamine

36. Suicide is a predominant concern in patients who suffer _____.
    a) catatonic schizophrenia
    b) paraphilia
    c) depression
    d) simple phobia

37. The psychoanalytic approach would assert that one's depression stems from faulty thinking and distorted perceptions.
    a) True
    b) False

38. Depression seems to be the result of _____.
    a) genetic and biological factors only
    b) both biological and environmental factors
    c) environmental factors only
    d) poor parenting in early childhood

39. Sexual masochism, sexual sadism, and exhibitionism are all examples of _____.
    a) paraphilias
    b) gender identity disorders
    c) sexual dysfunctions
    d) pedophilia

40. The good news is that, while we did not know much about the causes of mental disorders 100 years ago, today there is very little mystery—science has provided us with just about all the answers.
    a) True
    b) False

ANSWER KEYS

ANSWER KEY: OMSE#1

A. Quick Quiz		B. Matching
1. c	10. diathesis-stress	1. e
2. b	11. a	2. f
3. false	12. Seasonal Affect Disorder	3. a
4. schizophrenia	13. major depressive disorder	4. h
5. c	14. manic	5. c
6. d	15. b	6. g
7. c	16. false	7. i
8. negative	17. b	8. b
9. b	18. false	9. d

C. Complete the Table

	Perspective	Explanation
1.	Biological	Psychological disorders are symptoms of an underlying physical disorder caused by a structural or biochemical abnormality in the brain, genetic inheritance, or infection.
2.	Psychodynamic	Psychological disorders stem from early childhood experiences, unconscious sexual and aggressive conflicts, or an imbalance among the id, ego, and superego.
3.	Learning	Abnormal thoughts, feelings, and behaviors are learned and sustained like any other behaviors – or there is a failure to learn appropriate behaviors.
4.	Cognitive	Faulty and negative thinking can cause psychological disorders
5.	Humanistic	Psychological disorders result from blocking of normal tendency toward self-actualization.

ANSWER KEY: OMSE#2

A. Quick Quiz		B. Matching
1. d	9. conversion	1. c
2. true	10. false	2. i
3. panic	11. true	3. a
4. false	12. personality	4. f
5. agoraphobia	13. c	5. b
6. a	14. b	6. g
7. d	15. b	7. e
8. c		8. d
		9. h

C. Complete the Table

Disorder	Symptoms
1. Paranoid	Highly suspicious, untrusting, guarded, hypersensitive, easily slighted, lacking in emotion, holds grudges.
2. Antisocial	Callous disregard for the rights and feelings of others, is manipulative, impulsive, selfish, aggressive, irresponsible, reckless, is willing to break the law, lie, cheat, or exploit others for personal gain, without remorse; fails to hold jobs.
3. Histrionic	Seeks attention and approval; is overly dramatic, self-centered, shallow; is demanding, manipulative, easily bored, suggestible, craves excitement; often is attractive and sexually seductive.
4. Narcissistic	Has exaggerated sense of self-importance and entitlement and is self-centered, arrogant, demanding, exploitive, envious; craves admiration and attention; lacks empathy.
5. Borderline	Unstable in mood, behavior, self-image, and social relationships; has intense fear of abandonment; exhibits impulsive and reckless behavior, inappropriate anger; makes suicidal gestures and performs self-mutilating acts.

ANSWER KEY: LAB TO LIFE

1. Major Depression
2. Borderline Personality Disorder
3. Schizophrenia
4. Dissociative Identity Disorder
5. Bulimia Nervosa
6. Obsessive-compulsive Disorder

ANSWER KEY: COMPREHENSIVE PRACTICE TEST

1. b	11. d	21. d	31. c
2. c	12. c	22. b	32. b
3. b	13. d	23. true	33. b
4. d	14. d	24. true	34. d
5. a	15. c	25. b	35. c
6. c	16. a	26. c	36. c
7. false	17. false	27. d	37. false
8. a	18. b	28. c	38. b
9. b	19. b	29. b	39. a
10. d	20. d	30. true	40. false

16

THERAPIES

Analysis does not set out to make pathological reactions impossible, but to give the patient's ego freedom to decide one way or another.

–Sigmund Freud, 1923

CHAPTER OVERVIEW

If you ask the proverbial "person on the street," who knows little about psychology, that person will probably have heard of Sigmund Freud and psychoanalysis. While Freud's contributions to psychology go beyond psychoanalysis, he is certainly best known for that form of psychotherapy. Freud demonstrated to the world that the knowledge being gained in psychology could be used in the healing arts—psychoanalysis became psychotherapy. Prior to Freud's work, the treatment of mental illness took on a variety of often crude, dangerous, and unkind forms of restriction and unscientific attempts to "cure" the victim. Since the inception of psychoanalysis, psychotherapy has grown and progressed steadily. Today, one can find hundreds of references for different types of therapy for everything from schizophrenia to seasonal affective disorder. Fortunately, psychotherapy has become a much more sophisticated and helpful endeavor since the early days of exorcisms, mesmerism, and even psychoanalysis. New theoretical approaches and the discovery of effective therapeutic drugs have revolutionized the treatment of the mentally and emotionally ill. Yet, to this day, psychotherapy is a controversial issue. Eysenck (1952) denounced the effectiveness of psychotherapy by suggesting that talking to a friend would better help people with emotional problems than would seeking professional psychotherapy. The mass media often reminds us of the dangers of irresponsible and unscientific therapies, as former patients share their stories of misdiagnosis and mistreatment. This often leads to the belief that psychotherapy can be a dangerous alternative to real medicine. Given this, many who could benefit from scientifically supported forms of psychotherapy refuse to avail themselves of the opportunity.

As you become more familiar with the therapy options available for the treatment of mental, emotional, and behavioral disorders, you will be more prepared to make intelligent decisions regarding the role of psychotherapy in your life. This chapter will help you gain a more practiced and functional understanding of the modern therapies used to treat those afflicted with psychological and psychiatric disorders. The materials are divided into two OMSE sections: 1) psychotherapies, and 2) biological therapies and choosing a therapy/therapist.

By completing the exercised provided, you should gain a thorough understanding of the information provided in your text. In other words, you should be better prepared for tests, quizzes, class participation, and life itself.

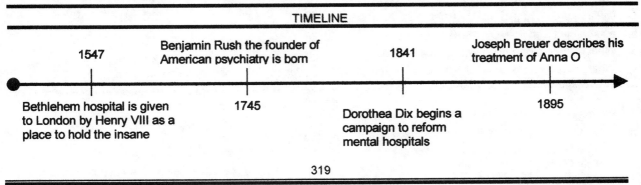

TIMELINE

1547 — Benjamin Rush the founder of American psychiatry is born — 1841 — Joseph Breuer describes his treatment of Anna O

Bethlehem hospital is given to London by Henry VIII as a place to hold the insane — 1745 — Dorothea Dix begins a campaign to reform mental hospitals — 1895

CHAPTER OUTLINE

Insight Therapies

Psychodynamic Therapies: Freud Revisited

Humanistic Therapies

Therapies Emphasizing Interaction with Others

Behavior Therapy: Unlearning the Old, Learning the New

Behavior Modification Techniques Based on Operant Conditioning

Therapies Based on Classical Conditioning

Therapies Based on Operational Learning Theory: Just Watch This!

Cognitive Therapies: It's the Thought That Counts

Rational-Emotive Therapy: Human Misery—The Legacy of False Beliefs

Cognitive Therapy: Overcoming "the Power of Negative Thinking"

The Biological Therapies

Drug Therapy: Pills for Psychological Ills

Electroconvulsive Therapy: The Controversy Continues

Psychosurgery: Cutting to Cure

Therapies and Therapists: Many Choices

Evaluating the Therapies: Do They Work?

Mental Health Professionals: How Do They Differ?

Selecting a Therapy: Finding One That Fits

Therapy and Race, Ethnicity, and Gender

Apply It! Finding a Therapist

Thinking Critically

Chapter Summary and Review

KEY TERMS

Insight Therapies

psychotherapy

insight therapy

psychoanalysis

free association

resistance

transference

person-centered therapy

self-actualization

nondirective therapy

Gestalt therapy

directive therapy

interpersonal therapy

family therapy

group therapy

psychodrama

encounter group

Behavior Therapy: Unlearning the Old, Learning the New

behavior therapy

behavior modification

token economy

time out

stimulus satiation

systematic desensitization

flooding

exposure and response prevention

aversion therapy

participant modeling

Cognitive Therapies: It's the Thought That Counts

rational-emotive therapy

automatic thoughts

cognitive therapy

The Biological Therapies

biological therapy

antipsychotic drugs

antidepressants

lithium

electroconvulsive therapy

psychosurgery

lobotomy

Therapies and Therapists: Many Choices

clinical psychologist

psychiatrist

psychoanalyst

OMSE # 1: PSYCHOTHERAPIES

LEARNING OBJECTIVES

1. What are the four basic techniques of psychoanalysis, and how are they used to help disturbed patients?

2. What are the role and the goal of the therapist in person-centered therapy?

3. What is the major emphasis in Gestalt therapy?

4. What four problems commonly associated with major depression is interpersonal therapy designed to treat?

5. What are some advantages of group therapy?

6. What is behavior therapy?

7. How do behavior therapists modify behavior using operant conditioning techniques?

8. What behavior therapies are based on classical conditioning?

9. How do therapists use systematic desensitization to rid people of fears?

10. What is flooding?

11. How does exposure and response prevention help people with obsessive compulsive disorder?

12. How does aversion therapy rid people of a harmful or undesirable behavior?

13. How does participant modeling help people overcome fears?

14. What is the aim of rational-emotive therapy?

15. How does cognitive therapy help people overcome depression and anxiety disorders?

LEARNING MASTERY SCORECARD: Update your score card as you work through the chapter. First, find and define key terms and concepts included in each section and note the page number(s) from the text that contain important references to the material. Next, gain a practical understanding of the concepts by considering the Laboratory to Life scenarios. Complete the *Objective-Mastery Self-Evaluation* (OMSE) exercises for this section and record your scores. Revisit the exercises, recording your score and the date completed until you have attained mastery (100%). Finally, prepare a lecture on each objective using the template provided, and practice presenting it. Keep an honest tally of your achievements and, when finished, you will have developed learning mastery.

Key Term	page #	Key Term	page #	Key Term	page #
psychotherapy	_____	directive therapy	_____	stimulus satiation	_____
insight therapy	_____	interpersonal therapy	_____	systematic desensitization	_____
psychoanalysis	_____	family therapy	_____	flooding	_____
free association	_____	group therapy	_____	exposure and response prevention	_____
resistance	_____	psychodrama	_____	aversion therapy	_____
transference	_____	encounter group	_____	participant modeling	_____
person-centered therapy	_____	behavior therapy	_____	rational-emotive therapy	_____
self-actualization	_____	behavior modification	_____	automatic thoughts	_____
nondirective therapy	_____	token economy	_____	cognitive therapy	_____
Gestalt therapy	_____	time out	_____		

Quick Quiz

Date	Score	Date	Score	Date	Score
__/__/__	_____	__/__/__	_____	__/__/__	_____
__/__/__	_____	__/__/__	_____	__/__/__	100%

Elaborate Rehearsal

Lecture Preparation	Completion Date
Key Terms, Persons, & Concepts	__/__/__
Learning Objectives	__/__/__
Lecture Notes	__/__/__

TIMELINE

1901 — Carl Rogers develops person-centered therapy — 1952 — Thorazine is first used as an antipsychotic drug

Sigmund Freud: *Interpretation of Dreams* — 1951 — Eysenck blasts psychotherapy as an ineffective treatment — 1954

A. QUICK QUIZ

1. Psychotherapy uses _____ rather than _____ means to treat emotional and behavioral disorders.

2. Helen is seeing a psychotherapist who believes that psychological well-being depends on self-understanding. Helen's therapist follows the notions of behavioral therapy.
   a) True
   b) False

3. Freud developed _____, the first formal psychotherapy.
   a) behaviorism
   b) psychoanalysis
   c) client-centered therapy
   d) interpersonal therapy

4. All of the following are basic techniques of psychoanalysis **except** _____.
   a) free association
   b) cognitive disputation
   c) dream analysis
   d) analysis of transference

5. What does the psychoanalyst think is happening when the client changes the subject, becomes angry, or misses appointments?
   a) transference
   b) insight
   c) resistance
   d) free association

6. Helen begins to behave toward the analyst in the same way she behaved toward a significant person from the past. The analyst would say that _____ is taking place.
   a) transference
   b) insight
   c) resistance
   d) free association

7. What is meant by nondirective therapy?
   a) The therapy is without any real focus.
   b) The therapist receives as much from the therapy as the client.
   c) The client determines the direction and focus of the therapy.
   d) The therapy is based on behaviors, not internal factors.

8. Which of the following theorists would be most associated with client-centered therapy?
   a) Skinner
   b) Ellis
   c) Freud
   d) Rogers

9. In non-directive therapy the focus is on the unconscious factors that block the individual's movement toward self-actualization.
   a) True
   b) False

10. Which of the following was **NOT** listed as a condition necessary for the client-centered therapist?
    a) unconditional positive regard
    b) empathy
    c) transference sensitivity
    d) genuine feelings toward the client

11. The term, "living in the moment," would be best matched with Gestalt therapy.
    a) True
    b) False

12. A therapy approach where the therapist takes an active role in determining the course of therapy sessions, and provides answers and suggestions to the client is known as _____ therapy.

13. An exciting new approach to treating depression is known as _____ therapy. This approach has been shown especially helpful in treating problems such as severe bereavement and difficulty in adjusting to role transitions.

14. An approach that has been shown to be helpful for problems such as troubled or troublesome teenagers, alcoholic parents, or abusive family situations is known as _____ therapy.
    a) interpersonal
    b) family
    c) cognitive relationship
    d) group dynamic

15. Group therapy has been identified as offering all of the following benefits **except**:
    a) lower expense
    b) sense of belonging
    c) collective transference
    d) giving and receiving feedback

16. Walt is receiving group therapy. In his group, members act out their problem situation or relationship. Other group members assist and participate in the process. This technique is known as _____.

17. Alcoholics Anonymous is the prototypical example of _____.
   a) psychodynamic group therapy
   b) self-help groups
   c) cognitive-behavioral group therapy
   d) humanistic group therapy

18. Which of the following would most likely suggest that, since people learn their emotional or behavioral problem, they can also unlearn the problem?
   a) a therapist who follows the ideas of Freud
   b) a Gestalt therapist
   c) a client-centered therapist
   d) a behavior therapist

19. The techniques of token economy, time out, and stimulus satiation are all based on the ideas of _____.
   a) operant conditioning
   b) classical conditioning
   c) cognitive learning
   d) psychodynamic therapy

20. Little Johnny has been acting out in class. He throws spit wads, makes funny noises, and writes bad notes to his classmates. When he does this his teacher scolds him and makes him stand in the front of the class. The problem is that he continues to do the bad behaviors. A school therapist finally suggested that the teacher avoid giving Johnny this apparent public reinforcement. The therapist based this suggestion on the learning theory concept of _____.
   a) negative reinforcement
   b) shaping
   c) negative punishment
   d) extinction

21. Systematic desensitization has been shown to be effective with a variety of phobia problems.
   a) True
   c) False

22. Rational Emotive Therapy is a type of _____ therapy.
   a) psychodynamic
   b) cognitive
   c) behavioral
   d) client-centered

B. MATCHING: Match the theory/therapy technique with the name of the theorist/therapist by placing the appropriate letter in the space provided.

	Theory/Technique	Theorist/Therapist
_____	1. Psychoanalysis	a. Perls
_____	2. Person-centered	b. Ellis
_____	3. Gestalt	c. Moreno
_____	4. Interpersonal	d. Wolpe
_____	5. Psychodrama	e. Freud
_____	6. Systematic Desensitization	f. Bandura
_____	7. Participant Modeling	g. Elkin
_____	8. Rational Emotive Therapy	h. Rogers

It's amazing that some people will get to the point of pulling their hair out before they will ask for help. Everybody has a rough stretch in life at one time or another, and your campus probably has a counseling office. If you're moving toward the breaking point, don't be too proud or too cool to admit it. Seek the help you need to get past your rough stretch. After all, counseling is only temporary—but your hair may not grow back in!

C. COMPLETE THE TABLE: Place the letter of the appropriate technique or concept in the space provided beneath the corresponding therapy. Boxes may contain more than one correct response.

Psychoanalysis	Client-Centered	Gestalt	Group Therapy	Behavioral Therapy	Cognitive Therapy
_____	_____	_____	_____	_____	_____
_____	_____	_____	_____	_____	_____
_____	_____	_____	_____	_____	_____
_____	_____	_____	_____	_____	_____

TECHNIQUES AND CONCEPTS

a. non-directive
b. psycho-drama
c. free association
d. time out

e. directive approach
f. aversion
g. unconditional positive regard
h. irrational beliefs

i. resistance
j. here and now
k. self-actualization
l. token economy

m. the "chair"
n. flooding
o. transference
p. sense of belonging

PREPARE A LECTURE: This activity is designed to offer you an opportunity to take advantage of a valuable mode of learning, elaborate rehearsal. Once you have finished the OMSE section, write a lecture using the instructional guide provided below. After your lecture is prepared, you can enhance your learning by writing a quiz covering the material. Now it is time to find some willing and inquisitive audience members. Your roommates or family may be a great place to start. Present the lecture as if you are teaching a class. Remember to ask for questions and quiz your students. This exercise can also serve to turn a *study-buddy* group into a very productive way to prepare for the test. Each member of the group can take different OMSE sections for their lecture/teacher role while the rest of the group serves as the class.

I. Key Terms, Names, Dates, and Concepts you will include in this lecture:

1. _____
2. _____
3. _____
4. _____

5. _____
6. _____
7. _____
8. _____

9. _____
10. _____
11. _____
12. _____

II. Learning Objectives (what do you want the student to know and be able to do as a result of your lecture):

1. _____
2. _____
3. _____
4. _____
5. _____

III. Lecture Notes (notes should be brief cues and serve as a guide).

Major topic #1: _____

  Sub-topics and notes: _____
_____
_____
_____

Major topic #2: _____

  Sub-topics and notes: _____
_____
_____
_____
_____

Major topic #3: _____

Sub-topics and notes: _____

_____

_____

_____

OMSE # 2: BIOLOGICAL THERAPIES AND CHOOSING A THERAPY/THERAPIST

LEARNING OBJECTIVES

1. What are the three main biological therapies?

2. How do antipsychotic drugs help schizophrenic patients?

3. For what conditions are antidepressants prescribed?

4. How does lithium help patients with bipolar disorder?

5. What are some of the problems with drug therapy?

6. For what purpose is electroconvulsive therapy (ECT) used, and what is its major side effect?

7. What is psychosurgery, and for what problems is it used?

8. What different types of mental health professionals conduct psychotherapy?

9. What therapy, if any, has proved to be the most effective in treating psychological disorders?

10. Why is it important to consider multicultural variables in the therapeutic setting?

LEARNING MASTERY SCORECARD: Update your score card as you work through the chapter. First, find and define key terms and concepts included in each section and note the page number(s) from the text that contain important references to the material. Next, gain a practical understanding of the concepts by considering the Laboratory to Life scenarios. Complete the *Objective-Mastery Self-Evaluation* (OMSE) exercises for this section and record your scores. Revisit the exercises, recording your score and the date completed until you have attained mastery (100%). Finally, prepare a lecture on each objective using the template provided, and practice presenting it. Keep an honest tally of your achievements and, when finished, you will have developed learning mastery.

Key Term	page #	Key Term	page #	Key Term	page #
biological therapy	_____	electroconvulsive therapy	_____	clinical psychologist	_____
antipsychotic drugs	_____	psychosurgery	_____	psychiatrist	_____
antidepressants	_____	lobotomy	_____	psychoanalyst	_____
lithium	_____				

Quick Quiz

Date	Score	Date	Score	Date	Score
__/__/__	_____	__/__/__	_____	__/__/__	_____
__/__/__	_____	__/__/__	_____	__/__/__	100%

Elaborate Rehearsal

Lecture Preparation	Completion Date
Key Terms, Persons, & Concepts	__/__/__
Learning Objectives	__/__/__
Lecture Notes	__/__/__

A. QUICK QUIZ

1. The class of drugs known as neuroleptics is mainly used to treat _____.
   a) mania
   b) schizophrenia
   c) anxiety
   d) depression

2. Elavil and Tofranil are examples of _____, and are used to treat _____.
   a) tricyclics; schizophrenia
   b) major tranquilizers; depression
   c) neuroleptics; schizophrenia
   d) tricyclics; depression

3. SSRIs and MAO Inhibitors are used mainly to treat _____.

4. Lithium is used to treat _____.
   a) anxiety
   b) bipolar disorder
   c) paraphilia
   d) schizophrenia

5. The minor tranquilizers are used mainly to treat the depression phase of bipolar disorder.
   a) True
   b) False

6. Prozac is an example of a(n) _____.
   a) SSRI
   b) minor tranquilizer
   c) MAO Inhibitor
   d) antipsychotic

7. Electroconvulsive therapy, although considered an extremely controversial method of therapy, may be the treatment of choice for _____.
   a) obsessive-compulsive disorder
   b) schizophrenia with paranoia
   c) suicidal depression
   d) extreme phobic anxiety

8. While it has never enjoyed a great deal of good public relations, ECT has returned as an important treatment tool in psychiatry.
   a) True
   b) False

9. Psychosurgery, while a dangerous and sometimes irresponsibly used procedure in the past, is now used almost as much as dangerous drugs such as the antipsychotics. This is due to the current use of laser technology and the ability to localize treatment to more precise brain areas.
   a) True
   b) False

10. If Hans Eysenck were to go for psychotherapy or psychological counseling, he would most likely prefer someone who:
    a) practiced Gestalt therapy
    b) practiced behavior modification
    c) practiced psychoanalysis
    d) practiced person-centered therapy

11. A _____ psychologist specializes in the assessment, treatment, and/or research of psychological problems and behavioral disturbances.

12. A clinical psychologist is to _____ as a psychiatrist is to _____.
    a) MD; Ph.D.
    b) Ph.D.; MD

13. Insight therapy seems best for problems such as _____.
    a) phobia and bad habits
    b) unhappiness and interpersonal problems
    c) sexual disorders
    d) schizophrenia

14. The text suggests that social phobia is best treated with _____.
    a) neuroleptics
    b) insight therapy
    c) psychoanalysis
    d) cognitive therapy

15. Which of the following biological treatments is used along with some types of therapy to treat obsessive-compulsive disorders?
    a) SSRIs
    b) MOA inhibitors
    c) ECT
    d) RET

B. COMPLETE THE TABLE: Record the classification and primary use of each listed drug in the space provided.

Drug Name	Classification	Primary Treatment Use
Thorazine		
Elavil		
Prozac		
Stelazine		
Valium		
Lithium		
Xanax		
Tofranil		

C. COMPLETE THE TABLE: Record the basic methods used by, and primary disorders treated by each of the major therapy approaches.

Therapy	Basic Methods	Used to Treat
Psychoanalysis		
Person-centered therapy		
Behavior therapy		
Cognitive therapy		
Biological therapy		

PREPARE A LECTURE: This activity is designed to offer you an opportunity to take advantage of a valuable mode of learning, elaborate rehearsal. Once you have finished the OMSE section, write a lecture using the instructional guide provided below. After your lecture is prepared, you can enhance your learning by writing a quiz covering the material. Now it is time to find some willing and inquisitive audience members. Your roommates or family may be a great place to start. Present the lecture as if you are teaching a class. Remember to ask for questions and quiz your students. This exercise can also serve to turn a *study-buddy* group into a very productive way to prepare for the test. Each member of the group can take different OMSE sections for their lecture/teacher role while the rest of the group serves as the class.

I. Key Terms, Names, Dates, and Concepts you will include in this lecture:

1. _____
2. _____
3. _____
4. _____

5. _____
6. _____
7. _____
8. _____

9. _____
10. _____
11. _____
12. _____

II. Learning Objectives (what do you want the student to know and be able to do as a result of your lecture?):

1. _____
2. _____
3. _____
4. _____
5. _____

III. Lecture Notes (notes should be brief cues and serve as a guide):

Major topic #1: _____

   Sub-topics and notes: _____
_____
_____
_____
_____

Major topic #2: _____

   Sub-topics and notes: _____
_____
_____
_____
_____

Major topic #3: _____

   Sub-topics and notes: _____
_____
_____
_____
_____

KEY TERMS AND CONCEPTS EXERCISE

The key terms and concepts are presented in order of their appearance in the text. Space is provided for you to include a personalized definition or example of each term or concept. As you encounter each term in the text, make a note of its meaning and context. Next, conceptualize the meaning of the term in a way that makes the most sense to you. Also, think about examples of the term from your own life. Write your definition and/or example in the space provided next to the word. The KEY TERMS exercise utilizes a modified *T-note* design so that you can self-evaluate your mastery of the definitions. First lay a sheet of paper over the terms and concepts side of the page so that you only see the definitions. Read the definition and try to recall the term or concept. Mark all those you are unable to answer so you can restudy them. When you have learned all of the terms and concepts in this way, move the paper to the definition side so that you can see only the term or concept, and try to recall both the textbook definition and your personal version. Repeat this until you know all of the terms by definition and personal understanding.

Psychotherapy	The treatment for psychological disorders that uses psychological rather than biological means and primarily involves conversations between patient and therapist. _____
Insight Therapy	Any type of psychotherapy based on the notion that psychological well-being depends on self-understanding. _____
Psychoanalysis	The psychotherapy that uses free association, dream analysis, and analysis of resistance to uncover repressed memories, impulses, and conflicts thought to cause psychological disorders. _____
Free Association	A psychoanalytic technique used to explore the unconscious by having patients reveal whatever thoughts or images come to mind. _____
Resistance	In psychoanalytic therapy, the patient's attempts to avoid expressing or revealing painful or embarrassing thoughts or feelings. _____
Transference	An intense emotional situation occurring in psychoanalysis, when one comes to behave toward the analyst as one had behaved toward a significant figure from the past. _____
Person-Centered Therapy	A nondirective, humanistic therapy in which the therapist creates a warm, accepting climate, freeing clients to be themselves and releasing their natural tendency toward positive growth. _____
Self-Actualization	Developing to one's fullest potential. _____
Nondirective Therapy	An approach in which the therapist acts to facilitate growth, giving understanding and support rather than proposing solutions, answering questions, or actively directing the course of therapy. _____
Gestalt Therapy	A therapy originated by Fritz Perls and emphasizing the importance of clients fully experiencing, in the present moment, their feelings, thoughts, and actions and taking responsibility for their behavior. _____
Directive Therapy	An approach to therapy in which the therapist takes an active role in determining the course of therapy sessions and provides answers and suggestions to the patient. _____

Interpersonal Therapy	A brief psychotherapy designed to help depressed people understand their problems in interpersonal relationships and develop effective ways to improve them. _____
Family Therapy	Therapy based on the assumption that an individual's problem is caused and/or maintained in part by problems within the family unit, and so the entire family is involved in therapy. _____
Group Therapy	A form of therapy in which several clients (usually 7 to 10) meet regularly with one or two therapists to resolve personal problems. _____
Psychodrama	A group therapy in which one group member acts out personal problem situations and relationships, assisted by other members, to gain insight into the problem. _____
Behavior Therapy	A treatment approach employing the principles of operant conditioning, classical conditioning, and/or observational learning theory to eliminate the inappropriate or maladaptive behaviors and replace them with more adaptive responses. _____
Behavior Modification	The systematic application of learning principles to help a person eliminate undesirable behaviors and/or acquire more adaptive behaviors; also called behavior therapy. _____
Token Economy	A behavior technique used to encourage desirable behaviors by reinforcing them with tokens that can be exchanged later for desired objects, activities, and/or privileges. _____
Time Out	A behavioral technique, used to decrease the frequency of undesirable behavior, that involves withdrawing an individual from all reinforcement for a period of time. _____
Stimulus Satiation	A behavioral technique in which a patient is given so much of a stimulus that it becomes something the patient wants to avoid. _____
Systematic Desensitization	A behavior therapy, used to treat phobias, that involves training clients in deep muscle relaxation and then having them confront a graduated series of anxiety producing situations (real or imagined) until they can remain relaxed while confronting even the most feared situation. _____
Flooding	A behavioral therapy used to treat phobias, during which clients are exposed to the feared object or event (or asked to imagine it vividly) for an extended period until their anxiety decreases. _____

Exposure And Response Prevention	A behavior therapy that exposes obsessive compulsive disorder patients to stimuli generating increasing anxiety; patients must agree not to carry out their normal rituals for a specified period of time after exposure. _____
Aversion Therapy	A behavior therapy in which an aversive stimulus is paired with an undesirable behavior until the behavior becomes associated with pain and discomfort. _____
Participant Modeling	A behavior therapy in which an appropriate response is modeled in graduated steps and the client attempts each step, encouraged and supported by the therapist. _____
Rational-Emotive Therapy	A directive, confrontational therapy designed to challenge and modify the irrational beliefs thought to cause personal distress; developed by Albert Ellis. _____
Automatic Thoughts	Unreasonable and unquestioned ideas that rule a person's life and lead to depression and anxiety. _____
Cognitive Therapy	Therapy designed to change maladaptive behavior by changing the person's irrational thoughts, beliefs, and ideas. _____
Biological Therapy	A therapy that is based on the assumption that most mental disorders have physical causes; treatments include drug therapy, ECT, and psychosurgery. _____
Antipsychotic Drugs	Drugs used to control severe psychotic symptoms, such as the delusions and hallucinations of schizophrenics; also known as neuroleptics or major tranquilizers. _____
Antidepressants	Drugs that are designed to treat depression and some anxiety disorders. _____
Lithium	A drug used in bipolar disorder to control the symptoms in a manic episode and to even out the mood swings and reduce recurrence of future manic or depressive states. _____
Electroconvulsive Therapy	A treatment in which an electric current is passed through the brain causing a seizure; usually reserved for the severely depressed who are either suicidal or unresponsive to other treatment. _____
Psychosurgery	Brain surgery to treat some severe, persistent, and debilitating psychological disorder or severe chronic pain. _____

Lobotomy	A psychosurgery technique in which the nerve fibers connecting the frontal lobes to the deeper brain are severed. _____ _____ _____
Clinical Psychologist	A psychologist, usually with a Ph.D., whose training is in the diagnosis, treatment, or research of psychological and behavior disorders. _____ _____ _____
Psychiatrist	A medical doctor with a specialty in the diagnosis and treatment of mental disorders. _____ _____
Psychoanalyst	A professional, usually a psychiatrist, with special training in psychoanalysis. _____ _____

FROM THE LABORATORY TO LIFE

Be an Intelligent Consumer

I often tell my students that the chances are good that, one way or another, each will become a consumer of mental health services some day. Unfortunately some will need these services for themselves. Others may need to make decisions about children or aging parents. Some may be in a position to assist employees or students. Being a consumer of mental health services need not be an embarrassment or involve feelings of shame. It is, however, an endeavor that should be understood and pursued with care. This exercise can help you become more aware of the issues and decisions that can help you become a beneficiary, not a victim, of the variety of mental health services available. Respond to each item and check your answers. Are you going to be an intelligent consumer?

1. A counselor is hosting a talk show on the radio and you call in with a question. You are on the phone with the counselor for one and a half minutes when he tells you that he understands your problem and then gives you advice to tell your mother about how mad you are at her. Should you run right over to mom's house and confront her?

   _____

2. You are feeling pretty bad lately. You are not sleeping or eating well and seem to always be sad. Even good news does not make you feel happy. You are beginning to wonder if you will ever start to feel good again. Your friend says that you are just in a rut and that you should start exercising—or something. Your friend also says that going to a counselor or psychologist will not help and that you will get in trouble at work for being crazy. Should you follow your friend's advice? _____

3. Your son has been acting up in school and you are advised by the school counselor to take him to your family doctor and get him on a medicine (Ritalin) for attention deficit disorder. Should you follow the school counselor's advice? _____

4. A psychiatrist tells you that the only real way to treat an emotional problem is through extensive psychotherapy and medicine. Is this advice necessarily correct? _____

5. You are trying to help your mother find a counselor. She is grieving your father's death. You accompany her to an appointment with a local therapist. The therapist advises you and your mother that her approach to dealing with grief is the best, and that type of approach is the most important factor in successful therapy. Is the therapist correct? _____

6. Your counselor suggests that, in addition to your sessions with him, you attend a local support group for people who suffer the problems you are currently experiencing. Is this good advice? _____

7. You have just been diagnosed with major depression and your psychiatrist is going to prescribe an antidepressant drug for your condition. When can you expect to start feeling better? _____

8. Do the initials behind a therapist's name really make a difference? _____

FROM THEORY TO PRACTICE

Turning Theory into Practice

Okay, you have studied and listened and taken notes—you have a mountain of theoretical knowledge taking up space in your brain and you are not even scheduled to be a participant on Jeopardy—so what are you going to do now? If you answered, "Go to Disneyland," you're wrong. If you answered, "I'm going to apply my theoretical knowledge in a way that will further my understanding of each psychological perspective," you're right. Below, you will notice that several disorders are listed. Your task is to consider the potential causes, conditions, and symptoms of each disorder and, based on your understanding of the various theories, determine which perspective might offer the most effective treatment possibilities. Of course, you may decide that certain therapies should be combined to offer the best hope for recovery—that is fine. Use your book, your notes, and, most importantly, your brain.

DISORDER	MAJOR CAUSES, CONDITIONS, AND/OR SYMPTOMS	PSYCHOLOGICAL PERSPECTIVE
Major Depression		
Schizophrenia		
Obsessive Compulsive Disorder		
Panic Disorder		
Bipolar Disorder		
Dissociative Fugue		
Antisocial Personality Disorder		

Based on this exercise, which theoretical perspective do you believe offers the greatest overall effectiveness? _____ Why? _____

_____

COMPREHENSIVE PRACTICE TEST

1. On your first visit to your new therapist, you are asked to reveal whatever thoughts, feelings, or images come to mind, no matter how trivial, embarrassing, or terrible they might seem. Your therapist is using a technique known as:
   a) analysis of resistance
   b) psychodrama
   c) free association
   d) stimulus satiation

2. When asked by your therapist to reveal your innermost feelings, you immediately begin to balk, trying all the while to avoid revealing certain embarrassing thoughts and feelings. Freud called this type of behavior:
   a) resistance
   b) flooding
   c) time out
   d) psychostalling

3. Which of the following is **NOT** considered an insight therapy?
   a) psychoanalysis
   b) Gestalt therapy
   c) rational-emotive therapy
   d) person-centered therapy

4. Your friend has been seeing a therapist for a few months when he tells you that he has strong feelings for his therapist because she reminds him of his late mother. He also tells you that he has been acting very affectionate toward his therapist like he wishes he had acted with his mother before she passed away. Your friend's reaction is called _____.

5. Traditional psychoanalysis can be a long and costly undertaking. Therefore, many psychoanalysts now practice a briefer form of therapy called _____.

6. Which of the following is **NOT** one of the three conditions that Carl Rogers believes are required of therapists?
   a) unconditional positive regard
   b) sympathy
   c) genuineness
   d) empathy

7. Person-centered therapy is most effective when the therapist proposes valuable solutions and offers solid advice while directing the therapeutic process.
   a) True
   b) False

8. In this directive form of therapy, the therapist prods and badgers clients to experience their feelings as deeply and genuinely as possible, and then to admit responsibility for them.
   a) behavioral
   b) psychodynamic
   c) rational-emotive
   d) Gestalt

9. Interpersonal therapy is designed to help patients cope with four types of problems commonly associated with depression. Which of the following is **NOT** one of the four types of problems?
   a) the misuse and abuse of controlled substances
   b) unusual or severe responses to the death of a loved one
   c) interpersonal role disputes
   d) deficits in interpersonal skills

10. In this therapy style, the therapist pays attention to the dynamics of the family unit.
    a) interpersonal therapy
    b) family therapy
    c) dynamic therapy
    d) unit analysis

11. The advantages of _____ therapy include the fact that it is usually less expensive, it gives the individual a sense of belonging, and it allows the individual to give and receive emotional support.

12. If you were having a relationship problem with your significant other, and your group therapist asked you to act out the problem, playing the role of your significant other, you would be using a technique called:
    a) group encounter
    b) couples therapy
    c) role reversal
    d) conjoint therapy

13. Which type of therapy seems to offer the most effective setting for treating adolescent drug abuse?
    a) family therapy
    b) Gestalt therapy
    c) person-centered
    d) behavioral therapy

14. This therapy involves the application of learning principles, like classical and operant conditioning, to eliminate inappropriate or maladaptive behaviors and replace them with more adaptive responses.
    a) Gestalt therapy
    b) behavior therapy
    c) psychodynamic therapy
    d) humanistic therapy

15. Your therapist, in trying to help you conquer your fear of heights, has taught you to use deep muscle relaxation and has asked you to prepare a hierarchy of anxiety-producing situations. What technique are you about to employ in attempting to conquer your phobia?
    a) flooding
    b) psychodrama
    c) systematic desensitization
    d) stimulus satiation

16. Your fear of heights is showing little improvement and your therapist takes you to the top floor of a tall building and asks you to look out the window toward the ground until she tells you that you have completed the assignment. What technique is she practicing?
    a) flooding
    b) psychodrama
    c) systematic desensitization
    d) stimulus satiation

17. This therapy emphasizes acceptance and unconditional positive regard:
    a) person-centered therapy
    b) cognitive therapy
    c) rational-emotive therapy
    d) psychodynamic therapy

18. About 10 sessions of this therapy over a 3 to 7 week period has been shown to be an effective treatment for patients suffering from obsessive compulsive disorder.
    a) client-centered therapy
    b) cognitive therapy
    c) rational-emotive therapy
    d) exposure and response prevention

19. Researchers have reported that *virtual reality* has been proven effective in treating spider phobias.
    a) True
    b) False

20. A technique based on Bandura's Social Learning Theory, observational learning, is:
    a) flooding
    b) participant modeling
    c) systematic desensitization
    d) implosive therapy

21. A type of therapy that assumes that maladaptive behavior results from irrational thoughts, beliefs, and ideas is combined with techniques such as relaxation training or exposure, resulting in a therapy called:
    a) cognitive-behavioral therapy
    b) behavior therapy
    c) psychodynamic therapy
    d) rational-exposure therapy

22. The premise of this therapy is that depression results from distorted thinking and the distortions tend to occur along three negative views—the future, the self and the world, or experience:
    a) client-centered therapy
    b) behavior therapy
    c) cognitive therapy
    d) gestalt therapy

23. Clinical psychologist, Albert Ellis, is credited for developing a therapy approach that challenges client's irrational beliefs about themselves and others. This therapy is known as:
    a) cognitive-behavior therapy
    b) progressive relaxation therapy
    c) nondirective therapy
    d) rational-emotive therapy

24. According to your text, rational-emotive therapy is based on a theory known as the ABC's of RET. What does the B stand for in ABC?
    a) behavior
    b) beliefs
    c) bereavement
    d) beauty

25. What does the C stand for in the ABC's of RET?
   a) consequences
   b) calibration
   c) conditioning
   d) collective unconscious

26. What does the A stand for in the ABC's of RET?
   a) acquired
   b) activating event
   c) accumulation
   d) attitude

27. Therapeutic groups where no professional leader is present & where participants share common concerns are called:
   a) existential groups
   b) group therapy
   c) T-groups
   d) self-help groups

28. The therapy style developed by Perls that focuses on the *here and now* is:
   a) Gestalt therapy
   b) existential therapy
   c) client-centered therapy
   d) psychodynamic therapy

29. Alcoholics are sometimes administered a drug, emetine, that produces nausea when mixed with alcohol in the client's bloodstream. This type of therapy is called:
   a) flooding
   b) implosive therapy
   c) aversion therapy
   d) ECT

30. This biomedical procedure helps reduce symptoms of severe depression by producing a seizure in the patient:
   a) psychosurgery
   b) prefrontal lobotomy
   c) electroconvulsive therapy
   d) chemotherapy

31. This type of biomedical procedure utilizes electrical current delivered through small electrodes to destroy a localized section of brain cells. While some proponents report that it has apparent benefits, it also has many detractors:
   a) psychosurgery
   b) prefrontal lobotomy
   c) electroconvulsive therapy
   d) chemotherapy

32. This group of drugs is used to treat disorders involving such symptoms as extreme hallucinations and delusions:
   a) antimania drugs
   b) antidepressant drugs
   c) antianxiety drugs
   d) antipsychotic drugs

33. This group of drugs includes tricyclics, MAO inhibitors, and SSRIs.
   a) antimania drugs
   b) antidepressant drugs
   c) antianxiety drugs
   d) antipsychotic drugs

34. The most severe side effect of typical antipsychotic drugs is:
   a) cramps
   b) muscle spasms
   c) tardive dyskinesia
   d) mania

35. About what percent of patients have a good response to standard neuroleptics?
   a) 25
   b) 75
   c) 50
   d) 82

36. One study of depression revealed that about 20% of individual differences in treatment outcomes were attributable to a close and positive relationship between therapist and patient.
   a) True
   b) False

37. In a major meta-analysis study, researchers concluded that people who received therapy were better off than those who did not.
   a) True
   b) False

ANSWER KEYS

ANSWER KEY: OMSE#1

A. Quick Quiz

1. psychological; biological
2. false
3. b
4. b
5. c
6. a
7. c
8. d
9. false
10. c
11. true
12. directive
13. interpersonal
14. b
15. c
16. psychodrama
17. c
18. d
19. a
20. d
21. true
22. b

B. Matching

1. e
2. h
3. a
4. g
5. c
6. d
7. f
8. b

C. Complete the Table

Psychoanalysis	Client-centered	Gestalt	Group	Behavioral	Cognitive
c, i, o	a, g, k	e, j, m	b, p	d, f, l, n	h

ANSWER KEY: OMSE#2

A. Quick Quiz

1. b
2. d
3. depression
4. b
5. false
6. a
7. c
8. true
9. false
10. b
11. clinical
12. b
13. b
14. d
15. a

B. Complete the Table

Drug Name	Classification	Primary Treatment Use
Thorazine	antipsychotic	schizophrenia
Elavil	tricyclic antidepressant	depression
Prozac	SSRI antidepressant	depression, obsessive-compulsive disorder
Stelazine	antipsychotic	schizophrenia
Valium	benzodiazepine	anxiety
Lithium	mood stabilizer	bipolar disorder
Xanax	benzodiazepine	anxiety, depression
Tofranil	tricyclic antidepressant	depression, generalized anxiety

Complete the Table

Type of Therapy	Basic Methods	Used to Treat
Psychoanalysis	interpret dreams, free association, resistance interpretation, transference	general feelings of unhappiness, unresolved problems from childhood
Person-centered therapy	empathy, unconditional positive regard, genuineness, reflection of feelings	general feelings of unhappiness, interpersonal problems
Behavior therapy	systematic desensitization, flooding, exposure and response prevention, aversion, reinforcement	fears, phobias, obsessive-compulsive disorder, bad habits
Cognitive therapy	identify irrational thoughts and negative thinking – replace with rational thinking	depression, anxiety, panic disorder, general feelings of unhappiness
Biological therapy	use of psychiatric drugs, ECT, psychosurgery	schizophrenia, depression, bipolar disorder, anxiety

ANSWER KEY: LAB TO LIFE

Be a Good Consumer

1.   No – the counselor has no idea of who you are, what your problem is, or what you need in just 90 seconds. Good counseling requires a thorough assessment and diagnosis in order to plan and carry out the treatment that will best fit your needs and help you solve your problem.

2.   No – your friend may have your best interest at heart, but if he or she is not a trained counselor, psychologist, or psychiatrist, you are not getting good advice. Some people do get in ruts that can be subdued through a change of activity, and exercise (for the individual who has been cleared by a physician) can be a great way to chase away the blues. But, you may also be suffering from a more serious problem—in this case, depression. If this is in fact the reason for your current problems, you need professional help. Also, getting this kind of help is not something to be ashamed of, and employers cannot base your employment on this. As a matter of fact, many employers now have programs to assist employees with these and other kinds of mental health problems.

3.   No – the counselor is not a doctor and cannot prescribe drugs. In addition, unless your family doctor specializes in childhood disorders, he or she would be well advised to make a referral to a psychiatrist or pediatrician that is specially trained in these matters. The use of drugs to treat behavioral problems in children can often lead to unnecessary complications in normal developmental processes, especially when they are used in response to an inaccurate diagnosis. At the same time, when a medicine is needed, refusal to take advantage of that treatment can be dangerous. Only a qualified doctor or psychiatrist can answer those questions for you.

4.   No, not necessarily – there are many modes of psychotherapy, counseling, and social-based support systems available and these are often effective in helping with life's trials and tribulations. Psychiatric-based psychotherapy and appropriate medicines are essential when the problem is one that has been shown to need this level of care. In that case, to not take advantage of this care could be dangerous. However, for the most part, psychiatric medicines do not cure the problems of life and there is really no one catchall therapeutic technique for all the ills of daily living. Each individual brings his or her own specific needs, strengths, and weaknesses, and each will need a therapeutic approach tailored to his or her specific case. Also, certain kinds of help, especially when not necessary, can be very expensive. The best advice in this situation is, "Get a second opinion."

5.   No – a good therapist would not say this to a client. First of all, research has been pretty consistent with the finding that the most important factor that predicts outcome is the quality of the relationship between the therapist and the client. Also, a good therapist will talk to you about their recommended approach, as well as possible alternatives. Remember, there is no such thing as a "one-size-fits-all" therapy, and each client needs an approach tailored to his or her specific case.

6.   Yes – group therapy and even nonprofessional social support groups such as Alcoholics Anonymous can be very helpful in many ways. Through the group process the client or participant can learn more about the particular problem

and discover that he or she is not alone. Other possible benefits include learning social skills, giving and receiving empathy-based support, and the instillation of hope as one sees others finding solutions to their own problems.

7.   Most antidepressant medications take at least a few weeks to have a significant beneficial effect. That is, if you are on the medication that will help you in the first place. Sometimes you will need to try several different kinds of medications or different doses before you and your doctor agree on the one that is right for you. This can be a frustrating time. You go to the doctor for relief and want that relief now – especially when you are seeking relief from the symptoms of a major psychological problem such as depression. You should talk with your doctor about the medication and what to expect in terms of effects. If you are feeling so bad that you believe you can no longer stand it, your doctor should know this and prescribe other supportive measures. In addition, many psychiatric medications have side effects that can range from mild irritations in life to dangerous interactions with other medicines or even certain foods. Make sure and learn about your medication and follow your doctor's orders.

8.   Yes – the initials can mean a lot. For one thing, only an M.D. can prescribe medications for you. Also, different initials can indicate different areas and levels of expertise. You would probably not feel comfortable buying a can of vegetables from the store without a label and some knowledge of the contents. You should use the same prudence when selecting a therapist or counselor. You have a right to ask questions and a good therapist or counselor will be glad to help you understand his or her areas and level of expertise. In addition, a good counselor knows when he or she is not qualified and will take steps to help you get to the person who can and should be treating you for your problem.

ANSWER KEY: COMPREHENSIVE PRACTICE TEST

1. c	11. group	20. b	29. c
2. a	12. c	21. a	30. c
3. c	13. a	22. c	31. a
4. transference	14. b	23. d	32. d
5. psychodrama	15. c	24. b	33. b
6. b	16. a	25. d	34. c
7. false	17. a	26. b	35. c
8. d	18. d	27. d	36. true
9. a	19. true	28. a	37. true
10. b			

17

SOCIAL PSYCHOLOGY

The tendency of the causal mind is to pick out or stumble upon a sample, which supports or defies its prejudices, and then to make it the representative of a whole class.

–Walter Lippmann, 1929

CHAPTER OVERVIEW

Social psychology is a fascinating sub-topic in psychology for several reasons. First, social psychology covers many of the issues and concepts explored in previous chapters, and integrates them in a way that allows for a better understanding and appreciation of human interaction and reciprocal behavioral influences. Social psychology introduces theories that attempt to explain how and why people behave in certain ways with certain people. So much of one's personal experience of the world and how he or she views that world and oneself is shaped by these interactions. We not only thrive on social contact, but also need this contact—we are a social animal. Additionally, social psychology has spawned some of the most interesting and clever research in the field. Milgram's study on obedience and Asch's research on conformity include just a few of the many fascinating methods used to shed light on the often surprising and sometimes less than complimentary ways we behave in social decision-making situations. In a way, we are each members of an ongoing experiment in social psychology. That experiment is life—living life each day as we interact with, influence and are influenced by the behaviors, attitudes, and decisions of others and ourselves. A third reason for the attraction of social psychology is that knowledge gained from this field of endeavor has served to have a direct beneficial impact on so many important social and interpersonal issues affecting people's daily lives. As we learn the ways and means of prejudice, aggression, helping behaviors, and social decision making, our discoveries can have important implications for social policy and interventions that can benefit all people.

This chapter will help you gain a more practiced and functional understanding of this interesting field of psychology and social behavior. The materials are divided into two OMSE sections: 1) social perception through group influence, and 2) attitudes and attitude change through aggression. You will examine the often-surprising ways our individual behavior can become a part of a much larger social dynamic. You will also gain an appreciation of the importance of research in psychology and how this research can have practical implications for daily life.

By completing the exercises provided, you should gain a thorough understanding of the information provided in your text. In other words, you should be better prepared for tests, quizzes, class participation, and life itself.

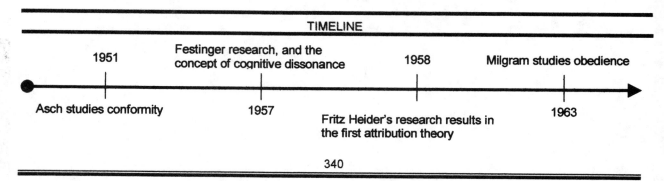

TIMELINE

1951 — Asch studies conformity

Festinger research, and the concept of cognitive dissonance — 1957

1958

Fritz Heider's research results in the first attribution theory

Milgram studies obedience — 1963

CHAPTER OUTLINE

Introduction to Social Psychology

Social Perception

Impression Formation: Sizing Up the Other Person

Attribution: Our Explanation of Behavior

Attraction

Factors Influencing Attraction: Magnets That Draw Us Together

Romantic Attraction

Mate Selection: The Mating Game

Conformity, Obedience, and Compliance

Conformity: Going Along with the Group

Obedience: Following Orders

Compliance: Giving In to Requests

Group Influence

The Effects of the Group on Individual Performance

The Effects of the Group on Decision Making

Social Roles

Attitudes and Attitude Change

Attitudes: Cognitive, Behavioral, and Emotional Patterns

Persuasion: Trying to Change Attitudes

Prejudice and Discrimination

The Roots of Prejudice and Discrimination

Discrimination in the Workplace

Combating Prejudice and Discrimination

Prejudice: Is It Increasing or Decreasing?

Prosocial Behavior: Behavior That Benefits Others

The Bystander Effect: The More Bystanders, the Less Likely They Are to Help

People Who Help in Emergencies

Aggression: Intentionally Harming Others

Biological Factors in Aggression: Genes, Hormones, and Brain Damage

Aggression in Response to Frustration: Sometimes, but Not Always

Aggression in Response to Aversive Events: Pain, Heat, Noise, and Crowding

The Social Learning Theory of Aggression: Learning to Be Aggressive

Apply It! Nonverbal Behavior—The Silent Language

Thinking Critically

Chapter Summary and Review

KEY TERMS

Introduction to Social Psychology

social psychology

confederate

naïve subject

Social Perception

primacy effect

attribution

situational attribution

dispositional attribution

fundamental attribution error

self-serving bias

Attraction

proximity

mere-exposure effect

halo effect

matching hypothesis

Conformity, Obedience, and Compliance

conformity

norms

compliance

foot-in-the-door technique

door-in-the-face technique

low-ball technique

Group Influence

social facilitation

audience effects

coaction effects

social loafing

group polarization

groupthink

social roles

Attitudes and Attitude Change

attitude

cognitive dissonance

persuasion

Prejudice and Discrimination

prejudice

discrimination

realistic conflict theory

in-group

out-group

social cognition

stereotypes

contact hypothesis

Prosocial Behavior: Behavior That Benefits Others

bystander effect

diffusion of responsibility

prosocial behavior

altruism

Aggression: Intentionally Harming Others

aggression

frustration

frustration-aggression hypothesis

scapegoating

personal space

density

crowding

FIRST IMPRESSIONS COUNT! Before you head out for that big job interview, lose the flannel shirt with the torn elbow, and the baggy jeans that open just enough to show your left kneecap. Get out your best business suit or outfit and polish your shoes. Smile and offer a firm handshake. You only get one chance to make a first impression. Make it your best impression.

OMSE # 1: SOCIAL PERCEPTION through GROUP INFLUENCE

LEARNING OBJECTIVES

1. Why are first impressions so important and enduring?

2. What is the difference between a situational attribution and a dispositional attribution for a specific behavior?

3. How do the kinds of attributions we tend to make about ourselves differ from those we make about other people?

4. Why is proximity an important factor in attraction?

5. How important is physical attractiveness in attraction?

6. Are people, as a rule, more attracted to those who are opposite or to those who are similar to them?

7. What did Asch find in his famous experiment on conformity?

8. What did Milgram find in his famous study of obedience?

9. What are three techniques used to gain compliance?

10. Under what conditions does social facilitation have either a positive or a negative effect on performance?

11. What is social loafing, and what factors lessen or eliminate it?

12. How are the initial attitudes of group members likely to affect group decision making?

LEARNING MASTERY SCORECARD: Update your score card as you work through the chapter. First, find and define key terms and concepts included in each section and note the page number(s) from the text that contain important references to the material. Next, gain a practical understanding of the concepts by considering the Laboratory to Life scenarios. Complete the *Objective-Mastery Self-Evaluation* (OMSE) exercises for this section and record your scores. Revisit the exercises, recording your score and the date completed until you have attained mastery (100%). Finally, prepare a lecture on each objective using the template provided, and practice presenting it. Keep an honest tally of your achievements and, when finished, you will have developed learning mastery.

Key Term	page #	Key Term	page #	Key Term	page #
social psychology	___	proximity	___	low-ball technique	___
confederate	___	mere-exposure effect	___	social facilitation	___
naïve subject	___	halo effect	___	audience effects	___
primacy effect	___	matching hypothesis	___	coaction effects	___
attribution	___	conformity	___	social loafing	___
situational attribution	___	norms	___	group polarization	___
dispositional attribution	___	compliance	___	groupthink	___
fundamental attribution error	___	foot-in-the-door technique	___	social roles	___
self-serving bias	___	door-in-the-face technique	___		

Quick Quiz

Date	Score	Date	Score	Date	Score
__/__/__	___	__/__/__	___	__/__/__	___
__/__/__	___	__/__/__	___	__/__/__	100%

Elaborate Rehearsal

Lecture Preparation	Completion Date
Key Terms, Persons, & Concepts	__/__/__
Learning Objectives	__/__/__
Lecture Notes	__/__/__

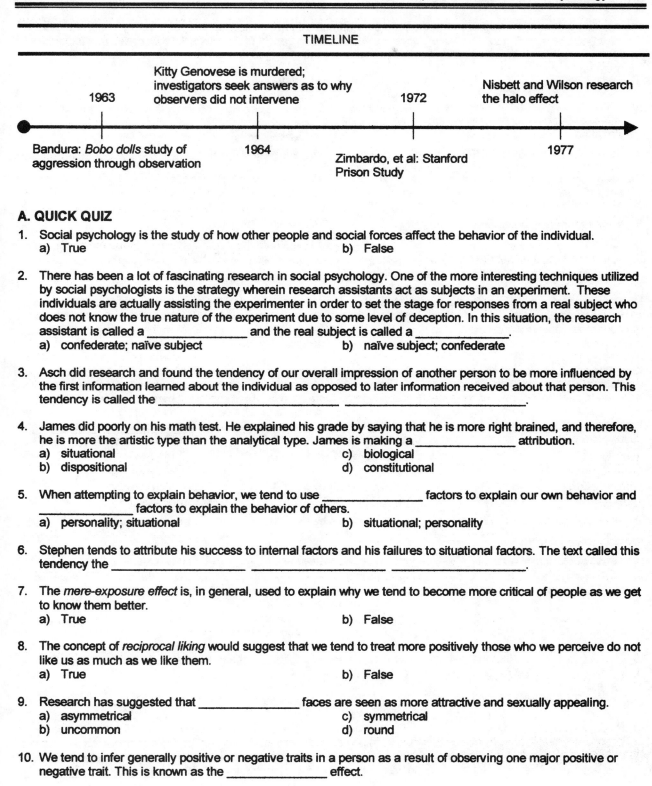

TIMELINE

1963

Kitty Genovese is murdered;
investigators seek answers as to why
observers did not intervene

1972

Nisbett and Wilson research
the halo effect

Bandura: *Bobo dolls* study of
aggression through observation

1964

Zimbardo, et al: Stanford
Prison Study

1977

A. QUICK QUIZ

1. Social psychology is the study of how other people and social forces affect the behavior of the individual.
    a) True
    b) False

2. There has been a lot of fascinating research in social psychology. One of the more interesting techniques utilized by social psychologists is the strategy wherein research assistants act as subjects in an experiment. These individuals are actually assisting the experimenter in order to set the stage for responses from a real subject who does not know the true nature of the experiment due to some level of deception. In this situation, the research assistant is called a _____ and the real subject is called a _____.
    a) confederate; naïve subject
    b) naïve subject; confederate

3. Asch did research and found the tendency of our overall impression of another person to be more influenced by the first information learned about the individual as opposed to later information received about that person. This tendency is called the _____ _____.

4. James did poorly on his math test. He explained his grade by saying that he is more right brained, and therefore, he is more the artistic type than the analytical type. James is making a _____ attribution.
    a) situational
    b) dispositional
    c) biological
    d) constitutional

5. When attempting to explain behavior, we tend to use _____ factors to explain our own behavior and _____ factors to explain the behavior of others.
    a) personality; situational
    b) situational; personality

6. Stephen tends to attribute his success to internal factors and his failures to situational factors. The text called this tendency the _____ _____ _____.

7. The *mere-exposure effect* is, in general, used to explain why we tend to become more critical of people as we get to know them better.
    a) True
    b) False

8. The concept of *reciprocal liking* would suggest that we tend to treat more positively those who we perceive do not like us as much as we like them.
    a) True
    b) False

9. Research has suggested that _____ faces are seen as more attractive and sexually appealing.
    a) asymmetrical
    b) uncommon
    c) symmetrical
    d) round

10. We tend to infer generally positive or negative traits in a person as a result of observing one major positive or negative trait. This is known as the _____ effect.

11. Whether we like to admit it or not, being physically attractive in this society appears to offer many advantages over being less attractive. This finding seems to hold true in a variety of situations for both males and females. Attractive babies even seem to enjoy an advantage over those judged less attractive—even with their own mothers.
    a) True
    b) False

12. Which of the following was **NOT** listed as one of the top four values cited by both men and women, across cultures, as among the most important values in selecting a mate?
    a) dependable character
    b) emotional stability and maturity
    c) seriousness
    d) pleasing disposition

13. Asch conducted a classic experiment on conformity. In this classic study he found that _____ of the subjects were not swayed by confederate assertions of a wrong answer.
    a) 50 percent
    b) 15 percent
    c) 75 percent
    d) 25 percent

14. Another classic study in social psychology is Milgram's research on _____. In this experiment it was found that most of the subjects (26 of 40) were willing to deliver the strongest possible shock to a confederate for giving wrong answers in a memory test.

15. Paul, a naïve subject in a variation of the study described above, tended not to comply with the order to provide stronger shocks when he was accompanied by others that also refused to comply. Was Paul's behavior consistent with similar studies?
    a) Yes
    b) No

16. While opening her mail one afternoon, Jan discovered an exciting announcement. She was about to win a million dollars. All she had to do was complete the contest form and send it in by the deadline date. In addition to the contest announcement, the letter told her about some fantastic deals on items the company was selling. The first thing she had to do was paste her address label on the contest form. The second thing she had to do was simply paste a picture of her favorite car on the contest form. As this continued she discovered an instruction to paste pictures of the products she would purchase from the company on the contest form. The company hoped that as Jan complied with the early, simple instructions, she would go ahead and order their products. This is an example of the _____ technique.
    a) door-in-the-face
    b) foot-in-the-door
    c) low-ball
    d) big-promise

17. Our individual performance may be affected sometimes by the mere physical presence of others. The text called this _____ _____.

18. Tim works in a grocery store. Sometimes he works by himself, stacking cans in an isle, while other times, he works alongside fellow employees who are performing the same job in the same area of the store. He has noticed that he seems to work harder when he is with others than when he is alone. The text called this the _____ effect.
    a) audience
    b) halo
    c) coaction
    d) convergence

19. Group polarization refers to the tendency of group members, following group discussion, to take a more _____ position on the issue at hand.
    a) extreme
    b) reaction based
    c) conservative
    d) rational

20. Hank is a member of a local community charity organization. The group is very close knit and such cohesion is important if the group is to remain effective in its goals. One night Hank was very concerned about the direction of a decision on allocating funds. He decided to go along with the popular opinion even though he had reservations. The book would say that Hank's decision was the result of the phenomenon called _____ _____.

B. Matching: Place the appropriate letter in the space provided.

_____	1.	acting according to the suggestion or request of others	a.	primacy effect
_____	2.	impact of passive spectators on performance	b.	attribution
_____	3.	effect of one major positive or negative trait	c.	proximity
_____	4.	equivalents attract	d.	mere-exposure effect
_____	5.	go with the group even though really disagree	e.	halo effect
_____	6.	large request may result in "yes" to small request	f.	matching hypothesis
_____	7.	cause of another's behavior	g.	conformity
_____	8.	repeated exposure results in positive evaluation	h.	norm
_____	9.	less effort when with others	i.	compliance
_____	10.	change attitude to be consistent with the group	j.	foot-in-the-door
_____	11.	small request leads to larger request	k.	door-in-the-face
_____	12.	geographic closeness	l.	audience effects
_____	13.	attitudes and standards of a group	m.	social loafing
_____	14.	overall impression influenced by first impression	n.	group think

C. COMPLETE THE TABLE: Describe the following major studies in social psychology:

1. Asch's study on First Impressions:

   Brief Description: _____

   _____

   _____

   _____

   Findings: _____

   _____

2. Asch's study on Conformity

   Brief Description: _____

   _____

   _____

   _____

   Findings: _____

   _____

3. Milgram's study on Obedience:

   Brief Description: _____

   _____

   _____

   _____

   Findings: _____

   _____

PREPARE A LECTURE: This activity is designed to offer you an opportunity to take advantage of a valuable mode of learning, elaborate rehearsal. Once you have finished the OMSE section, write a lecture using the instructional guide provided below. After your lecture is prepared, you can enhance your learning by writing a quiz covering the material. Now it is time to find some willing and inquisitive audience members. Your roommates or family may be a great place to start. Present the lecture as if you are teaching a class. Remember to ask for questions and quiz your students. This exercise can also serve to turn a *study-buddy* group into a very productive way to prepare for the test. Each member of the group can take different OMSE sections for their lecture/teacher role while the rest of the group serves as the class.

I. Key Terms, Names, Dates, and Concepts you will include in this lecture:

1. _____   5. _____   9. _____
2. _____   6. _____   10. _____
3. _____   7. _____   11. _____
4. _____   8. _____   12. _____

II. Learning Objectives (what do you want the student to know and be able to do as a result of your lecture):

1. _____
2. _____
3. _____
4. _____
5. _____

III. Lecture Notes (notes should be brief cues and serve as a guide).

Major topic #1: _____
    Sub-topics and notes: _____
    _____
    _____
    _____

Major topic #2: _____
    Sub-topics and notes: _____
    _____
    _____
    _____

Major topic #3: _____
    Sub-topics and notes: _____
    _____
    _____
    _____

Why are some people more aggressive than others? You've read all the theories and considered the possibilities, but maybe the best way to figure out what you believe to be the source of aggression is to look at your own aggressive tendencies and those of others you know. When are you most aggressive? What seems to trigger aggression in you? Do you react more aggressively behind the wheel of your car than at other times? Try a little experiment—the next time you begin to feel aggressive, stop and consider all the possible sources and triggers of your aggression. Can you change your attitude and/or mood? You might be able to—but you'll never know if you don't try. Being in control of your emotions is much cooler than letting your emotions control you.

OMSE # 2: ATTITUDES AND ATTITUDE CHANGE through AGGRESSION

LEARNING OBJECTIVES

1. What are the three components of an attitude?
2. What is cognitive dissonance, and how can it be resolved?
3. What are the four elements in persuasion?
4. What qualities make a source most persuasive?
5. What is the difference between prejudice and discrimination?
6. What is meant by the terms in-group and out-group?
7. How does prejudice develop, according to the social learning theory?
8. What are stereotypes?
9. What are several strategies for reducing prejudice and discrimination?
10. What is the bystander effect, and what factors have been suggested to explain why it occurs?
11. What biological factors are thought to be related to aggression?
12. What is the frustration-aggression hypothesis?
13. What kinds of aversive events and unpleasant emotions have been related to aggression?
14. What is the difference between density and crowding?
15. What are some psychological effects of crowding on humans?
16. According to social learning theory, what causes aggressive behavior?

LEARNING MASTERY SCORECARD:

Update your score card as you work through the chapter. First, find and define key terms and concepts included in each section and note the page number(s) from the text that contain important references to the material. Next, gain a practical understanding of the concepts by considering the Laboratory to Life scenarios. Complete the *Objective-Mastery Self-Evaluation* (OMSE) exercises for this section and record your scores. Revisit the exercises, recording your score and the date completed until you have attained mastery (100%). Finally, prepare a lecture on each objective using the template provided, and practice presenting it. Keep an honest tally of your achievements and, when finished, you will have developed learning mastery.

Key Term	page #	Key Term	page #	Key Term	page #
attitude	____	social cognition	____	aggression	____
cognitive dissonance	____	stereotypes	____	frustration	____
persuasion	____	contact hypothesis	____	frustration-aggression hypothesis	____
prejudice	____	bystander effect	____	scapegoating	____
discrimination	____	diffusion of responsibility	____	personal space	____
realistic conflict theory	____	prosocial behavior	____	density	____
in-group	____	altruism	____	crowding	____
out-group	____				

Quick Quiz

Date	Score	Date	Score	Date	Score
_/_/_	____	_/_/_	____	_/_/_	____
_/_/_	____	_/_/_	____	_/_/_	100%

Elaborate Rehearsal

Lecture Preparation	Completion Date
Key Terms, Persons, & Concepts	_/_/_
Learning Objectives	_/_/_
Lecture Notes	_/_/_

A. QUICK QUIZ

1. A(n) _____ is a relatively stable evaluation of a person, object, situation, or issue.

2. Jack has been wrestling with a dilemma—should he choose the blue car or the red car? He really loves them both. The red car has an automatic transmission and it is sportier than the blue car. Jack wants a sporty car with an automatic transmission. The blue car is not as sporty, and it has a manual transmission, but it is $3000.00 cheaper which puts it right in his price range. Also, the blue car has a sunroof and he really likes that. The text would say that Jack's dilemma over which car to purchase is an example of cognitive _____.
   a) evaluation
   b) restructuring
   c) dissonance
   d) accommodation

3. Which of the following was **NOT** identified as an element in persuasion?
   a) the source
   b) the authority
   c) the audience
   d) the message

4. Prejudice is to _____ as discrimination is to _____.
   a) a race; an individual
   b) a behavior; an attitude
   c) an attitude; a behavior
   d) an individual; a race

5. U.S. history books tell of increasing anti-immigrant prejudice in the 19th Century. The root of this sentiment was often based on the concern of Americans that the new immigrants would create undue competition for the limited jobs and other resources available in the country. The text would say that this prejudice is explained by the _____ _____ theory.

6. In the Sherif and Sherif experiment, while the "in-group – out-group" distinction did create a hostile relationship between the Rattlers and the Eagles, the establishment of social opportunities such as eating together and watching movies together seemed to settle the differences.
   a) True
   b) False

7. A child who grows up in a home that holds strong, negative opinions about members of another race will likely take on those same negative attitudes, especially if the child is reinforced for demonstrating these attitudes. This sounds like an assertion that would come from the _____ _____ theory of prejudice.

8. Social cognition refers to the way we typically process social information. This would include the processes we use to notice, interpret, and remember information about our social world.
   a) True
   b) False

9. A(n) _____ is a widely shared belief about the characteristics of members of various social groups and includes the assumption that all members of a social group are alike.

10. One approach, the _____ hypothesis, suggests that we can reduce prejudice and stereotypical thinking by increasing our contact and interaction with people from other groups.
   a) interaction
   b) contact
   c) out-group-in
   d) in-group-out

11. As the number of bystanders at an emergency increases, the probability of anyone helping a victim will decrease. This phenomenon is known as the _____ effect.
   a) bystander
   b) diffusion
   c) group apathy
   d) non-compliance to need

12. Ellen spends a lot of time engaging in behaviors that benefits others, such as offering help, cooperation, and sympathy. The text would say that Ellen engages in a lot of prosocial behavior.
   a) True
   b) False

13. Research has suggested that children can respond sympathetically to the distress of others, at least by their _____ birthday.
   a) third
   b) second
   c) fourth
   d) fifth

14. Jim jumped in front of the car in an attempt to save a child from being run over. While the child was saved, Jim suffered serious injury. Even though he was laid up in the hospital, Jim was glad that he was able to save the child. This would be identified in the text as an example of _____.

15. One of the earliest explanations for aggression was the _____ theory. Many current psychologists reject this theory but do suggest that biological factors can play a role in aggression.
   a) prosocial
   b) biosociological
   c) modeling
   d) instinct

16. The _____ - _____ hypothesis suggests that frustration can result in aggression.

17. Scapegoating occurs when a person is the victim of _____ aggression from another who is experiencing frustration, even though the victim is not responsible for the frustration.

18. Which of the following is a leading advocate of the social-learning theory of aggression?
   a) Festinger
   b) Milgram
   c) Sherif
   d) Bandura

B. MATCHING: Place the appropriate letter in the space provided.

_____ 1. relatively stable evaluation of a person, issue, etc.

_____ 2. state that can result from inconsistencies between one's attitudes

_____ 3. deliberate attempt to influence another's attitude or behavior

_____ 4. involves beliefs and emotions that can become hatred

_____ 5. actions toward any group based on a particular factor (e.g., race, sex, age)

_____ 6. a tight social group from which others are excluded

_____ 7. widely shared beliefs about traits of members of certain groups

_____ 8. reduction of prejudice through greater interaction among different groups

_____ 9. as more viewers gather, a victim's chances of help are reduced

_____ 10. behavior that benefits others

_____ 11. the intentional infliction of harm on another

_____ 12. the blocking of an impulse

_____ 13. displacing aggression onto innocent targets

_____ 14. number of people occupying a unit of space

_____ 15. subjective perception of too many people in one area

a. persuasion
b. crowding
c. bystander effect
d. frustration
e. attitude
f. density
g. contact hypothesis
h. cognitive dissonance
i. stereotypes
j. scapegoating
k. in-group
l. prejudice
m. discrimination
n. aggression
o. prosocial behavior

Is it getting a little crowded around you? Are you feeling a bit more stressed than usual. Be careful—crowding has been found to lead to increased aggression in some people. Try getting away from the crowds once in a while. Vacate your cramped lifestyle for a day at the beach or the park. Since crowding leads to stress, you may find that the lack of crowding leads to relaxation. Besides, you've probably earned a break.

C. Complete the Figure: Complete the figure on the three components of an attitude by 1) identifying a person, object, situation, or issue that is important to you, 2) writing in each of the three components of an attitude in the spaces provided, and 3) citing personal examples of each component in terms of how you would express your attitude.

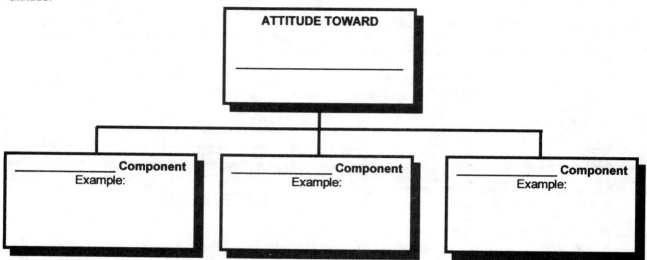

PREPARE A LECTURE: This activity is designed to offer you an opportunity to take advantage of a valuable mode of learning, elaborate rehearsal. Once you have finished the OMSE section, write a lecture using the instructional guide provided below. After your lecture is prepared, you can enhance your learning by writing a quiz covering the material. Now it is time to find some willing and inquisitive audience members. Your roommates or family may be a great place to start. Present the lecture as if you are teaching a class. Remember to ask for questions and quiz your students. This exercise can also serve to turn a *study-buddy* group into a very productive way to prepare for the test. Each member of the group can take different OMSE sections for their lecture/teacher role while the rest of the group serves as the class.

I. Key Terms, Names, Dates, and Concepts you will include in this lecture:

1. _____   5. _____   9. _____
2. _____   6. _____   10. _____
3. _____   7. _____   11. _____
4. _____   8. _____   12. _____

II. Learning Objectives (what do you want the student to know and be able to do as a result of your lecture?):

1. _____
2. _____
3. _____
4. _____
5. _____

III. Lecture Notes (notes should be brief cues and serve as a guide):

Major topic #1: _____
    Sub-topics and notes: _____
_____
_____
_____

Major topic #2: _____
   Sub-topics and notes: _____
_____
_____
_____

Major topic #3: _____
   Sub-topics and notes: _____
_____
_____
_____

KEY TERMS AND CONCEPTS EXERCISE

The key terms and concepts are presented in order of their appearance in the text. Space is provided for you to include a personalized definition or example of each term or concept. As you encounter each term in the text, make a note of its meaning and context. Next, conceptualize the meaning of the term in a way that makes the most sense to you. Also, think about examples of the term from your own life. Write your definition and/or example in the space provided next to the word. The KEY TERMS exercise utilizes a modified *T-note* design so that you can self-evaluate your mastery of the definitions. First lay a sheet of paper over the terms and concepts side of the page so that you only see the definitions. Read the definition and try to recall the term or concept. Mark all those you are unable to answer so you can restudy them. When you have learned all of the terms and concepts in this way, move the paper to the definition side so that you can see only the term or concept, and try to recall both the textbook definition and your personal version. Repeat this until you know all of the terms by definition and personal understanding.

Social Psychology	The study of how the actual, imagined, or implied presence of others influences the thoughts, the feelings, and the behavior of individuals. _____ _____
Confederate	Someone posing as a subject in an experiment but who is actually assisting the experimenter. _____ _____
Naïve Subject	A subject who has agreed to participate in an experiment but is not aware that deception is being used to conceal its real purpose. _____ _____
Primacy Effect	The tendency for an overall impression of another to be influenced more by the first information that is received about that person than by information that comes later. _____ _____ _____
Attribution	An inference about the cause of our own or another's behavior. _____ _____
Situational Attribution	Attribution of a behavior to some external cause or factor operating in the situation; an external attribution. _____ _____

Dispositional Attribution	Attribution of one's own or another's behavior to some internal cause such as a personal trait, motive, or attitude; an internal attribution.
Fundamental Attribution Error	The tendency to overemphasize internal causes and underemphasize situational factors when explaining the behavior of others.
Self-Serving Bias	Our tendency to attribute our successes to dispositional causes, and our failures to situational causes.
Proximity	Geographic closeness; a major factor in attraction.
Mere-Exposure Effect	The tendency of people to develop a more positive evaluation of some person, object, or other stimulus with repeated exposure to it.
Halo Effect	The tendency to infer generally positive or negative traits in a person as a result of observing one major positive or negative trait.
Matching Hypothesis	The notion that people tend to have spouses, lovers, or friends who are approximately equivalent in social assets such as physical attractiveness.
Conformity	Changing or adopting an attitude or behavior to be consistent with the norms of a group or the expectations of others.
Norms	The attitudes and standards of behavior expected of members of a particular group.
Compliance	Acting in accordance with the wishes, the suggestions, or the direct request of another person.
Foot-In-The-Door Technique	A strategy designed to secure a favorable response to a small request at first, with the aim of making the subject more likely to agree later to a larger request.
Door-In-The-Face Technique	A strategy in which someone makes a large, unreasonable request with the expectation that the person will refuse but will then be more likely to respond favorably to a smaller request at a later time.

Low-Ball Technique	A strategy to gain compliance by making a very attractive initial offer to get a person to agree to an action and then making the terms less favorable. _____ _____
Social Facilitation	Any positive or negative effect on performance due to the presence of others, either as an audience or as co-actors. _____ _____
Audience Effects	The impact of passive spectators on performance. _____ _____
Coaction Effects	The impact on performance caused by the presence of others engaged in the same task. _____ _____
Social Loafing	The tendency to put forth less effort when working with others on a common task than when working alone. _____ _____
Group Polarization	The tendency of members of a group, after group discussion, to shift toward a more extreme position in whatever direction they were leaning initially—either more risky or more cautious. _____ _____
Groupthink	The tendency for members of a very cohesive group to feel such pressure to maintain group solidarity and to reach agreement on an issue that they fail adequately to weigh evidence or to consider objections and alternatives. _____ _____
Social Roles	Socially defined behaviors considered appropriate for individuals occupying certain positions within the group. _____ _____
Attitude	A relatively stable evaluation of a person, object, situation, or issue. _____ _____
Cognitive Dissonance	The unpleasant state that can occur when people become aware of inconsistencies between their attitudes or between their attitudes and behavior. _____ _____
Persuasion	A deliberate attempt to influence the attitudes and/or behavior of another. _____ _____
Prejudice	Negative attitudes toward others based on their gender, religion, race, or membership in a particular group. _____ _____

Discrimination	Behavior, usually negative, directed toward others based on their gender, religion, race, or membership in a particular group. _____
Realistic Conflict Theory	The notion that prejudices arise when social groups must compete for scarce resources and opportunities. _____
In-Group	A social group with a strong sense of togetherness and from which others are excluded. _____
Out-Group	A social group specifically identified by the in-group as not belonging. _____
Social Cognition	Mental processes that people use to notice, interpret, understand, remember, and apply information about the social world and that enable them to simplify, categorize, and order their world. _____
Stereotypes	Widely shared beliefs about the characteristics, traits, attitudes, and behaviors of members of various social groups (racial, ethnic, religious) and including the assumption that they are usually all alike. _____
Contact Hypothesis	The notion that prejudice can be reduced through increased contact among members of different social groups. _____
Bystander Effect	The fact that as a number of bystanders at an emergency increases, the probability that the victim will receive help decreases, and help, if given, is likely to be delayed. _____
Diffusion Of Responsibility	The feeling among bystanders at an emergency that the responsibility for helping is shared by the group, so each person feels less compelled to act than if he or she alone bore the total responsibility. _____
Prosocial Behavior	Behavior that benefits others, such as helping, cooperation, and sympathy. _____
Altruism	Behavior aimed at helping another, requiring some self-sacrifice and not designed for personal gain. _____
Aggression	The intentional infliction of physical or psychological harm on another. _____

Frustration	Interference of the attainment of a goal, or the blocking of an impulse. _____ _____ _____
Frustration-Aggression Hypothesis	The hypothesis that frustration produces aggression. _____ _____ _____
Scapegoating	Displacing aggression onto minority groups or other innocent targets not responsible for the frustrating situation. _____ _____ _____
Personal Space	An area surrounding us; much like an invisible bubble, that we consider ours and that we use to regulate how closely others can interact with us. _____ _____ _____
Density	A measure referring to the number of people occupying a unit of space. _____ _____ _____
Crowding	A subjective perception that there are too many people in a defined space. _____ _____ _____

FROM THE LABORATORY TO LIFE

Emily was a bright, adventurous 6-year-old when her Great Aunt Ethel moved in with her, her parents, and her older sister Lisa who was 12. Emily took an instant liking to her great aunt, and she enjoyed helping Ethel and spending time with her. Ethel needed a great deal of help—she was 89 years old and partially paralyzed from a stroke. Emily would take her meals to her, fix her hair (as good as a 6-year-old can fix hair) and practice reading her children's books to her. Aunt Ethel enjoyed Emily's company and always acted excited when Emily announced that she had come to read a new story. Emily responded with equal joy at the fact that somebody seemed to take her seriously.

Lisa really did not care for Ethel. She said she smelled like mothballs, was grouchy, and always wanted others to drop what they were doing to wait on her every need. Her biggest complaints were that Aunt Ethel had taken over her bedroom and her parents were so busy caring for Ethel that they could not transport Lisa to all of the various athletic and social activities that she wanted to attend.

Years later, after Ethel had passed away and the girls had grown into adulthood, they both came home for the holidays. Emily, now a social worker who specialized in working with the elderly, and Lisa, now an aspiring fashion model, began the process of catching up on the last few years of their lives. Lisa and her husband, a handsome television actor, were appalled at the fact that Emily worked 40-hours a week with, as Lisa put it, "a bunch of old geezers." In trying to explain to Lisa the importance of caring for the elderly, Emily pointed out that she and her husband, a counselor who worked with troubled teens, actually volunteered another 16 hours a week with the elderly feeding and entertaining shut-ins on weekends. Lisa was incensed at this. She asked, "How can you stand it? They smell like mothballs. They're always whining to get their own way, and they're crabby all the time."

1. What is the term that best explains Lisa's attitude towards the elderly? _____.

2. Lisa may have developed her feelings toward the elderly as a result of competing with Aunt Ethel for her parents' time and attention. What theory, designed to explain the development of prejudice between social groups as an outcome of competition for resources, might explain Lisa's feelings toward the elderly? _____ _____.

3. Lisa holds certain attitudes and beliefs about the elderly that she probably developed while living with Aunt Ethel. These beliefs, which include the assumption that all older people are alike, are called _____.

4. Both Emily and Lisa have married men who are very much like themselves. What concept best explains this phenomenon? _____ _____.

5. Emily seems to be totally without prejudice toward the elderly. She barely remembers a time when she thought the elderly were "creepy," and she credits the time she was able to spend with Ethel as being the reason for her lack of prejudice today. What is the term that social psychologists would use to explain Emily's reduction in prejudice? _____ _____.

6. Emily's helping behavior as a child with Aunt Ethel, and her choice of a career as an adult would probably be considered _____ behavior.

7. The volunteer work that Emily and her husband do on weekends helps others, requires self-sacrifice, and does not result in personal gain. What is this type of behavior called? _____.

FROM THEORY TO PRACTICE

One of my coworkers, a male psychology professor in his early 40s, has long hair, a beard, wears denim and black leather, and rides a Harley Davidson to work (weather permitting). It's interesting to watch the reaction people have to him when we do speaking engagements together. Since this gentleman is a knowledgeable, gifted, and eloquent speaker, most people change their impressions of him shortly after he begins to speak. However, there are always a few who remain put-off by his appearance.

1. What concepts might come into play in explaining people's impressions of this biker-professor? _____
   _____
   _____

2. Can you think of a situation from your own life when something similar has happened? _____
   _____
   _____

I play a little golf—actually I'm not too bad, but I have little time for practice and tend to be inconsistent. When I am at my worst is when there are other golfers (especially good golfers) watching me tee off. I almost always shank the ball into the rough while being watched. Immediately, I say something about my new clubs, the high winds, poor course conditions, or the loud, distracting noise that only I could hear. Later, when I drive a 3-wood 250 yards onto the green, I might comment on my strength and finesse on the golf course.

3. What attributions come into play in this scenario, and when? _____
   _____
   _____

4. Can you think of a situation from your own life when something similar has happened? _____
   _____
   _____

COMPREHENSIVE PRACTICE TEST

1. Frank is participating in a social psychology experiment. He thinks that the experiment is about how people choose food preferences in social situations, but the experiment is really interested in how people change their decisions under different social pressure situations. Edwin, another participant, keeps asking Frank to change his selections. Frank doesn't realize it, but Edwin is actually working with the experimenter. In this case, Frank would be called a _____ and Edwin would be called a: _____.
   a) naïve subject; confederate
   b) confederate; naïve subject
   c) blind subject; confederate
   d) confederate; blind subject

2. Solomon Asch found that subjects who were given positive descriptions about someone prior to less positive descriptions were likely to rate those people high more often than people who were given less positive descriptions prior to positive descriptions. This tendency for an overall impression to be influenced more by first information received than by information that comes later is called the _____ effect.
    a) attribution
    b) fundamental
    c) primacy
    d) impression

3. Dispositional attribution is to _____ as situational attribution is to _____.
    a) external; internal
    b) others; self
    c) self; others
    d) internal; external

4. Jan watched as her classmate, Bill, fumbled through his speech, making many grammatical errors and even inaccurate statements such as the name of the current U.S. president. She attributed Bill's poor speech to his basic lack of motivation to be a good student and to be prepared for class. In this case, if Jan is wrong and Bill's performance is due to some other, external factor, Jan would be making what the book called the self-serving bias error.
    a) True
    b) False

5. The next time speech class was held, it was Jan's turn to present. She gave a relatively poor speech, fumbling over words and forgetting her lines. She rationalized this by blaming the students in the front row who were goofing off and distracting her. In this case, the text would suggest the possibility of the _____.
    a) primary attribution error
    b) fundamental self-bias error
    c) self-serving bias
    d) error of external factors

6. The concept of *proximity* was discussed in the text regarding _____.
    a) attribution
    b) attraction
    c) aggression
    d) prejudice

7. The mere-exposure effect would suggest that we:
    a) tend to form more positive opinions of a person, object, or other stimulus with fewer exposures to it
    b) tend to be more aggressive to people who are always in our immediate social settings
    c) tend to be more prejudice when we have increased exposure to minority groups
    d) tend to form a more positive opinion of a person, object, or other stimulus with repeated exposure to it

8. The idea that we tend to like people who like us, or at least those whom we believe like us, was identified in the text as _____.
    a) reciprocal attraction
    b) reciprocal liking
    c) social reciprocity
    d) social disinhibition

9. The good news is that people in the last few decades seem to be less influenced by physical attractiveness and more influenced by internal factors such as personality when it comes to who we are attracted to and how we respond to people.
    a) True
    b) False

10. Just before Jessie left for his college admission interview his mother reminded him to check his tie and comb his hair before meeting the interviewer. His mother was probably concerned about the _____ effect.
    a) attenuation
    b) Solomon
    c) Harvard
    d) halo

11. The old adage, "Birds of a feather flock together," was cited in the text with regards to the concept of _____ and factors that influence attraction.
    a) attribution
    b) social influence
    c) similarity
    d) proximity

12. The _____ hypothesis would suggest that couples who are mismatched in attractiveness will be more likely to end a relationship than those who are better matched.
    a) similarity
    b) matching
    c) physical conformity
    d) mate selection

13. Characteristics such as dependable character, emotional stability and maturity, and pleasing disposition were cited in the book as values identified by many people as important in _____.
   a) mate selection
   b) social role model selection
   c) employee selection
   d) factors that influence physical attractiveness

14. _____ are the attitudes and standards of behavior expected of a particular group.
   a) Values
   b) Social rules
   c) Norms
   d) Social postures

15. In his classic experiment on conformity, Asch found that subjects were willing to deliver what they believed was a very strong electrical shock to others (actually confederates) even when it was highly stressful for the subject to continue the delivery of those shocks.
   a) True
   b) False

16. Wood, et al would suggest that a minority opinion will have more influence on a majority group if:
   a) the opinion is vague and stresses a major departure from the majority opinion
   b) the opinion is clearly stated and well organized while differing from the majority opinion
   c) the opinion is clearly stated and generally agrees with the majority opinion
   d) the opinion is stated with qualifications that compliment the majority opinion

17. Another classic experiment cited in the text was Milgram's study on _____.
   a) obedience
   b) attraction
   c) prejudice
   d) social rules and group conformity

18. One strategy to induce compliance to a request is known as the _____ technique. In this strategy, the person making the request will secure a favorable response to a small request with the aim of making the person more likely to agree to a larger request later.
   a) door-in-the-face
   b) low-ball
   c) foot-in-the-door
   d) risky shift

19. A good example of the door-in-the-face technique would be to ask $10,000.00 for a car hoping that the buyer, who will likely refuse to pay this much, will then be willing to agree to pay $8,000.00, the price you wanted in the first place.
   a) True
   b) False

20. Social loafing refers to:
   a) the tendency to avoid social contact and interpersonal relationships
   b) the tendency to exert less effort with working with others on a common task
   c) the tendency to be less productive when working alone than with others
   d) the tendency to see others' work as more externally motivated than our own

21. A common finding on audience effects seems to be that we tend to do better at tasks we are just learning, or more difficult tasks at which we are proficient, when we are being watched.
   a) True
   b) False

22. Dave, a new member of the city council, is not convinced that the new zoning law is a good one, but he finally votes with the majority who originally supported the new law. This is an example of _____.
   a) social counter-conformity
   b) group polarization
   c) group unification
   d) cognitive dissonance

23. The city council decision was a bad one. While several members of the council recognized this, they voted for the law anyway because they wanted to preserve the cohesive nature of the group. This was identified in the book as the concept of groupthink.
   a) True
   b) False

24. Which of the following is not listed as a component of an attitude?
   a) social
   b) behavioral
   c) cognitive
   d) emotional

25. Repeated studies on the relationship between attitudes and behavior indicate that an attitude will predict an observed behavior about _____ percent of the time.
    a) 50
    b) 40
    c) 25
    d) 10

26. Festinger studied _____ _____, the unpleasant state that can occur when people become aware of inconsistencies between their attitudes or their attitudes and their behavior.

27. Strategies such as changing a behavior, changing an attitude, explaining away an inconsistency, or minimizing the importance of an inconsistency are all used to reduce _____.
    a) cognitive distortion bias
    b) relative attribution frustration
    c) cognitive dissonance
    d) inconsistency anxiety

28. A one-sided persuasion approach is most effective _____.
    a) with an audience consisting of intelligent but skeptical listeners
    b) with an audience who is not well informed and less intelligent
    c) with an audience who is less intelligent but very skeptical
    d) with an intelligent audience which is split in terms of original attitudes about the issue

29. A negative attitude based on another's gender, religion, race, or other group membership is known as _____.
    a) discrimination
    b) prejudice
    c) stereotype
    d) social dissonance

30. The realistic conflict theory would predict _____.
    a) that stereotypes increase with inter-group diversity
    b) that prejudice increases with inter-group competition for resources or opportunities
    c) that stereotypes are more pronounced when there is inter-group cooperation
    d) that discrimination stems from differences in basic attitudes between groups

31. A recent explanation for attitude-based behaviors is founded on the concept of _____, the ways in which we typically process social information. A good example of this is the use of stereotypes.
    a) social learning theory
    b) inter-group cognition
    c) social cognition
    d) cognitive learning theroy

32. The terms, *stereotype* and *prejudice,* are actually different ways to say the same thing.
    a) True
    b) False

33. Carl is the kind of person who tends to regularly put others down, especially those already vulnerable to prejudice, as a way to feel better about himself. The text includes research, which indicates that this strategy is _____.
    a) common
    b) common for majority members
    c) rare
    d) common for minority members

34. Ronnie is a student at a small, private college that is dominated by several major fraternity/sorority organizations and a great deal of academic and other kinds of competition. If Ronnie is like most of the people studied in social psychology, he will tend to see more _____ in his fraternity and more _____ in other fraternities.
    a) similarity; diversity
    b) diversity; similarity

35. The _____ hypothesis would suggest that there are conditions under which people can reduce prejudice and stereotypical thinking through increased contact and interaction between the groups.
    a) social interaction
    b) proximity
    c) social contract
    d) contact

36. You are preparing for a trip to a large metropolis. Your mother had previously expressed concern regarding your going to the city by yourself. You responded to her concern with the argument that with all the people around, even if someone tried to mug you, you would be OK. After all, people are basically good and they would surely come to your immediate aid in a time of need. Would social psychologists say that this is probably the case?
   a) no – they would cite research on things like prosocial behavior and altruism to support the probably lack of support in such an emergency
   b) yes they would – they would say that research proves that people tend to help others in emergencies like the one you used to calm your mother's fears
   c) no – they would cite evidence of the contrary based on phenomena such as the bystander effect and the diffusion of responsibility
   d) yes – the diffusion of responsibility and the bystander effect seems to motivate people to help strangers in these kinds of situations

37. You finally get to the big city and, shortly after leaving the train station, you watch as another person, seemingly distressed and disoriented, darts back and forth across the wide sidewalk looking for help. You are surprised that, while numerous people stop and watch the spectacle, most show no reaction, and nobody offers assistance. You are even more surprised that you remain passive and offer no help. Would this also surprise the social psychologists?
   a) no – your response to such situations can be influenced by the reactions of others
   b) yes – your apathy would be predicted by the concept of prosocial behavior
   c) no – prosocial behavior would occur only if no-one else offered assistance
   d) yes – the bystander effect phenomenon would predict that you would offer assistance

38. The frustration–aggression hypothesis suggests that frustration can lead to _____.
   a) passive resistance   c) aggression
   b) escape-avoidance behaviors   d) prosocial reactions

39. An interesting finding in the relationship between biology and aggression is that *low* autonomic nervous system arousal levels seem to be related to aggressive behavior.
   a) True   b) False

40. Which of the following seems to be true about testosterone levels and aggression?
   a) Testosterone is not, in the long run, positively correlated with aggressive behavior.
   b) Testosterone is correlated with aggression in males but not females.
   c) Testosterone is correlated with aggression in females but not males.
   d) Testosterone is correlated with aggression in both males and femalse.

41. The cognitive-neoassociationistic model would suggest that _____ is(are) the basic source of aggression.
   a) prejudice   c) negative affect
   b) negative social learning   d) genetic factors

42. Jan told Alice that there are 200 people who live in one square block in her neighborhood. Alice replied that that was too many people for such a small area. Jan is talking about _____ and Alice is talking about
_____.
   a) density; crowding   c) population parameters; subjective parameters
   b) subjective parameters; population parameters   d) crowding; density

When we focus on the differences between us as being negatives, we miss important opportunities to gain new perspectives and an increased understanding of others and ourselves. When we view the differences as positives—opportunities to grow and learn—we find that our combined perspectives and efforts can lead to personal benefit and shared success.

ANSWER KEYS

ANSWER KEY: OMSE # 1

A. Quick Quiz

1. true
2. a
3. primacy effect
4. b
5. b
6. self-serving bias
7. false
8. false
9. c
10. halo
11. true
12. c
13. d
14. obedience
15. a
16. b
17. social facilitation
18. c
19. a
20. group think

B. Matching

1. i
2. l
3. e
4. f
5. n
6. k
7. b
8. d
9. m
10. g
11. j
12. c
13. h
14. a

C. Complete the Table

1. Brief Description:
Asch gave a group of subjects a list of characteristics that began with the positive characteristic of intelligence and ended with the less complimentary characteristic of envious. He then asked the subjects to write their impressions of the person described. Asch then gave the list to another group of subjects but in the opposite order – envious first and intelligence last. He had this second group also rate the person.

Findings:
The subjects who were given the list with the positive traits appearing first rated the person higher than the subjects who responded to the list with the less complimentary characteristics listed first.

2. Brief Description:
Asch designed an experiment to see if a subject would select an obviously wrong answer to a simple test if other subjects (confederates) all selected the wrong answer.

Findings:
Five percent conformed to the wrong answer all of the time, 70 percent conformed some of the time, and 25 percent never conformed.

3. Brief Description:
Milgram had a subject (the teacher) deliver electric shocks to another subject (a confederate) whenever the confederate appears to miss an answer on a memory test. The subject is instructed to deliver stronger and stronger shocks each time the confederate misses an item.

Findings:
Of 40 subjects, no one stopped before what they thought was the delivery of 300 volts and 65 percent followed the experimenter's instructions all the way to the maximum 450 volts – even though the subjects believed they were delivering severe pain and discomfort to the confederate.

ANSWER KEY: OMSE # 2

A. Quick Quiz

1. attitude
2. c
3. b
4. c
5. realistic conflict
6. false
7. social learning
8. true
9. stereotype
10. b
11. a
12. true
13. b
14. altruism
15. d
16. frustration-aggression
17. displaced
18. d

B. Matching

1. e
2. h
3. a
4. l
5. m
6. k
7. i
8. g
9. c
10. o
11. n
12. d
13. j
14. f
15. b

C. Complete the Figure

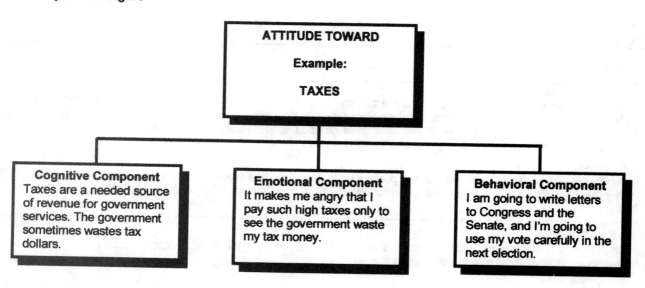

ATTITUDE TOWARD

Example:

TAXES

Cognitive Component
Taxes are a needed source of revenue for government services. The government sometimes wastes tax dollars.

Emotional Component
It makes me angry that I pay such high taxes only to see the government waste my tax money.

Behavioral Component
I am going to write letters to Congress and the Senate, and I'm going to use my vote carefully in the next election.

ANSWER KEY: LAB TO LIFE

1. prejudice
2. realistic conflict theory
3. stereotypes
4. matching hypothesis
5. contact hypothesis
6. prosocial behavior
7. altruism

ANSWER KEY: COMPREHENSIVE PRACTICE TEST

1. a	12. b	23. true	33. a
2. c	13. a	24. a	34. b
3. d	14. c	25. d	35. d
4. false	15. false	26. cognitive dissonance	36. c
5. c	16. b	27. c	37. a
6. b	17. a	28. b	38. c
7. d	18. c	29. b	39. true
8. b	19. true	30. b	40. d
9. false	20. b	31. c	41. c
10. d	21. false	32. false	42. a
11. c	22. b		

STATISTICAL METHODS

What makes statistics unique is its ability to quantify uncertainty, to make it precise. This allows statisticians to make categorical statements with complete assurance about their level of uncertainty.

–Source Unknown

INTRODUCTION TO STATISTICS

When friends in college discovered my selected major, psychology, I was warned over and over again to watch out for the statistics classes. I was advised that I would suffer many times over as I wandered aimlessly, lost in a maze of mile-long formulas that seemed to haunt statistics students for no apparent reason. By the time I got to my first such class I was so frightened that I missed the point of the whole thing. Besides, they were right—all we did was solve monster equations, one after another, and we were never told why. We were psychology students and we knew by then that there was a lot of research going on in our chosen field. We had heard about the white rats, all of the interesting discoveries in Social Psychology, Piaget's studies, and the fact that the use of the scientific method had been one of the important parental factors in the history of psychology. We understood the scientific responsibility of doing things that would help verify our observations and theories. But none of that helped us to understand why we had to endure this seemingly torturous thing called statistics. And, unfortunately, nobody bothered to explain it to us.

Students need to understand *why*—to have a reason to work and to comprehend the *what*, and the *how*. With statistics, the *why* is really quite simple. As a matter of fact, it can be summarized in the form of what I believe is one of the most important formulas in all of science—a formula that can often deceive the casual reader in terms of its simplicity. The formula reads as follows: $O = T + e$. According to this Trojan Horse, the observations (O) made in psychology are equal to the sum of the true event or situation (T) and an inevitable amount of error in observation or measurement (e). In other words, we never have the luxury of exclusive truth when we look at things in science, and this is especially the case in a discipline with the amount of subjectivity in observation and interpretation that we often find in psychology. One of the earliest and most enduring controversies in psychology has been the issue of what psychology should attempt to measure in the first place. Wundt, the father of modern psychology, studied the structure of the mind. Freud spoke of how the structures of the mind (in his case, the id, ego, and superego) shaped personality. Meanwhile the behaviorists were, and are asserting that only overt, observable behaviors are legitimate topics in the science of psychology. A review of your text will indicate that there is much we attempt to understand that is not quite that simple. Psychology is a science of constructs—concepts or theories that are often inferred through indirect and sometimes imperfect observations. Look at the illustrations of the brain in Chapter Two of your text. There you will find arrows pointing to things like the cerebellum, the frontal lobe, and the pituitary gland, but do you see any arrows pointing to the id, the happy, the sad, or the personality? Not likely! These are constructs and we know about them only through indirect evidence and inference. When we attempt to manipulate and measure these kinds of constructs we will always be faced with the reality of $O = T + e$. However, while we accept this reality, we will forever be motivated to make it go away. The whole point of following the scientific method in psychology is to make the "e" in the formula as small as possible. We follow rules in science and following those rules helps us have confidence that our observations and measurements represent more truth than error. In other words, we know there will be some measure of error in our results. We will attempt to control that error through the design of an experiment that will control the sources of that error. Return for a moment to chapter one of your text, and review the basics of the experimental method and terms such as bias, control group, and random assignment. These are some of the ways in which we attempt to control the potential for error in our observations. The problem is that we will never know for sure if we have completely succeeded in that control. That is where statistical analysis becomes important in psychology.

Statistics is really just another way to say "calculating probability." In this case, we are talking about the probability that what we find when we do our experiment is the result of error or chance instead of the thing we were interested in when we decided to do the experiment. Again (from Chapter One of your text), we manipulate something (the *independent variable*) and then measure what that does to something else (the *dependent variable*). If we see that the dependent variable seems to change when we do specific manipulations with the independent variable, statistics gives us an index of the extent to which we can have confidence that the change was actually due to the independent variable and not error or chance. If I compare the differential effect of *lecture-format* versus *discussion-format* psychology classes on unit test scores and find that the discussion format resulted in higher average scores, can I assume that the type of class format has caused the higher scores? What if the discussion students were more interested in psychology, had better study skills, or suffered less test anxiety than the students who received the lecture format? If any of these alternative explanations are actually the case, then, at least relative to the issue of type of format (the independent variable in this case), our results would be said to be based on error in our observation or measurement. We would report that the discussion format is better than the lecture format and this may not be the case at all. The next step could be to make important decisions about how we should teach based on inaccurate information. Now imagine if the same kind of erroneous information had an influence on how we treated a particular psychological disorder. Because of the importance of what we do with the information we gather through experiments in psychology, we need to be confident that what we observed in the experiment was based as much as possible on the true relationship between the independent and dependent variable. We may achieve an adequate level of confidence by following the rules of a sound experimental design and then applying statistical analysis to our data. If our analysis indicates that we can have confidence that what we see appears to be more truth than error, we can then make certain assertions about the independent-dependent variable relationship. We do statistical analysis so that we can determine the degree to which we can have confidence in our results!

In our criminal justice system, we assume there is no relationship between the defendant and the crime until there can be shown evidence of that relationship to some predetermined level of confidence (called beyond reasonable doubt). The same is true in psychological research. We assume there is no relationship between the independent variable and the dependent variable until we can show evidence of that relationship to some predetermined level of confidence (called statistical significance). In court, the prosecuting attorney uses logic and other kinds of evidence to illustrate that a relationship exists beyond a reasonable doubt. In psychological research we use some basic math to determine our level of confidence. Think of tossing a coin six times. In the long run, we could expect three heads and three tails. But what if we observe five heads and one tail? Is our observation the result of chance or is there some other reason for the unexpected outcome? Statistical analysis can give us a number that represents the possibility that we could toss a coin six times and get heads five of those times simply by chance. We then decide if that number is small enough to determine that the event was the result of some systematic influence—hopefully our independent variable. By the way, the chances of tossing a coin six times and getting heads five of those times is .03125. Is this probability small enough to say that there is a good chance the five heads did not happen just by chance? If so, you had better check that coin before you flip to decide who is going to do the dishes tonight!

Developing an understanding of the basic *whys* and *hows* of statistics is important because so much of your life is affected in one way or another by someone having done a statistical analysis. The medicines you take were scrutinized through rigid statistical analyses before they were made available to you. The items you but at the grocery store or the department store probably endured a marketing and statistical analysis before they were put on the shelf. Even the food you eat is, somewhere along the line, involved in the wonderful world of statistics. This appendix should help you gain a more practiced and functional understanding of the relationship between statistical analysis and human behavior. The materials are presented in two forms, 1) a quick quiz on the basic terms and concepts of statistics, and 2) a basic example of a hypothetical research project with statistical analysis that will help you interpret the results. You will become the decision-maker based on the analysis.

By completing the exercises provided, you should gain a thorough understanding of the information provided in your text. In other words, you should be better prepared for tests, quizzes, class participation, and life itself.

Quick Quiz

1. There are two basic kinds of statistics. _____ statistics are used to organize, summarize, and describe information gathered from actual observations, while _____ statistics are procedures that allow researchers to make inferences about the characteristics of the larger population and derive estimates of how much confidence we can have about those inferences.

2. A measure of _____ _____ describes the center or middle of a distribution of scores.

3. The _____ is the arithmetic average of a group of scores.
    a) mode
    b) median
    c) mean
    d) range

4. The _____ is the middle value or score when a group of scores are arranged from highest to lowest.
    a) mode
    b) median
    c) mean
    d) range

5. The _____ is the most often occurring score in a group of scores.
    a) mode
    b) median
    c) mean
    d) range

6. Brenda has added each test score for the third unit test in her psychology class and then divided that sum by the number of scores she added together. She then reports that the average score on the test was 83 points. She has calculated the _____ of the test scores.
    a) mode
    b) median
    c) mean
    d) range

7. Brenda listed the scores she calculated above in a table showing the frequency, or number of scores that fall within equalized class intervals. In other words she created a frequency _____.

8. A histogram is a bar graph that depicts the frequency, or number of scores, within each class interval in the distribution.
    a) True
    b) False

9. The bell shaped or normal curve is probably the best known example of a frequency _____.

10. When Brenda examined the test scores from her psychology class, she was also interested in how the scores were different from each other. Measures of _____ provide an index of how the scores in a distribution spread out, away from the mean.

11. The _____ is the difference between the highest score and the lowest score in a distribution of scores.
    a) standard deviation
    b) median
    c) standard variation
    d) range

12. The _____ is a number that reflects the average amount that scores in a distribution vary or are different from the mean.
    a) standard deviation
    b) average deviation
    c) standard variation
    d) average variation

13. Under the normal curve, what percentage of scores fall between −1 and +1 standard deviations?
    a) 99.72
    b) 95.44
    c) 68.26
    d) 34.13

14. The normal curve can give us an indication of how two or more scores are related in terms of their relative strength and the direction of that relationship.
    a) True
    b) False

15. What two things do we learn about the relationship between two variables from a correlation coefficient?
 a) mean and median   c) range and deviation
 b) strength and direction   d) cause and effect

16. A correlation of +.75 is stronger than a correlation of -.81.
 a) True   b) False

17. It was found that as study time increased so did average scores on tests. It could be said that there was a
 _____ correlation between study time and average test scores.

18. When doing research, is it better to get a positive correlation than a negative correlation?
 a) Yes – this indicates a strong cause-effect relationship.
 b) No – the terms *positive* and *negative* are not related to the quality of the information gained from the analysis.

19. The range of a correlation coefficient is from –1 to +1.
 a) True   b) False

20. Sue and John are doing a research project for their psychology class. They are interested in whether or not college student attitudes about different races or cultures can be influenced by cooperative intergroup contacts. From a student body of 15000 students they let a computer randomly select 100 ID numbers. They contact these students and ask them to participate in their experiment. After they do their experiment they conclude that intergroup contact can influence college student attitudes about different races and cultures. In this experiment, the population was _____ and the sample was _____.
 a) the students who participated in the experiment; college students in general
 b) college students in general; the students who participated in the experiment

21. Your current psychology class has too few people in it to ever be considered a population in psychological research.
 a) True   b) False

22. Using a _____ sample is important if we are going to generalize our findings from the sample to the population.

23. Sue and John did inferential statistics using the probability of .05 to determine if their results were due to chance or to the effects of intergroup contacts. In this case, .05 refers to _____.
 a) the probability that they detected a real difference (intergroup effect) 5 times out of 100
 b) the probability that their data was the result of chance was no more than 95 percent
 c) the probability that their data was the result of chance was no more than five percent
 d) the strength of the correlation coefficient they needed to say that their experiment worked

24. If I do an experiment and claim statistical significance—that means I have proven that a relationship exists between two variables.
 a) True   b) False

Of course it looks menacing at first, but statistical equations involve nothing more difficult than 6th or 7th grade math once you break the equations down into their simplest components. Even the most terrifying formula contains nothing more difficult than a square or a square root. Look, it's statistics—not *sadistics*. You don't need a fancy computer. Get out your calculator, break down the equation, and make some answers happen.

FROM THE LABORATORY TO LIFE

An Example: Using Statistics in Psychology

Professor Smith knows that many of the students at the college where he teaches psychology must take his class in order to fulfill their general education requirements. Of these students, many either do not really want to take the psychology class and/or do not see how the class will ever be of use to them. He has been keeping track of test scores and has noticed that while the overall (all his students combined) average test score is 81, the average score for his non-psychology majors is seventy-seven. Again, many of these non-psychology majors just do not see the need, and so do not seem motivated to do well in the class. Professor Smith believes that doing better in psychology class would benefit students for several reasons. The first of which is the fact that doing well in any class will help the student acquire a more well rounded education. The second reason is the fact that when students do not do well in a class, it will have a negative effect on their GPA. And finally, Professor Smith believes that a general introduction and knowledge of basic psychology can be useful and relevant to students no matter what they are going to do in their future personal and professional lives. Because of this, he has decided to try a little experiment to determine if a particular type of motivational seminar on how psychology can be used by non-psychology majors will help raise the average scores of these students' test scores. From Professor Smith's current population of non-psychology majors with a mean score of 77, 15 students are randomly selected to participate in a seminar where they will hear about the different ways psychology can play a role in their lives. The seminar will focus on how psychology is a part of a variety of professions such as health care, teaching, sales and marketing, and working with people in general. It is also emphasized that future parents will learn a lot about child development and other relevant issues. While the selected students are attending the special seminar, they are also participating in the regular psychology class with the other students (major and non-major). Finally, at the end of the unit, all the students take the same unit examination. After the students take the unit examination Professor Smith collects the following data.

➢ The average score for non-psychology majors is 77.
➢ The scores on this test for the 15 students who participated in the special seminar are represented in the table below:

77	69	68
85	76	83
76	84	79
83	83	82
91	90	75

See the instructions below for help on how to calculate these basic descriptive statistics.

You have agreed to help Professor Smith analyze the data. The ultimate question is will the special seminar on how knowledge of psychology can be useful for non-psychology majors result in a higher average score on psychology tests. Your first task is to calculate some descriptive statistics from the data provided.

1. What is the mean of the sample distribution?   _____
2. What is the median of the sample distribution?   _____
3. What is the mode of the sample distribution?   _____
4. What is the range of the sample distribution?   _____
5. What is the standard deviation of the sample distribution?   _____

It's a Piece of Cake!

The mean isn't really mean—it's easy to figure out.
The median—think of the median on a highway—it's the thing that runs right down the middle.
The mode—add an "L" to mode and you get model. The model of a distribution is the score you see the most often in that distribution.

A Primer on Calculating Descriptive Statistics

I. Some basics on math and symbols:
  A. The order of math operations are:
    1. Evaluate within parenthesis values first.
    2. Evaluate powers.
    3. Calculate multiplication and division starting at the right and working left.
    4. Calculate addition and subtraction starting at the right and working left.
  B. Some important symbols:
    1. Σ – is the symbol that means to sum (add) up the values that follow the symbol.
    2. N – refers to the number of scores in the distribution.
    3. X – refers to an individual score.
    4. $\overline{X}$ – refers to the Mean Score.

II. Some important formulas:

    1. The Mean = Σ X/N.
    2. The Median = $\dfrac{N+1}{2}$ this value will tell you how far to count down from the top of the ordered distribution (from lowest score to highest score) to find the middle score in the distribution.
    3. The Mode is the most often occurring score in the distribution.
    4. The Range is the highest score minus the lowest score.
    5. The Standard Deviation =

$$\sqrt{\frac{\Sigma(X-\overline{X})^2}{N-1}}$$

The above formula, while it may look a little intimidating, is really quite simple. What it tells you to do is to take each score (X) and subtract the mean of the distribution (X) from that score – then square that difference. You will do that for each score and then add up all the squared differences (Σ). Your next step is to divide that sum by the number of scores in the distribution minus one (N-1). Finally, you will take the square root of that number. You now have your standard deviation! Beginning statistics students may find it helpful to create a table with the following headings:

Each score	Each score minus the mean	Square the result of each score minus the mean

Of course, calculators and computers do these mundane calculations for us now, but, try doing it the old-fashioned way – it is good practice and a lot of fun.

Now it is time to use your calculated descriptive statistics to help Professor Smith decide if there is evidence of the special seminar increasing average psychology test scores. To do this you must now enter the realm of *inferential statistics*. As your text indicates, inferential statistics are used to help the researcher decide two important things. First, does there appear to be a meaningful relationship between the variables of interest (the independent variable and the dependent variable) as opposed to the idea that the results are due simply to chance. The second issue refers to the amount of confidence you can have in your assertion that the evidence is strong enough to determine that the results are due to the relationship between the independent and the dependent variable.

In the case of Professor Smith, you are helping to test the hypothesis that the special seminar will significantly increase psychology test scores. However, there may another explanation for the data you have recorded – the scores could be the result of chance factors. In essence you are testing two opposing hypothesis statements.

The **Null Hypothesis** (H_0) will predict that the results are because of chance factors and that the scores you are currently working with actually are part of the same scores that resulted in a mean score of, in this case, seventy-seven. At this point we will need to introduce another important symbol - μ - refers to the population mean. The population mean in our experiment is, again, seventy-seven. The Null Hypothesis will be listed as:

$$H_0: \overline{X} = \mu$$

Stated: There is no difference between the sample mean and the population mean. In other words, the manipulation (special seminar) will have no significant effect on test scores.

The **Experimental Hypothesis** (H_1) will predict that there is indeed a relationship between the independent variable and the dependent variable, and that the special seminar actually increased test scores. The Experimental Hypothesis will be listed as:

$$H_1: \overline{X} > \mu$$

Stated: There is a significant difference between the sample mean and the population mean. In other words, the manipulation will produce a significant effect on test scores.

We will now test our hypotheses statements by converting our sample mean into what is called a t-score. Once we obtain our t-score we will compare our obtained score to a table of scores that tells us the probability of having obtained our score strictly by chance. We will find a probability value based on how much confidence we want to have in our research decision. Recall that the text talked about .05 – the score beyond which we would expect chance to have been responsible only five percent of the time. We will find that .05-based score in a special table of t-score probabilities. We will call that score our *critical value.* If our obtained score is higher than the critical value, we will decide that our results are due to something (hopefully the independent variable) other than chance and *reject* the Null Hypothesis.

We now need to meet one more formula, the formula to convert our mean score into our t (obtained) score. This formula is:

$$t = \frac{\overline{X} - \mu}{s}$$

In this formula, the *s* in the denominator is the standard deviation of the data (recall descriptive statistics). The formula is instructing you to subtract the population mean from the sample mean and divide that difference by the standard deviation.

We will now find our critical value from the table. For our current experiment, the critical value is 1.761.

Now it is time to test our hypothesis statements and make our research decision.

6. What is your *t* obtained? _____
7. When you compare your *t* obtained to the above critical value, should you reject the Null Hypothesis? _____
8. In Professor Smith's experiment, what was the independent variable? _____
9. In Professor Smith's experiment, what was the dependent variable? _____
10. Based on the decision made in item 7 above, what should you infer regarding the relationship between the independent and dependent variable? _____

Well, that is statistics! While actual research in psychology will usually involve more complex experimental and analysis designs, you have just performed the essence of the whole thing. It really is that simple. In fact, in many ways, it is even simpler than what you just did. Computer programs now perform most of the analyses and help reduce human error.

KEY TERMS AND CONCEPTS EXERCISE

The key terms and concepts are presented in order of their appearance in the text. Space is provided for you to include a personalized definition or example of each term or concept. As you encounter each term in the text, make a note of its meaning and context. Next, conceptualize the meaning of the term in a way that makes the most sense to you. Also, think about examples of the term from your own life. Write your definition and/or example in the space provided next to the word. The KEY TERMS exercise utilizes a modified *T-note* design so that you can self-evaluate your mastery of the definitions. First lay a sheet of paper over the terms and concepts side of the page so that you only see the definitions. Read the definition and try to recall the term or concept. Mark all those you are unable to answer so you can restudy them. When you have learned all of the terms and concepts in this way, move the paper to the definition side so that you can see only the term or concept, and try to recall both the textbook definition and your personal version. Repeat this until you know all of the terms by definition and personal understanding.

Descriptive Statistics	Statistics used to organize, summarize, and describe information gathered from actual observations. _____
Measure of Central Tendency	A measure or score that describes the center or middle of a distribution of scores (examples: the mean, the median, and the mode). _____
Mean	The arithmetic average of a group of scores; one calculates the mean by adding up all the single scores and dividing the sum by the number of scores. _____
Median	The middle value or score when a group of scores are arranged from highest to lowest. _____
Mode	The score that occurs most frequently in a group of scores. _____
Frequency Distribution	An arrangement showing the frequency, or number of scores that fall within equal-sized class intervals. _____
Histogram	A bar graph that depicts the frequency or number of scores within each class interval in a frequency distribution. _____
Frequency Polygon	A line graph that depicts the frequency or number of scores within each class interval in a frequency distribution. _____
Variability	How much the scores in a distribution spread out, away from the mean. _____
Range	The difference between the highest score and the lowest score in a distribution of scores. _____

Standard Deviation	A descriptive statistic reflecting the average amount that scores in a distribution vary or deviate from their mean. _____
Normal Curve	A symmetrical, bell-shaped frequency distribution that represents how scores are normally distributed in a population; most scores fall near the mean, and fewer and fewer scores occur in the extremes either above or below the mean. _____
Correlation Coefficient	A numerical value indicating the strength and direction of relationship between two variables, which ranges from +1.00 (a perfect positive correlation) to −1.00 (a perfect negative correlation). _____
Positive Correlation	A relationship between two variables in which both vary in the same direction. _____
Negative Correlation	A relationship between two variables in which an increase in one variable is associated with a decrease in the other variable. _____
Inferential Statistics	Statistical procedures that allow researchers (1) to make inferences about the characteristics of the larger population from their observations and measurements of a sample, and (2) to derive estimates of how much confidence can be placed in those inferences. _____
Population	The entire group of interest to researchers and to which they wish to generalize their findings; the group from which a sample is selected. _____
Sample	The portion of any population that is selected for study and from which generalizations are made about the entire population. _____
Random Sample	A sample of subjects selected in such a way that every member of the population has an equal chance of being included in the sample; its purpose is to obtain a sample that is representative of the population of interest. _____

ANSWER KEYS

QUICK QUIZ

1. descriptive; inferential	9. polygon	17. positive
2. central tendency	10. variability	18. b
3. c	11. d	19. true
4. b	12. c	20. b
5. a	13. c	21. false
6. c	14. false	22. random
7. distribution	15. b	23. c
8. true	16. false	24. false

LAB TO LIFE

1. 80.066
2. 82
3. 83
4. 23
5. 6.68
6. .458
7. no
8. whether or not the student received the special seminar
9. test scores
10. it appears that the special seminar did not have the expected effect (significantly raise test scores) on the dependent variable